SPECTRAL NATIONALITY

SPECTRAL NATIONALITY

Passages of Freedom from Kant to Postcolonial
Literatures of Liberation

PHENG CHEAH

COLUMBIA UNIVERSITY PRESS
NEW YORK

Columbia University Press
Publishers Since 1893
New York   Chichester, West Sussex

© 2003 Columbia University Press

Library of Congress Cataloging-in-Publication Data

Cheah, Pheng.

    Spectral nationality : passages of freedom from Kant to postcolonial
literatures of liberation / Pheng Cheah.
      p. cm.
    Includes bibliographical references and index.
    ISBN–0–231–13018–X (cloth : alk. paper) —ISBN 0–231–13019–8 (pbk. :
alk. paper)
    1. Postcolonialism. 2. Decolonization. 3. Nationalism. 4. State, The.
5. National characteristics 6. National state. 7. Culture. 8. Liberty.
9. Internationalism. 10. Philosophy, German—18th century. 11. Philosophy, German—19th century. I. Title.

JV51.C457 2003
325'.3'01—dc22

                          2003055361

Columbia University Press books are printed
on permanent and durable acid-free paper.
Printed in the United States of America
Designed by Lisa Hamm
c 10 9 8 7 6 5 4 3 2 1
p 10 9 8 7 6 5 4 3 2 1

For L.G.S., who taught me to love books, not knowing that it would lead me on this errant path.

CONTENTS

Acknowledgments xi
List of Selected Works Cited and Abbreviations xiii

Introduction. The Death of the Nation? 1

PART I CULTURE AS FREEDOM: TERRITORIALIZATIONS
AND DETERRITORIALIZATIONS 15

1. The Rationality of Life: On the Organismic Metaphor of the Social
   and Political Body 17

   Myths of the Organic Community 17
   The Transition from Mechanistic to Organismic Metaphors of the
     Social and Political Body 25
   Freedom, Culture, and Organism 34

2. Kant's Cosmopolitanism and the Technic of Nature 61

   How Can Freedom Be Objectively Real? Antimechanism Before the
     Third Critique 64
   Taking Credit from Nature: Culture as Freedom in Kant's Historical
     Writings 74
   Organized Products of Nature: Organismic Causality and Freedom in
     the *Critique of Judgment* 80

The Political Body as Organism: Cosmopolitan Culture and
the Reorganization/Organicization of the State-Machine 89
The Technic of Nature: Effacing Nature's Favor and the Absolute
Recuperation of *Techne* 99
The Technic of the Other: Sheer Exposure 106

3. Incarnations of the Ideal: Nation and State in Fichte and Hegel   115

The Original People: Fichte's *Addresses to the German Nation* 117

The Nation as a Community of Language and the Overcoming
of Death 121
The *Kulturnation* as Spiritual Organism 125
The State as Instrument of the People: Why National *Bildung* Is Not
an Official Ideology 129
The Originary Infection of the Nation-People 136

The Actualization of Reason: Hegel's Organic State and the Ghost of
National Culture 141

Wirklichkeit and the Idea of the State 144
Becoming Other While Staying at Home: The Animal Organism
149
The Vital State and the Machine of Civil Society 153
Bildung as the Paradigm of Spiritual Work and Freedom 161
Volksgeist: The Apparitional Supplement of the Rational
State 169

4. Revolutions That Take Place in the Head: Marx and the National
Question in Socialist Decolonization   179

The World Community of Productive Laborers: Marx's
Deterritorialization of Freedom 181
Epigenesis of Labor: The *Verwirklichung* of Humanity and the
Proletarian Revolution as Appropriation 191
Ghostly Consciousness, Haunted Actuality 200
Acts of Culture: The Return of the Nation-People in Socialist
Decolonization 208

PART II SURVIVING (POSTCOLONIALITY) 233

5. Novel Nation: The *Bildung* of the Postcolonial Nation as Sociological
   Organism   235

6. The Haunting of the People: The Spectral Public Sphere in Pramoedya
   Ananta Toer's Buru Quartet   249

   The Buru Quartet's Function: Reanimating a Critical Public Sphere in
   New Order Indonesia 253
   The Birth and Arrested Life of the Indonesian Nation Circa 1900 264
   The Modernity of National Consciousness: The Spectral World of
   Modern Knowledge 269
   The Comparative Gaze and the Desire for National *Bildung* 273
   Freedom Through the Nation: The Critique of Colonialist Instrumen-
   tal Reason as the Reenchantment of the World 281
   Conjuring the People, Giving Life to the National Body: Organization
   as Vital Movement and Power 289
   "*Landasan [yang] lebih mengikat*": What Binds a Healthy Nation-
   People Together 296

7. Afterlives: The Mutual Haunting of the State and Nation   307

   The Negation of Life: The State as the Agent of Death 307
   The Negation of Death 312
   The Haunting of the Colonial State by Minke's Afterlife 319
   Morbid Interrogations: The Constitutive Possibility of Death Within
   the Living National Body 329
   Publicness and the Spectral Gaze of State Surveillance 331
   Counterfeit Life 341

8. The Neocolonial State and Other Prostheses of the Postcolonial
   National Body: Ngũgĩ wa Thiong'o's Project of Revolutionary
   National Culture   349

   National Culture as Self-Recursive Mediation 354
   The Onus of Narrative Fiction 363

Monstrous Bodies and Nonfunctional Organs 365
The Surviving of Surviving 371

Epilogue. Spectral Nationality: The Living-On of the Postcolonial Nation in Globalization 381

Index 397

ACKNOWLEDGMENTS

ooks do not spring fully formed from their authors' foreheads. The help and advice of my teachers were indispensable to the making of this one. Jonathan Culler made "theory" a legitimate field in literary studies and enabled me to write on Derrida in an English department dissertation. Without his cheerful encouragement and guidance, I would have left academia to pursue a legal career. Benedict Anderson's brilliant work provoked me to think about the complexities of national belonging and "Southeast Asia." He patiently checked my translations of Pramoedya and then translated all my quotations from the last two volumes of the Buru quartet when the going got tough. His self-sacrificing generosity as a teacher is a constant reminder that academia has not been completely professionalized. I am deeply indebted to György Márkus, who first taught me how to read Kant and Hegel and generously reread Hegel and Fichte with me line by line in early 1996 despite his own unforgiving schedule. During the writing of this book, he patiently answered all my queries about German philosophy. What I have learnt from him cannot be quantified. Elizabeth Grosz infected me with her passion for contemporary French theory and taught me how to read it philosophically. My critique of organismic vitalism parallels her current work on Darwin and Bergson. I am grateful for her support and friendship. I am also grateful to Walter Cohen and Laura Brown who always found the time to give sound advice.

I have been fortunate to have Peter Fenves and Harry Harootunian as reviewers of my manuscript. The book is stronger as a result of their careful and incisive comments. Judith Butler, John McCumber, and Larry Lipking generously commented on various portions of the manuscript, and Allen Wood, Alan Code, and Eckart Förster gave me much needed help with aspects of Kant, Fichte and Aristotle. All philosophical shortcomings of the book remain mine. The work of Gayatri Chakravorty Spivak and Dipesh Chakrabarty were important examples. Thanks also to Jennifer Crewe and Michael Haskell at Columbia University Press for their commitment to the project and their editorial insight.

Many colleagues and friends at Berkeley, where most of this book was completed, provided stimulating conversation and encouragement. My thanks to David Bates, Anthony Cascardi, Carol Clover, David Cohen, Michael Mascuch, Aihwa Ong, Chris Berry, Deniz Gökturk, Lydia Liu (now at Michigan), Tony Kaes, and David Hollinger. I am fortunate to have had Carol Hau for a classmate at Cornell. Her warm friendship and that of Tsao Heng-Kwong, Sheng Yu-Jane, Martha Said, Wahyu Utomo, Ben Abel, and Andrew Abalahin made the long and hostile winters of Ithaca a bit more bearable. I am thankful also for the continuing friendship of Madhu Dubey and Susannah Gottlieb.

The book was completed with the help of the following research support from the University of California at Berkeley in 2000 and 2001: the Townsend Center for the Humanities Fellowship, the Humanities Research Fellowship, and the Regents' Faculty Fellowship. An abridged version of chapter 1 appeared in *Radical Philosophy* no. 112 (March/April 2002): 9–24. Portions of chapters 6 and 7 were published as "Spectrality and Reincarnation: Pramoedya Ananta Toer's Buru Quartet as Historical Memory," in *Imagining the Past, Remembering the Future: War, Violence, and Memory in Asia*, ed. Maria Serena I. Diokno (Japan Foundation Asia Center and University of Philippines: Quezon City, 2001), 131–44. Parts of chapter 4 and the epilogue draw on an earlier essay, "Spectral Nationality: The Living-on of the Postcolonial Nation in Neocolonial Globalization," in *Becomings: Explorations in Time, Memory, and Futures*, ed. Elizabeth Grosz (Ithaca: Cornell University Press, 1999), 176–200.

SELECTED WORKS CITED AND ABBREVIATIONS

WORKS BY IMMANUEL KANT

Citations to the *Critique of Pure Reason* use A and B pagination. All other references to Kant's work cite the volume and page number of the twelve volume *Werkausgabe* by Wilhelm Weischedel (Frankfurt: Suhrkamp, 1968). For the reader's convenience, I have also provided references (preceded by Ak.) to the volume and page number of the Akademie edition of the Second and Third Critiques and other main texts (*Kants Gesammelte Schriften,* ed. Königliche Preußiche [later Deutsche] Akademie der Wissenchaften [Berlin: Walter de Gruyter, 1902–]). Citations are followed by the page number of an available English translation (preceded by a semicolon), as listed below. I have modified these translations where appropriate.

Anthropology from a Pragmatic Point of View. Trans. Mary J. Gregor. The Hague: Martinus Nijhoff, 1974.

Critique of Judgment. Trans. and ed. Werner S. Pluhar. Indianapolis: Hackett, 1987.

Critique of Pure Reason. Trans. and ed. Paul Guyer and Allen W. Wood. Cambridge: Cambridge University Press, 1997.

Education. Trans. Annette Churton. Ann Arbor: University of Michigan Press, 1960.

Opus Postumum. Ed. and trans. Eckart Förster. Cambridge: Cambridge University Press, 1993.

Political Writings. Ed. Hans Reiss, trans. H. B. Nisbet. Cambridge: Cambridge University Press, 1991. Abbreviated *Pol. Writ.* in the text.

Practical Philosophy. Trans. and ed. Mary Gregor. Cambridge: Cambridge University Press, 1996. Abbreviated *Prac. Phil.* in the text.

WORKS BY J. G. FICHTE

All references to Fichte's work are, as is customary, to *Johann Gottlieb Fichtes sämmtliche Werke,* ed. I. H. Fichte, 8 vols. (Berlin: Veit, 1845–46), and *Johann Gottlieb Fichtes nachgelassene Werke,* ed. I. H. Fichte, 3 vols. (Bonn: Adolph-Marcus, 1834–1835; treated in the text as vols. 9–11 of *Fichtes sämmtlichte Werke*), and cite volume and page numbers, although I have actually used the variorum edition of the *Gesamtausgabe,* ed. Reinhard Lauth and Hans Jacob, Bayerischen Akademie der Wissenschaften (Stuttgart-Bad Cannstatt: Friedrich Frommann Verlag, 1964–). I have used the Medicus text of *Reden an die Deutsche Nation,* reprinted, with new introduction by Reinhard Lauth (Hamburg: Felix Meiner, 1978). Citations are followed by the page number of an available English translation (preceded by a semicolon), as listed below. I have modified these translations where appropriate.

Addresses to the German Nation. Ed. George Armstrong Kelly, trans. R. F. Jones and G. H. Turnbull. New York: Harper and Row, 1968.

Early Philosophical Writings. Trans. and ed. Daniel Breazeale. Ithaca: Cornell University Press, 1988. Abbreviated *EPW* in the text.

Foundations of Natural Right According to the Principles of the Wissenschaftslehre. Ed. Frederick Neuhouser, trans. Michael Baur. Cambridge: Cambridge University Press, 2000.

The Science of Knowledge (Wissenschaftslehre [1794]). Ed. and trans. Peter Heath and John Lachs. Cambridge: Cambridge University Press, 1982.

The Vocation of Man. Trans. Peter Preuss. Indianapolis: Hackett, 1987.

WORKS BY G. W. F. HEGEL

References to Hegel's work are to *Werke in zwanzig Bänden,* ed. Eva Moldenhauer and Karl Markus Michel (Frankfurt: Suhrkamp, 1970). Anmerkungen and Zusätze are indicated by A and Z, respectively, following the paragraph number. I have used Johannes Hoffmeister's editions of *Die Vernunft in der Geschichte,* vol. 1 of *Vorlesungen über die Philosophie der Weltgeschichte* (Hamburg: Felix Meiner, 1955), and *Jenaer Realphilosophie: Vorlesungmanuskripte zur Philosophie der Natur und des Geistes von 1805–1806* (Hamburg: Felix Meiner, 1969), and the 2d edition of Georg Lasson's *System der Sittlichkeit* (Hamburg: Felix Meiner, 1967). Citations are followed by the page number of an available English translation (preceded by a semicolon), as listed below. I have modified these translations where appropriate.

Aesthetics: Lectures on Fine Art. 2 Vols. Trans. T. M. Knox. Oxford: Clarendon Press, 1998.

The Difference Between Fichte's and Schelling's System of Philosophy. Trans. H. S. Harris and Walter Cerf. Albany: SUNY Press, 1977.

Elements of the Philosophy of Right. Ed. Allen W. Wood, trans. H. B. Nisbet. Cambridge: Cambridge University Press, 1991.

The Encyclopaedia Logic. Part 1 of *The Encyclopaedia of the Philosophical Sciences.* Trans. T. F. Geraets, W. A. Suchting, H. S. Harris. Indianapolis: Hackett, 1991.

Hegel and the Human Spirit: A Translation of the Jena Lectures on the Philosophy of Spirit, 1805–6, with Commentary. Trans. Leo Rauch. Detroit: Wayne State University Press, 1983.

Hegel's Philosophy of Mind. Part 3 of *The Encyclopaedia of the Philosophical Sciences* (1830). Trans. William Wallace. Oxford: Clarendon Press, 1971.

Hegel's Philosophy of Nature. Part 2 of *The Encyclopaedia of the Philosophical Sciences* (1830). Trans. A. V. Miller. London: Clarendon Press, 1970.

Hegel's Political Writings. Trans. T. M. Knox. Oxford: Clarendon Press, 1964.

Hegel's Science of Logic. Trans. A. V. Miller. Atlantic Highlands, N.J.: Humanities Press, 1989.

Lectures on the Philosophy of World History: Introduction: Reason in History. Trans. H. B. Nisbet. Cambridge: Cambridge University Press, 1980.

Phenomenology of Spirit. Trans. A. V. Miller. Oxford: Oxford University Press, 1977.

System of Ethical Life (1802–3) and First Philosophy of Spirit, part II of *The System of Speculative Philosophy 1803–4.* Trans. and ed. H. S. Harris and T. M. Knox. Albany: SUNY Press, 1979.

WORKS BY KARL MARX AND FRIEDRICH ENGELS

References to Marx's and Engels's works in German are to *Karl Marx Friedrich Engels Gesamtausgabe (MEGA)*, ed. Institut für Marxismus-Leninismus (Berlin: Dietz, 1973–). References to *Die Deutsche Ideologie,* "Marx über Feuerbach," and *Manifest der kommunistichen Partei* (1848) are to *Marx/Engels Gesamtausgabe,* ed. V. Adoratskij (Berlin: Marx-Engels Verlag, 1932). The first two texts are in vol. 1:5, the *Manifest* is in vol. 1:6.

Citations are followed by the page number of an available English translation (preceded by a semicolon), as listed below. I have modified these translations where appropriate.

Capital: A Critique of Political Economy. Volume 1. Trans. Ben Fowkes. Harmondsworth, U.K.: Penguin, 1976.

Capital: A Critique of Political Economy. Volume 3. Trans. David Fernbach. Harmondsworth, U.K.: Penguin, 1981.

Early Writings. Trans. Rodney Livingstone and Gregor Benton. Harmondsworth: Penguin, 1975. Abbreviated *EW* in the text.

The First International and After. Vol. 3 of *Political Writings*. Ed. David Fernbach. Harmondsworth, U.K: Penguin, 1974. Abbreviated *First International* in the text.

The German Ideology. 3rd rev. ed. Moscow: Progress Publishers, 1976.

Grundrisse: Foundations of the Critique of Political Economy. Trans. Martin Nicolaus. Harmondsworth, U.K.: Penguin, 1973.

The Revolutions of 1848. Vol. 1 of *Political Writings*. Ed. David Fernbach. Harmondsworth, U.K.: Penguin, 1973. Abbreviated *Rev* in the text.

Surveys from Exile. Vol. 2 of *Political Writings*. Ed. David Fernbach. Harmondsworth, U.K.: Penguin, 1973.

SPECTRAL NATIONALITY

INTRODUCTION. THE DEATH OF THE NATION?

Nationalism has almost become the exemplary figure for death. The millenium's end is marked (and marred) by an endless catalogue of fanaticist intolerance, ethnic violence, and even genocidal destruction, which are widely regarded as extreme expressions of nationalism: patriarchal fundamentalism in Afghanistan and other parts of "the Islamic world"; the atrocities designated by the proper names of Rwanda and Bosnia; the recent revival of the nuclear race in South Asia as a result of official religious nationalism in India and Pakistan; and so on. The common association of nationalism and the desire for the archaic suggests that nationalism destroys human life and whatever future we may have because its gaze is fixed on the frozen past. Yet all this seems so antithetical to the universalistic aims of Third World decolonization and the nation-building projects of the nonaligned countries of the Bandung group of Asia and Africa, wherein nationalism's sacrificial tendencies were thought to guarantee an eternal future because the nation stands as the enduring substrate through which individuals are guaranteed a life beyond finite, merely biological life. This alleged organic power of origination is intimated by the nation's etymological link to "nativity" and "natality."

I initially set out to write a book about the tribulations of revolutionary postcolonial national culture. I wanted to examine whether the spirits of decolonization and Bandung had a future in view of recent arguments about the nation-form's imminent obsolescence because of its continuing erosion by an emerging cosmopolitanism, by a global political community in contemporary globalization, and by the ethical critique of nationalism's totalitarian and fundamentalist tendencies that is the dominant impetus of postcolonial studies. This is still the central theme of this book's second half. However, it quickly became clear that I could not adequately address the issue without first understanding revolutionary nationalism's genealogical roots in late-eighteenth- and early-nineteenth-century German philosophical thought. In his famous distinction between "good" and "evil" nationalism, Hans Kohn argued for the modularity of "bad" German cultural national-ism for the Asian and African experiences: "German nationalism, with its anti-Western, anti-Enlightenment, and Germanophile attitude, became the model for many similar conservative nationalist trends, from Russia to India, from Spain to Latin America—an overcompensation for political backwardness in the modern world by claims to 'spiritual' superiority based upon the legendary glories of pre-modern traditions."[1] But what struck me about Amilcar Cabral's and Frantz Fanon's theories of revolu-tionary national culture was their universalistic humanism and trenchant critique of elite nativism.

Two other features of decolonizing nationalist discourse suggested a more progressive association with German philosophy. First, the concrete goals of political and economic freedom presuppose a philosophical understanding of freedom as the transcendence of finitude through rational purposive endeavor. Second, the repeated representation of the people and their revolutionary culture as the bearer of life is directly continuous with the organismic metaphor of the social and political body inaugurated by German idealism, which associated freedom with the causality of culture and organic life. Indeed, from this perspective, the putative antithesis between cosmopolitan universalism and nationalist particularism mislead-ingly obscures the fact that both philosophical nationalism and cosmopoli-tanism articulate universal institutional models for the actualization of freedom and are underwritten by the same organismic ontology. I was thus led to this book's central premise: instead of trying to exorcise postcolonial nationalism and replace it with utopian, liberal, or socialist cosmopoli-

---

1. Hans Kohn, *Prelude to Nation-States: The French and German Experience, 1789–1815* (Princeton, N.J.: Van Nostrand, 1967), p. 32.

tanisms, we ought to address its problems in terms of the broader issue of the actualization of freedom itself.

This approach is contrary to the general trend of contemporary criticism. The shift toward cultural studies reveals an impatience with philosophy. Studies of postcolonial nationalism in particular are historicist and sociological in orientation. They favor "the concrete" over abstract rumination, which is dismissed as obfuscatory. It is as if nationalism is evaluated positively or negatively in terms of its affinity to philosophy. This is best evidenced in the work of Benedict Anderson and that of the subaltern-studies scholars, the two most influential approaches to Third World nationalism today. Nationalism, Anderson argues, is so tenacious because it is more like religion and kinship than a set of ideas. Its political power is to be contrasted with its "philosophical poverty and even incoherence." "Unlike most other isms, nationalism has never produced its own grand thinker: no Hobbeses, Toquevilles, Marxes or Webers."[2] Whereas Anderson sees nationalism as unphilosophical and therefore populist in spirit, the subaltern-studies historians argue that Indian nationalism is impoverished because it is *too* philosophical. It is a historical repetition in colonial space that reveals the particularistic limits of the European Enlightenment's universalist pretensions. In colonial South Asia, Ranajit Guha writes, Western humanism took the form of a nationalism which, "armed with quasi-universalist pretensions of its own . . . would [in turn] claim to speak for all Indians lumped together by the sameness David Hume had attributed to all mankind."[3] Similarly, Partha Chatterjee notes that "if nationalism expresses itself in a frenzy of irrational passion, it does so *because* it seeks to represent itself in the image of the Enlightenment and *fails* to do so. . . . [The Cunning of Reason] has seduced, apprehended and imprisoned [nationalism]."[4] Accordingly, one should search for the non-Western (and therefore, non-Enlightenment-philosophy) elements within

2. Benedict Anderson, *Imagined Communities: Reflections on the Origin and Spread of Nationalism*, 2d ed. (London: Verso, 1991), p. 5. Hereafter referred to in the text as *IC*.

3. Ranajit Guha, *A Construction of Humanism in Colonial India: The 1993 Wertheim Lecture* (Amsterdam: Centre for Asian Studies), p. 11.

4. Partha Chatterjee, *Nationalist Thought and the Colonial World: A Derivative Discourse?* (London: Zed, 1986), p. 17.

nationalism, especially the heterogeneous subaltern voices left out by nationalist historiography.

The quarantine of philosophy is contradictory in both cases. When Anderson describes the common conception of the nation "as a solid community moving steadily down (or up history)," he glosses it through a "precise" *philosophical* analogy with "the idea of a sociological organism moving calendrically through homogeneous, empty time" (*IC*, 26). Similarly, the idea of spontaneous popular subaltern resistance to the postcolonial state and capital is rooted in a conception of "the people" as a self-actualizing vital force that can transcend limitations imposed upon it. What is at stake is precisely a philosophical *idea* of the "concrete," of how universal freedom can be actualized in a concrete proper body. As Jacques Derrida notes,

> The self-positing or self-identification of the nation always has the form of a *philosophy* which, although better represented by such and such a nation, is none the less a certain relation to the universality of the philosophical. This philosophy, the structure of nationality, does not necessarily take the form or the representation of a system stated by professional philosophers in philosophical institutions; it can show up as spontaneous philosophy, an implicit philosophy but one that is very constitutive of a non-empirical relationship with the world and a sort of potentially universal discourse, "embodied," "represented," "localised," . . . by a particular nation.[5]

Nationalism's philosophical structure is not to be found in the thought or work of any particular philosopher, but in a constellation of concepts that are the necessary (but not sufficient) condition of nationality. These concepts are "freedom," "culture," and "organic life." Michel Foucault has observed that from the nineteenth century onwards, "the great struggles that have challenged the general system of power" have taken as their paramount objective "life, understood as the basic needs, man's concrete essence, the realization of his potential, a plenitude of the possible."[6] But

---

5. Jacques Derrida, "Onto-Theology of National Humanism (Prolegomena to a Hypothesis)," *Oxford Literary Review* 14 (1992):10.
6. Michel Foucault, *The History of Sexuality*, vol. 1, *An Introduction*, trans. Robert Hurley (New York: Vintage, 1980), pp. 144–45.

this watershed association of freedom and life is not only the consequence of the historical rise of biopower (power that fosters life instead of repressing it). It is also part of a philosophical history that sees organic life qua organized matter as an analogue of freedom and, therefore, as the paradigmatic metaphor for social organization and political life. This organismic vitalism is the thread linking Frantz Fanon's assertion that "each man or woman brings the nation to life by his or her action," to Marx's idea of living labor as the source of proletarian revolution, and Fichte's characterization of the German nation as a self-originating and self-organizing living whole.[7]

We cannot grasp postcolonial national culture's radical legacy without an adequate understanding of the organismic metaphor of German idealism that conventional knowledge has buried alive with its myths and caricatures. There are, of course, also important historical and conjunctural affinities between the rise of German cultural nationalism in various political states following Napoleonic conquest and Third World decolonization. First, the revivification of a vernacular national culture was as important to Fichte writing in a Prussia where even in the time of Frederick the Great (who described German as a semibarbarous tongue), the social and aesthetic ideals and the lingua franca of the court were French, as it was to the Kenyan novelist, Ngũgĩ wa Thiong'o, who insisted on writing in Gikuyu in the 1980s to reverse the linguistic and cultural alienation imposed by British colonial education policies and American neocolonial global culture. Second, like the German nation prior to 1871, decolonizing Asian and African nations did not coincide with the colonial or feudal/monarchical territorial state. They were prestatized nationalisms. This nonidentity between nation and state gave rise to the nationalist desire to inspirit and transform the existing state structure in the nation's image. Finally, both forms of nationalism were initially reactive movements catalyzed by an awareness of the nation's economic, social, and political backwardness in comparison to the European imperial center or the hegemonic power.[8]

---

7. Frantz Fanon, *The Wretched of the Earth*, trans. Constance Farrington (New York: Grove Weidenfeld, 1963), p. 132.

8. For Germany, this is France and England. Marx's scathing comments on the retarded character of the German bourgeoisie are almost identical to Fanon's and Cabral's denigration of the native comprador bourgeoisie. This is why Partha Chatterjee can employ the idea of passive revolution that Gramsci derived from the Italian Risorgimento as an analytical schema for Indian nationalism.

These similarities have been noted before. But they have only served the diagnosis of organic cultural nationalism as a Romantic mystification that resists enlightened rational progress or the historical/sociological deterministic argument (pioneered by Marx and reformulated by Norbert Elias) that national culture is the ideology of a retarded bourgeoisie. Such arguments rely on a genetic fallacy whereby the organismic metaphor's significance is predetermined and limited by the material conditions of its emergence. The same similarities can, however, also indicate a common historical experience of modernity's exhilarating and shocking impact. In the centers of the Industrial Revolution (France and England), the experience was less intense because modernity came at a more moderate pace. But for peoples elsewhere (Germany, Africa, and Asia, for example), the encounter was abrupt and greatly accelerated. Thus, instead of being an ideological mystification, the organismic metaphor can be seen as fundamental to a new rational understanding of human action and purposive causality that tried to make sense of this intense experience. The fact that these ideas received their first elaborate formalization in German philosophy does not make decolonizing and postcolonial nationalisms derivative of a European model. They are comparable responses to a common experience of intense structural transformation—whether this takes the form of Napoleonic invasion, nineteenth-century territorial imperialism, or uneven globalization.

This alternative interpretation is more productive for three reasons: First, it leads to a more judicious understanding of the liberatory dimension of the organismic metaphor in German philosophy and its legacy in postcolonial nationalism. Second, once the metaphor's rational basis is acknowledged, we can see that it is not limited to nationalism, but also informs various cosmopolitanisms and other progressive political philosophies. These political organicisms, which are in polemical dialogue with each other, form a continuing series of territorialized and deterritorialized models for realizing freedom. Third and most importantly, if postcolonial nationalism has emerged at the end of this series as the most efficacious model for the actualization of freedom for the world's masses, its vicissitudes have a far greater significance than that accorded to it by postcolonial theory. Instead of merely revealing the Eurocentric limits of Enlightenment universalism, the failure of decolonization problematizes the very idea of freedom as the incarnation of ideals. It leads us to ask: is organismic vitalism an adequate framework for understanding postcolonial nationalism's persistence in the contemporary global order and its future as an emancipatory project? If not, how should we rethink the ideas of freedom and emancipation?

Such an interrogation necessarily touches on a central problem in contemporary theory: the relation between culture and politics. In philosophical modernity, culture qua incarnation of human ideals supplies the ontological paradigm of the political because it is purposive activity through which we transcend our finitude and become free. Heidegger succinctly outlines this privileging of culture:

> A fourth modern phenomenon manifests itself in the fact that human activity is conceived and consummated as culture [*Kultur*]. Thus, culture is the actualization [*Verwirklichung*] of the highest values, through the nurture and cultivation [*Pflege*] of the highest goods of man. It lies in the essence of culture as such nurturing, to nurture itself in its turn and thus to become the politics of culture [*Kulturpolitik*].[9]

The idea that political activity is a case of and finds its truth in culture is quite foreign to contemporary understandings of the political. It is a measure of the poverty of contemporary academic discourse that we have lost this axiomatic sense of culture's cobelonging with politics. The division of academic labor into specialized disciplines with their own jargon sets up politics and culture as intrinsically distinct concepts designating separate bounded realms that are the exclusive objects for political science and the humanities or, more recently, cultural studies. Our attempts to bridge these realms via cultural politics or neo-Marxist notions of ideology and hegemony that modify Marx's dismissal of culture as merely superstructural only point to their intersection in the mediating zone of cultural hegemony. In contradistinction, the organismic metaphor of the political body, which views cultural incarnation as an analogue of freedom, underscores the point that culture is the ontological paradigm of the political. This emerges even more clearly in postcolonial national *Bildung*, where radical political activity patently reverts to revolutionary literary culture.

---

9. Martin Heidegger, "Die Zeit des Weltbildes," in *Holzwege* (Frankfurt: Vittorio Klostermann, 1950), pp. 73–74; translated as "The Age of the World Picture," in *The Question Concerning Technology and Other Essays*, trans. William Lovitt (New York: Harper and Row, 1977), p. 116.

Contemporary cultural studies is premised on the belief that analyses of politics have not paid enough attention to culture and that we should remedy this by focusing on how culture shapes politics. I am proposing, however, that there is a surfeit of culture because political activity is always already modeled on the incarnational power of culture. But culture's transformational capacity is precisely what the impossible imperativity of postcolonial nationalism puts into question: It is not that human ideals cannot be incarnated because reality is never adequate to ideals, but that any process of actualization is inevitably haunted and can go awry. This might be a better way to account for the vicissitudes of nationalism than the dichotomies of nationalist particularism vs. cosmopolitan universalism and cultural nationalism vs. political nationalism or civic patriotism that inform most studies of nationalism. These dichotomies pathologize nationalism either by opposing it to Enlightenment universalism, from which it is allegedly a fall, or by distinguishing a "bad" chauvinistic cultural nationalism from a "good" universalistic nationalism centered on constitutional structures that enshrine humanistic ideals. The first position fails to recognize that nationalism is also a universalism because both it and cosmopolitanism are based on the same normative concept of culture. Many German philosophers of national *Bildung* (e.g., Herder, Schiller, Humboldt, and Fichte) were also cosmopolitanists who saw the nation and its culture as the most effective actualization of universal ethical ideals. The second position, which contrasts real political-institutional guarantees of freedom to the mystical promise of freedom through culture, defines culture in the narrower anthropological sense and ignores the fact that all political institutions are *of* culture in the normative sense. It forecloses the fact that the successful working of civic patriotism depends on national *Bildung* understood not as ideological indoctrination, but as a cultivational process where universal ideals are incarnated in the daily practices of a collective's individual members. As I will show, neither the nation-form nor culture are per se particularistic or chauvinistic. We need a different way of understanding national culture's degeneration into an oppressive ideology.

I am keenly aware that by arguing that normative political activity has been conceived in terms of culture's incarnational causality, I am open to the accusation of having performed, unwittingly or otherwise, the sort of ideological inversion that Marx diagnosed in *The German Ideology* when he took Hegel and his heirs to task for making spiritual and ideational forms the basis of concrete reality. Put differently, is not my approach to the genesis of political organicism and nationalism and their fate in decolonization and postcoloniality ahistorical, insofar as I do not primarily focus on the material conditions that give rise to various organicist-nationalist claims in political history? Do I not then lapse into a mystifying apologia for the more fascistic turns of political organicism that draw precisely on the invisible spiritual ties of national culture? As I have already mentioned, my argument is not historicist in character. Instead, it questions the very view of human history at the heart of Marxist historicism, namely, history as the realm of human self-activity and self-actualization, the sphere in which human beings materially produce the actual conditions under which they live through labor and social intercourse. This understanding of history as actualization, which is necessarily teleological, underwrites both the protocol of immanent critique that seeks to re-embed ideological forms in the concrete, actual conditions from which they have sprung and Marx's idea of the proletarian revolution. It is my contention that the ideas of actualization and the concrete derive from German idealism and that cultural activity is their original paradigm. Marx is also Hegel's son, and culture is the occulted model for creative labor and the proletarian revolution.

A historicist approach locates the link between political organicism and fascism in an unfortunate constellation of historical factors, or it places the blame on historical actors. It implies that these historical conditions of political oppression can be exposed through rational critique and corrected in due (teleological) time. I try instead to situate the contamination of political organicism as an irreducible possibility within freedom conceived as human self-actualization itself. This is not because I think that historical analyses are unimportant and that the contamination should not be corrected, but partly because the historicist axioms of the correction and transcendence of contingent limitations through analysis of concrete history are sufficiently intertwined with totalitarianism's drive toward purification that we should exercise appropriate caution. I therefore remain skeptical about any claim about forms of collective life (social, political, or cultural) in which freedom is fully self-actualizing. We can call the irreducible possibility of contamination in the movement of self-actualization "history" if this is not taken to mean the comprehensible regularity of empirical processes of human interaction plotted by historical materialism, but the absolute surprise or chance of the event that affects natural phenomena and historical processes alike. Historical analyses remain invaluable for reconstructing the concrete conditions under which contamination occurs in specific cases, but they do not acknowledge the irreducible character of contamination and its radical implications for the theory and practice of freedom.

This book is divided into two parts. The first part asks why freedom was characterized through metaphors of organic life from the late eighteenth century onwards and explores the origin and development of the organismic metaphor of the political body in the thought of Kant, Hegel, Fichte, Marx, and socialist decolonization. Kant conceived of transcendental or moral freedom as a special power of causality opposed to the arational mechanism of nature. But because freedom needs to be actualized in the empirical world, he argued that the existence of "teleological time"—a special mode of temporality characterizing the self-recursive, purposive causality of culture and organic life—gives us hope that freedom can be actualized. Culture and the organism thereby became, for Kant, phenomenal analogues of freedom, and the operation of the ideal political body was likened to an organism's epigenetic processes. For Kant, the ideal political body was a cosmopolitan federation. Elaborating on the idea of freedom's "actualization/actuality" (*Verwirklichung/Wirklichkeit*), Fichte and Hegel insist that moral freedom can only be concrete in a territorialized political community. Respectively, they oppose the living nation to the machine-state and the organic state to mechanical civil society. These oppositions and the underlying thematic opposition between empty phantasmatic form and living concrete reality have become axiomatic in social-scientific discourse.

For Hegel, culture is the paradigm of reason's self-actualization because it is a process of self-recursive mediation where reason returns to itself from the external world through a beneficial mediating device. Despite Marx's anticulturalism, this schema informs his idea of "appropriation" (*Aneignung*), the process by which the products alienated from living labor by dead capital are returned back to their producers. Appropriation is the central principle of the proletarian world revolution, whereby freedom becomes deterritorialized once again and the nation is dismissed as a bourgeois phantasm. However, with the insistence on *national* reappropriation in Marxist debates about the national question, especially in Third World socialist decolonization, as exemplifed by the theories of Frantz Fanon and Amilcar Cabral, the proletariat is reterritorialized and the nation is reincarnated. The failure of socialist cosmopolitanism, I argue, indicates that the popular nation in the former Third World, or today's postcolonial South, is the last effective bearer of the idea of transcendental freedom for the majority of the world's masses.

Teleological time is a fundamental structure of all political organicisms. However, in each case, their self-recursive causality is disrupted even as it is enabled by an alterity that is not within rational control. In Kant, this takes the form of an inhuman technic of nature. This vulnerability to self-loss also opens up Fichte's nation to the state; Hegel's ideal state to the supplement of the national spirit; and Marx's proletarian revolution to the national question.

The second part of the book focuses on the vicissitudes of postcolonial nationalism. The supplementary relationship between nation and state in Hegel's and Fichte's philosophies is especially pertinent to postcoloniality, where it is played out as a mutual haunting of the popular organism and the state: the nation tries to reappropriate the state from authoritarian and global capitalist forces so that it can fully incarnate itself. As Cabral's famous dictum that "national liberation is necessarily an act of culture"[10] indicates, this project of reappropriation is literally a form of radical *Bildung*. Patriotic culture is a form of self-recursive mediation, an organic prosthesis of the living national body. It aims to resurrect the national spirit through the formation of a critical public sphere that continually presses against the state in order to inspirit it and transfigure the degraded present. The success of nationalist *Bildung* is therefore a crucial test case for the continuing viability of organismic vitalism.

Because postcolonial nationalist *Bildung* draws a lot of its strength from narrative fiction, especially that of the bildungsroman, I focus in particular on the difficulties of narrating the postcolonial nation in contemporary Asia and Africa through readings of Pramoedya Ananta Toer and Ngũgĩ wa Thiong'o. The uncontrollable recurrence of figures of ghosts and malignant prostheses in Pramoedya's and Ngũgĩ's attempts to reincarnate

---

10. Amilcar Cabral, "National Liberation and Culture," in *Unity and Struggle: Speeches and Writings,* trans. Michael Wolfers (New York: Monthly Review Press, 1979), p. 143.

the national organism indicate that something has gone awry with their projects. The national organism and the culture that was supposed to preserve its life and resurrect it are constitutively possessed by the neocolonial state and other phantomatic processes such as the global culture industry. This requires us to rethink the idea of freedom as the transcendence of finitude. I conclude by suggesting that the most apposite metaphor for freedom today is not the organism but the haunted nation. Here, I draw on the theoretical alternative to organismic vitalism provided by Jacques Derrida's work on spectrality and examine its implications for the future of postcolonial nationalism.

I wrote this book as an organic whole. The problems of postcoloniality are an exemplary performance and undoing of the fundamental concepts of organismic vitalism. Just as it is impossible to understand postcoloniality without some grasp of the philosophemes of freedom, culture, and organic life, it is also impossible to understand the future of these ideas without a consideration of their displacement outside the North Atlantic. Philosophy has retreated into the insular sphere of specialized exegesis. Its continuing relevance to our contemporary globalized world is increasingly doubtful. I have tried to make the book as "user-friendly" as possible because I want to persuade readers who may be unfamiliar with Kant, Hegel, Marx, and others why it is still important to read them. However, readers who are interested in postcoloniality and find philosophical discourse recondite will probably skip the first half of the book. Conversely, philosophically trained readers who are not interested in events outside the North Atlantic will probably confine themselves to those parts on European philosophy.

I have tried to cross various disciplinary borders because unless they are bridged, it is impossible to follow the multiple threads of the global fabrication of the contemporary human being. Philosophy formulates ethical concepts and normative ideals by abstracting from "prototypical" evidence confined to the limited sociohistorical situation of the North Atlantic. In my view, political phenomena need to be understood in terms of the philosophical lenses through which they were initially conceptualized because these formative philosophemes leave long-lasting residues. Conversely, philosophemes are also actualized and have a future that may be quite different from what their originators envisioned when they are performed in/as history in other spaces. Finally, in arguing that postcolonial nationalism performs the undoing of organismic vitalism and the modern philosopheme of culture as freedom, I attempt to cross and recross the border between theory (and philosophy), which is always regarded as universal even though it is implicitly geographically marked as "made in the North Atlantic," and area studies, which is always regarded as particularistic and explicitly geographically marked as "of the rest of the world outside the North Atlantic." For such a task, one needs to have several languages at one's disposal; to be at the same time area-studies trained, but also not so area-bound that one is incapable of making broader generalizations. Although I do not have all these credentials, I am comforted by the thought that all work should ultimately be comparative and collaborative, open to the disruption of the other. This is also the uncanny promise of life, which is always pregnant with the specter of alterity.

PART 1

Culture as Freedom: Territorializations and Deterritorializations

THE RATIONALITY OF LIFE: ON THE ORGANISMIC
METAPHOR OF THE SOCIAL AND POLITICAL BODY

MYTHS OF THE ORGANIC COMMUNITY

In "What Is a Nation?" (1882), Ernest Renan provides an exemplary definition:

> The nation, like an individual, is the culmination of a long past of endeavours, sacrifice, and devotion. . . . A nation is therefore a large-scale solidarity, constituted by the feeling of the sacrifices that one has made in the past and of those that one is prepared to make in the future.[1]

As the subject and object of a common inheritance that requires repeated affirmation, the nation is a quasi-natural force from the past that constrains the present and future actions of its members. As a personality in its own right, it exacts sacrifice from them. Renan thus unintentionally captures for posterity the two fundamental characteristics of the idea of organic community. We are told often enough that the nation holds itself together by means of atavistic hallucinations and the violent and oppressive subordination of its members to the larger whole. Accordingly, the idea of organic community is often associated with "bad" nationalism—

---

1. "What Is a Nation?" trans. Martin Thom, in *Nation and Narration*, ed. Homi Bhabha (London and New York: Routledge, 1990), p. 19. Hereafter cited in the text as "WN."

the Prusso-Germanic nationalism of Bismarck, the National Socialism of Hitler, ethnic fundamentalism and cultural chauvinism in decolonized Asia and Africa, and with totalitarianism in general.[2] In the conventional history of ideas, the organismic theory of the political body is said to entail the permanent inequality of members within the collective because the individual is seen as an abstraction that must be subordinated to its function within the larger whole qua living organism.[3] Moreover, these oppressive consequences are said to issue directly from the theory's intellectual origins in the German romantic movement understood as a mystical, irrationalist view of life that arose in ideological reaction to the Enlightenment. As Hans Kohn puts it, "the connection between nationalism and tradition received its strongest expression in German romanticism. . . . Starting as extreme individualists the German romanticists developed the opposite longing for a true, harmonious community, an organic folk community, which would immerse the individual in the unbroken chain of tradition. . . . To the optimistic idealization of the future, so characteristic of the Age of Enlightenment, the romanticists opposed a similar idealization of the national past."[4] Their ideal of the organic state "represented a flight from reality into mythology. It was not a return to any real past; it was an idyllic myth and poetic dream which transfigured the past into a Golden Age."[5]

One feature of Renan's definition of the nation is, however, not so easily reconciled with this received understanding of the organic community. For instead of defining organic bonds in terms of biological race or geographical

---

2. See, for instance, the representative claim in C. L. Wayper, *Political Thought* (New York: Philosophical Library, 1954), 155, that "if through Bismarck and the triumph of an armed and organic nationalism, Hegel's influence can be seen leading to Nazism and Fascism, through Marx and Engels it can also be shown operating strongly on Lenin, Stalin, and Communist Russia."

3. See H. S. Reiss, "Introduction," in *The Political Thought of the German Romantics, 1793–1815,* ed. H. S. Reiss (New York: Macmillan, 1955), p. 8.

4. Hans Kohn, *Nationalism: Its Meaning and History* (Princeton: Van Nostrand, 1955), p. 34. For an elaboration of the link between romanticism and the conception of the German nation as an organic community, see Hans Kohn, *Prelude to Nation-States: The French and German Experience, 1789–1815* (Princeton, N.J.: Van Nostrand, 1967), chap. 24; and Liah Greenfeld, *Nationalism: Five Roads to Modernity* (Cambridge: Harvard University Press, 1992), chap. 4.

5. Kohn, *Prelude to Nation-States,* p. 172.

and ethnolinguistic descent, he suggests that the nation is first and foremost a moral project that involves rational willing and consensual acts of self-renunciation. "A nation is a soul, a spiritual principle" ("WN," 19):

> Man is a slave neither of his race nor his language, nor of his religion, nor of the course of rivers nor of the direction taken by mountain chains. A large aggregate of men, healthy in mind and warm of heart, creates the kind of moral conscience which we call a nation. So long as this moral consciousness gives proof of its strength by the sacrifices which demand the abdication of the individual to the advantage of the community, it is legitimate and has the right to exist. ("WN," 20)

The nation is spiritual because its life issues from purposive moral work in which individualistic interests are sacrificed so that the ideals of the community can be incarnated and given objective existence. This work binds together the nation qua organic whole.

Renan's definition of the nation is significant because it implies that the concept of "organism," from which the organismic metaphor of the social and political body is derived, is an important philosophical basis of nationalism. It is difficult to grasp the moral dimensions of the organismic metaphor today because both it and the nation-form are unfailingly read under the sinister sign of ideology and subjected to the profoundest caricature and misunderstanding. In fact, the metaphor was first formulated in German idealist philosophy before the advent of Jena Romanticism. It had a crucial role in Kant's and Fichte's moral and political philosophy because it was a response to the question of how freedom could be realized in the world of experience. The historical coincidence of the rise of European nationalism with the decline of the mechanistic metaphor of the state and the corresponding articulation of the organismic metaphor is part of the complex traffic between German idealism and nationalism, philosophy and politics. In the first half of this book, I examine the metaphor's origins in the German philosophy of the late eighteenth and early nineteenth centuries in order to understand its inherent rationality and to reconstruct a more progressive genealogy for it and the nation-form from which it is indissociable. The organismic metaphor persists in the discourse of Third World revolutionary decolonizing nationalism. The second part of the book assesses the metaphor's continuing feasibility and whether post-colonial nationalism has a future in our global conjuncture. It is important to stress from the outset that I am offering a critique of political organicism. I argue that the organismic metaphor is not plausible in contemporary globalization and that its apparent plausibility in the past masked an entire complex of unanswered questions concerning the transcendence of finitude that it promised. But instead of rehearsing tired arguments about the irrationalism of organic community, I proceed from an understanding of the rationality of organic life itself.

———◆———

It is useful to begin with a brief consideration of the confusions riddling earlier critiques of organic community that follow from a resolute refusal to acknowledge the organismic metaphor's rational underpinnings. Written in the aftermath of National Socialism, many of these critiques remain extremely influential in contemporary discourse. They have perpetrated an intellectual-historical myth about the organic community that reduces the organismic metaphor to a manipulative mystification. These critiques can be divided into two main positions. They are not mutually exclusive and can be found in various combinations in a given thinker. The first position is a socioeconomic determinist argument that holds that German organic nationalism is the tendentious hallucination of a marginal intelligentsia who overcompensated for its political inactivity and economic backwardness in the realm of speculative thought. This was, of course, Marx's view. A harsher formulation holds that early German nationalism was a psychosocial pathology of a socially disgruntled *Bildungsburgertum* irresponsibly out of touch with political and economic reality. This lack of a reality principle led to disastrous historical consequences when others put their ideas into practice. In Hans Kohn's words, "the idealism of Fichte, of Hegel, the dreams of Novalis, the brilliant formulations of Schlegel and Adam Muller opened no doors to a responsible mastery of reality. They were, at their best, lofty excursions in the realm of thought . . . , but dangerous by reason of their claims to explain or change reality through their surrealistic concepts. Yet they exercised a disturbing and profound influence on politics and history in Germany and other lands where the cautious and sober empiricism of a Locke or a Hume, the skeptical and rational clarity of a Descartes or a Voltaire, the critical analysis of a Kant, never took root.[6]

This type of argument invariably conflates German idealism with romanticism and views the organic community as a romantic product, which is denounced as mystical, fantastic, or irrational because it appeals to faith, imagination, and the passions. But this denunciation is not always convincing or unequivocal. Since the same idea is also found in the work of many idealist philosophers who were the architects of elaborate philosophical systems, it is also paradoxically characterized as *overly* rational to the point that it lacks realism.[7] The complex links and discontinuities between German idealism and romanticism, especially that of the Jena period, and an evaluation of romantic social and political thought are beyond the scope of this book.[8] But even if the romantic use of the organismic metaphor is mystical and may have led to an oppressive form of nationalism, this is not an inevitable consequence of the idea of organic community per se. Indeed, the charge that the idea of organic community is irrational is often based on a terminological confusion wherein a critique of the mechanical state based on the understanding (*Verstand*) is taken as a complete flight from reason without consideration of the philosophical

---

6. Kohn, *Prelude to Nation-States*, p. 124. Cf. H. S. Reiss, "Introduction," in *The Political Thought of the German Romantics*, who accuses Fichte of the same lack of realism (pp. 11, 21); and Greenfeld, *Nationalism*, pp. 309–10, 314, 325–26.

7. Kohn's views on the metaphor's irrationality are especially confused when he discusses Hegel. Having argued that the romantics saw the nation-state as "an organic personality, God's creation like the individual himself, only infinitely greater . . . and the fountainhead of all individual life," he notes that "though . . . Hegel . . . was not a romanticist but a rationalist, his concept of the state resembled that of the romanticists" (Kohn, *Nationalism*, 35). Kohn also overlooks that Kant, the philosopher of critical reason and liberal individualism, was the metaphor's originator.

8. For a detailed intellectual-historical reconstruction of the relationship between Jena romanticism and idealism, see Frederick C. Beiser, *Enlightenment, Revolution, and Romanticism: The Genesis of Modern German Political Thought, 1790–1800* (Cambridge, Mass.: Harvard University Press, 1992). Hereafter cited in the text as *ERR*. For a philosophically nuanced argument that Jena romanticism is the transformation of the philosophy of spirit into an aesthetic philosophy, see Philippe Lacoue-Labarthe and Jean-Luc Nancy, *The Literary Absolute: The Theory of Literature in German Romanticism*, trans. Philip Barnard and Cheryl Lester (Albany: SUNY Press, 1988), pp. 34–35. One should distinguish the early romanticism of Friedrich Schlegel, Novalis, and Schelling from the later romanticism of Adam Mueller.

distinction between the understanding and reason (*Vernunft*) in Kantian and post-Kantian thought.[9]

The second conventional critique points to the inner affinity between the organismic metaphor and German conservatism although it concedes that the metaphor has also been deployed in progressive and democratic political theories. It is argued that since an organism implies slow evolution and growth, the organismic metaphor is fundamentally conservative and, hence, has been more readily used by historicists, such as Gentz and Savigny, to justify conservative politics.[10] In his accounts of the organismic theory of the political body and German conservatism, Karl Mannheim combines both of the above arguments. He suggests that there is an elective affinity between political conservatism and the irrational mysticism of organismic thinking: "conservative thinking tends to favour theological-mystical, or, in any case, transcendental definitions" of state legitimation and mythical transcendence is easily given a historicist inflection.[11] However, he gives a sociological-determinist explanation for why German romanticism took on an irrational and mystical cast. Echoing Marx, he suggests that this hypertrophy of metaphysical abstraction is a reflection of and compensation for the political and economic underdevelopment of Germany, especially the political inefficacy of romantic intellectuals and their detachment from their bourgeois class origins.

Romanticism, Mannheim argues, is the first oppositional critique of the capitalist rationalization of the world. It "is . . . a reception, a collecting of

---

9. In order to argue that the organic spirit is the antithesis of reason, Liah Greenfeld creatively amends an English translation of Friedrich Schlegel's Athanaeum Fragment no. 366 ("Understanding [*Verstand*] is mechanical, wit is chemical, genius is organic spirit") by translating *Verstand* as "reason" (Greenfeld, *Nationalism*, 335, 543–44 n114).

10. See Reinhold Aris, *History of Political Thought in Germany from 1789 to 1815* (London: Allen and Unwin, 1936), p. 294. Cf. Aira Kemiläinen, *Nationalism: Problems Concerning the Word, the Concept, and Classification,* Studia Historica Jyväskyläensia, vol. 3 (Jyväskylä, Finland: Kustantajat Publishers, 1964), p. 112.

11. Karl Mannheim, *Conservatism: A Contribution to the Sociology of Knowledge,* trans. David Kettler and Volker Meja (London and New York: Routledge and Kegan Paul, 1986), p. 56; hereafter cited in the text as *C*. This text was Mannheim's 1925 *Habilitationschrift*, posthumously published in full in 1984. See also his "The History of the Concept of the State as an Organism: A Sociological Analysis," in *Essays on Sociology and Social Psychology* (London: Routledge and Kegan Paul, 1953): 165–82, hereafter cited in the text as "Org."

all the [irrational] elements and ways of life, derived ultimately from the religious consciousness, which were pushed aside by the onmarch of capitalist rationalism" (*C*, 66). "It made it its task to salvage these elements, to lend them a new dignity and to save them from extinction. 'Community'-bound experience is pitted, in various forms, against manifestations of the turn to 'society' . . . : family against contract, intuitive certainty against rationality, inner experience as a source of knowledge against the mechanistic" (*C*, 65). But because these intellectuals are socially anomalous and politically inactive, their ideas were incorporated into the ideologies of more politically active social strata such as the feudal powers and landowners. They were also "without interest in the capitalist process or even threatened by it with extinction, and . . . were, moreover bound by tradition to the lost world forms [*Weltgestalten*] of the various stages of the pre-capitalist past," and they used romantic ideas as resources against bourgeois industrialism (*C*, 66). The strong affinity between mystical organismic ideas and conservatism thus obeys a strict sociological law governing German conditions.

Mannheim's critique of organismic theory is more incisive because he emphasizes that romanticism is not entirely irrational. "The romantic solution does not destroy the Enlightenment faith in reason, but merely modifies it. The faith in the power of reason, in the capacity of thought, is not abandoned. Only one type of thinking is rejected, the immobile thought of the Enlightenment with its deductions from single principles and mere combinations of rigid conceptual components, and the horizon of potential thinking is expanded only in contrast to this one type" (*C*, 142). This distinction between the static rationality of the Enlightenment and a more dynamic form of thought is precisely the distinction between the understanding's mechanical operations and reason's living procedures. But Mannheim's repeated identification of organismic thought with romantic mysticism prevents him from affirming the organismic metaphor's inherent rationality. He is clearly aware that Kant, who provided the first thorough philosophical elaboration of the idea of organism, "foreshadows the growth of the spirit of nationalism and the theory of the '*Volksgeist.*'" "The great builders of philosophical systems such as Fichte, Schelling and Hegel could only free themselves from the spell of eighteenth century mechanism by starting with Kant's seemingly dry and abstract definitions" ("Org.," 172). Yet, in the same breath, Fichte, Schelling, and Hegel are equated with "romantics like Adam Mueller" and criticized as examples of "a projection of political experiences on to the metaphysical or aesthetic plane" (Ibid.).[12]

From Mannheim's criticism, we can see that critiques of organicism are concerned with the nature of the political itself. They repeatedly suggest that political experiences should be understood rationally and not mystically. But at the same time, one should also not be overly rational to the point that one loses touch with reality and becomes carried away, transported to metaphysical heights, thereby losing sight of practical exigencies. The political thus involves conformity to reality. But one could also argue the exact opposite, that it is the essence of the political to waver unceasingly between reality and ideals, between what is and what ought to be, in the endeavor to realize the ideal and to idealize reality. This is what distinguishes it from a mere pragmatics or technics. It is a practice with a critical-normative dimension. It is precisely the problem of reality that is at stake in a moral politics or political morality, the problem of how norms can be actualized and how reality can be transformed in the image of normative ideals through critical practice. As Frederick Beiser aptly notes, the myth of the apolitical German intellectual who escapes from the harsh world of political reality into an ideal world of metaphysics and aesthetics "has blinded scholars to the political motivations of so much German philosophy and literature in the eighteenth century. . . . [The ideas of Kant, Fichte, et al.] were not harmless abstractions floating in Plato's world of forms, but potent weapons engaged in political struggle" (*ERR*, 8).[13]

But a definition of the political as the site of the critique of reality and the incarnation of ideals would involve "metaphysics" if by that we mean a dimension that is beyond brute facticity and finite existence, a state of being higher than a merely given reality. As we will see in subsequent chapters, when idealist philosophers like Kant, Fichte, and Hegel speak of moral freedom as the basis of political freedom, they have in mind this higher state where we transcend our finitude through the causality of ideas. It is moreover not accidental that critiques of the mystical nature of idealist moral and political philosophy always focus on the organismic metaphor

---

12. This theme of "yes, philosopher X is a rationalist, but still too metaphysical" is repeated in Mannheim's reading of Hegel as a dynamic rationalist. See *C*, esp. 154–55. Hegel would pose problems for Mannheim's characterization of organismic thought as an irrational mysticism, but his unfinished text breaks off before a full analysis of Hegel.

13. Beiser suggests that the myth originates from Madame de Staël's *De l'Allemagne*.

of the social and political body. For the idea of organic life was formulated in idealist philosophy precisely to capture a form of being in which reality and ideality, matter and rational-purposive form, can coexist.

The main purpose of this critical exposition of the dominant intellectual-historical myth of organic community is to suggest that organismic conceptions of collectivity do not necessarily repudiate normative reason. The idea of organic life represents a rupture from rigidly mechanistic conceptions of the world, and different conceptualizations of the organism give rise to different uses of the organismic metaphor in moral and political philosophy. To take an obvious instance, while Mannheim and others seem to understand organic life in preformationist terms, that is, as a static form of evolution in which the past is a germinal essence from which the present and future unfolds, most idealist philosophers were influenced by Blumenbach's theory of epigenesis and saw organic life as a dynamic process of self-formation and self-generation, a spontaneous, rational-purposive and autocausal becoming.[14] This dynamic understanding of organic life informs Marxism and the discourse of revolutionary decolonization, where the organic is seen as a rational response to capitalist rationalization under the sign of colonialism.

THE TRANSITION FROM MECHANISTIC TO ORGANISMIC METAPHORS OF THE SOCIAL AND POLITICAL BODY

But what motivated the change from the dominant eighteenth-century understanding of collective existence in mechanical terms to seeing society and the political body as an organism? And what exactly did "organism" as the antonym of "machine" mean? Friedrich Meinecke's account of the rise of German nationalism between 1795 and 1815 is a useful starting point:

> Modern man now entered the political organism with the intent of conquering it. It was nothing new for men with modern attitudes to occupy positions of central authority; they were in evidence from the days of Emperor Frederick II in the Middle Ages to the Frederican age. But on the whole they had driven

---

14. For Mannheim's preformationist understanding of organismic thought, see *C*, pp. 95–102.

the state from the outside, as it were; guiding it as one would a machine. The reformers, on the contrary, wanted to possess the state, and infuse it with their blood.[15]

In the intervening years between the French Revolution and the formation of the German Confederation after Napoleon's decline, Napoleon had invaded Germany, dissolved the Holy Roman Empire, and subjugated various territorial states including Prussia. This is the historical catalyst of the political reform of the absolutist state and German nationalism. What is striking is Meinecke's analogy between the absolutist state and a machine and how he distinguishes the machine-state's organization from that of a warm-blooded living being. A machine is organized from the top down, by an external force. In contradistinction, a living being is organized from within and self-perpetuating. The reform of the absolutist state, figured as the transformation of a machine into a living creature, involves imparting it with the capacity of self-organization, or organic life. By the end of the quoted passage, the meaning of "organism" in the metaphor of the state as political organism has mutated from "technical instrument" to its complete opposite: a nonartificial life-form.

The discursive allusions and references signalling this paradigm change or rupture are necessarily diacritical and operate in two registers. First, in the philosophy of nature, which is not yet clearly divorced from the natural sciences, the study of living forms as phenomena that cannot be explained by efficient or mechanical causality represents a clear "shifting of scenes" that sets new limits on the field and transforms its legitimate areas of inquiry. For the victory of the emergent epigenetic concept of life over preformationist theories meant that divine creation could no longer be a legitimate issue in the scientific study of the natural world.[16] At the same time, the new idea of organism stimulated an equally revolutionary epistemic shift in political philosophy: the repudiation of the mechanistic model of the state that had been dominant since Hobbes.[17] The rationalistic aspect of

---

15. Friedrich Meinecke, *The Age of German Liberation, 1795–1815,* trans. Peter Paret and Helmuth Fischer (Berkeley: University of California Press, 1977), p. 45.
16. See Nicholas Jardine, *The Scenes of Inquiry: On the Reality of Questions in the Sciences* (Oxford: Clarendon, 1991), p. 53.

the organismic metaphor of the political body often goes unrecognized simply because most contemporary political theorists are unaware of debates about organic life in the history and philosophy of the life sciences. Let us first consider the shift in political philosophy.

The use of the organism as an extended metaphor for the political body was first explicitly formulated by Kant in the *Critique of Judgment* (1790, 2d ed. 1793). Prior to this, the political body was predominantly imagined in terms of mechanistic models of state and society that had succeeded the hylozoistic Aristotelian-Galenic tradition. In his formulation of the state as "an artificial man," Hobbes had been the first to characterize the political body within the mechanistic framework of Descartes's description of the human body qua complex animal body as an automaton.[18] For Hobbes, the artificial life of automata are imitations by human art of the animal life created by a divine Artificer.[19] The absolutist state or commonwealth is produced when human art undertakes the even more ambitious attempt of imitating *human* life itself with its superior trait of reason. It is in this sense that Leviathan is an artifical man.[20]

On the one hand, Hobbes's metaphor of the state as a human machine significantly modifies the classical analogy of the body politic, which is

---

17. For more detailed reconstructions of this intellectual-historical shift that also touch on the adventures of mechanistic and organismic metaphors of the political body from ancient Greek philosophy to the contemporary era, see Ahlrich Meyer, "Mechanische und organische Metaphorik politischer Philosophie," *Archiv für Begriffsgeschichte* 13, no. 2 (1969): 128–99; Ernst-Wolfgang Böckenförde, "Organ, Organismus, Organisation, politischer Körper," in *Geschichtliche Grundbegriffe: Historisches Lexikon zur politisch-sozialen Sprache in Deutschland,* ed. Otto Brunner, Werner Conze, and Reinhardt Koselleck (Stuttgart: Ernst Klett, 1978) 4:519–622; the entries on *Organ, organik, Organisation, Organismus,* and *Organizismus* in *Historisches Wörterbuch der Philosophie,* ed. Joachim Ritter, vol. 6 (Basel: Schwabe, 1984): 1317–61; Manfred Frank, *Der kommende Gott: Vorlesungen über die Neue Mythologie* (Frankfurt: Suhrkamp, 1982), chap. 6; F. W. Coker, *Organismic Theories of the State: Nineteenth Century Interpretations of the State as Organism or as Person* (New York: AMS Press, 1967); and C. L. Wayper, *Political Thought.*

18. For Descartes's comparison of animate bodies to clocks and hydraulically operated automata, see *Discourse on the Method of Rightly Conducting One's Reason and Seeking the Truth in the Sciences,* part 5, in *The Philosophical Writings of Descartes,* trans. John Cottingham, Robert Stoothoff, and Dugald Murdoch (Cambridge: Cambridge University Press, 1985), 1:139–41; and "Treatise on Man," ibid., 1:99.

19. Thomas Hobbes, *Leviathan* (Harmondsworth, U.K.: Penguin, 1981), p. 81.

20. Ibid., pp. 81–82.

fused with ideas of covenant and contract theory. Hobbes's commonwealth is not the well-integrated and harmonious living unity of the Greek body politic, since it has to be regulated by the force of law. On the other hand, Hobbes still retains the Aristotelian understanding of the relationship between members of the state and the sovereign: Leviathan's members are likened to the different functional parts or limbs of the individual human body as organs or instruments of the soul qua source of life and movement, even if these body parts have to be made to cooperate through the mediating agency of joints (the executive and judicial powers) and nerves (coercion and reward). One glimpses here three fundamental motifs in Hobbes's metaphor from which the more concrete features of the mechanistic model of the political body are derived. In the first place, the state is characterized by *hierarchy* since its relation to its members is said to correspond to the vertical relationship of subordination between an alien soul and bodily parts. Second, the commonwealth is *artificial* since the harmony of the political body is not given, but established by the device of a social contract and continually maintained by enlightened despotism. But finally and most importantly, because these political bonds replicate the soul–limbs relationship found in nature, artifice is itself a mimesis of nature. The mechanistic model of the state is thus premised upon *the absence of a sharp distinction between the artificial and the naturally living.*

The mechanical state's characteristics can be understood as elaborations of these underlying motifs, which function as lenses to apprehend and give cognizable shape to sociopolitical relations and even as a means of justification. For instance, the absolutist state's hierarchical nature is understood and justified by recourse to the idea that the sovereign and its various powers articulate the common good because it is the external agent that sets the sociopolitical machine into motion. The account of the emergence of society and state from a contract between atomistic individuals who associate in order to pursue self-interest is understood in terms of the separate components in a mechanical assemblage that are only put together for a specific purpose, and the coercive force used to maintain the association is understood in terms of the physical forces that hold a machine together. Finally, the mimetic relationship between the rational designs of political art and those of divine artifice in the creation of humanity and nature can serve as a more rational basis for the sovereign's divine right.

Of course, there were vitalist conceptions of society and the political body pre-dating the organismic model of German idealism that challenged the absolutist implications of the mechanistic model, especially in the discourses immediately preceding and during the French revolution. But generally speaking, despite their egalitarian and progressive implications, these—unlike those of the second generation French Romantics such as Renan and Michelet—remained within the mechanistic paradigm for at least three reasons. First, as Hegel pointed out, social-contract theory was mechanistic since it presupposed that society and state were artifacts brought into being by an act of association which must, by definition, be prior and external to the collectivity that was formed. But more significantly, although the living people were opposed to the machine-state, the body politic's life process was still conceived under principles of mechanical causality because its source of movement was attributed to something qualitatively and substantively alien to the body parts—namely, a soul. The important point here is not whether the corporate will is autocratic or formed through rational consensus: its mechanistic nature necessarily follows from the idea that it is different from and superior to the individual wills from which it is composed because it is thereby conferred the same intelligible principle of animation ascribed to the soul.[21] In contradistinction, in a genuinely organismic conception of the political body, the relationship between whole and parts can no longer be understood in terms of the soul–limbs relationship because the parts are both cause and effect of the whole and not subordinate to it. Finally, to the extent that the totality of nature was conceived as the creation of a divine artificer, no genuine idea of organism and, hence, no genuinely organismic conception of collective existence was possible. In the original instance, nature itself is not self-creating but a product of something else!

Rousseau's writings best exemplify the awkwardness of a vitalism that has not completely freed itself from mechanism. In his description of the

---

21. In *Qu'est-ce que le Tiers État?*, Abbé Sieyès famously defines the nobility as "a people apart, a false people which, unable to exist by itself for lack of useful organs, latches on to a real nation like those vegetable growths which can only live on the sap of the plants they exhaust and suck dry" (quoted in Greenfeld, *Nationalism*, p. 172). The model of the body politic is clearly that of a giant human body, a supreme cause that is more powerful than its parts, on which a parasite is attached.

body politic as "a moral and collective body" or "public person" with a general will formed by a social contract between private persons with particular wills, Rousseau rejects Hobbes's absolutist model.[22] Insofar as each individual member is in unity with other members and forms "an indivisible part of the whole," Rousseau's idea of the general will is partially organismic. Indeed, in the earlier *Discourse on Political Economy* (1755–56), he explicitly compares the body politic to a living organic body where the parts are united in such a way that there is reciprocal connection and internal correspondence. The source of life is the interdependence of the parts:

> The body politic, taken by itself, can be looked upon as an organized body, alive and similar to a man's. The sovereign power represents the head; the laws and customs are the brain, . . . public finances are the blood which a wise economy, performing the functions of the heart, sends out to distribute nourishment and life throughout the entire body.
>
> The life of the one as well as the other is the self common to the whole, the reciprocal sensitivity and the internal correspondence of all the parts. What if this communication should cease, the formal unity vanish, and the contiguous parts no longer belong together except by being next to one another? The man is dead, or the state is dissolved.
>
> The body politic is, then, also a moral being that has a will, and this general will . . . always tends towards the preservation and the well-being of the whole and of each part.[23]

Yet, in *The Social Contract,* the body politic is explicitly described as "an artificial body."[24] Indeed, Rousseau also understands the organic body itself in mechanistic terms. In the same passage from the *Discourse on Political Economy,* he notes that "the citizens are the body and the members that make the machine move, live, and work."[25] Hence, regardless of whether

---

22. Jean-Jacques Rousseau, *Of the Social Contract,* book 1, chap. 6 [9–10], in *The Social Contract and Other Later Political Writings,* ed. and trans. Victor Gourevitch (Cambridge: Cambridge University Press, 1997), p. 50.

23. Rousseau, *Discourse on Political Economy,* in *The Social Contract and Other Later Political Writings,* p. 6.

24. Book 3, chap. 1 [21], p. 86. Cf. book 3, chap. 11 [2], p. 109.

25. Cf. *Of the Social Contract,* book 3, chap. 11 [3], p. 109, where the heart as the source of life is described in the mechanical-functional terms of a hydraulic pump.

he characterizes the body politic as natural or artificial, as a natural telos of human freedom or as an artificial mechanism of contract, Rousseau continues to conceive of the living human body metaphorically as a mechanical assemblage of internal organs and limbs governed by the mind.[26]

In its inaugural formulations, the organismic metaphor of society and state in German philosophy is a polemical response to the mechanistic model outlined above. There were, of course, sociohistorical conditions for its emergence: for instance, the suitability of the organismic metaphor for expressing the strong desires for active political participation and political unity and for greater identification of individuals with the state felt by the growing bourgeois stratum in the transition from an autocratic, administrative mercantilist state to a modern capitalist state.[27] What interests us is the metaphor's ideational structure and the philosophical work it was designed to accomplish. In the hands of the Jena romantics with whom it is most frequently associated, the organismic metaphor was used to articulate a new concept of society that was opposed not only to the mechanical model of enlightened despotism, but also to the modern civil society celebrated by theories of social contract and liberal individualism.[28] *The Oldest Systematic Programme of German Idealism,* an anonymous manuscript in Hegel's handwriting, denounced the state as inimical to freedom because it was nothing other than a machine and championed its abolition: "We must therefore go beyond the state! For every state must treat free human beings as if they were cogs in a machine; but that it should not do; therefore it should *cease* to exist."[29] Novalis spoke of transforming the state-machine "into a living autonomous creature," "a poetic state" in which "the unruliness of nature and the forced order of artifice would interpenetrate one another

---

26. For more detailed discussions of the tension between organismic and mechanistic conceptions in Rousseau's account of the political body, see, for instance, Ahlrich Meyer, "Mechanische und organische Metaphorik politischer Philosophie," pp. 142–47; and C. L. Wayper, *Political Thought,* p. 151.

27. See Aris, *History of Political Thought in Germany from 1789 to 1815,* pp. 292–93.

28. For a fair-minded and thorough assessment of early romantic political theory, see Beiser, *ERR,* esp. ch. 9.

29. Anon., *The Oldest Systematic Programme of German Idealism* (1796–1797), in *The Early Political Writings of the German Romantics,* ed. and trans. Frederick C. Beiser (Cambridge: Cambridge University Press, 1996), p. 4. Available in German in Georg Wilhelm Friedrich Hegel, *Das älteste Systemprogramm des deutschen Idealismus,* in *Werke I: Frühe Schriften,* ed. Eva Moldernhauer and Karl Markus Michel (Frankfurt: Suhrkamp, 1986), pp. 234–35.

and be resolved into *spirit*."[30] The mechanical state of enlightened despotism is based on self-interest. It is a state "where the interests of the state were as self-centred as those of its subjects, yet where the interests of both are so artificially connected that they reciprocally promoted one another."[31] In contradistinction, Novalis's poetic state is an organized society bound together by the living ties of reason and not the artifice of self-interested calculative understanding: "The drive toward society is the drive toward *organization*. Through this *spiritual assimilation* there often arises from the most common ingredients a good society centred around one spiritual individual."[32] This spiritual state is *an organism,* a form of life higher than mere existence. Likewise, speaking of life as an approximation of the concept of freedom, Friedrich Schlegel points to the importance of a harmonious relation of the individual to the whole: "we cannot consider human beings individually. The question of the vocation of man concerns, therefore, not the individual but the whole of humanity. We have constructed it as *an organic concept*. Practical philosophy should not construct therefore the ideal of an individual person, but the idea of the whole, of society."[33]

The common theme in all these examples is the link between spirit as a concrete form of reason, freedom, self-perpetuating life, and the harmonious unity of individuals in a society that preserves their autonomy. As opposed to both the paternalistic state-machine and artificial modern bourgeois civil society, such a society is a rationally organized totality, or living organic whole, wherein freedom is concretely approximated or even realized. The early conception of the organismic model of society thus overturns the key motifs of the mechanistic model. First, the hierarchical relationship of the different limbs of the individual human body to the soul or mind is replaced by a complete interdependence of parts and whole. Instead of receiving its movement from an alien source, the collectivity is self-animating. Instead of being subordinated to the government, each individual actively

---

30. Novalis, *Mixed Remarks*, no. 122, in *The Early Political Writings of the German Romantics*, p. 84, emphasis added.

31. Novalis, *Faith and Love* (1798), no. 36, in *The Early Political Writings of the German Romantics*, p. 45.

32. Novalis, *Pollen* (1798), no. 59, in *The Early Political Writings of the German Romantics*, p. 19, emphasis added.

33. *Philosophical Lectures: Transcendental Philosophy* (Jena, 1800–1801), part 2, excerpted in *The Early Political Writings of the German Romantics*, p. 156, emphasis added.

participates in the collective's life just as the parts and whole of an organism mutually determine each other. Second, society is not formed by a contract for the pursuit of individual self-interest. It is instead a harmonious whole in which individual self-fulfillment and self-development are fostered through social interaction and cooperation. The community is therefore held together not by external force and coercion, but by bonds with the permanence of a higher nature, the rational bonds of spirit and all its products: art, philosophy, and, more generally, culture. Culture is not necessarily territorially bound, although for many romantic thinkers it took the form of the culture of a nation or a people. Finally, such a society is not merely an imitation of nature, but a higher form of life. As a self-originating being, its ends, its structure or form, and its development are internally prescribed and inseparable from its parts. In this respect, it transcends mere nature conceived as mechanism. Thus, for the first time in philosophical history, "organism" sharply breaks with artifice and derivation.

One sees here how mistaken the caricature of Jena romanticism as the purveyor of the theory of the organic state actually is. As Frederick Beiser points out, Schlegel, Novalis, and Schleiermacher, who articulated their ideal of organic community in the late 1790s at the height of their individualistic period, did not have a proto-Nazi organic theory of the state, but a rationalist organic theory of society in which the autonomy and unique self-development of the individual was actively cultivated (*ERR*, 226–27). Indeed, *The Oldest Systematic Programme of German Idealism* exemplifies the strong anarchistic streak in the early romantics who thought that the state would wither away because it is unnecessary to an ideal organic society. Although later German romantics like Adam Mueller developed the organismic metaphor into a conservative theory of the state, unless we are blinded by anachronism it is clear that "what the organic concept meant to Mueller in 1808 was not what it meant to Friedrich Schlegel, Schleiermacher, and Novalis in 1798" (*ERR*, 238).

I have outlined some of the key differences between organismic and mechanistic metaphors of society and the political body. But we have yet to grasp exactly why the rational ideals of political morality find their most apposite expression in the organismic metaphor. Why was it important to characterize society and the political body as an organism? This implies a series of other questions: for instance, why is mechanism inimical to the rational ideal of freedom? What is an organism and in what manner of speaking is reason isomorphic with organic vitality? How are reason and organic life connected to freedom? The significance of the organismic metaphor can only be properly understood if we see it as a braiding-together of three fundamental philosophemes that emerged in late-eighteenth- and early-nineteenth-century philosophy: a transcendental idea of freedom, the concept of culture, and the idea of organism. As we will see, we are very far from having renounced organicism in contemporary political discourse.

FREEDOM, CULTURE, AND ORGANISM

The idea of freedom as a special power (*Vermögen*) of causality, a capacity for willing and acting, doing and making, through which rational beings could transcend the finitude or contingency of their natural existence, is obviously not original to German idealism. What was new was the broaching of freedom's possibility without reference to divine providence. The canonical formulation of this transcendental idea of freedom, which Fichte, Hegel and others develop and modify, belongs to Kant:

> By freedom in the cosmological sense . . . I understand the faculty [*Vermögen*] of beginning a state from itself, the causality of which does not in turn stand under another cause determining it in time in accordance with the law of nature.[34]

But this auto-causality contradicts causality according to natural laws, whereby every occurrence must have a cause that must in turn have a prior cause. Hence, Kant adds that freedom can only be comprehended when "reason creates the idea of a *spontaneity*, which could start to act from itself, without needing to be preceded by any other cause that in turn determines it to action in accordance to the law of causal connection" (*KrV*, A 533/B 561; p. 533, emphasis added).

In the entire post-Kantian idealist tradition, moral and political freedom are derived from and grounded on transcendental freedom. This is why

---

34. Immanuel Kant, *Kritik der reinen Vernunft* (*Critique of Pure Reason*), A 533/B 561; p. 533. Hereafter cited in the text as *KrV*.

mechanism is inimical to freedom. The laws of causality governing nature defined as the totality of appearances dictate that each thing or event must have a prior cause within the linear succession of time. Such laws are characterized as mechanical in analogy with the fundamentally dependent nature of a machine. The sensible natural world is a mechanism in two senses: the movement of its different parts exhibits a blind necessity or predetermined regularity that can be expressed through mathematical formulae. More importantly, no part of nature is self-sufficient because no occurrence or movement is possible that is not caused by something else, just as no automaton can operate without being first set in motion by something other, and no moving machine can work without being connected to an external source from which it takes its energy.

The spontaneous self-causality of freedom is thus antithetical to mechanical causality. Without this auto-causality, no moral autonomy is possible because "freedom in the practical sense is the *independence* of the power of choice [*Willkür*] *from necessitation* by impulses of sensibility" (*KrV*, A 534/B 562; p. 533, emphasis added). If our actions are determined by sensuous impulses, we are no better than machines because such impulses are part of the blind necessity of nature. In contradistinction, the moral will belongs to a self-determining being, an autonomous subject whose actions are determined by its own universal reason and not an external source. Such a practical being would be self-originating and an end-in-itself because it would contain the ground of its own existence within itself, a ground which moreover possesses universal validity or rational necessity. Because the moral will exhibits a spontaneous auto-causality similar to transcendental freedom, "the abolition [*Aufhebung*] of transcendental freedom would also simultaneously eliminate all practical freedom" (*KrV*, A 534/B 562; p. 534).

In the First and Second Critiques, what Kant juxtaposes to mechanism is freedom, and not organism. However, because the causality of freedom lies beyond spatiotemporal conditions, it is "outside" the sensible world of experience. Hence, the idea of transcendental freedom logically leads to the problem of how this auto-causality can be manifested or have effects in the empirical world. How can freedom operate in the world of appearances in which we live? Since practical freedom is linked to the causality of reason, what is broached here is precisely the ability of reason to incarnate or realize its ideals. Phrased in this way, the problem has implications that extend beyond the corpus of German idealist political thought. As I have noted, any normative theory of the political must be concerned with the question of how rational ideals can be made real. Albrecht Wellmer similarly observes that "the question how freedom can be realized in the modern world has inspired and haunted European political philosophy for centuries. This is true at least if we only regard those political thinkers who belong to the tradition of the Enlightenment in the broadest sense of the word . . . [such as] Locke, Rousseau, Kant, Hegel, Marx, Mill, Tocqueville, and, in our day, Jürgen Habermas, Charles Taylor and John Rawls."[35] The modern conception of freedom implies something more than a rigid neo-Platonic distinction between the existing world and an ideal condition. Insofar as freedom must be regarded as an ideal that is capable of being realized, the distinction between the ideal and the real can and must be crossed. Conversely, one must regard the existing world as something that can be transformed in accordance with a rational and universal image.

The idealist formulation of transcendental freedom merely brings out in the profoundest relief the central paradox of the modern conception of freedom. In intellectual-historical terms, this understanding of freedom arose in the wake of the separation of mechanism from human reason effected by the Newtonian/Cartesian predication of the natural or material world as the totality of objects governed by arational mechanical laws. For humanity to be free from the constraints and dictates of natural necessity, the world of mechanism must first be sundered from the sphere of human reason, to the point that they are regarded as two ontologically distinct realms. Henceforth, freedom is precisely what is not or cannot be blindly determined or given by something else: for example, past events that are part of the mechanism of nature. Freedom is, first and foremost, freedom from the given. This sundering of the realm of human freedom from the material world of mechanism is part of the larger shift from a cosmological to an anthropologistic worldview. As opposed to a natural-teleological conception of the cosmos, a mechanistic conception of the world shifts the burden of responsibility for the current state of social and political existence

---

35. Albrecht Wellmer, "Models of Freedom in the Modern World," *Philosophical Forum* 21 (1989–90): 227.

from an inscrutable divinity to finite humanity. Modern freedom is self-grounding. Its paradoxical crisis, however, is that in order to be realized, the sphere of freedom must somehow be reconciled with or conjoined to the arational world of mechanism from which it was constitutively sundered.

The modern philosophemes of culture and organism that emerged at around the same time became invaluable for articulating a response to the problem of freedom's actualization. Both concepts shared a striking conjunctural affinity: they were formulated in reaction to the impact of industrial modernity and were therefore opposed to mechanism in a more concrete sense. It has been argued that the theory of mechanism is a symptom of the industrial age and reflects its various features: the use of simpler kinds of machines such as the automaton and the clock in early industrial life; the nascent capitalist economy and the individualistic norms of its rising bourgeois class; and the subsequent specialization and division of labor required by the expansion of manufacture that led to the dismemberment of a product into its component parts.[36] Similarly, the harmonious unity of parts and whole in the modern idea of organism can be seen as the displaced figuration of a desired solution to the vicissitudes of industrial society—the decline of communal spirit as a result of the atomistic pursuit of selfish interests and socioeconomic division.

The concept of culture was also a response to the shock of modernity. The philosophy of culture sought to correct the mechanistic understanding of the world and the entropy of civil society, which were factors contributing to the accelerated erosion of time-honored traditions and customs that had held society together. According to a well-known narrative about modernity, "an instrumental-pragmatic conception of knowledge as power, as a tool of mastery . . . destroyed the traditional conception of nature as meaningful cosmos or divine creation," and as the repository of natural laws that provided commonly accepted guiding norms for human conduct.[37] Consequently, the concept of culture, as György Márkus points out, was invented "in order to make up this norm- and value-deficit."[38] More concretely, the institutions, skills, and spiritual powers of culture were seen as a shelter

---

36. See Karl Mannheim, "Org.," p. 169.
37. György Márkus, "Antinomien der Kultur. Das Projekt der Moderne zwischen Aufklärung und Romantik," *Lettre International* (Berlin), no. 38 (1997): 13.
38. Ibid.

from and antidote to the vaporizing forces of industrial capitalist civil society. Although the division of labor was crucial for technical and social progress and, hence, important for the advancement of the outer aspects of culture such as urbanity, civility, and the autonomization of the cultural sphere itself, the occupational specialization of individuals in civil society and the ensuing division of society into socioeconomic classes with special functions had stunted human development and fragmented and separated the powers of the human personality. The human vocation for freedom had been degraded with this dismemberment of humanity's social character. If social regulation was left solely to the modern centralized state or the self-regulating market, the result would be "civilized barbarism," the glittering misery Rousseau excoriated in the First and Second Discourses.[39] Thus, the intense preoccupation with *Bildung* in the late eighteenth century by thinkers such as Wilhelm von Humboldt, Fichte, Schiller, and Goethe was an attempt to remedy this etiolation of humanity without lapsing into a Rousseauistic idealization of the state of nature.[40]

The concepts of culture and organism thereby became interconnected, most notably in the use of *"Bildung"* to refer to processes of human cultivation as well as organic forms. This locution was popularized by Goethe, and the two concepts were used to elucidate each other.[41] Alloyed to the more abstract antimechanism of the transcendental idea of freedom, these concepts formed the basis for the organismic metaphor of the social and political body. One must also note here a special conjunctural affinity to nationalism, which was also a response to the deep crisis and upheaval of modernity and a search for regeneration and stronger social foundations. Consequently, the nation-form was most readily characterized as an organic community although the organismic metaphor was also used to describe other sociopolitical forms. But what is the deeper philosophical

---

39. The phrase "civilized barbarism" is from Agnes Heller, "Culture, or Invitation to Luncheon with Immanuel Kant," in *A Philosophy of History in Fragments* (Oxford: Blackwell, 1993), p. 137.

40. See Roy Pascal, "'Bildung' and the Division of Labour," in *German Studies Presented to Walter Horace Bruford* (London: George Harrap, 1962), pp. 14–28.

41. Goethe repeatedly drew parallels between works of art and organic forms—for instance, in his suggestion, *"Die höchste und einzige Operation in der Natur und Kunst ist die Gestaltung."* *"Gestaltung"* is a cognate of *"Bildung."* For a detailed discussion, see Elizabeth M. Wilkinson, "Goethe's Conception of Form," *Proceedings of the British Academy* (1951): 175–97. The quotation from Goethe's correspondence is cited on p. 190 of Wilkinson's essay.

affinity between the ideas of culture and organism and the auto-causality of modern freedom?

The problematic of culture is expressed through a series of cognate terms that include most notably, "*Kultur,*" "*Bildung,*" "*Aufklärung,*" "*Erziehung,*" and "*Geist.*" As late as 1784, Moses Mendelssohn wrote that

> the words "enlightenment [*Aufklärung*]," "culture [*Kultur*]" and "education [*Bildung*]" are still newcomers to our language. At the present time they belong merely to the language of books. The common masses scarcely understand them. . . . Linguistic usage, meanwhile, appears to want to make a distinction among these words which have similar meanings, but it has not yet had time to establish their borders. Education, culture and enlightenment are modifications of social life, effects of the hard work and efforts of human beings to improve their social condition.[42]

The philosopheme of culture articulates the formative power over nature that co-belongs with humanity, not only as an animal capable of rational contemplation, but as a purposive being with the ability to shape its natural self and external conditions in the image of rationally prescribed forms.[43] Mendelssohn points to its two crucial moments: culture as the individual-pedagogical process of cultivation and its objective results.

The first aspect and basic meaning of culture was formed through a metaphorical extension of cultivation as agrarian activity (the Latin

---

42. Moses Mendelssohn, "On the Question: What Does 'to Enlighten' Mean?" in *Philosophical Writings,* ed. and trans. Daniel O. Dahlstrom (Cambridge: Cambridge University Press, 1997), p. 313.

43. The following discussion draws heavily on the work of the Budapest School philosopher, György Márkus. See Márkus, "Culture: The Making and the Make-Up of a Concept (An Essay in Historical Semantics)," *Dialectical Anthropology* 18 (1993): 3–29 (hereafter cited in the text as "Culture"), and "A Society of Culture: the Constitution of Modernity," in *Rethinking Imagination: Culture and Creativity,* ed. Gillian Robinson and John Rundell (London: Routledge, 1994), pp. 15–29 (hereafter cited in the text as "SC"). See also Rudolf Vierhaus, "Bildung," in *Geschichtliche Grundbegriffe* 1 (1972); Jörg Fisch, "Zivilization, Kultur," in *Geschichtliche Grundbegriffe* 7 (1992); W. H. Bruford, *Culture and Society in Classical Weimar, 1775–1806* (Cambridge: Cambridge University Press, 1962), esp. appendix 2, pp. 432–40; and Raymond Guess, "*Kultur, Bildung, Geist,*" in *Morality, Culture, and History: Essays on German Philosophy* (Cambridge: Cambridge University Press, 1999): 29–50. The ethical and social dimension that follows from the idea of tending and improving by education or training is rarely found in English formulations of the culture concept before Matthew Arnold.

cultura) into the educational task of the ethical and intellectual development of the mind or the soul. Cicero's idea of "*cultura animi*" is the most notable formulation of this. Thus, "*Bildung*" is often linked to "*Erziehung*" and used to refer to processes of training, development, education, and formation.[44] But "*Bildung*" also refers to the results and products of cultivation. This was already implied by the term's religious roots in German mystical discourse from the Middle Ages to the Renaissance and in seventeenth- and eighteenth-century Pietism. The process of spiritual forming (*bilden*) involved the remaking or transforming of the soul into the picture or image (*Bild*) of God through individual activity.[45] Because *Bildung* involved the creation of an object corresponding to an ideal model, it always contained an objective moment. When the term was secularized in the Enlightenment and used as a synonym of "*Kultur*," "*Bildung*" designated the inner-directed formation of an individual in the image of a personality prescribed by moral norms. Its product was, in the first instance, the resultant state of mind or the way of existence of the cultivated moral person. But the incarnational dimension of "*Bildung*" with its self-reflexive causality that belonged to a spiritual or metaphysical plane was gradually extended to objects in the external world such that one could speak of a "world of *Bildung*." This realm of spiritual works was deemed to play a fundamental role in the education of humanity to full maturity and the furthering of universal progress because its contents evoked and stimulated a similar spiritual activity in the minds of other perceivers. Hence, in the 1770s and 1780s, culture "became the synonym for all those *objectified results* of human creativity by, and due to which the "natural constitution" of human individuals—their inborn needs, drives and propensities—

---

44. "*Erziehung*" refers more narrowly to the process of education and training that is imposed by a person or group on another and implies socialization, whereas "*Bildung*" can also be used to refer to a process of self-formation, the form ("*Bild*") that is imparted in such a process, and the results of self-cultivation. Different authors used the terms differently. Kant uses "*Kultur*" to refer to the vocational development of the full powers of each individual. Fichte rarely used "*Kultur*," speaking instead of various forms of education using "*Bildung*" and "*Erziehung*." For Hegel, the process of *Bildung* and its various products such as the arts, philosophy, and social institutions were all manifestations of *Geist*. *Kultur* and *Bildung* remained synonyms until the second half of the nineteenth century, when *Bildung* was restricted to the educational process and its results. See Geuss, "*Kultur, Bildung, Geist*," pp. 32–33, 36–37.

45. See Márkus, "Culture," p. 15.

become modified, developed and supplemented" ("Culture," 18; emphasis in original).

Culture is a crucial agent for the realization of freedom because of its incarnational causality. Its individual-pedagogic dimension already involves an internal link between autonomous rational effort and the shaping of some naturally given ground into cultivated form. This ability to transform and improve *human* nature through rational endeavor, which cannot be understood solely in terms of mechanical causality, implies that humanity possesses a degree of freedom from nature. In *Bildung*, the ideal form is not separate from the process and resulting product in the same way a model is separate from its copy. A model is temporally prior and external to the copy, which is a reproduction or duplication of the original by mechanical means. In *Bildung*, however, the form is simultaneously a dynamic forming. *Bildung* is a rational inner-directed process we undertake or submit to precisely because it brings out and develops natural dispositions or capacities (*Naturanlagen*) already in us. Thus, although it has regulative and normative functions, the ideal form to be stamped on us also inheres in and is inseparable from the material and process of production. Heidegger captures *Bildung*'s peculiar temporality in his observation that

> *Bildung* means two things. On the one hand, *Bildung* is a *Bilden* [forming/stamping] in the sense of an unfolding stamping [*ein Bilden im Sinne der entfaltende Prägung*]. This *Bilden*, however, *bildet* [stamps or impresses; *"Bilden" aber "bildet" (prägt)*] by antecedently taking measure in terms of a paradigmatic image [*maßgebenden Anblick*; literally, a glimpse that gives measure], which for that reason is called the proto-type [*Vor-bild*; literally, pre-image]. *Bildung* is at once stamping and guidance by an image [*Prägung zumal und Geleit durch ein Bild*].[46]

Bildung is the stamping of something, the giving of form to what is formless but only insofar as the form conforms to something within the thing to be formed. Yet, this "inner something" must be brought out or developed by

---

46. Martin Heidegger, *Platons Lehre von der Wahrheit* (Bern: Francke, 1947), p. 24. I have benefited from discussing the passage with Peter Fenves who helped me with my translation. Heidegger's criticism of *Bildung* is directed at the concept's Platonic origins.

the process of formation which is an unfolding or guiding through an image or picture. Although Heidegger is primarily interested in the onto-logical underpinnings of *Bildung* rather than its development into the anthropologistic theme of human cultivation in the eighteenth and nine-teenth centuries, his comments help us understand the peculiar nature of *Bildung*'s causality, where the ideal form's inseparability from the process of its materialization is a spontaneity that cannot be captured by linear mechanical causality. Thus, although *Bildung* takes place in the sensible world, it is also a process of auto-causality through reason. As we will see, because the inherent dispositions *Bildung* brings out are not preformed instincts or innate knowledge, it can only be explained in terms of an organism's spontaneous auto-causality.

When *Bildung* is extended to designate the realm where ideal forms materialize as external objects with a reality or life independent of the con-tingent circumstances of their creation, this world of objectified mind or spiritual being ("*geistige Sein*") is seen as exhibiting the same spontaneous auto-causality. Because they are stamped or imprinted by spiritual and rational activity, these objects are dematerialized or idealized. Conse-quently, they become portals admitting an individual subject into the world of *Bildung*. When they stimulate or revive a similar spiritual or for-mative activity in the minds of their perceivers, they do so not as external objects, but as an integral part of an eternally ongoing process of spiritu-alization and formation. Hence, culture is regarded as the process and realm of the transcendence of finitude in at least two senses. More obvi-ously, it is the inheritable works and accomplishments of earlier genera-tions that endure beyond the finite life span of mortal individuals and can therefore preserve for posterity humanity's significant achievements with the hope of resurrecting these ideals in succeeding generations. But more importantly, these inherited works can reinspirit us because they are objectifications of universally valid norms. Because these norms are not just blindly given by tradition but need to be rationally justified through changing conditions of existence, they can be used to guide us in our self-determined activity of remaking ourselves and the world. Thus, Ernst Cassirer speaks of cultural symbolic activity as the process by which we transcend the finite world: "Human culture taken as whole may be described as the process of man's progressive self-liberation. Language, art, religion, science, are various phases of this process. In all of them man discovers and proves a new power—the power to build up a world of his own, an 'ideal' world."[47]

Consequently, culture in its utopian face is often described as an objective reality that is superior to nature—or the realm where humanity overcomes nature through reason. For Kant, cultural progress will undermine the state of nature "until art [*Kunst*], when it reaches perfection, once more becomes nature—and this is the ultimate goal [*letzte Ziel*] of man's moral destiny."[48] Similarly, Hegel suggests that "after the creation of the natural universe, man appears on the scene as the antithesis of nature; he is the being who raises himself up into a second world. . . . The province of the spirit is created by man himself," and it is man's translation of the kingdom of God into actuality.[49] This recurring theme of culture as a second, higher nature underscores the unique combination of autonomous transformation and stability that characterizes cultural causality. Culture is simultaneously like and unlike nature. It is similar to nature because it is an objective realm. But it is opposed to nature because it works upon nature to transform it. However, for this transformation to be more than arbitrary change, the world of culture must consist of products embodying universally valid ideas. Unlike the senseless regularity of the mechanism of nature, actions in the realm of culture must be governed by rationally binding ideals. But unlike the purposiveness of a meaningful cosmos which is predetermined by an ultramundane force, these ideals must issue from and express the self-determining character of human reason, its "ability to create an order of meanings and values and to superimpose it upon the senseless causal sequence of events" (Márkus, "SC," 18). Culture is thus a second or higher nature, a nature that has been spiritualized.[50]

---

47. Ernst Cassirer, *An Essay on Man: An Introduction to a Philosophy of Human Culture* (New Haven: Yale University Press, 1944), p. 228.

48. Kant, "Mutmasslicher Anfang der Menschengeschichte," 11:95; "Conjectures on the Beginning of Human History," in *Pol. Writ.,* 228.

49. Georg Wilhelm Friedrich Hegel, *Lectures on the Philosophy of World History: Introduction: Reason in History,* trans. H. B. Nisbet (Cambridge: Cambridge University Press, 1975), p. 44.

50. Note, however, that "second nature" can also refer to an artificially produced nature that is not infused with morality and lacking in harmonious unity. Schelling refers to the legal order in this way in *System of Transcendental Idealism* (1800), trans. Peter Heath (Charlottesville: University of Virginia Press, 1978), pp, 193–98. For Georg Lukács, the crisis of the novel stems from the loss of organic unity in modernity. See *The Theory of the Novel,* trans. Anna Bostock (Cambridge: MIT Press, 1971), pp. 62–65.

Hence, *Bildung* is rigorously distinguished from mere civilization, which is concerned with external, sensuous, or material refinement. In Humboldt's formulation,

> *Civilization* is the humanization of peoples in their outward institutions and customs. . . . *Cultur* adds science and art to this refinement of the social order. But when we speak in our language of *Bildung,* we mean by this something at the same time higher and more inward, namely the disposition that, from the knowledge and feeling of the entire spiritual and moral endeavour [*geistigen und sittlichen Strebens*], pours out harmoniously upon temperament and character.[51]

Hence, "*Bildung*" was generally reserved for higher, inner-directed activities that directly embody and progressively realize the human *Geist* and its rational values, such as religion, philosophy, the arts, and also law and forms of political and social life.[52] It is precisely this autonomy of culture qua incarnational power and spiritualized nature that makes it a phenomenal analogue of the spontaneous auto-causality of transcendental freedom. This is why Kant, Fichte, and Hegel, as well as Schiller, Humboldt, Herder, and the early Romantics, saw cultural education (*Bildung* or *Kultur*) as important to progress and freedom and, more specifically, to the political state. Indeed, some of them regarded education as the state's most important task.[53] My

---

51. Wilhelm von Humboldt, *On Language: On the Diversity of Human Language Construction and its Influence on the Mental Development of the Human Species* (1836), ed. Michael Losonsky, trans. Peter Heath (Cambridge: Cambridge University Press, 1999), pp. 34–35. I have substituted the key German nouns in this translation.

52. "*Zivilisation*" is mildly perjorative and "is used to refer to the external trappings, artifacts and amenities of an industrially highly advanced society and also to the overly formalistic and calculating attitudes and habits that were thought to be characteristic of such societies" (Geuss, "*Kultur, Bildung, Geist,*" p. 32). The standard study of the sociological context of the "culture"/"civilization" distinction is Norbert Elias, *The Civilizing Process*, trans. Edmund Jephcott (Cambridge, Mass.: Blackwell, 1994), esp. pp. 3–33.

53. For a fuller account of the widespread argument about the importance of education for the state and Schiller's, Humboldt's and, the Jena Romantics' views on whether or not the modern state should play an active role in education, see Frederick Beiser, *ERR*, pp. 25–26, 92–110, 130–37, 229. See also Bruford, *Culture and Society in Classical Weimar*, pp. 184–292; and Friedrich Meinecke, *Cosmopolitanism and the National State,* trans. Robert Kimber (Princeton: Princeton University Press, 1970).

point is not only that these philosophers and thinkers, who were shocked by the atrocities and violence of the French Terror, regarded spiritual education as an essential precondition for fundamental change that would establish political freedom because such education would prepare the people for freedom by instilling in them social responsibility, civic virtues, and a knowledge of public affairs. These are obviously intended consequences and concrete aims of *Bildung*. What is important here is why these philosophers saw *Bildung* as a prerequisite for achieving (political) freedom. The self-realization and perfection of a person's characteristic powers is seen as necessary for political freedom because of the similarity between the causality of *Bildung* and transcendental freedom. Culture's political import is a consequence of the derivation of political freedom from transcendental freedom.

Thus, far from being a retreat from the political as we commonly assume today, far from being superstructural or secondary to the realm of the political, culture—the normative process by which humanity transforms itself and its external reality through the prescription of purposive forms, and the realm where human interaction is ordered according to laws and norms prescribed by collective reason—actually supplies the ontological paradigm for the political. In this view, political freedom is the spontaneous auto-causality of a collective body in which an individual's humanity can be realized because its norms embody universal ideals. By ensuring the internalization of these ideals, which become incarnated in individual actions, *Bildung* creates a firm basis of unity for collective existence. Any society or state based on *Bildung* would be free because it would be a harmonious self-determining whole that exhibits in its daily functioning a spontaneous auto-causality akin to that of transcendental and moral freedom.

Bildung is thus the imparting of freedom. It makes whole again the human character dismembered by modern life and forms a social totality in harmony with itself. One can find countless examples of this presupposition as well as its corollary, the polemical metaphor of the unnurturing modern state as a calculating machine. After characterizing *Kultur* as "the ultimate and highest means to . . . [man's] final goal [as a rational sensuous creature]: complete harmony with himself," Fichte proclaims that "the true vocation of the scholarly class *is the supreme supervision of the actual progress of the human race in general and the unceasing promotion of this progress*," and that "the vocation of the scholar [is] to be the *teacher* of the human race."[54] Novalis similarly defines the relationship between the state and the people as fundamentally cultural and pedagogical in nature: "Politics. The need of the state is the most pressing need of a person. To become and remain a person one has need of *a state*. . . . A person without a state is a savage. All culture springs from the relationship of a person with the state. The more cultivated one is, the more one is the member of a cultured state."[55]

This ontological primacy of culture to the political is not an antiquated feature of German idealism but an enduring legacy in contemporary ethical and political thought. Insofar as it is a fundamental axiom of any *normative* political theory that the political involves the transcendence of what is merely given, *the political is by definition a species of spiritual or cultural activity*. In Cassirer's words, "all the great ethical philosophers . . . do not think in terms of mere actuality. . . . It follows from the very nature and character of ethical thought that it can never condescend to accept 'the given.' The ethical world is never given; it is forever in the making. . . . The great political and social reformers are indeed constantly under the necessity of treating the impossible as though it were possible."[56] Heidegger is entirely correct to say (in the passage discussed in my introduction) that in modernity "human activity is conceived and consummated as culture" and that "it lies in the essence of culture . . . to become the politics of culture."[57] Philippe Lacoue-Labarthe has likewise suggested that

> The political (the City) belongs to a form of *plastic art,* formation and information, fiction in the strict sense. This is a deep theme which derives from Plato's politico-pedagogic writings . . . and reappears in the guise of such concepts as *Gestaltung* (configuration, fashioning) or *Bildung,* a term with a revealingly polysemic character (formation, constitution, organization, education, culture etc.).[58]

---

54. Fichte, *Lectures Concerning the Scholar's Vocation,* in *Early Philosophical Writings,* trans. and ed. Daniel Breazeale (Ithaca: Cornell University Press, 1988), pp. 150, 172, 174.

55. *The Universal Brouillon: Materials for an Encyclopaedia* (1798–99), no. 394 in *The Early Political Writings of the German Romantics,* p. 88.

56. Cassirer, *An Essay on Man,* pp. 60–61.

57. Martin Heidegger, "Die Zeit des Weltbildes," in *Holzwege* (Frankfurt: Vittorio Klostermann, 1950), pp. 73–74; translated as "The Age of the World Picture," in *The Question Concerning Technology and Other Essays,* trans. William Lovitt (New York: Harper and Row, 1977), p. 116.

58. Philippe Lacoue-Labarthe, *Heidegger, Art, and Politics,* trans. Chris Turner (Oxford: Blackwell, 1990), p. 66; emphasis in original.

But in a desacralized world where nature, including human nature, is primarily governed by mechanical causality, how can we grasp the incarnational causality of cultural activity? The emergent concept of organism became aligned to culture precisely because organic life-forms were natural phenomena that could not be explained solely in mechanical terms. Indeed, there is an intrinsic thematic connection between culture and organism in addition to the extrinsic affinity outlined above. The obvious organismic overtones of spiritual cultivation became especially clear from the late eighteenth century onward, when *Bildung* as an inner-directed process of spiritual formation was distinguished from the artifice of mere civilization and external refinement. But more importantly, the autonomous and, indeed, autochtonous character of culture means that like organic life-forms conceived epigenetically, culture is self-impelling, self-producing, and self-generating. Culture as a second, higher nature was therefore logically connected to the newly articulated idea of the organism as a natural purposive being. As Gadamer points out, *Bildung* resembles the Greek notion of *physis*. It is not a technical process that involves the instrumental use of nonintegral means by a power external to the process and its product:

> Like nature, *Bildung* has no goals outside itself. . . . In having no goals outside itself, the concept of *Bildung* transcends that of the mere cultivation of given talents, from which the concept is derived. The cultivation of a talent is the development of something that is given, so that practicing and cultivating it is a mere means to an end. . . . In *Bildung*, by contrast, that by which and through which one is formed becomes completely one's own. . . . What is absorbed is not like a means that has lost its function. Rather, . . . nothing disappears, but everything is preserved.[59]

But Gadamer's comparison of *Bildung* to *physis* is not entirely accurate. *Physis* cannot be resurrected to explain the causality of *Bildung* because in a desacralized world, where nature is blind mechanism, there cannot be any intelligent causality other than the technical causality of rational human action. Moreover, unlike *Bildung*, *physis* is continuous with *techne*

---

59. Hans-Georg Gadamer, *Truth and Method,* 2d rev. ed., trans. Joel Weinsheimer and Donald G. Marshall (New York: Continuum, 1995), pp. 11–12.

because their relationship is mimetic. *Bildung,* however, is a type of purposive causality that outstrips mere artifice. But its purposiveness cannot stem from an intelligent, dynamic nature or a divine creator. To understand how the modern idea of organism satisfied these needs, we must contrast it with Aristotle's classical theory of epigenesis, which remained influential until the seventeenth century, and the mechanistic, preformationist, and early vitalist theories of organism that succeeded neo-Aristotelian biological theory.

Aristotle is generally credited with the earliest formulation of the organismic metaphor of the political body and its central tenet, the priority of the state qua self-sufficient whole to the individual citizens that are its parts. He famously compared the isolated individual to a lifeless, nonfunctioning hand that has been cut off from the body, a simile that resurfaces in Hegel.[60] The state is like a natural living being because it is the final cause and end of the human individual.[61] Like *physis,* it is self-sufficient, self-developing, and contains the principle and cause of its movement, change, and rest within itself.[62] Aristotle's definition of life is crucial to the organismic metaphor because it underscores the self-generating character of organic forms. Unlike nature, artificial, crafted things (*techne*) do not have an inherent tendency to change. They do not contain within themselves the principle of their own making because they are brought into existence or altered by "some external agent" from which they receive all causality.[63] Whereas nature exists, causes itself, and creates itself sponta-

60. Aristotle, *Politics* 1.2.1253a, in *The Politics and the Constitution of Athens,* ed. Stephen Everson, trans. B. Jowett (Cambridge: Cambridge University Press, 1996). See also *Politics* 2.2.1261a; 2.5.1263b; 3.1.1274b (on the relationship of individuals and family to the state as one of unity of parts and whole); 4.4.1290b–1291a (comparison of the different parts of the state to the different functioning organs of an animal body).

61. Ibid., 1.2.1252b–1253a.

62. In *Movement of Animals,* trans. E. S. Forster, vol. 12 of *Aristotle in Twenty-Three Volumes* (London: Heinemann, Loeb Classical Library, 1968), Aristotle suggests that the constitution of animals resembles a well-ordered state. There is no need for a soul in each part or organ because each performs its natural function as a result of their natural and structural interconnections within the living body as a whole (703a–b). I am grateful to Alan Code for taking the time to discuss Aristotle's views on the body-soul relation with me. The shortcomings of the following paragraphs are solely mine.

63. *The Physics,* vol. 1, trans. Philip Wicksteed and Francis M. Cornford, vol. 4 of *Aristotle in Twenty-Three Volumes* (London: Heinemann, Loeb Classical Library, 1957), 2.1.192b.

neously and directly without the mediation of something other, *techne,* which is concerned with making something other, has no spontaneity and necessarily involves mediation.[64] The principle of dynamism within nature is its form (*eidos*), which is able to propagate and actualize itself. Consequently, nature possesses an auto-causality and power of self-generation that is oriented towards a final, intelligible end.[65] A living body is a natural body capable of "self-nourishment, growth and decay."[66] Its source of vitality is the soul, which gives it formal organization. The soul is "the first actuality of a natural body which has life potentially," and "whatever has organs will be a body of this kind."[67] The living body is thus higher than mere matter because it is a body with organs, an organized whole where its parts receive their vital movement and intelligible organization from the soul.[68]

Now, although Aristotle distinguishes artificial from living bodies because of the latter's intrinsic dynamism and auto-causality, he also characterizes the body and its limbs as "*organa*" or technical instruments. Insofar as the living body is an intermediary force that the soul moves to move other things, it is like a hinge joint of the soul. Although the soul is spatially inseparable from the body, it is qualitatively superior to it.[69] Hence, Aristotle

---

64. Compare *The Nicomachean Ethics,* trans. H. Rackham, vol. 19 of *Aristotle in Twenty-Three Volumes* (London: Heinemann, Loeb Classical Library, 1934), 6.4.4–5; and the suggestion in *De Generatione Animalium* 1.22.730b, in *De Partibus Animalium I and De Generatione Animalium I,* trans. D. M. Balme (Oxford: Clarendon Press, 1972), p. 55, that nature "acts like modellers, not carpenters, since it fashions the thing being constituted not by touching it through something else but directly by using its own parts."

65. *Physics,* vol. 1, 2.2.194a.

66. *De Anima: Books 2 and 3,* trans. D. W. Hamlyn (Oxford: Clarendon, 1993), 2.1.412a11. This is the nutritive faculty basic to all living beings (2.4.415a-b).

67. *De Anima* 2.1.412a22–28.

68. Cf. Georges Canguilhem, *A Vital Rationalist: Selected Writings from Georges Canguilhem,* ed. François Delaporte (New York: Zone, 1994), p. 205. Hereafter cited as *VR*.

69. *De Anima* 3.10.433b, pp. 70–71. The issue of whether Aristotle's views on the soul-body relation is a dualism or a hylomorphism has been a subject of much debate. See the essays in Martha C. Nussbaum and Amélie Oksenberg Rorty, eds., *Essays on Aristotle's De Anima* (Oxford: Clarendon Press, 1992). Although commentators have suggested that Aristotle's instrumentalist vocabulary is compatible with hylomorphism and that the soul is not alien to or separable from the living body (as in Cartesian dualism) but constitutive of its very organization and nature, the characterization of the soul as alien is a (mis)reading Aristotle's text calls for because the imagery of instruments and organs necessarily suggests that it is distinct from the body.

elucidates the soul-body relationship by a technological analogy of the craftsman and his tools.[70] The organic body is only self-moving by virtue of its fundamentally slavish dependence on the soul: "the body is the soul's tool born with it, a slave is as it were a member or tool of his master, a tool is a sort of inanimate slave."[71] Hence, the body has a subordinate status. It exists for the *sake of something else*—a purpose and a final cause.[72] The *organon* is an instrument that serves a function, end, or activity set by the soul. Different bodily organs exist to fulfill specific functions according to their place within the whole body as a larger organ. All are means to the soul's higher end.[73] Consequently, Aristotle's biological writings repeatedly characterize the body and its various organs using technological metaphors and analogies with saws, axes, hammers, drills, and so on. He compares the motion of animals to that of marionettes and catapults and describes the multifunctional hand as the instrument of all instruments.[74] This means that living nature, which creates itself spontaneously from itself without mediation from anything foreign or other, becomes constitutively infected with its very opposite or other, *techne*.

This technological modulation of organic life is not entirely surprising. Aristotelian teleology cannot rigorously distinguish between artificial and living beings because the relationship between *techne* and *physis* is mimetic. Art and life are both purposive and exhibit final causality because nature is the ur-artificer that art imitates.[75] However, with the gradual erosion of a cosmological worldview, the instrumentalist characterization of the life process opens classical epigenesis up to an entirely opposite interpretation: mechanism. Prima facie, Cartesian mechanism breaks with Aristotle's theory of the four kinds of causality. It reduces all causality to efficient causality by defining all nature as matter in extension and eliminates the

---

70. *De Generatione Animalium* 1.22.730b, p. 55.

71. *The Eudemian Ethics*, trans. H. Rackham, vol. 20 of *Aristotle in Twenty-Three Volumes* (London: Heinemann, Loeb Classical Library, 1952), 7.9.1241b.

72. *De Partibus Animalium* I 1.1, in *De Partibus Animalium I and De Generatione Animalium I*, pp. 3–11, esp. 641b–642a. I am grateful to Alan Code for alerting me to this passage.

73. Ibid. 645b, p. 19.

74. See *Movement of Animals* 701b; *Parts of Animals*, trans. A. L. Peck, vol. 12 of *Aristotle in Twenty-Three Volumes*, (London: Heinemann, Loeb Classical Library, 1968) 4.10.687a, p. 373.

75. See *The Physics* 2.2.194a, 2.8.199a. For characterizations of Nature as maker, clay-modeler, or smith, see *De Generatione Animalium* 1.20.730b, p. 55, and *The Politics* 1.2.1252b.

conception of life as self-animating nature through a gradually expanded sense of mechanism that incorporates vital functions. This literalization of Aristotle's technological analogies is epitomized by Descartes's definition of the animal body as an automaton, but especially by La Mettrie's 1747 description of the human body as a vital clockwork or perpetual-motion machine.[76] But the apparent elimination of final causality is misleading. For like classical teleology, a mechanistic conception of life does not allow for an ontological distinction between art and nature, made things and organic/organized beings. Both are equally machines and products of technical design. Leibniz saw the organic body as "a kind of divine machine or natural automaton, which infinitely surpasses any artificial automaton, because a man-made machine is not a machine in every one of its parts. . . . But nature's machines—living bodies, that is—are machines even in their smallest parts, right down to infinity."[77]

Thus, mechanism is not incompatible with teleology and even necessarily presupposes it.[78] All machines have a rational maker external to them, who made them for a purpose or to produce certain effects. Purposiveness is merely displaced from a final cause within the organic body to the moment of its technological construction. To be sure, in this scheme the soul is no longer the source of movement for living beings. Yet, even a complex machine such as a self-propelling automaton or motor still needs to be constructed by an artificer alien to it and set in motion by an external energy source.[79] The continuity between mechanism and teleology repeats

76. Julien Offray de La Mettrie, *Machine Man*, in *Machine Man and Other Writings,* trans. Ann Thomson (Cambridge: Cambridge University Press, 1996), pp. 7, 31.

77. G. W. Leibniz, "Monadology" (1714), in *Philosophical Texts,* ed. and trans., R. S. Woolhouse and Richard Francks (Oxford: Oxford University Press, 1998), p. 277.

78. Descartes explicitly blocked any move to finalism on the grounds that the nature of God as an infinite being cannot be grasped by finite human reason. The conception of organic bodies as self-sustaining automata without any design leads to French materialism, where living machines are seen as outcomes of purely natural causal processes. See Aram Vartanian, *Diderot and Descartes: A Study of Scientific Naturalism in the Enlightenment* (New Jersey: Princeton University Press, 1953). On the other hand, György Márkus has pointed out to me in private correspondence that in Newtonian physics, finalist ideas are necessary partly because of the absence of conservation laws. The winding up of the clock of Nature by divine intervention is a physical necessity. This is why Newton insisted that "natural theology" organically belongs to a philosophy of nature (i.e., physics).

79. See Canguilhem's extended discussion of the deep complicity between mechanism and teleology in Descartes's theory of the animal-machine and the continuity between Descartes's and Aristotle's

the mimetic interplay between *physis* and *techne* in Aristotle. This is the philosophical backdrop for the debates between preformationists and epigeneticists in late-eighteenth-century biological theory that led to the modern concept of organism.[80]

Preformationism sought to address two major deficiencies in neo-Cartesian accounts of organic life: the inability to solve the problems of how a body-machine could be self-moving and how the complex organization of functional parts found in living bodies came into existence in the process of generation. Although it was possible, with some difficulty, to explain automatic movement by recourse to the art of the motor, the attempt to derive the complex formation of organic beings from movement and the combination of material particles through collision was far less plausible. Thus, in the late seventeenth and eighteenth centuries, "organism" was used as a semantic substitute for the neo-Aristotelian idea of the soul "in order to explain how systems composed of distinct components nevertheless work in a unified manner to perform a function," where the reciprocal relations between the components were such that "the word 'part' seemed ill-suited to denote the 'organs' of which the organism could be seen as the 'totality' but not the 'sum'" (Canguilhem, *VR*, 81–82). Preformationists such as Charles Bonnet and Albrecht von Haller appealed to the implicit teleological presuppositions of Cartesian mechanism, which they articulated

---

conceptions of organic life in *VR*, pp. 207, 227–36, and "Machine and Organism," trans. Mark Cohen and Randall Cherry, in *Incorporations*, ed. Jonathan Crary and Sanford Kwinter (Cambridge, Mass.: Zone, 1992). Hereafter cited as "M.O."

80. The polemics between preformationism and earlier epigenetic accounts should not be understood as a conflict between teleology and mechanism. Both applied various combinations of teleological and mechanical principles and, prior to Blumenbach, failed to make a sharp distinction between the causality exhibited by an organism and a machine. The conflict between preformation and epigenesis should be distinguished from the conflict between vitalism and mechanism, the latter being concerned with specifying the causal nature of biological processes. In biological debates, mechanism is used in a narrower sense to refer to physicochemical forces and not to the laws of classical Newtonian-Cartesian mechanics. One can subscribe to the epigenetic view of organic nature as a self-producing system and explain this epigenesis in either vitalist or mechanical terms. And although preformationism is opposed to the reduction of organic processes to physicochemical forces, a preformationist can also subscribe to mechanism in the broader philosophical sense. Unless indicated otherwise, I use "mechanism" in the broader sense. See Clark Zumbach, *The Transcendent Science: Kant's Conception of Biological Methodology* (The Hague: Martinus Nijhoff, 1984), pp. 79–86.

into a theory of *evolutio*. The successive appearance of anatomical forma-tions (morphogenesis), they argued, was the result of the gradual unfolding or geometrical development of a preexisting germ and its latent structures.[81] Indeed, one could say that for preformationists, nature generates nothing! As Georges Canguilhem notes,

> Living machines implied a mechanic of their own, and that implication pointed toward a *Summus opifex*, God. It was therefore logical to assume that all living machines had been constructed in a single initial operation, and thence that all the germs of all the preformed living things—past, present or future—were, from the moment of creation, contained one inside the other. (*VR*, 79)

In this view, the formation of living beings also involves a teleological cause. But this purposiveness is not *of* the organism or *proper to it*, for unlike the Greek *physis*, which is self-moving and self-generating, its origins are in a divine maker beyond the natural world. Consequently, unlike Aristotle's idea of the soul qua form governing the actualization of new organic beings, the final cause is no longer united to the efficient cause. Because it evacuates physical nature of any purposiveness, preformationism is resolutely mecha-nistic in the philosophical sense although in the history of biology it is regarded as opposed to mechanistic and materialist explanations of life. Moreover, as Canguilhem points out, the organism is also a machine because every facet of its formation and its subsequent activity strictly adheres to the blueprint of the original germ (Canguilhem, "M.O.," 58).

In contradistinction, modern epigenesis argued that anatomical forma-tions could not be geometrically derived from a preformed germ and that a mechanism of formation had to exist that could organize simple unor-ganized matter into complex organic forms. This theory of spontaneous generation, which views the formation of living beings as "essentially a

81. For an account of preformationism and epigenetic challenges to it between 1745 and 1790, see James L. Larson, *Interpreting Nature: The Science of the Living Form from Linnaeus to Kant* (Balti-more: Johns Hopkins University Press, 1994), chap. 5. My thanks to David Bates for alerting me to this study. This otherwise fine study is not alert to the mechanistic underpinnings of preforma-tionism. For a more philosophical reconstruction, see Peter McLaughlin, *Kant's Critique of Teleol-ogy in Biological Explanation: Antinomy and Teleology* (Lewiston: Edwin Mellen, 1990), pp. 8–24. See also Helmut Müller-Sievers, *Self-Generation. Biology, Philosophy, and Literature Around 1800* (Palo Alto: Stanford University Press, 1997), chap. 1.

matter of the apposition of material particles moved by the forces dwelling in matter," gained more credence in the second half of the eighteenth century because the improved technology of microscopic examination revealed the presence of a series of nonpreformed structures in the generative process.[82] But although modern epigenesis broke with the finalist presuppositions of preformationism, its earlier proponents (Buffon, Maupertuis, and Wolff), who argued that organic forms arose out of the combination of various seminal and nutritional fluids, were nevertheless forced to appeal to a soul-like, intelligible mechanism of formation. Yet, it was unclear how simple mechanical forces that were mysterious and unobservable (such as affinity, which was loosely based on Newtonian attraction, or a *vis essentialis*) could give rise to the complex systematicity of organic structures and their unfailing development from simple elements. Early epigenetic theories enabled generation to be conceived as a self-contained and self-causing process. But the autonomy accorded to living nature remained very limited since nature was also emptied of purposiveness. The organism remains imprisoned by a mechanistic framework and is not fundamentally different from a machine.

Blumenbach's vitalist theory of epigenesis (first formulated in 1781) was pathbreaking because it sharply distinguished the living organism from an artificial machine. He argued that a living body was created by a *Bildungstrieb*, a formative drive which was also responsible for the body's continuing regeneration: "in all living creatures, there is a particular, innate, lifelong, active, effective force (*Trieb*) that confers a determinate form, afterward preserves it, and when this is deranged, where possible, restores it."[83] He cautioned that *"Bildungstrieb"* was merely a name by which we could understand a group of observable a posteriori effects and not a principle that explained the ultimate end of generation. Nevertheless, from a philosophical perspective, it was a purposive causality within vital processes, a final cause constitutive of and immanent to the organism. Regular harmony in fertilization and morphogenesis indicated a purposive causality that exceeded the mechanism of nature. But since no preformed germ was detected in seminal fluids prior to fertilization, this organic form did not issue from a divine hand. It was spontaneously generated from

---

82. Larson, *Interpreting Nature*, p. 161.

83. Blumenbach, *Über den Bildungstrieb und das Zeugungsgeschäfte,* quoted in Larson, *Interpreting Nature*, p. 159. See also Nicholas Jardine, *The Scenes of Inquiry*, pp. 22–28.

within the organism, and could undergo deviations as a result of changes in physical conditions that acted as external stimuli.[84]

Blumenbach's theory liberated life processes from divine preformation because it defined the organism as a self-organizing being that causes its own motility and self-perpetuation, an internally organized complex structure or totality capable of auto-construction, auto-maintenance, auto-regulation, auto-repair, and auto-genesis. As Larson suggests, Blumenbachian epigenesis is the organic counterpart of the declaration of human rights. It is "a declaration of the rights of nature in the name of rational science" that "opposed the prejudice of immutability in the world of living forms and treated nature as an autonomous power, pursuing, by means of her own forces, the continuities of her own development."[85] Henceforth, the organism is differentiated from the machine in three respects: first, whereas a machine cannot construct or repair itself and therefore always presupposes a fundamental dependence on a creator external to it to give it purpose and movement, an organism is self-forming. It grows and develops from within with reference to an end immanent to its own nature. Second, whereas a machine is merely the sum of its parts, an organism is a totality that is greater than the combination of its organs. The organs coexist and are intrinsically related to the whole with which they form a harmonious unity. Finally, despite its immanent purposiveness, an organism exhibits greater variability in its activity than a machine because its causality is more vulnerable to changes in surrounding conditions. Life is aleatory.

Most importantly, this definition of a living organism as spontaneously self-organizing enforced a strict ontological distinction within nature between living and nonliving beings. As Michel Foucault points out, in most of eighteenth-century natural history, "the terms organized and non-organized defined merely two categories; these categories overlapped, but did not necessarily coincide with, the antithesis of living and non-living." However, in the period between 1775 and 1795, "the organic becomes the living[,] . . . that which produces, grows, and reproduces; the inorganic is

---

84. See Larson, *Interpreting Nature,* pp. 159–60. For a fuller account of the difference between Blumenbach's theory and earlier accounts of epigenesis, see Timothy Lenoir, "Teleology Without Regrets: the Transformation of Physiology in Germany, 1790–1847," *Studies in the History and Philosophy of Science* 12, no. 4 (1981): esp. pp. 309–12.

85. Larson, *Interpreting Nature,* p. 133. Cf. Jardine, *The Scenes of Inquiry,* p. 33; and Michel Foucault, *The Order of Things,* trans. Alan Sheridan (New York: Vintage, 1973), p. 272.

the non-living, that which neither develops nor reproduces; it lies at the frontiers of life, the inert, the unfruitful—death. And although it is intermingled with life, it is so as that element within it that destroys and kills it."[86] Life, Xavier Bichat wrote in 1800, "is the collection of functions that resist death" (quoted in Canguilhem, *VR*, 69). Life is the momentary transcendence of finitude.

Herein lies the conceptual affinity between culture and the modern conception of the organism's causality. As the incarnation of rational ideals, *Bildung* is a purposive nonmechanical causality. This makes it a phenomenal analogue of the spontaneous auto-causality of transcendental freedom. But because *Bildung* is a dynamic process of forming immanent to the subject of *Bildung* in its collective setting and does not involve the instrumental use of external means, it also exceeds *techne* or artifice. This kind of purposive but nontechnical causality is inconceivable within a mechanistic worldview. The organism, however, displays a type of natural causality that is isomorphic with *Bildung* in several respects. Its *Bildungstrieb* is similar to *physis*. It is spontaneous, purposive and self-generating. But unlike Aristotelian epigenesis and preformationism, the organism's power of self-movement and final causality is intrinsic and does not come from an outside source. The organism is also sharply distinguished from artificial things. This makes it an important means for understanding the nontechnical purposiveness of cultural processes. Moreover, the ontological distinction between self-organized/organic being as life and nonorganic being as death accords to the organism the same finitude-transcending powers attributed to culture.

The striking isomorphism is reflected in the use of the same word, "*Bildung*," to refer to both phenomena. Goethe famously points to the epigenetic quality of organic forms as well as the products of cultivation:

> when we study forms [*Gestalten*], the organic ones in particular, nowhere do we find permanence, repose, or termination. We find rather that everything is in ceaseless flux. This is why our language makes such frequent use of the term "*Bildung*" to designate what has been brought forth and likewise what is in the process of being brought forth.[87]

---

86. Foucault, *The Order of Things*, p. 232.

87. *Goethe's Botanical Writings*, trans. Bertha Mueller (Woodbridge, Conn.: Ox Bow Press, 1989), pp. 23–24. Cf. Bruford, *Culture and Society in Classical Weimar, 1775–1806*, p. 258. For a fascinating

For Goethe, natural processes of organic formation and humankind's "possibility of endless development through always keeping his mind receptive and disciplining it in new forms of assimilation and procedure" constitute "a twofold infinitude."[88] The characterization of the cultural sphere as an organismic totality or the culture of a people as an organic body is a development of this analogy, which was also gradually extended to describe specific cultural phenomena such as genres or even individual works of literature.

The analogy between culture and organism had a special significance for German idealist philosophy. The organism is quite literally the basis of culture and of a teleological view of history, for the analogy was elaborated into an organismic conception of nature as a self-organizing whole, a system of purposes that historically culminates in the world of culture. Because the purposiveness of culture and of organism are natural analogues of the spontaneous auto-causality of transcendental freedom, they were grounds for the hope or conviction that freedom was actualizable in an otherwise blindly mechanical natural world. As Philippe Lacoue-Labarthe and Jean-Luc Nancy point out, Kant's attempt to bridge the gulf between nature and freedom is distinctly organismic-cultural:

> the resolution was envisaged in the *Darstellung* of the "subject" by means of the Beautiful in works of art (the formation of *Bilder* able to present liberty and morality analogically), by means of the "formative power" (*bildende Kraft*) of nature and life within nature (the formation of the organism), and finally by means of the *Bildung* of humanity (what we retain under the concepts of history and culture).[89]

Understood within the philosophical framework of its genesis, the organismic metaphor of the social and political body accrues a more progressive and rationalist genealogy. At the very least, one ought to regard it with less

---

account of Blumenbach's influence on Goethe and his economic theory, see Myles W. Jackson, "Natural and Artificial Budgets: Accounting for Goethe's Economy of Nature," in *Accounting and Science: Natural Inquiry and Commercial Reason,* ed. Michael Power (Cambridge: Cambridge University Press, 1994): 57–80. See also H. B. Nisbet, *Goethe and the Scientific Tradition* (London: Institute of Germanic Studies, University of London, 1972), esp. pp. 57–58.

88. *Goethe's Botanical Writings,* p. 21.

89. *The Literary Absolute,* p. 32.

cynicism and see it as more than an irrational reactionary myth in the initial moment of its formulation. If it is a myth, then it is a myth of enlightened reason itself (double genitive), with all the dialectical contradictions implied by such a statement after Adorno.[90] The organismic conception of culture was transferred directly to the ideal form of society or political body, which was viewed as an organism for two reasons. In the first place, the undesirable sociopolitical formations to which it was counterposed—the bureaucratic state of enlightened despotism or civil society—were repeatedly described as machines. But more importantly, insofar as the ideal collective is regarded as both the material condition for optimum self-cultivation and the highest ideal and product of *Bildung,* its functionings are by nature organismic.

Broadly speaking, all normative conceptions of the political characterized the relationship between individual, society, and state by the same immanent purposiveness and harmonious unity of an organism: on the one hand, the individual can only fully develop his or her powers within the collective. On the other hand, society and the state can only achieve optimal stability and growth through the individual's inner development. Only if both conditions are fulfilled can the collective and the individual be considered as a self-organizing whole and end in itself. To be sure, the ontological dimension of the organismic metaphor of the social and political body intersects in complex and interesting ways with the sociohistorical context of its enunciation. In this regard, one can mention the increasing uneasiness about the impact of complex machines on the character of life under industrial capitalism. But it is the ontological moment that has greater priority in German idealism. The state or society as organism signifies refuge from the atomism of industrial modernity because it is, in the first instance, an analogue for the spontaneous auto-causality of transcendental freedom. Modernity's destabilizing forces are a manifestation of the blind mechanism of nature, and the freedom offered by the collective qua organism is essentially the inner worldly transcendence of this finitude, that is to say, immanent transcendence.

The idea of immanent purposiveness put forward by modern theories of organism is undoubtedly connected to the increasing use of "immanen-

---

90. Cf. Manfred Frank, *Der kommende Gott,* pp. 168–69.

tist" principles in nineteenth-century political philosophy recognized by Carl Schmitt among others.[91] Once it came into being, the organismic metaphor of the social and political body was deployed in a variety of political philosophies, idealist and materialist, republican or despotic, monarchical or democratic, and even socialist and anarchist. It was used to characterize various forms of territorialized or deterritorialized political community such as the nation, the state, a cosmopolitan world federation, or a global community of laborers. The multiple forms that the organismic metaphor can take indicate that it is not inherently pathological or reactionary as is commonly assumed when we focus on some of its less salutary instantiations—for example, the connection between ideas of *Kulturnation* or late-romantic theories of the state and the violent history of German nationalism. Indeed, it is arguable that in their description of the *Kulturnation,* or the state as an eternally unchanging primordial totality that functions as a genetic principle throughout history, such theories espouse preformationist rather than epigenetic ideas. My intention is not to excuse these aberrations but to suggest a different way to account for them. Instead of dismissing them as irrational, we need to link them to the rationality of the organismic metaphor itself.

All political forms that rely on the organismic metaphor are different models intended to provide the optimal institutional basis for the actualization of freedom. Because the vital organism is a phenomenal figure for the auto-causality of freedom, these forms have as their common substrate a dynamic that subordinates death and artifice to organic life. That which has the capacity to regenerate itself spontaneously lives forever in some form or other. Hence, that which is free is that which has eternal life. This is the logical consequence of the definition of freedom as that which is the ground and end of its own existence, or which amounts to the same thing, the determination of freedom as the transcendence of finitude. We will now examine how this vitalist dynamic is set in place by Kant and its relationship to his idealist cosmopolitanism.

---

91. Carl Schmitt, *Political Theology: Four Chapters on the Concept of Sovereignty,* trans. George Schwab (Cambridge: MIT Press, 1985), pp. 49–52. Similarly, Jean-Luc Nancy points out that communitarianism (including communism) and individualism are both based on figures of human immanence. See *The Inoperative Community,* trans. Peter Connor (Minneapolis: Minnesota University Press, 1991), p. 13.

KANT'S COSMOPOLITANISM
AND THE TECHNIC OF NATURE

2

mmanuel Kant's vision of a cosmopolitical world order is widely regarded as the single most important philosophical source for contemporary normative theories of international relations, including accounts of global civil society and the international public sphere.[1] What Kant calls "a universal *cosmopolitan existence*" is nothing less than the *regulative idea* of "a perfect civil union of mankind."[2] This constitutional global federation of all existing states, which is also more ambitiously described as "a universal federal state [*allgemeiner Völkerstaat*]," is "based on *cosmopolitan right* [*Weltbürgerrecht*], in so far as individuals and states, coexisting in an external relationship of mutual influences, may be regarded as citizens of a universal state of mankind [*allgemeinen Menschenstaats*] (*ius cosmopoliticum*)."[3] Although this union would not possess

1. See James Bohman and Matthias Lutz-Bachmann, eds. *Perpetual Peace: Essays on Kant's Cosmopolitan Ideal* (Cambridge: MIT Press, 1997), esp.: Jürgen Habermas, "Kant's Idea of Perpetual Peace, with the Benefit of Two Hundred Years' Hindsight," pp. 113–53; and Allen W. Wood, "Kant's Project for Perpetual Peace," in *Cosmopolitics: Thinking and Feeling Beyond the Nation,* ed. Pheng Cheah and Bruce Robbins (Minneapolis: University of Minnesota Press, 1998), 59–76.
2. "Idee zu einer allgemeinen Geschichte in weltbürgerliche Absicht," 11:47; "Idea for a Universal History with a Cosmopolitan Purpose," *Pol. Writ.,* 51. Hereafter cited as "Idee."
3. "Über den Gemeinspruch: Das mag in der Theorie richtig sein, taugt aber nicht für die Praxis," 11:172; "On the Common Saying: 'This May be True in Theory, But It Does Not Apply in Practice,'" *Pol. Writ.,* 92. Hereafter cited as "TP." "Zum ewigen Frieden. Ein philosophischer Entwurf," 11:203n; "Perpetual Peace—A Philosophical Sketch," *Pol. Writ.,* 98n. Hereafter cited as "PP."

the coercive means of enforcement available to a world-state, it would nevertheless be able to make rightful claims on its constituent states regarding their treatment of individuals and other states. Individual states would retain their sovereignty but would be held accountable by a universal citizenry—humanity—with regard to issues such as disarmament and imperialist expansion. Kant's world federation would therefore fall somewhere between the political community of the state in its lawful relations with other states and a world-state.

Yet, Kant's cosmopolitanism is not opposed to the organic political community of the nation. His world federation is clearly an association of sovereign territorial states. His vision, articulated in 1795, prior to the age of nationalism in Europe, is a prenationalist attempt to reform absolutist statism.[4] It is also irrigated by an organismic discourse. The world federation's establishment depends on a teleological view of nature as a system of ends, and takes as its basic unit a political body conceived as an organism. Kant suggests that the guarantor of everlasting peace is nature herself as an ur-artificer (*große Künstlerin*).[5] Nature makes the world a bounded sphere so that society amongst men and intercourse between nations is physically inevitable, thereby implying the right to communal possession of the earth's surface.[6] In *Anthropology from a Pragmatic Point of View*, Kant argues that the organism is the basis for realizing the ideal constitution because its self-preserving life is the most immediate instance of nature's purposiveness for us:

> Only from Providence does . . . [man] expect his species to tend toward the civil constitution it envisages. . . . Providence means precisely the same wisdom that we observe with admiration in the preservation of species of organic [*organisierter*] natural beings, constantly working toward their destruction

---

4. I have elaborated this in "The Cosmopolitical—Today," in *Cosmopolitics*, ed. Cheah and Robbins, pp. 23–25.

5. "PP," 12:217; *Pol. Writ.*, 108.

6. Nature's other contrivances include the spirit of commerce (*Handelsgeist*), which appeals to the mutual self-interest of citizens and nations alike and is incompatible with despotism and war between nations. See "PP," 11:214, 226; *Pol. Writ.*, 106, 114; "Idee," 11:46; *Pol. Writ.*, 50–51; and *Die Metaphysik der Sitten*, § 62, 8:475–76; *The Metaphysics of Morals*, in *Prac. Phil.*, 489–90. The latter is cited hereafter as *MS*.

and yet always protecting them; and we do not assume a higher principle in its provisions for man than we suppose it is already using in the preservation of plants and animals.[7]

Organized natural beings exhibit a purposive auto-causality that enables the individual organism to overcome its finitude in the preservation of the species. The causality of organic beings involves a natural process of self-supplementation where nature replenishes what has become lacking in, departed from, or become absent from it by substitution. As Kant puts it in the Third Critique, "while nature works toward the destruction of individuals, it also continually compensates [*ersetzt*] for their disappearance [*Abgang*]."[8] This auto-causality makes the organism a phenomenal analogue of transcendental freedom.

This intrinsic connection between Kant's account of organic life and his political thought has rarely been broached because of a double myopia.[9] Appropriations of Kant in mainstream political theory cannot engage with the ontological underpinnings of his ethical and political philosophy because these are studied only after being detached from his philosophical architectonic. On the other hand, systematic studies of Kant's philosophy have notoriously neglected his anthropological, historical, and political writings on the basis of their peripheral status.[10] Yet Kant only became interested in strictly political and institutional questions after the Third Critique's publication in 1790, indicating that his political thought should

---

7. *Anthropologie in pragmatischer Hinsicht*, 12:683; Ak., VII:328; 189. Cited hereafter as *Anthropologie*.

8. *Kritik der Urteilskraft*, 10:379; Ak., V:422; *Critique of Judgment*, 309. Hereafter cited as *KU*.

9. Susan Meld Shell's work is a notable exception. See *The Embodiment of Reason: Kant on Spirit, Generation, and Community* (Chicago: University of Chicago Press, 1996); and "Cannibals All: The Grave Wit of Kant's Perpetual Peace," in *Violence, Identity, and Self-Determination*, ed. Hent de Vries and Samuel Weber (Stanford: Stanford University Press, 1997): 150–61. For another sustained engagement with Kant's troubled attempts to overcome finitude in his historical and political writings, see Peter Fenves, *A Peculiar Fate: Metaphysics and World-History in Kant* (Ithaca, N.Y.: Cornell University Press, 1991), and "Under the Sign of Failure," *Idealistic Studies* 26 (spring 1996):135–51.

10. As Hans Saner notes, "lack of a system; scant space; late writing (at a time of senility, as some have said); placement outside of the main works; non-committal tone—all these moments have resulted in the very modest place assigned to political thought in the history of Kant interpretation" (*Kant's Political Thought: Its Origins and Development*, trans. E. B. Ashton [Chicago: University of Chicago Press, 1973], p. 2).

be read within the broader framework of the Third Critique's teleology of nature and theory of culture.[11]

For present purposes, Kant is exemplary for two reasons: he was the first to link the realization of freedom to organic life understood as a spontaneous auto-causal process sharply distinguished from human artifice. Second, the *Critique of Judgment* contains the first modern formulation of the organismic metaphor of the political body. This chapter retraces how transcendental freedom gradually gains an organismic shape in and after Kant's Third Critique. Why is freedom conceived in terms of organic life, and what are its implications? But although Kant inaugurates a sharp distinction between the organism and artifice and forbids the association of the former with instrumentality, his elucidation of organized natural beings in terms of a technic of nature also implies an aporetic interplay between *physis* and *techne,* the inhuman and the human, that complicates the realization of freedom at various levels. It is my broader argument that these aporias are deeply sedimented in the organismic metaphor, which assumes more concrete sociological shapes in Fichte's, Hegel's, and Marx's writings.

HOW CAN FREEDOM BE OBJECTIVELY REAL?
ANTIMECHANISM BEFORE THE THIRD CRITIQUE

As is well known, Kant defines moral freedom as the causality of ideas and opposes this nonsensibly conditioned causality to the blind mechanical causality of nature. This special causality issues from our ontological constitution as beings with a rational will. Action (*Handlung*) in general is a physical body's movement that produces effects within a temporal sequence. But whereas nonhuman action is empirically conditioned and can only be understood according to mechanical laws, human action has a nonempirical dimension. As the power of choice exercised in accordance to principles or conceptions of laws, the human will (*Willkür*) is the ability

---

11. See Hannah Arendt, *Lectures on Kant's Political Philosophy*, ed. Ronald Beiner (Chicago: University of Chicago Press, 1982), pp. 15–16. The exception is "Idee zu einer allgemeinen Geschichte in weltbürgerlicher Absicht" (1784).

to deviate from the blind compulsion or necessitation of external nature.[12] Human action is thus contingent. It will remain marked by contingency as long as our will is determined by sensuous inclinations. But if our will is determined by principles issuing from reason (*Vernunft*), our actions will have universal necessity because reason is a faculty that is not empirically conditioned. A person determined by reason "is a merely intelligible object, because the actions of this object cannot at all be ascribed to the receptivity of sensibility."[13] For Kant, moral freedom is essentially a will that is determined by itself, from the *inside* of itself as reason rather than by what is *outside* itself, the necessitation of external nature or natural inclinations within us as sensible beings. Moral reason's two fundamental features are self-determination and spontaneity. A will determined by ideas of reason can only be determined by itself because ideas are independent of all appearances. Such a will is also spontaneous. A rationally determined will is motivated by something that is not empirically given. Hence, it is not part of any causal time series that governs appearances and does not have any prior cause other than itself.

The moral will is therefore strikingly intractable or obstinate. "Reason," Kant writes, "does not give in to those grounds which are empirically given [*so gibt die Vernunft nicht demjenigen Grunde, der empirisch gegeben ist*], and it does not follow the order of things as they are presented in intuition, but with complete spontaneity it makes its own order according to ideas, to which it fits the empirical conditions" (*KrV*, A 548; 541). Moral reason is effectively the practice of ontological abstinence. In practical action, reason will not give or yield anything to nature; it will also not take or accept anything that nature gives to it, but rather tries to make given existence yield to its ideas. Kant links reason's intractability, its staunch refusal to receive what is given, to something positive that cannot be found in nature: the power of origination. "An original [*ursprüngliche*] action, through which something happens that previously was not, is not to be expected from the causal connection of appearances" (*KrV*, A 544; 538). Reason, however, "can not only be regarded negatively, as independence from empirical

---

12. Cf. *Grundlegung zur Metaphysik der Sitten*, 7:41; Ak., IV:412–13; *Prac. Phil.*, 66. Hereafter cited as GM.

13. Kant, *Kritik der reinen Vernunft*, B 574–75; *Critique of Pure Reason*, 540; hereafter cited as *KrV*.

conditions . . . , but also indicated positively by a faculty of beginning a series of occurrences from itself [*eine Reihe Begebenheiten von selbst anzu-fangen*]" (*KrV*, A 553–54; 543).

But reason's originality or originariness is more than just the making of things or the achieving of certain effects in time. It involves the giving of time itself. Reason is outside of time but is nevertheless capable of giving time *in practical situations* because it is a "before" before any "before" in the temporal sense:

> Pure reason, as a merely intelligible faculty, is not subject to the form of time, and hence not subject to the conditions of the temporal sequence. The causality of reason . . . does not arise or start working at a certain time in producing an effect. For then it would itself be subject to the natural law of appearances, to the extent that this law determines causal series in time, and its causality would then be nature and not freedom. Thus . . . if reason can have causality in regard to appearances, then it is a faculty through which the sensible condition of an empirical series of effects first begins. For the condition that lies in reason is not sensible and does not itself begin [*fängt also selbst nicht an*]. Accordingly, there takes place here what we did not find in any empirical series: that the condition of a successive series of occurrences could itself be empirically unconditioned. For here the condition is outside the series of appearances (in the intelligible) and hence not subject to any sensible condition or to any determination of time through any passing cause. (*KrV,* A 551–52; 542–43)

As an original condition that cannot be properly considered a beginning since it is itself unconditioned, the practical "ought" (*Sollen*) is the only example of transcendental freedom—a special, totally other form of causality that violates the mechanical causality of nature—available to us. It "expresses a species of necessity and a connection with grounds which does not occur anywhere else in the whole of nature" (*KrV*, A 547; 540). This means that practical freedom cannot be figured in spatiotemporal terms. As long as we are *inside* nature's spatiotemporal coordinates, we will always be determined by something other than ourselves qua reason. To be free, we have to reach for and act from a ground that is totally outside the form of nature. This "outside" lies beyond what is empirically outside us. But it is also paradoxically within us in our reason. Hence, in order that we can act from within ourselves, in order that we can regain or return to ourselves and be with and inside ourselves, we have to first go beyond nature, including the nature of our empirical selves.

This is why Kant initially denies to all nature, including organic life, the spontaneous auto-causality that confirms the existence of transcendental freedom.[14] The Third Critique will retract this denial of an organic power of origination. To understand this gradual turn to organicism, we need to consider the explicit antimechanism of Kant's moral philosophy. Kant calls the determination of the will by anything other than reason "heteronomy." Heteronomy is literally a lawfulness that is given by what is other to me and outside of me. It is described through a metaphor of political ownership. A heteronomous will is subject to an alien (*fremde*) power. It is no longer in possession of or proper to itself because it has been possessed by a foreign other. Conversely, a free will is a will of its own, one that is proper to itself. As the author (*Urheberin*) of its own principles, it gives the law to itself and only obeys its own governance, regulation, or direction (*Lenkung*). Thus, freedom is a causality independent of alien influences:

> *Will* [*Wille*] is a kind of causality of living beings insofar as they are rational [*vernünftig*], and *freedom* would be that property [*Eigenschaft*] of such casuality that it can be efficient [*wirkend*] independently of alien causes determining it, just as *natural necessity* is the property of the causality of all nonrational beings to be determined to activity by the influence of alien causes.
>
> (*GM*, 8:81; Ak., IV:446; 94)

> One cannot possibly think of a reason that would consciously receive direction [*Lenkung*] from any quarter with respect to its judgments, since the subject would then attribute the determination of his judgment not to his reason but to an impulse. Reason must regard itself as the author of its principles independently of alien influences; consequently as practical reason or as the will of a rational being it must be regarded of itself as free, that is, the will of such a being cannot be a will of his own [*eigener Wille*] except under the idea of freedom. (*GM*, 8:83; Ak., IV:448; 96)

---

14. *KrV*, B 574; 540. Elsewhere (B 374; 397), Kant suggests the opposite: "A plant, an animal, the regular arrangement of the world's structure . . .—these show clearly that they are possible only according to ideas." Cf. *KrV*, A 833–35; 691–2, where Kant compares the architectonic of reason as an organized unity to the growth and development of an animal body.

The *Critique of Practical Reason* develops this contrast between moral freedom's spontaneous auto-causality and the dependent character of causality under natural laws by mixing the metaphor of political ownership with images of mechanical objects and their technical construction. Kant's account of moral freedom is punctuated with a series of pejorative figures of the turnspit, the automaton, the clockwork machine, and the marionette, which he obsessively counterposes to freedom's spontaneity. Mechanical causality is represented by its most appropriate synecdoche, the machine:

> All necessity [*Notwendigkeit*] of events [*Begebenheiten*] in time in accordance with the natural law of causality can be called the *mechanism* of nature, although it is not meant by this that the things which are subject to it must be really material *machines*. Here one looks only to the necessity of the connection of events in a time series as it develops in accordance with natural law, whether the subject in which this development takes place is called *automaton materiale*, when the machinery is driven [*betrieben*] by matter, or with Leibniz *spirituale,* when it is driven by representations; and if the freedom of our will were none other than the latter (say, psychological and comparative but not also transcendental, i.e., absolute), then it would at bottom be nothing better than the freedom of a turnspit, which, when once it is wound up, also accomplishes its movements of itself.[15]

An automaton is only free in a relative sense. Because it is dependent on an external source of energy which sets it in motion and moves itself only by conserving this prior force, it has no spontaneity. Its movements are merely given events in a time series. An automaton does not possess the free will's power of origination because it is not the absolute condition of its own movement. Kant stresses the fundamental dependence of any machine, its secondariness as *techne* with respect to its maker or the subject that sets it in motion. The relationship of an artificial object to its artificer is analogous to subjugation and subservience to another's commands and directions.

Indeed, Kant argues that moral freedom is so exacting that it should not be compared to any causality in the sensible world. God may have created

---

15. *Kritik der praktischen Vernunft,* 7:222; Ak., V:97; *Prac. Phil.,* 217. Hereafter cited as *KpV.*

in us the capacity for freedom. But if we confuse this creation with the causality of human actions in the sensible world, we reduce freedom to a marionette's movement because the moral will would be determined in the last instance by a supreme maker qua external cause. We must instead see freedom as a determination of supersensible man beyond spatiotemporal coordinates:

> In fact, if a human being's actions insofar as they belong to his determinations in time were not merely determinations of him as appearance but as a thing in itself, freedom could not be saved. A human being would be a marionette or an automaton, like Vaucanson's, *built and wound up by the supreme artist* [*obersten Meister aller Kunstwerk*]; self-consciousness would indeed make him a thinking automaton, but the consciousness of his own spontaneity, if taken for freedom, would be mere delusion inasmuch as it deserves to be called freedom only comparatively, because the proximate determining causes of its motion and a long series of their determining causes are indeed internal *but the last and highest is found entirely in an alien hand* [*fremden Hand*]. (*KpV*, 7:227; Ak., V:101; 221; emphasis added)

Kant's moral antimechanism can be summarized as follows: the existence of nature as a whole and any nonrational beings within it is fundamentally heteronomous. Because the self-moving machine is the clearest case of nature's other-directedness, Kant figures any alien influence as an alien hand that is instrumental in the making of automata. Thus *techne*, the sum of all artificial objects that bear the mark of this alien hand, is the paradigm of nature's heteronomy.

At this point, Kant's antimechanism is not yet an organicism. The spontaneity of moral freedom is not yet linked to the purposive vitality of organisms. This turn is a response to the problem of how to connect freedom with the mechanism of nature. Because freedom is distinct from and opposed to mechanical causality, it is an absent cause in the mechanism of nature. Although it can initiate a series of appearances within nature, the finitude of our cognitive powers prevents us from determining its connection to this series. An infinite and self-causing absolute being such as God would possess an intellectual intuition that can actively grasp the world as it is in itself because it can create the world as it is in itself. But for human creatures, the world and even our own existence is merely given to us as a world of appearances within spatiotemporal coordinates. We apprehend the world passively through our intuition, which is not active, but sensible and receptive. We are not gifted with an originary intuition that can originate objects. These are the marks of our finitude:

> Our kind of . . . intuition . . . is called sensible because it is not *original* [*ursprünglich*], i.e., one through which the existence of the object of intuition is itself given [*gegeben*] (and that, so far as we can have insight, can only pertain to the original being [*Urwesen*]); rather it is dependent on the existence of the object, thus it is possible only insofar as the representational capacity of the subject is affected through that.
>
> It is also not necessary for us to limit that kind of intuition in space and time to the sensibility of human beings; it may well be that all finite [*endliche*] thinking beings must necessarily agree with human beings in this regard (though we cannot decide this), yet even given such universal validity this kind of intuition would not cease to be sensibility, for the very reason that it is derived [*abgeleitet*] (*intuitus derivatus*), not original (*intuitus originarius*), thus not intellectual intuition, which for the ground already adduced seems to pertain only to the original being, never to one that is dependent as regards both its existence and its intuition (which determines its existence in relation to given objects). (*KrV*, B 72; 191–92)

Practical power of origination and independence of practical reason, yes; but also derivativeness of our cognitive powers and their dependency on given objects. Infinity and transcendence, on the one hand; irreducible finitude, on the other. This is the infamous gulf between the realms of freedom and nature, practical reason and theoretical reason.

This separation of the two realms is not necessarily bad. For Kant, the criterion for evaluating the will's morality is *how* it is determined and not its *effectivity* (*Wirksamkeit*), or what its actions can *effect*. Any will determined by an object is heteronomous and governed only by a rule of skill (*Geschicklichkeit*), which is either "technical [*technisch*] (belonging to art [*Kunst*])" or pragmatic, if that object is happiness (*GM*, 7:46; Ak., IV:416; 69). The equation of *techne* with dependency and heteronomy thus applies not only to artificial objects but also to the technical attitude of human subjects. For despite the common view that *techne* indicates that humans possess a certain power of influence or mastery over nature, the etymological connection between *Geschicklichkeit* (skill/technical ability) and *Schicksal* (fate) firmly places technical and artificial causality within the mechanical order of the given. Hence, Kant notes that "a good will is not good because of what it effects [*bewirkt*] or accomplishes, because of its fitness to attain some proposed end, but only because of its volition" (*GM*, 7:19; Ak., IV:394; 50). A will would still be good even if it were completely technically unskilled, utterly inept, or inefficacious, "even if, by a special disfavor of fortune [*besondere Ungunst des Schicksal*] or by some niggardly provision of a stepmotherly nature, this will should wholly lack the capacity to carry out its purpose—if with its greatest efforts it should yet achieve nothing" (ibid.).

However, because the free will also acts, and action necessarily takes place in nature, freedom must also be connected to the mechanism of nature. Here, effectivity and actuality (*Wirklichkeit*) would be crucial. In moral action, we attempt to reorder empirical reality in the ideal image of universal moral form (*natura archetypa*) by acting as if the sensible world is a rational system of ends that is no longer governed by mechanical laws. The moral law, Kant writes,

is to furnish [*verschaffen*] the sensible world, as *sensible nature* . . . , with the form of a world of the understanding, that is, of *supersensible* nature, though without infringing upon the mechanism of the former . . . . And since the laws by which the existence of things depends on cognition are practical, supersensible nature, so far as we can make for ourselves a concept of it, is nothing other than *a nature under the autonomy of pure practical reason*. The law of this autonomy [i.e. the moral law] . . . is therefore the fundamental law of a supersensible nature and of a pure world of the understanding, the counterpart of which is to exist in the sensible world but without infringing upon its laws. The former could be called the *archetypal world* [*urbildliche*] (*natura archetypa*) which we cognize only in reason, whereas the latter could be called the *ectypal world* [*nachgebildete*] (*natura ectypa*) because it contains the possible effect [*mögliche Wirkung*] of the idea of the former as the determining ground of the will. For the moral law in fact transfers us, in idea, into a nature in which pure reason, if it were accompanied with suitable [*angemessenen*] physical power [*Vermögen*], would produce the highest good, and it determines our will to confer on the sensible world the form of a whole of rational beings. (*KpV*, 7:156–57; Ak., V:43; 174–75)

Moral action is quite literally an imprinting or impressing of an ideational form onto the sensible world, the *Bildung* of the *nachgebildete* in the image of the *urbildliche*. But as *action,* morality has a highly qualified character. Because of the finitude of our faculties, Kant expresses the gravest uncertainty as to whether we can even know if the ideal form we seek to imprint onto sensible nature will be received by it and realized. He repeatedly stresses the distinction and distance between the possible (*möglich*) and the actual (*wirklich*); between what I want to do in pursuance of what ought to be done and what I am physically able or empowered to do.

This quandary of how to connect transcendental freedom to nature is exacerbated in Kant's practical philosophy. Because the former is elaborated as a moral world of intelligent beings, a noumenal or supersensible world that transcends the world of appearances, the impossibility of theoretical knowledge and proof of the objective reality of freedom receives even greater emphasis. Thus, Kant notes that "freedom . . . is a mere idea, the objective reality of which can in no way be presented in accordance with laws of nature and so too cannot be presented in any possible experience; and because no example of anything analogous can ever be put under it, it can never be comprehended or even only seen" (*GM,* 7: 96; Ak., IV: 459; 105). Moral action may lift us up from the mechanism of nature into an intelligible, supersensible world. But this has no bearing on what moral actions can actually achieve because their optimal effect is projected in terms of their taking place in the supersensible. Since we cannot experience supersensible nature, we cannot connect our moral actions to actual effects in the sensible world where we exist. When we try to impart rational form to sensible nature, the best that we can say is that this rational form contains the *possible effect* of an ideal world, which we could bring into existence *if* we had sufficient capabilities.

But because the moral law is not an empty "ought" but also a "would do," there must be a basis for hoping that our moral actions can have actual effects in the mechanism of nature. The demonstration that freedom and mechanism are merely compatible is insufficient as an incentive or interest of moral action.[16] Some help or favor (*Gunst*) must come from

---

16. The most convincing case for the position that holds that Kant intends moral freedom to be realized is made by Yirmiyahu Yovel, who argues that in addition to the categorical imperative, there is an imperative to act to promote the highest good, which is an accompanying idea and not a direct motivation. See Yovel, *Kant and the Philosophy of History* (Princeton, N.J.: Princeton University Press, 1980).

the side of a nature that is not the supersensible nature revealed to us by practical reason but is nevertheless more than mere mechanism. What is needed is an intimation of *teleological time*.[17] An infinite, self-causing, absolute being does not require temporal progression. But we need time to develop morally and to bring about what we morally will. This is what makes us historical beings. However, the time we have is blindly given to us. It is measured by the aimless mechanical succession of cause and effect. There is no guarantee that there can be any meaningful regularity of phenomena and their rational interconnection within given time. Hence, we must look for some further sign that nature is favorable (*günstig*), amenable, or well-disposed to moral action—some indication of an underlying unity of practical reason's causality with natural causality that would be the basis for the realization of moral freedom in the sensible world. The Third Critique's teleological conception of nature as an organized system of ends and culture as the ultimate end of such a system is formulated to bridge the gulf between freedom and nature, and to reconcile these two different causalities.

The need for a natural teleology was always already implied in Kant's moral philosophy. *The Foundations of the Metaphysics of Morals* describes it as a nonmechanical view of nature that reverses the direction of moral action: "*Teleology* considers nature as a kingdom of ends [*Reich der Zwecke*], *morals* considers a possible [*mögliches*] kingdom of ends as a kingdom of nature. In the former the kingdom of ends is a theoretical idea for explaining what exists. In the latter, it is a practical idea for the sake of bringing about, in conformity with this very idea, that which does not exist but which can become real [*wirklich*] by means of our conduct" (*GM*, 7:70n; Ak., IV:437n; 86n). Teleology is the counterpart of an ideal realm of ends in the realm of nature, the *actuality* of a purposive order in nature where morality can only think of a *possible* purposive order that it will try to actualize through action. Teleology is therefore connected to morality by a striking symmetry, although critical philosophy cannot justifiably

---

17. "Teleological time" is the term used by Amihud Gilead's extremely suggestive essay, "Teleological Time: A Variation of a Kantian Theme," *Review of Metaphysics* 38 (March 1985): 529–62. Gilead defines it as the time of incarnation where the architectonic of reason becomes realized, and he links it to culture: "without teleological time man cannot proceed towards his aim, which is the whole vocation of man in the moral act; without this time, the complete development (rather, culture [*Kultur*]) of human reason is impossible or precluded" (541).

assume any harmonious accord between nature and us or count on purposive nature as a partner and fitting member (*schicklichen Gliede*) of the moral realm of ends.[18]

Indeed, Kant's idea of a moral community of all rational beings as a realm of ends is implicitly organismic. It draws a striking analogy between moral ties and the organic connection of ends in living forms. The idea of a *Reich* refers to a systematic union (*systematische Verbindung*) or harmonious connection (*Verknüpfung*) of all ends into a whole (*Ganze*) by universal rational laws. Such laws are given by each member (*Glied*), and "have as their purpose . . . the relation of these beings to one another as ends and means [*Zwecke und Mittel*]," such that each member of such a *Reich*, as a giver of its own laws, relates to other members "*never merely as a means* but always *at the same time as ends in themselves [Zweck an sich]*" (*GM*, 7:66; Ak., IV:433; 83). This is precisely the harmonious interconnection of natural ends and the reciprocity of parts and whole in a living organism, where the end of each part serves the ends of all the other parts and the whole organism, and the whole arises from the parts.[19] The organic analogy is confirmed by Kant's suggestion that we might see our own faculty of reason as something given to us by teleological nature for an end (i.e., moral freedom), just as the constitutions of natural living organisms have ends: "In the natural constitution [*Naturanlagen*] of an organized being, that is, one constituted purposively for life [*eines organisierten, d.i. zweckmäßig zum Leben eingerichteten Wesens*], we assume as a principle that there will be found in it no instrument [*Werkzeug*] for some end other than what is also most appropriate to that end and best adapted [*schickliste*] to it" (*GM*, 7:20; Ak., IV:395; 50).

TAKING CREDIT FROM NATURE: CULTURE AS FREEDOM IN KANT'S HISTORICAL WRITINGS

Kant initially sought evidence of nature's purposiveness in the historical regularity of cultural progress. The theory of culture in his pre-1790 historical

---

18. See *GM*, 7:72–73; Ak., IV:438; 87–88.
19. My thanks to Allen Wood for alerting me to the analogy.

writings addresses the issue of what human beings can do in the sensible world to actualize freedom without compromising its unconditioned causality by reducing it to technics. What grounds does nature give us to believe that our moral actions can change the sensible world and that moral progress is possible? He argues that cultural progress gives us hope that moral freedom can be actualized because the sphere of culture is an empirical simulacrum or asymptotic approximation of the realm of ends. What, then, is culture's ontological status and mode of causality? Exemplifying the late-eighteenth- and early-nineteenth-century German philosophical understanding of *Bildung* as a phenomenal analogue of transcendental freedom, Kant transposes the moral will's ontological abstinence and staunch refusal to accept the given into cultural activity. But he makes a crucial qualification: this refusal to accept anything from nature is itself a predisposition given by nature. There is thus a qualified acceptance of an original favor, at the undeterminable moment of creation, from a purposive nature which is more than mere mechanism, although no gratitude whatsoever can be shown towards nature as mechanism in the course of our lives as cultural beings.

Human beings, Kant argues, have certain naturally given, original predispositions (*Naturanlagen, ursprüngliche Anlagen*), such as reason and freedom of will that are directed toward rational activity. But these predispositions are not instincts. They are germs (*Keime*) that need to be developed (*entwickeln*) through our own efforts. These capacities remain dormant and ineffectual if they are not frequently exercised. But because we are finite and they take a long time to develop, they can only be fully developed in the species (*Gattung*). Culture (*Kultur*), as an objective realm broadly defined to include legal and political institutions and the arts and sciences, is the historical medium for the development of our rational capacities. Culture is thus a power for transcending the mechanism of nature found in nature itself. It is the prosthetic compensation for the limitations human finitude imposes on our development. It is also a subjective attitude and a set of end-oriented processes that display our ability to transcend nature. "Nature," Kant suggests,

has willed that man should produce entirely by his own initiative [*gänzlich aus sich selbst herausbringe*] everything which goes beyond the mechanical ordering of his animal existence, and that he should not partake of any other happiness or perfection than that which he has procured for himself without instinct and by his own reason. . . . Nature gave man reason, and freedom of will based upon reason, and this in itself was a clear indication of nature's intention as regards his endowments. For it showed that man was not meant to be guided by instinct or equipped and instructed by innate knowledge; on the contrary, he was meant to produce everything out of himself. Everything had to be entirely of his own making [*eigen Werk*]—the discovery of a suitable diet, of clothing, of external security and defence . . . as well as all the pleasures that can make his life agreeable, and even his insight and prudence [*Klugheit*] and the goodness of his will. Nature seems here to have taken pleasure in exercising the strictest economy and to have measured out the basic animal equipment so sparingly as to be just enough for the most pressing needs of the beginnings of existence. It seems as if nature had intended that man, once he had finally worked his way up from the uttermost barbarism [*Rohigkeit*] to the highest degree of skill [*Geschicklichkeit*], to inner perfection in his manner of thought . . . , should be able to take for himself the entire credit for doing so and have only himself to thank for it. ("Idee," 11:36; *Pol. Writ.*, 43)

The key ideas of Kant's philosopheme of culture thus reinscribe the fundamental features of moral freedom. First, as the human power of making things that are beyond the mechanical existence of animals and the remaking and improving of oneself, culture is a form of auto-causality not only capable of origination but also of incarnating ends as objective works in the sensible world. A qualified recuperation of techne from the taint of heteronomy occurs. *Techne* is here not merely the making of things for the satisfaction of individual desires; it refers to artificial products and institutions that lift humanity beyond an animal existence and develop the species and improve its fabric of existence. Second, this intramundane power of origination is a taking of credit for oneself from nature. It is not that nature does not give, but that she is miserly: she gives us reason and free will, but only as predispositions, the development of which we owe to ourselves and for which we must thank ourselves. What we are now has not been given to us but has been achieved by our own making: this is what nature intends. Culture is thus the capacity for radical ingratitude to nature with which nature favors us. Third, culture is the transcendence of finitude in two senses. As reason's incarnational power and practical effectivity, culture is the concrete, inner worldly transcendence of natural mechanism. It is also the transcendence of finite existence because it inscribes the immortality of the species in the individual. This means that culture itself is a form of freedom.[20]

The idea of cultural freedom introduces a bifurcation between lower (heteronomous) and higher (autonomous) forms of *techne*. On the one hand, culture is heteronomous because it is part of and conditioned by the mechanism of nature: "all the culture and art [*Kunst*] which adorn mankind and the finest social order man creates are fruits of his unsociability" ("Idee," 11:40; *Pol. Writ.*, 46). Following Rousseau, Kant argues that the rise of culture and art coincides with inequality because their precondition is an exchange economy.[21] Their historical development leads to war because they are symbolic markers of self-aggrandizement on the part of states, and the technological and material means of asserting state egotism.[22] Such evils follow from man's finitude as a technical being conditioned by sensuous inclinations. Our role on earth is so thoroughly artificial (*sehr künstlich*) that no perfection can be expected ("Idee," 11:41n; *Pol. Writ.*, 47n). But at the same time, Kant also recuperates *techne* as the higher "enforced art" (*abgedrungene Kunst*) of discipline that curbs our inclinations ("Idee," 11:40; *Pol. Writ.*, 46). This higher culture is closer to morality. It is rationally directed and does not rely on sensuous forms that appeal to the inclinations. There is therefore an inner isomorphism between the subject of *Bildung* and the individual moral subject. Because cultural education can actively foster a way of thinking conducive to the formulation of clear moral principles, the process of *Bildung* positively incarnates the moral will in an anthropological personality and gradually realizes the realm of ends in the sensible world: "by a continued process of enlightenment, a beginning is made towards establishing a way of thinking which can with time transform the primitive natural capacity for moral [*sittlichen*] discrimination into definite practical principles; and thus a

---

20. Cf. Emil Fackenheim, "Kant's Concept of History," in *The God Within: Kant, Schelling, and Historicity* (Toronto: University of Toronto Press, 1996): 34–49. Fackenheim uses the apposite phrase, "cultural freedom," to refer to a social mode of freedom that produces institutions and forms of government. "It may enlarge, transform, or even pervert . . . [natural desires]; but . . . does not emancipate itself from them" (41).

21. Kant, "Conjectures on the Beginning of Human History," 11:97; *Pol. Writ.*, 230.

22. "TP," 11:170; *Pol. Writ.*, 90.

pathologically enforced social union is transformed into a *moral* whole [*moralisches Ganze*]" ("Idee," 11:38; *Pol. Writ.*, 44–45).

The two forms of *techne* correspond to the distinction between civilization and culture:

> We are *cultivated* [*kultiviert*] to a high degree by art and science. We are *civilised* [*zivilisiert*] to the point of excess in all kinds of social courtesies and proprieties. But we are still a long way from the point where we could consider ourselves *morally* mature [*moralisiert*]. For while the idea of morality [*Moralität*] is indeed present in culture [*Kultur*], an application of this idea which only extends to semblances of morality [*Sittenähnliche*], as in love of honour and outward propriety, amounts merely to civilisation [*Zivilisierung*].
>
> ("Idee," 11:44; *Pol. Writ.*, 49)

Unlike Rousseau, Kant suggests that under- or misdeveloped culture, which is the source of evil, remains part of the mechanism of nature. It is typified by the artificial, external refinement of mere civilization. But when culture is properly developed "in accordance with the true principles of man's *education* [*Erziehung*] as a human being and citizen," we will develop our capacities (*Anlagen der Menscheit*) according to our destiny as a moral species (*sittlichen Gattung*) ("Conjectures," 11:93; *Pol. Writ.*, 227). We will no longer be a merely physical species. Properly developed culture mediates between nature and morality and elevates us beyond mere mechanism into a higher nature in which our culture and nature do not conflict. "Art [*Kunst*], when it reaches perfection, once more becomes nature—and this is the ultimate goal of man's moral destiny" ("Conjectures," 11:95; *Pol. Writ.*, 228).

Kant's ideas about the cosmopolitan world federation and the republican constitutional state are inseparable from his philosophy of culture. His solution to the problem of how to develop a sphere of moral culture is primarily political. It is the state's duty to maximize the *Bildung* of its citizens. This means that the highest, most ideal relation between a state and its members is primarily cultural. Political freedom is an example of cultural freedom, and the political relation is the cultural relation par excellence. A state with a just civil constitution and a cosmopolitan order are material conditions that enable universal culture to flourish and bring about nature's greatest purpose, the development of our moral and rational predispositions. Moral development requires the technic of *Bildung*, "the slow and laborious efforts of . . . citizens to cultivate their minds [*der inneren Bildung der Denkungsart*]" ("Idee," 11:45; *Pol. Writ.*, 49). For the state to be a material support of this *Bildung*, its inner workings must mirror the arduous task of its citizens: "a long internal process of careful work [*Bearbeitung*] on the part of each commonwealth [*gemeinen Wesens*] is necessary for the education [*Bildung*] of its citizens" (ibid.). But to establish a state where *Bildung* is the primary political relation requires establishing a state of legality between states. As long as states devote their attention and resources to their expansionist war efforts, their citizens' *Bildung* will be thwarted: either held up and left unsupported for want of funds or obstructed by carnage or the distractions of endless preparation for war. Thus, only a universal cosmopolitan existence can serve "as the matrix [*Schoß*] within which all the original capacities of the human race may develop" ("Idee," 11:47; *Pol. Writ.*, 51).

But Kant's recuperation of *techne* cannot be absolute. Because cultural freedom remains within finitude, it is premised on a prior favor of nature. The reconciliation of nature and culture in a second nature necessarily appeals to a teleological nature. The realization of a cosmopolitan order depends on a cunning ruse of nature. Kant argues that unknown to us, nature deploys the mechanical factors of self-interest, egotistical strife, and unsocial sociability to reach a higher good.[23] War is detrimental to all states, which are linked by trade, and self-interest will lead to the formation of a world federation. The gradual spreading of enlightenment, he suggests, will influence rulers so that even those who have no money for public educational institutions will not hinder private efforts at support. But by relying on the cunning of nature to explain the course of history, Kant risks making transcendent or dogmatic claims about providential intentions and a hidden teleological plan that we cannot possibly experience and know. It also implies that the sphere of cultural freedom is itself heteronomous because the external political preconditions for its fullest development are produced by a purposive agency other than the human will. Freedom explicitly takes on an organismic shape in response to such objections. The *Critique of Judgment* reformulates the central themes of Kant's theory of

---

23. "The cunning of nature" is Yirmiyahu Yovel's quasi-Hegelian phrase. See *Kant and the Philosophy of History*, pp. 8–9. The idea is summed up in Kant, "Idee," 11:38–39; *Pol. Writ.*, 45.

culture in organismic terms. It attempts to recuperate *techne* absolutely by obliterating all trace of nature's favor. It derives the purposiveness of natural organisms from the artificial and rational capacity for organization found in human beings by appealing to a technic of nature that mirrors human *techne*.

ORGANIZED PRODUCTS OF NATURE: ORGANISMIC CAUSALITY AND FREEDOM IN THE *CRITIQUE OF JUDGMENT*

The *Critique of Judgment* attempts to bridge the gulf between nature and freedom by seeking an intelligible natural substrate that unites the noumenal ground of appearances with the supersensible realm of ends.[24] If "the concept of freedom is to actualize [*wirklich machen*] in the world of sense the end [*Zweck*] enjoined by its laws," Kant writes, "it must be possible to think of nature as being such that the lawfulness in its form will harmonize with at least the possibility of [achieving] the ends that we are to achieve in nature [*zur Möglichkeit der in ihr zu bewirkenden Zwecke*] according to laws of freedom" (*KU*, 10:83–84; Ak., V:176; 15). The passageway between cultural progress and moral freedom would also be reinforced by locating teleological time in nature since cultural progress would be continuous with natural purposiveness (*Zweckmäßigkeit*). But although such purposiveness is similar to the providence in the historical and anthropological writings, it does not involve a transcendent claim. Instead, it is an a priori principle we need to use in relating to nature because of the finitude of our faculties. This purposiveness is intimated by the apparent harmony between nature as a system of contingent particular empirical laws and our cognitive faculties. Without this accord, we could not specify the manifold forms of natural phenomena left undetermined by the understanding's a priori laws. More specifically, beautiful things suggest the subjective purposiveness of nature, and natural organisms even suggest objective purposiveness. We are concerned with the latter.

The principle of purposiveness implies that the regularity of nature can be explained neither by blind mechanism nor in terms of chance, for

---

24. See Kant, *KU*, 10:288, 297; Ak., V:346, 353; 219–220, 229, for formulations of the connection between the three forms of supersensible.

instance, an Epicurean random collision of bodies.[25] Chance is also inimical to freedom because it is as blind as any mechanism. To ground freedom's realization on chance is to abolish freedom. It deprives the final end of rational lawfulness, making it the outcome of a fortunate accident (*Glück-szufall*). Likewise, Kant repeatedly stresses that organisms cannot be explained by chance. As an objective end, the organism is the natural exorcism of chance as a governing principle in nature. Since its purposiveness includes a capacity for self-perpetuation and spontaneous generation, the organism is also the annihilation of death and the overcoming of finitude. Purposiveness is thus aligned with life, and chance, with death.

The organism is moreover a serendipitous phenomenal analogue of moral freedom because of its peculiar causality. Whereas beautiful or sublime things merely suggest a purposiveness of *form* for the subject's cognitive faculties (formal, subjective purposiveness), organized bodies (*organisierte Körper*) in nature imply intrinsic purposiveness in the object's material constitution, as if an end has been realized in it. However, such material, objective purposiveness is anomalous. The only two forms of causality we know are efficient causality governed by mechanical natural laws and the human will's final causality. The former has universal necessity but is blind. The latter, whose paradigmatic case is human artifice or technical capability (*Kunst* or *techne*), is action determined by concepts. It is, however, contingent. Kant characterizes these forms of causal connection by two different temporal series. Following the First Critique, efficient or real causality is a descending, nonreversible series of causes and effects in which any given effect cannot in turn be a cause of that which caused it. In contradistinction, final or ideal causality involves a reversible series that is both ascending and descending. In final causality, an effect can also be the cause of that which caused it because a prior presentation (*Vorstellung*) of a desired effect can determine one to bring about the existence of the thing that will cause that effect. As a conceived end, the desired effect is also the final cause of that which causes it. In Kant's example, a house is the cause of rental income but the conception of rental income may also be its ideal cause, the reason why it was built in the first place (*KU*, 10:320; Ak., V:372; 251).

---

25. J. D. McFarland points out that this unity of nature as a system of empirical laws is the necessary basis for making inductive inferences, which would otherwise by plagued by "the spectre of chance." See *Kant's Concept of Teleology* (Edinburgh: Edinburgh University Press, 1970), p. 75.

But apart from the qualified exception of *Bildung,* technical purposive causality is just as inimical to moral freedom. Although *techne* involves a reversible causal series and introduces some interference into the determinism of efficient causality, it is still not a spontaneous auto-causality. The technical attitude is heteronomous because it is action determined by an external object. Moreover, *techne* is the operation upon existing matter by an external concept. Hence, a technical causal series is marked by "*dependence [Abhängigkeit]* both as it ascends and as it descends" (*KU,* 10:320; Ak. V: 372; 251; emphasis added). In contradistinction, an organism is a natural end (*Naturzweck*), both a natural being and an end. This is its fundamentally paradoxical character: it appears to have been brought into existence by something more than blind mechanism. Yet, unlike a technical product, its end cannot be related to an external will. As exemplified by the ability of a tree to produce itself as species and individual in generation and growth and the capacity of its reciprocally dependent parts to produce each other through auto-repair, auto-maintenance, and preservation, a natural end seems to be a purposive auto-causality within nature itself! Kant characterizes this puzzling causality, which I will call organismic, as follows: "I would say, provisionally, that a thing exists as a natural end if it is *both cause and effect of itself* [*es von sich selbst . . . Ursache und Wirkung ist*] (although [*of itself*] in two different senses). For this involves a causality which is such that we cannot connect it with the mere concept of a nature without regarding nature as acting from an end; and even then, though we can think this causality, we cannot grasp it" (*KU,* 10:318; Ak., V:370–71; 249)[26]

By definition, any thing that is an end is an *organized* being (*organisiertes Wesen*) in which the material content and form of its parts (*Teile*) "are possible only through their relation to the whole [*Ganze*]" (*KU,* 10:320; Ak., V:373; 252). This is because a concept of the whole governs the thing's production such that the form of the whole and every aspect it contains (the content and form of its parts) are organized and determined a priori by the

---

26. Kant does not use the term "*Organismus*" and only uses the adjective "*organisch*" very sparingly in the Third Critique. But a natural end can be called an organism because of its self-organization. "*Organisch*" is frequently employed in Kant's *Opus Postumum,* ed. and trans. Eckart Förster (Cambridge: Cambridge University Press, 1993), where "organic body" is synonymous with "organized body in nature."

concept. But a natural end is a special kind of organized being that needs to be rigorously distinguished from a work of art (*Kunstwerk*). The latter is merely a product of a rational cause that preexists, is external to, and is distinct from the matter or parts of the thing. Technical causality is heteronomous. It involves the combination of various preexisting parts into an aggregate. The idea determining the process and the thing produced is foreign to the thing's nature. The maker artificially imposes this idea on the thing, which comes into being for the sake of another, to whom it is subjected.

In contradistinction, a natural end's purposiveness must originate solely from within the natural product itself. This auto-causality is only thinkable as a combination of "the parts of the thing . . . into the unity of a whole because they are reciprocally cause and effect of their form" (*KU*, 10:321; Ak., V:373; 252). There must be a complete interdependence between parts and whole, material content and purposive form, whereby the former is simultaneously the cause and effect of the latter and vice versa. What is formed in the process is not merely an aggregate but a systematic unity. Kant outlines three essential moments or aspects of organismic causality: "what is needed is that all its parts, through their own causality, produce one another as regards both their form and combination, and that in this way they produce a whole whose concept ([if present] in a being possessing the causality in terms of concepts that would be adequate for such a product) could, conversely, be the cause of this body according to a principle" (ibid.). First, the causal relationship between each of the parts and the other parts must be one of reciprocity. Second, the parts produce the whole. Third, the whole at the same time also produces the parts such that the parts are possible only in relation to the whole. This implies a reciprocity not only between the parts, but also between the parts and the whole, which indicates an inner confluence between final and efficient causality, where the final cause appears as immanent in the thing itself. Hence, a more precise definition of a natural end is an organized being that is at the same time also self-organizing (*organisiertes und sich selbst organisierendes Wesen*). It brings itself into being and exists by its own accord and not by another hand. Organismic causality is thus autonomous in two senses. In a negative sense, it exhibits a certain independence from mechanical principles. In a positive sense, it is superior to *techne* because it is self-causing.

Kant's account of the organism is a unique form of vitalism.[27] Vitalism is the view that organic matter contains a special nonmaterial property, a vital force (i.e., life) that gives it a purposive dynamism and distinguishes it from matter in general, which is inanimate, unorganized, and governed by mechanical laws. In biological theory, vitalism is associated with the position that life cannot be explained in physicochemical terms. Kant, however, does not appeal to a preexisting life force. He rejects hylozoism and emphasizes the autonomous character of organismic causality:

> In considering nature and the ability [*Vermögen*] it displays in organized products we say far too little if we call this an *analogue* of art [*Kunst*], for in that case we think of an artist [*Künstler*] (a rational being) apart from nature. Rather, nature organizes itself, and it does so within each species of its organized products. . . . We might be closer if we call this inscrutable property [*Eigenschaft*] of nature an *analogue* of *life*. But in that case we must either endow matter, as mere matter, with a property (for instance, the property of life, as hylozoism [does]) that conflicts with its nature [*Wesen*]. Or else we must supplement matter with an alien principle (a soul) *conjoined* to it [*fremdartiges mit ihr in Gemeinschaft stehendes Prinzip (eine Seele) beigesellen*]. But [that also will not work. For] if an organized product is to be a natural product, then we cannot make this soul the artificer [*Künstlerin*] that constructed it, since that would remove the product from (corporeal) nature. And yet the only alternative would be to say that this soul uses as its instrument [*Werkzeug*] organized matter; but if we presuppose organized matter, we do not make it a whit more intelligible. Strictly speaking, therefore, the organization of nature has nothing analogous to any causality known to us.
>
> (*KU*, 10:322–23; Ak., V:374–75; 253–54)

Dogmatic vitalism, he argues, forces the organism into community with something foreign, thereby taking it away from its very nature, alienating it from what is proper to it. If we derive the organism's purposiveness from a soul, we reduce it to an artificial product and instrument and subject it to an alien agency because the soul functions as an artist-maker external to

---

27. For a comprehensive account of Kant's theory of life, see Reinhard Löw, *Philosophie des Lebendigen: Der Begriff des Organischen bei Kant, sein Grund und seine Aktualität* (Frankfurt: Suhrkamp, 1980).

and distinct from the organism's matter. Kant rejects the hylozoistic doctrine of living matter (*belebten Materie*) on the grounds that life is a property that is improper to matter and contradicts its essence, which is lifelessness (*Leblosigkeit*) or inertia (*KU*, 10:345; Ak., V:394; 276). Moreover, hylozoism relies on a circular argument. It claims to derive the purposiveness of organisms from the life of matter. But since organisms are the only examples we have of life, the concept of life depends on our experience of organisms and cannot be formulated a priori.

Although he is often regarded as repudiating vitalism, Kant is actually a critical vitalist because he safeguards the autonomy of organic life and insists on its distinctiveness from both nonorganized and technical bodies.[28] Although he argues that the purposiveness of organic beings cannot be reduced to physicochemical causes and can only be understood as issuing from an immaterial principle, which operates in the reciprocal relationship between an organism's form and its parts, he stops short of equating this principle with a determinate life force within matter because he insists that we cannot know anything about it but can only think it in analogy with the final causality of human concepts. The critical nature of Kant's vitalism is clearly seen in his reliance on Blumenbach's epigenetic theory of *Bildungstrieb,* which points to the spontaneous, autonomous nature of generation.[29] Kant is attracted to Blumenbach's theory for two

---

28. W. H. Werkmeister, "Kant's Philosophy and Modern Science," *Kant-Studien* 66, no. 1 (1975): 50–55; and Clark Zumbach, *The Transcendent Science: Kant's Conception of Biological Methodology* (The Hague: Martinus Nijhoff, 1984), pp. 79–113, regard Kant as an anti-vitalist.

29. Kant refers to Blumenbach in three texts: § 81 of the Third Critique (*KU*, 10:381; Ak., V:424; 311); "Über den Gebrauch teleologischer Prinzipien in der Philosophie," 9:164n; and a letter to Blumenbach on 5 August 1790, in Immanuel Kant, *Correspondence,* trans. and ed. Arnulf Zweig (Cambridge: Cambridge University Press, 1999), p. 354. The following paragraphs on Kant's use of Blumenbach refer to the passage from *KU.* For extended discussions of Blumenbach's theory of *Bildungstrieb,* his relationship of reciprocal influence with Kant, and Kant's influence on the program to integrate teleology with mechanism and vitalism with materialism in German philosophy of biology in the first half of the nineteenth century, see Timothy Lenoir, "Teleology Without Regrets: The Transformation of Physiology in Germany, 1790–1847," *Studies in the History and Philosophy of Science* 12, no. 4 (1981): 293–354; Lenoir, "Kant, Blumenbach, and Vital Materialism in German Biology," *ISIS* 71, no. 256 (1980): 77–108; Lenoir, *The Strategy of Life: Teleology and Mechanics in Nineteenth Century German Biology* (Dordrecht: Reidel, 1982), esp. chap. 1; and Nicholas Jardine, *The Scenes of Inquiry: On the Reality of Questions in the Sciences* (Oxford: Clarendon Press, 1991), pp. 25–43.

reasons: Blumenbach's explanation of biological formations (*Bildungen*) begins with what is already a living, self-preserving, purposive body or organized matter instead of lifeless, unorganized raw matter from which life then miraculously springs forth as an additional causal principle to explain how matter could have originally formed (*gebildet*) itself into a self-preserving form. Blumenbach argues that organic forms cannot be accounted for by the nonintentional apposition and combination of particles either through mechanical forces of attraction and repulsion, chemical reaction, or by the chance collision of particles (Epicureanism). But he neither derives organization from preformed structures (preformationism) nor from life as an inexplicable purposive causal agent found in physical nature (hylozoism). Instead, he sees life as equiprimordial with organization, as organization's spontaneous effect. Blumenbach calls this capacity (*Vermögen*) of an organic body's matter for original organization (*ursprünglichen Organisation*) the *Bildungstrieb*. It is a purposiveness immanent to organized natural bodies and cannot be reduced to the blind mechanical and chemical forces constituting matter. But it is also not an alien principle imposed upon matter. As Timothy Lenoir puts it, it is "a teleological agent which had its antecedents ultimately in the inorganic realm but which was an emergent vital force."[30]

Kant also endorses the *Bildungstrieb*'s heuristic character. It is "factual confirmation" of "the union of two principles that people have believed to be irreconcilable, namely the physical-mechanistic and the merely teleological way of explaining organized nature."[31] Although we can witness the effects of its organizing activity, which suggests that nature is more than mere mechanism, it remains inscrutable and we cannot arrive at any knowledge about how it comes about or discover the final cause for the organization of nature and the origins of life. Its existence does not refute materialist or mechanical explanations of organic nature. It merely suggests that they are insufficient for the study of organisms but does not allow us to determine anything about a higher purposive nature.[32]

---

30. "Kant, Blumenbach, and Vital Materialism," p. 83.
31. Letter to Blumenbach, *Correspondence*, p. 354.
32. Cf. Kant's criticism of Herder for indulging in dogmatic metaphysics and an exercise in the poetic imagination in Herder's claim of having discovered the invisible forces that give rise to organization of organic forms, in Kant, *Rezension zu Johann Gottfried Herder: Ideen sur Philosophie der Geschichte der Menscheit*, 12:791–92; *Pol. Writ.*, 209.

Kant's account of organismic causality is a vitalism without life because he posits self-organization as the source of life and not vice versa. Organismic causality is the spontaneous auto-causality of life without life! We cannot speak of life as a property of the organism that preexists and causes its organization, but there are nevertheless life effects that follow from its purposive self-organization. Strictly speaking, the life of the organism is life without a prior essence of life. There are only spontaneous life effects, that is, life as its own effect, although even the "own" is misleading because it suggests a preexisting life force, while spontaneous self-organization is all there is. This spontaneous activity cannot be referred back to a soul. But it is both immaterial and has material effects.[33]

Herein lies organismic causality's ontological superiority vis-à-vis the causality governing inorganic beings, even technical beings like machines. It is a formative power (*bildende Kraft*). "An organized being," Kant writes, "is not a mere machine. For a machine has only motive force [*bewegende Kraft*]. But an organized being has within it formative force [*bildende Kraft*], and a formative force that this being imparts to the kinds of matter that lack it (thereby organizing them). This force is therefore a formative force that propagates itself—a force that a mere ability [of one thing] to move [another] (i.e. mechanism) cannot explain" (*KU*, 10:322; Ak., V:374; 253). Whereas a watch cannot repair itself, a tree is able to reproduce itself and its own parts precisely because it has a formative power that makes it self-organizing. Moreover, this power can also be exercised on external matter, which is conferred the organism's proper form and assimilated by it in such a way that this matter is also imbued with the same formative power. This organismic appropriation of external raw matter bears a striking similarity to culture because it involves the imparting of one's own proper form to matter, the reworking of matter in one's own *Bild* so that it can be

---

33. Extensive consideration of the *Opus Postumum* is beyond the scope of this book, but in it Kant clearly gestures towards what I have called "vitalism without life." Kant repeats the argument that "matter does not organize itself but is organized by what is immaterial" even though one cannot thereby assume a soul (149). He defines life as the activity of an immaterial principle, the unity of an organic body thought of in analogy with the end of human willing (137). For an interesting attempt to relate Kant's account of the organism to contemporary theories of chemistry that see life as a property that emerges at the systemic level from self-organizing principles (e.g., Prigogine's theory of dissipative structures), see Alicia Juarrero Roqué, "Self-Organization: Kant's Concept of Teleology and Modern Chemistry," *Review of Metaphysics* 39 (September 1985): 107–35.

made part of one's proper self. The process of growth is not a mere increase in size through mechanical laws, but a form of *Bildung:* "the matter that the tree adds to itself is first processed [*verarbeitet*] by it until the matter has the quality proper [*spezifisch-eigentümlicher*] to the species . . . and the tree continues to develop [*bildet*] itself by means of a material that in its composition is the tree's own product. . . . the separation and recombination of this raw material show that these natural beings have a separating and forming ability [*Scheidungs- und Bildungsvermögens*] of very great originality" (*KU*, 10:318–19; Ak., V:371; 250). The *bildende Kraft* and *Bildungsvermögen* of an organism, like the Blumenbachian *Bildungstrieb*, is thus a capacity for purposive form-giving work, a power of self-origination in the sensible world that infinitely outstrips the ability of human art (*Kunst*).

Kant's account of organic life is pathbreaking because it sharply distinguishes organismic causality from artificial and technical causality. Both are purposive. But whereas an artificial object always bears the mark of a foreign hand, an organism seems to exhibit some autonomy because its purposive activity originates from within itself, from the complete reciprocity between its parts and its whole, content and form. Kant's idea of the organism therefore breaks with its etymological roots in the Greek "*organon.*" As we saw in the previous chapter, Aristotle's definition of the living being as a body with organs and the living body as an instrument/organ of the soul suggests a mimetic continuity between *physis* and *techne* that continues through Descartes and Leibniz to the reduction of final causality to human technics in eighteenth-century mechanism. Kant breaches this mimeticism. Even as he insists on the importance of final causality in the study of organisms, he sharply distinguishes the auto-causality of organisms from heteronomous technical causality. The organism is not an artificial instrument (*Werkzeug*) because an instrument, like anything created for an end, is brought into existence by and for the sake of another. A natural end may appear to be an instrument to the extent that each of its parts "exists only *as a result* of all the rest" and, hence, can be regarded as "existing *for the sake* of the others and of the whole" (*KU*, 10:321; Ak., V:373; 253). But strictly speaking, the organism is functionality generalized throughout an entire being. Because of its self-organizing, self-causing nature, the causality producing it and each of its parts never issues from or serves anything alien, but only itself. In an organism "everything is an end [*Zweck*] and reciprocally also a means [*Mittel*]," and this reciprocity distinguishes it from an artificial instrument (*KU*, 10:324; Ak., V:376; 255). Each part of an organism is an organ only in a paradoxical sense because it also "*produces the other parts* (so that each reciprocally produces the other)." Hence, "something like this cannot be an instrument of art [*Werkzeug der Kunst*], but can be an instrument only of nature, which supplies all material for instruments (even for those of art)" (*KU*, 10:321–22; Ak., V:374; 253).

This is precisely why organismic causality is an analogue of freedom. Since an organism is not fashioned according to an external concept, its purposiveness is not the work of a foreign hand. Its circular, self-recursive character implies a peculiar temporality somewhere in between the linear time of mechanical and technical causality and the timelessness of moral willing, which spontaneously originates a temporal series but remains outside it. We see here the inseparability of Kant's interest in the organism from the problem of how a finite creature can incarnate moral freedom in the sensible world. The circular temporality of organismic causality, in which each moment is ordered and related to all other moments according to a final end to be achieved, is the gift of teleological time at the immediate level of objective existence that does not require a dogmatic appeal to providence.[34] As Ernst Cassirer notes, the organism is a symbolic counterpart in objective existence of the idea of end-in-itself and self-value that can otherwise only be found in the ethical sphere.[35]

THE POLITICAL BODY AS ORGANISM: COSMOPOLITAN CULTURE AND THE REORGANIZATION/ORGANICIZATION OF THE STATE-MACHINE

Kant's organismic vitalism is the fundamental philosophical condition for the genesis of *political organicism,* the conceptualization of the ideal social or political body as a living organism sharply distinguished from the nonliving,

---

34. For a broader formulation of the link between Kant's teleology of nature and his philosophy of history, see Friedrich Kaulbach, "Der Zusammenhang zwischen Naturphilosophie und Geschictsphilosophie bei Kant," *Kant-Studien* 56, nos. 3–4 (1966): 430–51. Cf. Yovel, *Kant and the Philosophy of History*, pp. 128–29.

35. Cassirer, *Kant's Life and Thought*, trans. James Haden (New Haven: Yale University Press, 1981), p. 340.

especially the machine as a product of human *techne*. Lexical similarity already indicates an isomorphism between the *"bildende Kraft,"* *"Bildungsvermögen,"* and *"Bildungstrieb"* of organismic causality and the higher technic of *"Bildung,"* which is also a sensible form of purposive auto-causality. Since the constitutional political body is culture's highest achievement and synecdoche, culture's association with organic life is easily transferred to the operations of the political body itself. Hence, despite his repeated insistence that the organization of nature is not analogous to any causality we know, Kant immediately suggests that a new form of political organization may be an exception to the rule:

> On the other hand, the analogy of these direct natural ends can serve to elucidate a certain [kind of] association [*Verbindung*] [among people], though one found more often as an idea than in actuality: in speaking of the complete transformation [*Umbildung*] of a large people into a state, which took place recently, the word *organization* was frequently and very aptly applied to the establishment of legal authorities, etc., and even to the entire body politic. For each member [*Glied*] in such a whole should indeed be not merely the means [*Mittel*], but also an end [*Zweck*]; and while each member contributes to making the whole possible [*der Möglichkeit des Ganzen mitwirkt*], the idea of that whole should in turn determine the member's position and function.
>
> (*KU*, 10:323n; Ak., V:375n; 254n)[36]

This is not a casual analogy. In § 59, Kant had described a constitutional monarchy and a despotic state as resembling in their causalities "an animate [*beseelten*] body," and "a mere machine (such as a hand mill)" (*KU*, 10:296; Ak., V:352; 227).

Kant's organismic metaphor is thus an attempt to elucidate the associative ties of the emergent republican state. "Organization" refers to a previously unprecedented inner articulation of individual citizens into legal institutions and even the formation of the state itself from individual members. This kind of state exhibits the same purposive auto-causality of an organism because it is a self-organizing whole in which there is a reciprocity between parts and whole, means and end. The being of such a political

---

36. It is unclear whether this reference is to the American Revolution (1776–83) or the French Revolution, which was in its early months at the time of the writing of the Third Critique.

body and its individual members, like that of an organism and its parts, is not subordinate to a foreign hand. This broad homology between an organism's autonomous constitution and political freedom elucidates the sociopolitical values of liberty and equality in terms of the organism's three moments. The reciprocal causal relationship between an organism's parts implies equality amongst citizens. That the parts produce each other and the whole at the same time that the whole produces the parts implies the liberty of the citizens vis-à-vis the polity. The reciprocity of parts and whole clearly contradicts the myth that the organismic metaphor justifies a despotic and instrumentalist relation between the political body and its citizenry because it subordinates the latter to the whole. Kant's critique of preformationism indicates that the organic whole is not a preexisting germ that precedes its parts. Moreover, an organism's parts are only organs in a qualified sense. No individual part is subordinate to anything else because it is both a means and an end.

The organismic metaphor thus clearly breaks with the traditional analogy of the body politic. In the mechanistic model, as in the Greek tradition, the idea of the body politic elaborated correspondences between society or the state and the different functional parts or limbs of the human body, which were organs of the soul or mind. Kant's organismic metaphor, which rejects the derivation of life from an alien soul, replaces the hierarchical relationship between head and limbs with an egalitarian interdependence between citizens and the state similar to the relation of parts and whole in an organism. This is the seam where the Third Critique is stitched onto the theory of political morality in Kant's post-1790 political writings. Two decisive changes take place. First, ideal political institutions, which are simulacra of moral freedom, are described as organisms because organismic causality is a phenomenal analogue of moral freedom. Second, culture is now regarded as the ontological paradigm and ultimate end of the ideal constitutional state because its causality is isomorphic with organismic causality.[37]

---

37. On the cobelonging of culture and politics, see also Patrick Riley's suggestion that public legal justice is a strand of culture and "the legal realization of moral ends, coupled with the creation of a legal environment for *motiva moralia*, is the telos of politics-as-culture." (Patrick Riley, *Kant's Political Philosophy* (Totowa, N.J.: Rowman & Littlefield, 1983), p. 98) Cf. George Armstrong Kelly's suggestion that Kant saw the state as the culture preserver. See Kelly, *Idealism, Politics, and History: Sources of Hegelian Thought* (Cambridge: Cambridge University Press, 1969), p. 145.

In Kant's view, moral principles actively influence politics by analogy. Pure principles of right impart the universal form of moral reason to political practice: "a true system of politics cannot therefore take a single step without first paying tribute to morality. . . . [A]ll politics must bend the knee before right" ("PP," 11:243–44; *Pol. Writ.*, 125). Political right is a simulacrum of morality that mediates between it and the merely pragmatic art (*Kunst*) of politics, enabling moral reason to influence and infuse politics. Thus, although moral freedom cannot appear in the sensible world, it can take the asymptotic form of increasing legality and socio-political freedom.[38] The two paradigmatic institutions embodying political right are publicness (*Öffentlichkeit*) and the republican civil constitution. Following the figural schema established in the Third Critique, these political institutions situated between freedom and the mechanism of nature exhibit the decidedly organismic attributes of reciprocity, harmonious unity, and rational purposive spontaneous activity. The ideal form of social contract is a civil state in which external relations between individuals are governed by laws derived from public right. This system of rights secures external freedom by ensuring harmony and reciprocity amongst individuals. The *Metaphysics of Morals* takes the organismic metaphor further. Kant argues that the citizens of a constitutional state or commonwealth formed by an original contract can be divided into merely passive parts (*Teile*) and active members (*Glieder*) who possess the right to vote and administrative and legislative powers. While everyone within the state should be treated according to natural laws of freedom and equality, only genuine citizens who are independent and want to be "a part of the commonwealth acting from his own choice in community with others [*mit anderen handelnder Teil*]" are active members of the state who "have the right to manage the state itself, . . . the right to organize it or to cooperate [*mitzuwirken*] for introducing certain laws" (*MS*, 8:432–34; Ak., VI:314–15; *Prac. Phil.*, 458–59).

One sees quite clearly how the organism's capacity for self-preservation is translated into the socioeconomic independence of an active individual bourgeois citizen who runs state institutions. Passive citizens lack a civil personality (*bürgerliche Persönlichkeit*). They do not possess civil indepen-

---

38. *Der Streit der Fakultäten*, 11:365; "A Renewed Attempt to Answer the Question: 'Is the Human Race Continually Improving?'" *Pol. Writ.*, 187–88. Hereafter cited as *SF*.

dence because they rely on others for protection or economic welfare. Women, minors, domestic servants, and "anyone whose preservation (*erhalten*) in existence . . . depends not on his management of his own business but on arrangements made by another (except the state)" are all passive parts and mere associates of the state (*MS*, 8:433; Ak., VI:314; *Prac. Phil.*, 458). Their heteronomous mode of socioeconomic existence is mere inherence (*Inhärenz*). However, one can be elevated from this passive condition through one's own efforts. The organismic political body is thus an ideal horizon that cannot be actualized in the present because of empirical division and economic inequality in society.

The *spontaneity* of rational-critical publicness (*Öffentlichkeit*) is likewise an analogue of the organism's spontaneity. Publicness can take the form of enlightened public opinion, which continually presses upon the state and puts it in touch with the needs of society (a theme brilliantly elaborated by Jürgen Habermas), or a universal, disinterested sympathy that rationally informed onlookers express publicly about great world historical events such as the French Revolution.[39] Kant also describes the cosmopolitan world federation as a system of organic relations, "a progressive organization of citizens of the earth [*Erdbürger*] into and towards the species, as a system held together by cosmopolitan bonds" (*Anthropologie*, 12:690; Ak., VII:333; 193).

Because its causality is even closer to organismic causality than the technic of political organization, culture further strengthens this correlation between the organization of living forms and forms of legal and sociopolitical organization that promote political freedom. By itself, the political state cannot achieve moral freedom because it is a coercive organization and a product of skill directed toward improving the material conditions of life. It belongs to the realm of external freedom and, hence, the mechanism of

---

39. On Kant's view of publicness as a vehicle for fostering the unity of an empirical consciousness in general and its importance for Habermas's theory of the public sphere, see Jürgen Habermas, *The Structural Transformation of the Public Sphere: An Inquiry into a Category of Bourgeois Society,* trans. Thomas Burger (Cambridge: MIT Press, 1989), pp. 102–17. On the public reaction to the French Revolution, see Kant, *SF*, 11:357–60; *Pol. Writ.*, 182–83. Despite Kant's republicanism and his insistence on the oppositional character of the public sphere, he does not endorse the right to civil disobedience or revolution against an illegitimate government. Kant remained supportive of enlightened monarchical authoritarianism. He believed that although the authorities should heed the public sphere, change should take place from the top downwards.

nature. Thus, although the constitutional state is "a great step . . . taken *towards* morality . . . this is still not the same as a moral step" ("PP," 11:238n; *Pol. Writ.,* 121n). Establishing a republican constitution "does not involve the moral improvement of man; it only means finding out how the mechanism of nature can be applied to men in such a manner that the antagonism of their hostile attitudes will make them compel one another to submit to coercive laws, thereby producing a condition of peace within which the laws can be enforced" ("PP," 11:224; *Pol. Writ.,* 113).[40] Hence, although "a civil constitution artificially raises to its highest power the human species' good predisposition to the final end [*Endzweck*] of its destiny . . . *animality* [still] manifests itself earlier and, at bottom, more powerfully than pure *humanity.* . . . This is because nature within man tries to lead him from culture to morality and not (as reason prescribes) from morality and its law, as the starting point, to a culture designed to conform with morality" (*Anthropologie,* 12:681–82; Ak., VII:327–28; 188).

Herein lies the importance of cultural education. Our pure humanity can only be brought out with the full development of a moral culture because moral education (*Erziehung/Edukation*) alone can foster the harmonious unity of an empirical consciousness in general.[41] By organizing individuals into a coherent whole, culture infuses the resulting collective with rational dynamism. It changes the state by strengthening the ties between it and its citizens. Through its relation to culture, the state becomes organicized. Instead of being an artificial machine imposed upon the people, it becomes united with them into a self-organizing whole imbued with organismic causality. The state can participate in cultural education in two ways. It can encourage popular enlightenment (*Volksaufkärung*), "the public instruction of the people upon their duties and rights towards the state to which they belong" directed by an independent, nonofficial stratum of intelligentsia (*SF,* 11:362; *Pol. Writ.,* 186). This is a populist extension of Kant's earlier argument about the formation (*bilden/Bildung*) of educated

---

40. Hence Kant's famous remark that "the problem of setting up a state can be solved even by a nation of devils (so long as they possess understanding)" ("PP," 11:224; *Pol. Writ.,* 112).

41. "Man is destined [*bestimmte*] by his reason to live in a society with men and in it to *cultivate* [*kultivieren*] himself, to *civilize* [*zivilisieren*] himself, and to make himself *moral* [*moralisieren*] by the arts and sciences. . . . Man must, therefore, be *educated* [*erzogen*] to the good" (*Anthropologie,* 12:678; Ak., VII:324–25; 186).

(*gebildet*) citizens capable of "the public use of reason," who play an active role in reforming the political body either by participating in the rational debate of the critical public sphere, or by occupying a public position within the state-apparatus.[42] Popular cultural education generates a form of enlightened public mediation that opens up the state to the people. Such publicity (*Publizität*) is essential for the nation's progress because it is the avenue for the people to voice their grievances and make rightful demands.

The state can also undertake the *Bildung* of its youth in spiritual and moral culture by establishing a schooling system that "will eventually not only make them good citizens, but will also bring them up to practise a kind of goodness which can continually progress and maintain itself" (*SF*, 11:366; *Pol. Writ.*, 188–89). Hence, there is an imperative not only to treat the people as more than mere instruments but also to *organicize* the state and bring it into a harmonious unity with the people through the agency of culture. Such a plan is necessary to the development of moral culture on a large scale. It enables the organic evolution of the state, which "will reform itself from time to time, pursuing evolution instead of revolution, and will thus make continuous progress" (*SF*, 11:367; *Pol. Writ.*, 189).[43]

The Third Critique locates culture's organicizing power in its incarnational ability. The organism's intrinsic purposiveness makes us ask whether organized natural beings are extrinsically connected so that the whole of nature is a system of ends and whether this system has a final end (*Endzweck*), an unconditioned end-in-itself, a being whose ground of existence lies solely in itself. Kant argues that moral freedom is the only unconditioned end we know. But although no final end can be found within nature (since all natural beings are conditioned), nature can still have an ultimate end (*letzter Zweck*). The culture (*Kultur*) of human beings is the highest goal nature can accomplish. Culture is the point toward which the whole of nature is oriented, the principle that organizes individual

---

42. See "Beantwortung der Frage: Was ist Aufklärung," 11: 55; "An Answer to the Question: 'What is Enlightenment?' " *Pol. Writ.*, 55.

43. But Kant is pessimistic about the plan's success. He argues that states are still mere machines who use up their finances to wage war. Many rulers have a purely instrumentalist view of education. They only consider improving the skill of their citizens so that they can be better instruments for their ends. See *Über Pädagogik*, 12:706; *Education*, 17–18. Hereafter cited as *UP*. The organicization of the state thus requires the education of rulers.

natural ends into a system. We may regard the human species as equally subject to "a natural mechanism without an end," and merely a link (*Glied*) in the chain of ends like any other natural end because we have sensuous inclinations (*KU*, 10:384; Ak., V:427; 315). "Nature . . . is very far from having adopted [man] . . . as its special darling and benefited him [*mit Wohltun begünstig habe*] in preference to the other animals, but has in fact spared him no more than any other animal from its destructive workings" (*KU*, 10:388; Ak., V:430; 318). Kant observes, however, that we are actually the paramount and most favored member of nature as a teleological system. Humankind is gifted with rational capacities without which nature could not have been conceived as purposive in the first place:

> But he is also a means for preserving [*Mittel zur Erhalthung*] the purposiveness in the mechanism of the other links. Man is indeed the only being on earth that has understanding and hence an ability to set himself ends of his own choice [*willkürlich Zwecke*], and in this respect he holds the title of lord of nature; and if we regard nature as a teleological system, then it is man's vocation [*Bestimmung*] to be the ultimate end of nature, but always subject to a condition: he must have the understanding and the will [*Willen*] to give both nature and himself reference to an end [*Zweckbeziehung zu geben*] that can be independent of nature, self-sufficient, and a final end.
>
> (*KU*, 10:389; Ak., V:431; 318)

This a priori definition of culture as the ultimate end reinscribes the key themes of Kant's earlier philosophy of culture—the recuperation of *techne* in *Bildung* as a higher, autonomous form of culture that mediates between freedom and nature; culture as ingratitude to nature and a refusal to accept nature's gifts, and so on—within organic life itself. Because the human will's purposive causality preserves nature's purposiveness, we can regard humankind as having an organismic causality. Indeed, our understanding's causality is organismic causality raised to the highest level since it *originates* the *conception* of organized nature. Thus, we become the originators of organismic causality, which was initially regarded as nature's gift. An acknowledgment of nature's favor to man is immediately followed by an act of ingratitude toward nature. Second, culture is the site for transcending finitude because it mediates between the mechanism of nature and the final end that lies beyond nature (moral freedom). But the formation of culture is no longer passively dependent on providential nature. Culture actively gives purposiveness to mechanical nature and refers nature beyond itself. One could say, in Hegelian fashion, that culture is the dynamic unfolding or development of the implicit truth of natural organisms, the substrate and end of natural purposiveness.

This is why cultural work is an epigenetic process. Culture

> is a formal and subjective condition, namely, man's aptitude in general for setting [*setzen*] himself ends, and for using nature (independently of [the element of] nature in man's determination of ends [*Zweckbestimmung*]) as a means [for achieving them] in conformity with the maxims of his free ends generally. Producing in a rational being an aptitude for ends generally (hence [in a way that leaves] that being free [*folglich in seiner Freiheit*]) is *culture*.
>
> (*KU*, 10:389–90; Ak., V:431; 319)

Culture is the subjective capacity for prescribing rational ends to nature and the activity of actualizing them. But more importantly, it is a self-reflexive activity that brings forth in a rational creature this ability to set ends at all. Because it enables us to be independent of nature, culture frees us. Our capacity for freedom comes from ourselves, from an aptitude we bring out in ourselves. Unlike animals, we are our own work and not that of a foreign hand. Thus, although our rational powers are propitious, naturally given dispositions, they are not instincts preformed by an alien reason (*fremde Vernunft*), but have to be brought out by our own efforts.[44] Culture is self-incarnational work: "man has a character which he himself creates, insofar as he is capable of perfecting himself according to the ends that he himself adopts. Because of this, man, as an animal endowed with *the capacity for reason* [*mit Vernunftfähigkeit begabtes Tier*] (*animal rationabilis*), can make of himself a *rational animal*" (*Anthropologie*, 12:673; Ak., VII:321; 183).

As the work of freedom that arises from ourselves, culture exceeds mere skill (*Geschicklichkeit*). Kant refines his earlier distinction between civilization and culture by distinguishing between cultures of skill and discipline.[45]

---

44. See *Anthropologie*, 12:683–84; Ak., VII:329; 189; and *UP*, 12:697; 2.

45. Kant's terminology is not always consistent. The *Anthropology* associates both civilization and discipline with the pragmatic disposition, which is lower than the moral disposition, and not skill. Civilization, however, is lower than discipline (12:676; Ak., VII:323–24; 185). In *UP*, education is

Skill concerns the promotion of ends in general. As a technical predisposition involving the manipulation (*Handhabung*) of things and nature in general as instruments, it is "a mechanical predisposition joined with consciousness" (*Anthropologie*, 12:674; Ak., VII:322; 183). Because the culture of skill does not teach us how to discriminate morally between ends, its freedom is merely technical mastery over external nature. In contradistinction, the culture of discipline (*Zucht*) involves the self-reflexive formation of the human will so that it can select ends that are most right or rational. Its freedom from nature is literally a freeing of ourselves from *our own* nature, the animal nature *in* us: "It is negative and consists in the liberation [*Befreiung*] of the will from the despotism of desires, a despotism that rivets us to certain natural things and renders us unable to do our own selecting" (*KU*, 10:390; Ak., V:432; 319). Discipline is the recuperation of *techne* in a higher form of culture that we perform on our own bodies to actualize purposive moral form in them. It makes the individual natural body more amenable to the influence of rational ideas and moral principles and facilitates the frequent exercise of our moral will by transforming the body into an intelligible sign.

In Kant's view, culture is deterritorialized and cosmopolitan despite its connection to the territorial state. Cultural education can only be carried out fully in a state of peace under the aegis of a world federation. The material conditions under which culture can attain its highest development are therefore cosmopolitan. But more importantly, prior to the establishment of this cosmopolitan whole, our attempts at developing our humanity through discipline are aided by our attraction to cultural forms that have a universal ideational or affective content such as the fine arts, the sciences, and also the humanities (*humaniora*).[46] Exposure to these forms humanizes us for they stimulate "a universally communicable pleasure" (and the capacity for universal communication) as well as a universal feeling of sympathy, which together constitute the sociability (*Geselligkeit*) proper to humanity (*KU*, 10:392, 300; Ak., V:433, 355; 321, 231). Self-cultivation gradually

---

divided into many categories, and both discipline and moral culture (*moralische Kultur*) are different modes of education.

46. Cf. Kant's insistence on the cosmopolitan basis of any educational scheme in *UP*, 12:704; 15.

organizes us into an empirical consciousness in general. This form of humane sociability is an asymptotic incarnation of moral freedom. It actively mediates between unsocial sociability and the moral realm of ends, and it refers nature to a final end that lies beyond nature but nevertheless has effectivity in it. These forms of culture "make man, not indeed morally better for [life in] society, but still civilized for it [*nicht sittlich besser, doch gesittet machen*]: they make great headway against the tyranny of man's propensity to the senses, and so prepare him for a sovereignty in which reason alone is to dominate" (*KU*, 10:392; Ak., V:433; 321).

THE TECHNIC OF NATURE: EFFACING NATURE'S FAVOR AND THE ABSOLUTE RECUPERATION OF *TECHNE*

Kant's greatest bequest to moral and political thought is neither a deontological theory of rights, nor his cosmopolitan vision, but his organismic metaphor of the political body. This legacy is even more enduring because it is generally unacknowledged or even unperceived. By establishing connections between organismic causality and culture as the highest form of *techne,* the metaphor privileges culture as the site of transcendence and the actualization of freedom. Henceforth, almost all modern ethical and political philosophy will be marked by a strict habitual correlation of freedom with the purposive dynamism of organic life, even if the latter is not named as such. Conversely, death and artifice will be linked to finitude and what is inimical to freedom—for instance, domination or ideological manipulation by the authoritarian bureaucratic state-apparatus; exploitation under capital (Marx); instrumental reason (Horkheimer and Adorno); the invasion of the life-world by the system-world (Habermas); and even the crafting of life by techniques of biopolitical power (Foucault). And although Kant saw the organismic political body as subsisting within a cosmopolitan system, the same constellation of philosophemes gradually assumes different, more specific sociological shapes, such as the nation, the territorial state, or the global community of workers. These various models are regarded by their proponents as the optimal institutional or organizational basis for the realization of freedom across different historical contexts. Whatever particular political ends they articulate, they are underwritten by the same organismic vitalism. As we will see, the ties to nation and state affirmed by Fichte and Hegel are grounded in the same concepts of freedom, culture, and organism that Kant uses to elaborate the attachments constituting a global community. The fact that the ideal political forms of cosmopolitanism and nationalism are rooted in the same organismic metaphor means that they cannot be understood in terms of a polarity between rational, universalistic and irrational, particularistic political ideologies.

However, the organismic metaphor is plagued by a series of aporias from its inception. For Kant is only able to ground the teleological time of cultural progress in natural purposiveness and subordinate both to moral purposiveness by means of a certain sleight of hand. His account of organismic causality forecloses the radical heteronomy of nature's favor in the gift of organic life. Because natural purposiveness is the apparent but inexplicable lawfulness of the contingent (*zufällig*), it always involves an element of surprise and luck, which Kant figures as an unexpected favor (*Gunst*) from nature: "this is also why we rejoice (actually we are relieved of a need) when, just as if it were a lucky chance favoring our aim [*ein glücklicher unsre Absicht begünstiger Zufall*], we do find such systematic unity among merely empirical laws" (*KU*, 10:93; Ak., V:184; 23–24). This inexplicability is especially pronounced in the organism: because its purposiveness is objective, we naturally assume that it cannot issue from us but must come about by nature's favor.

Dependency and heteronomy are therefore introduced into the realization of freedom. Just as Kant had defined culture as the taking of credit from nature, nature's favor also has to be eliminated because it too closely resembles the cunning of nature. This is achieved in at least two ways: through the idea of a technic of nature and through the archetypal understanding it points to. The technic of nature is the idea of nature itself as *Kunst*.[47] It reinscribes the theme of culture as ingratitude to nature at the transcendental level of the constitution of our cognitive faculties. This technic operates at two levels: in our general ability to determine nature in its specificity and in the existence of organisms. In the first case, our

---

47. The use of the phrase changes in emphasis between the First and Second Introductions. In the former (published posthumously in 1914), "the technic of nature" is used frequently to refer to the purposiveness of organisms and the purposiveness of nature in general for our cognitive faculties. In the Second Introduction, it only refers to the presentation of a natural product as an end.

understanding possesses a priori universal laws we prescribe to nature to constitute it as the general object of experience. However, we also discover a certain lawfulness in nature's diverse particularity that allows us to determine nature in its specificity. But since this more specific lawfulness (of particular empirical laws) does not issue from our finite understanding, we have to assume that it is the gift of another understanding that mirrors ours: "the particular empirical laws must . . . be viewed in terms of such a unity as [they would have] if they too had been given by an understanding (even though not ours) so as to assist [*Behuf*] our cognitive powers [*Erkenntnisvermögen*] by making possible a system of experience in terms of particular natural laws" (*KU*, 10:88–89; Ak., V:180; 19). This assumption of another understanding is itself a principle our reflective judgment gives to us.

There are therefore two acts of giving. First, nature seems to give itself to us via specific empirical laws. We comprehend the lawfulness of nature in its specificity by thinking of it as nature's purposiveness for our cognitive faculties, as nature favoring us. Quite independently of what we will or need, nature gives us a gift, which is figured as favorable fortune and good chance because it is independent of us. However, Kant argues that although such purposiveness is "quite distinct from practical purposiveness (in human art or in morality)," we "think it by analogy with practical purposiveness" because nature cannot relate its products to ends (*KU*, 10:89; Ak., V:181; 20). Nature cannot give itself to us in any other way but mechanically. So to receive the favor of nature's purposiveness, to accept the gift of empirical nature, we must think of it in analogy with our technical purposiveness, as the gift of another understanding that is not ours. We must practice radical ingratitude. We must efface the gift by denying nature itself, for we can only present (*vorstellen*) nature's favor to ourselves as the gift of another understanding, which nature is not. This presentation is a second gift. We give ourselves this principle in reflective judgment that supervenes over and effaces the first gift.

The same double stricture guides our presentation of organismic causality as a technic of nature. We think of nature as having a technical capability in its production of organisms because they are systems requiring a concept of an end and not merely mechanically produced aggregates (*KU*, 10:30; Ak., XX:217–18; 405–6). "Given that we find something purposelike in nature's products," Kant writes, "let us call nature's procedure [*Verfahren*] (causality) a technic" (*KU*, 10:341; Ak., V:390; 271). But when we speak of nature as *Kunst*, "we only borrow this causality from ourselves and attribute it to other beings without wishing to assume that they and we are of the same kind" (*KU*, 10:307; Ak., V:361; 237). On the one hand, there is an acknowledgement of nature's alterity to our own constitution as artificial technical beings. There is a prohibition against a mimetic relationship between organic life and *techne*. But on the other hand, insofar as the technic of nature is a heuristic principle for investigating nature and not a new form of natural-scientific causality, we also borrow something from ourselves and project it onto nature. We anthropomorphize. Instead of receiving what nature gives us in a straightforward manner, we lend to nature so that we can receive it (or receive back from it/take from it) in an appropriative manner, in a style proper to us. Indeed, nature might as well not be there because we only receive back what we imposed on it: "we put [*legen*] final causes into things, rather than, as it were, lifting them out of our perception of things" (*KU*, 10:34; Ak., XX:220; 408n27).

A surreptitious subordination of nature to human purposiveness thus occurs in the very gesture of granting purposive nature autonomy. For our faculties necessarily assume an a priori technical and instrumental attitude when we cognize nature in its particularity. Our judgment assumes the reflective principle of natural purposiveness for its own use (*ihren eigenen Gebrauch*), like an instrument, to get a handle on (*fassen, begreifen*) nature's particular laws and products. We use the principle of natural purposiveness to enable a more specific cognitive possession of nature. It is a mediating device or tool allowing us to appropriate nature's gift/favor by thinking of it as our gift to nature. Instead of fortunately finding purposiveness in nature, we attribute purposiveness to nature. The technic of nature is, therefore, not really *of* nature. It is not found in nature but instead derives from our judgment, which itself operates technically: "So it is the *power of judgment* that is properly [*eigentlich*] technical; nature is presented as technical only insofar as it harmonizes with, and so necessitates, that technical procedure of judgment" (*KU*, 10:32; Ak., XX:220; 408).

The extended analogy between organismic causality and *technical* causality arises from this technical operation. This anthropomorphic projection of human purposiveness onto nature makes natural purposiveness appear continuous with and amenable to human purposiveness. Consequently, the theme of culture as the stealing of credit from nature and the definition of culture as nature's ultimate end are made to appear as the historical unfolding of an a priori scene of giving and receiving by and from nature. While organic life remains opposed to lower forms of artifice such as mere civilization and skill, higher forms of *techne* such as discipline become continuous with natural purposiveness. They are forms of rational ordering that exhibit a purposive auto-causality and teleological time similar to the organization of nature.

It is impossible to overstate the ingenuity of Kant's recuperation of *techne*. In his moral philosophy, technical imperatives, which determined the will through a posteriori principles, were devalued for depriving the will of its rightful infinity and autonomy. However, the actualization of moral freedom requires technical capabilities we do not possess because of our finitude. Here, Kant purifies *techne* of human artifice by attributing it to a teleological nature. The technic of nature reconciles *techne* with nature in the service of actualizing freedom. Purposive nature remains distinct from artifice, for we only regard nature as technical by *analogy:* "All precepts of skill belong, as consequences, to the *technic* of nature. . . . But I shall henceforth use the term technic in other cases too, namely, where we merely *judge* [certain] objects of nature *as if* they were made possible through art [*ihre Möglichkeit sich auf Kunst gründe*]" (*KU*, 10:14; Ak., XX:200; 390). At the same time, the actualization of freedom is also saved from dependency on an actual favor from nature because the technic of nature is a mere principle of reflective judgment.

The same sleight of hand occurs in Kant's idea of a nonsensible archetypal understanding. The technic of nature can only be a reflective principle for us because we have a discursive understanding that is separate from our sensible intuition. We can only intuit appearances because our intuition is dependent on the senses. Likewise, our understanding can only cognize objects given to us through universal concepts, copies or images (*Bilder*) it possesses a priori. When we cognize nature, our understanding can only move from these universal concepts to blindly given particulars, which it synthesizes and subsumes under the categories. From the standpoint of our understanding, the lawfulness of the particular (natural purposiveness) is contingent because our concepts cannot determine anything about the diversity of nature in its particularity. Thus, although an organism seems to be a natural end, we cannot cognize it as such because our understanding does not have such a concept. But, Kant argues, we can think of another understanding that is different from ours, an intuitive understanding, that does not need to use images or copies in cognizing the world because it can grasp the original world, the world as it is in itself.[48] Such an understanding would be able to grasp the lawfulness of the particular because it can proceed from an *intuited* universal—a universal that is already *synthetic* because it is actual—to the particular. The intuitive understanding can see the rational basis behind how parts are lawfully synthesized and combined to make an actual unity or a determinate form of the whole. For such an understanding, which Kant also calls an archetypal understanding (*intellectus archetypus*), there would be no difference between the mechanism and technic of nature.

This contrast between the two understandings brings us back to the quandary of human finitude that obstructed freedom's actualization. We have a discursive understanding because we are finite beings. Possibility (*Möglichkeit*) and actuality (*Wirklichkeit*) are distinct for us. Something is possible if it is thinkable, if it corresponds to the formal conditions of experience in accordance with concepts. But it will only be actual if it is exhibited as a material object. Because we cannot create the objects we intuit, there will always be things that are transcendent for our understanding, for example, ends in nature. The limits of our understanding thus ultimately point back to the finitude of our intuition. Although the archetypal understanding is not identical to the original intuition or intuitive understanding (which can give rise to its own objects through its representations) postulated in the First Critique, it points to the latter through a parallelism. For just as our finite understanding leads us to think of an archetypal understanding, we can also think of the noumenal substrate of the world we receive through our sensible intuition as "based on a corre-

---

48. For a fuller discussion of the origins of the concept of an intuitive understanding in Plotinus and Kant's explicit reference to it in his letter of 21 February 1772 to Marcus Herz, see Cassirer, *Kant's Life and Thought*, pp. 280–87. In the First Critique, the intuitive understanding that grasps things in themselves is synonymous with a non-sensible or intellectual intuition (*KrV*, B 308–9, 311–12; 361, 363). Note, however, that there is a more powerful, productive kind of intuitive understanding or intellectual intuition whose representations can give rise to objects, which Kant calls divine (*KrV*, B 72, B 145; 191–92, 253). For an insightful discussion of the differences between the receptive and creative senses of intellectual intuition and intuitive understanding, see Eckart Förster, "Die Bedeutung von §§ 76, 77 der *Kritik der Urteilskraft* für die Entwickelung der nachkantischen Philosophie [Teil 1]," *Zeitschrift für philosophische Forschung* 2 (2002): 169–90.

sponding intellectual intuition (even though not ours)" (*KU*, 10:363; Ak., V:409; 293). The distinction between actuality and possibility would not apply to such a *productive* intellectual intuition, which is an absolute self-causing being and the ground of its own existence because it can intuit its own objects and originate that which it thinks.

More importantly, this supersensible cause that the technic of nature points to is a basis in which the supersensible world of moral freedom is united with the supersensible as undetermined substrate of nature.[49] Only this time, the bridge between nature and freedom is more secure. It is not a speculative postulate, but is intimated by the existence of organisms, which reflect the limitations of our finite understanding back to us. Herein lies the hope of transcendence. When confronted with organisms, "the character of the human cognitive powers forces us to seek the supreme basis for such combinations in an original understanding [*ursprünglichen Verstande*], as cause of the world" (*KU*, 10:364; Ak., V:410; 294). Although Kant insists that the archetypal understanding is not an actually existing primal being about which we have insights, but rather something we think of in analogy with our faculties, it nevertheless strongly suggests the presence of a higher, non-mechanical nature that is conducive to the actualization of moral freedom.

But as with the technic of nature, the subordination of the natural purposiveness of organisms to moral teleology also occurs through an anthropomorphic projection. Strictly speaking, our finite understanding should be derived from the archetypal understanding. Kant suggests this by noting that when we cognize organic beings in terms of the reciprocity of parts and whole, we take the infinite understanding as a model and mimic its operations: "Let us suppose, then, that we try to present . . . the possibility of the parts, in their character and combination, as dependent on the whole, so that we would be following the standard set by intuitive (archetypal [*urbildlichen*]) understanding" (*KU*, 10:361; Ak., V:407; 292). But the archetypal understanding is actually derived from us. It mirrors our understanding because it is an infinite or intuitive *understanding*. It is simultaneously like and unlike our understanding. We grasp the possibility of transcending finitude only by means of an anthropomorphic projection.

---

49. Cf., "judgment finds itself referred to something that is neither nature nor freedom and yet is linked with the basis of freedom, the supersensible, in which the theoretical and the practical power are in an unknown manner combined and joined into a unity" (*KU*, 10:297; Ak., V:353; 229).

THE TECHNIC OF THE OTHER: SHEER EXPOSURE

But nature still does not completely harmonize with our moral ends because the continuity between cultural progress, moral purposiveness, and natural purposiveness Kant posits is fundamentally unstable. Instead of safeguarding moral freedom from heteronomy, his formulation of organic life is itself disrupted by a heteronomy that is essential to the teleological time needed for moral freedom's incarnation, but that cannot be subordinated to this final end.

In the first place, Kant can only dissociate *techne* from finitude by compromising the autonomy that organismic causality initially seemed to exhibit. The technic of nature is nothing other than the a priori instrumentalization of nature, its subordination to human purposiveness. Instead of confirming that purposive nature enables us to transcend the heteronomy of both natural mechanism and human artifice, Kant's argument is an a priori invasion of organic life by human *techne*. Prima facie, the technic of nature grants organic life autonomy and elevates it above the dependent status of human technical objects, which *exist merely for the sake of another*. By insisting on the organism's irreducibility to human artifice, Kant breaks with the Aristotelian view of a mimetic continuity between *physis* and *techne*. However, the technic of nature makes organic nature dependent on us because it is a principle that we anthropomorphically project onto nature so that we can view it as an instrument of practical reason. Mimeticism returns. Only this time, it is *physis* that mimes *techne!* We "use a remote analogy with our own causality in terms of ends generally, to guide our investigation of organized objects and to meditate regarding their supreme basis . . . *for the sake of* [assisting] that same practical power [*praktischen Vernunftvermögens*] in us by analogy with which we were considering the cause of the purposiveness in organized objects" (*KU*, 10:323–24; Ak., V:375; 255; emphasis added). We need the existence of organisms so that we can postulate purposive nature as ground for actualizing our freedom from the mechanism of nature. But such a ground is thereby also a means towards a higher end that lies beyond it. Paradoxically, we need nature to be independent of us so that it can finally be subjected to us via the technic of judgment!

This return of mimeticism destabilizes the organismic metaphor's teleological time. Kant initially suggests that organized nature cannot be thought of in analogy with human artifice and that we know no other causality analogous to it. Then, by suggesting that we can better elucidate republican forms of political association if we consider them organic, he implies the priority and originality of organic life to political organization. But this presupposition is overturned if we remember that political organization is adduced as the only example of human creation available to us that is like the organization of nature. Without this example, we would find it very difficult to understand the organism's peculiar causality. Hence, if it earlier seemed that organic life supplied the model for the technic of political organization, it now turns out that it is through an at best "remote" analogy with political craft that we can better understand organismic causality. Organic life and *techne* change places ceaselessly. This oscillation has a radical significance. The hope that we can incarnate moral freedom rests on an analogy between organismic causality and the moral will's autonomous causality. Moral freedom was explicitly distinguished from *techne* because of its fundamentally heteronomous nature. But we are now told to understand organismic causality by means of technical causality! The basis for freedom's incarnation is thus contaminated by *techne*, which Kant had initially distinguished from organismic causality.

Second, and more importantly, the projection of human purposiveness onto nature obscures the many occasions littering Kant's corpus where nature *prompts* or *directs* (*veranlassen*) us in what it gives us to experience.[50] For teleological judgments are concerned with the purposiveness of *objects*. The principle of objective purposiveness is not an a posteriori principle of determinative judgment because the actuality of natural ends cannot be proven by experience. However, unlike the principle of subjective purposiveness employed in judgments of taste, which our faculties possess a priori, objective purposiveness is not an a priori principle. This is because teleological judgments arise in response to certain cases or occasions (*in vorkommenden Fällen*) or certain products, on the occurrence of which they necessarily depend (*KU*, 10:105; Ak., V:193; 34).[51] The idea of a natural end

---

50. "Now in a way this principle [of objective purposiveness] must be derived from experience: experience must prompt us to [adopt] it [*seiner Veranlassung nach, von Erfahrung abzuleiten*]" (*KU*, 10:324; Ak., V:376; 256).

51. Objective purposiveness is an application of the a priori principle of formal or subjective purposiveness of nature in specific cases where the need arises. Unlike aesthetic judgment, teleological judgment is not a special faculty. See *KU*, 10:105–6; Ak., V:194; 34–35.

is unlike all other Kantian ideas because it relies on a commensurate object given in nature. For us to even employ teleological principles, the ordering or arrangement (*Anordnung*) of nature must have been favorable to our judgment in the first place (KU, 10:26; Ak., XX:214; 402).

In the Third Critique, Kant actually suggests that it may be the case that "nature gives us a hint [*ein von der Natur uns gleichsam gegebener Wink*], as it were, that if we use the concept of final causes we could perhaps reach beyond nature and connect nature itself to the highest point in the series of causes" (*KU*, 10:340; Ak., V:390; 271). Such promptings or hints belong to the same figural chain as the propitious natural dispositions that providential nature has placed in us, such as morality and reason. To this chain, one must also add the French Revolution as a *Begebenheit* (occurrence) that functions as a sign emitted in history indicating moral progress, which should ideally lead to another *Begebenheit* of superior moral import, "the *evolution* of a constitution governed by *natural right*" (*SF*, 11:360; *Pol. Writ.*, 184). "In human affairs, there must be some experience or other which, as an event which has actually occurred [*Begebenheit*], might suggest [*hinweiset*] that man has the quality or power of being the cause and . . . the author [*Urheber*] of his own improvement. . . . [T]he event originally chosen as an example would not in itself be regarded as the cause of progress in the past, but only as a rough indication [*hindeuten*] or *historical sign* [*Geschichtszeichen*] (*signum rememorativum, demonstrativum, prognostikon*)."[52] These gifts are examples of nature's favor (*Gunst*) on which we must depend as finite creatures to actualize freedom. The motif of the favor is repeated throughout the Third Critique but only explicitly thematized in the suggestion that the existence of organisms entitles us or gives us a right, like a right of possession, to see nature as a system of ends:

> Once nature has been judged teleologically, and the natural ends that we find in organized beings have entitled us [*uns berechtigt hat*] to the idea of a vast system of the ends of nature, then . . . [we] may regard nature as having held us in favor [*eine Gunst, die die Natur für uns gehabt hat*] when it distributed not

---

52. *SF*, 11:356–57; *Pol. Writ.*, 181. Cf. Jean-François Lyotard, *The Differend: Phrases in Dispute*, trans. Georges Van Den Abbeele (Minneapolis: University of Minnesota Press, 1988), pp. 164–65. Lyotard points out that the *Begebenheit* is more than just an intuitive given (*Gegebene*), which would be blind or without rational justification.

only useful things but a wealth of beauty and charms as well. (*KU*, 10:329–30; Ak., V:380; 260)

We can formalize the problem posed by nature's gift of organic life as follows: Because of our finitude, we need nature's favor to actualize moral freedom. But this neediness subjects the incarnation of moral freedom to a contingency that is not that of our understanding. It disrupts the continuity between natural purposiveness and moral teleology. Hence, it needs to be repeatedly effaced. The technic of nature and the archetypal understanding are anthropomorphic projections deployed to foreclose these secrets emitted by nature. They are bandages covering over our effacement of nature's favor. Just as Kant defines culture as radical ingratitude to nature, such anthropomorphisms subordinate purposive nature to cultural and moral teleology by effacing its alterity.

For there is ultimately no reason why the technic of nature we attribute to organisms needs to be related back to an archetypal *understanding* and its teleological time. This necessarily follows from Kant's point that because our finite cognitive powers cannot determine the supersensible substrate, the technic of nature is merely a principle of reflective judgment. Nature could indeed be speaking to us of its intentions, and they may be favorable to us. But we do not and cannot know this. But this does not mean that everything subsumed under the principle of natural purposiveness is merely projected onto nature by reflective judgment. All that Kant has established is that a natural object cannot be produced by an understanding, although our cognitive faculties may make sense of the purposiveness of organic life by reflecting on it as the product-effect of an original understanding or intellectual intuition. It does not follow that natural purposiveness is completely saturated by our judgment of it as arising from an understanding that is like ours, that it is completely governed by teleological time.

Strictly speaking, in view of the radical alterity of the supersensible substrate, it would be more appropriate to characterize nature's favor or technic as a secret that may not be a secret, an encryption that may not after all hide any intention to be revealed, but which nevertheless unceasingly prompts us to try to decipher it.[53] When we make regulative use of an analogy with our

---

53. I have borrowed this formulation from Jacques Derrida, "Passions: 'An Oblique Offering,'" in *On the Name,* ed. Thomas Dutoit (Palo Alto, Calif.: Stanford University Press, 1995), p. 143.

own understanding and regard the technic of nature as the product of an archetypal understanding so that we can think of it as purposive for our moral vocation, we reduce this secret that may not be a secret to our alter ego, to an understanding that mirrors our own. Through an anthropomorphic projection, we make organic life mime human *techne* and subordinate it to our purposiveness.[54]

But our dependency on such secrets suggests another, entirely different understanding of the technic of nature. Kant's characterization of the technic of nature as the causality of an archetypal understanding emphasizes its intentional nature, thereby reducing it to human *techne*. But the other essential feature of *techne* that Kant repeatedly underscores is its heteronomy. One might speak of *techne* in a more general sense as the originary opening up of a being to the influence of another, a constitutive exposure to the other. The technic of nature is more accurately conceived as an opening up to an other that is not an understanding like ours, but an assymetrical, even inhuman other. In Kant's words, "ends, i.e., presentations that themselves are regarded as conditions of the causality for their objects (their effects), must always be given [*gegeben*] from somewhere before judgment [can] concern itself with the conditions under which the manifold [will] harmonize with these ends" (*KU*, 10:46; Ak., XX:232; 421). This "somewhere" is an inhuman substrate absolutely other to our cognitive faculties. But it nevertheless emits various secrets that are instances of a more originary *techne* (if it can be so called) that does not issue from human causality. Unlike organismic causality proper and the higher forms of human *techne* such as discipline and moral culture, nature's favor is a nonselfrecursive form of *techne*. It is the aporetic infection and haunting of life that disrupts even as it inaugurates the teleological time that grounds human freedom's actualization.

Our dependency on nature's favor to actualize freedom and to solve the many secrets of human existence—the secrets of how to establish the ideal constitution or the perfect pedagogical plan—would then make us, as moral *actors*, the products of an inhuman *techne* that is unknowable to us. We would be dependent on a purposiveness that we cannot know definitely as favoring our moral endeavors, although we sometimes see hints and

---

54. This mirroring is even more pronounced in the *Opus Postumum*, which bases the concept of an organic body on our experience of ourselves as an organic body (137).

glimpses that it may. For instance, "the precise time" at which the moral *Begebenheit* of a republican constitution's evolution "will occur must remain indefinite [*unbestimmt*] and dependent upon chance" (*SF*, 11:361; *Pol. Writ.*, 185). The intimation of a secret that may not be a secret that we find in such *Begebenheiten* and in organic life would open us up without return or recuperation to another *techne*, the *techne of the other*.

The other's *techne* is not mere mechanism. It is also not a substantial presence like human moral reason or a divine creator, unless these are themselves effects of this secret that may not be a secret. What is important in Kant's characterization of the technic of nature as a nondeterminable substrate is its *nondeterminability*, and not its *substantiality*. The technic of nature is not a concealed presence that can be revealed if we refrain from projecting onto it. Our anthropomorphic projections of *techne* in the narrow sense onto it are impositions, but nature also opens itself up to these invasive supplementations insofar as the secrets it emits induce responses. Indeed, the technic of nature is nothing other than the process of sending and giving that renders nature vulnerable to supplementation. It is a heteronomy that is the condition of possibility of the actualization of moral freedom, but also its condition of impossibility. One could call this condition of (im)possibility *sheer exposure* provided that this is understood as coextensive with the irreducible finitude and givenness of nature as well as our constitution as human beings.[55]

This inhuman *techne* has unsettling implications for political organicism in general. The organismic metaphor of the social and political body attempts to ground human transcendence in the purposiveness of organic life as a

---

55. The trace of a peculiar heteronomy in moral freedom is already intimated by Kant's paradoxical description of our consciousness of the moral law as "a fact [*Faktum*] of reason." See Jean-Luc Nancy, *The Experience of Freedom*, trans. Bridget McDonald (Palo Alto, Calif.: Stanford University Press, 1993), pp. 21–25; Lyotard, *The Differend*, pp. 120–22. The moral law is a fact because it cannot be deduced but simply exists in our reason (*KpV*, 7:141–42; Ak., V:31; *Prac. Phil.*, 164). Yet, at the same time, it is a self-announcing *Faktum* of reason, and not merely given (*gegeben*) like other givens within the mechanism of nature (*KpV*, 7:142; Ak., V:31; *Prac. Phil.*, 165). Before it is understood as pure reason's giving of laws to itself, the moral law's facticity is that which opens us up through reason to something other that is neither the mechanism of nature nor something already present in reason. Just as the trace of the inhuman other is reduced to the technical causality of an archetypal understanding in the case of organic life, this opening-out is attenuated by being interned within the faculty of reason as the most proper characteristic of human beings. It is confined to their transportation into an infinite realm of ends.

phenomenal analogue of moral reason's spontaneous auto-causality. But life itself turns out to be the gift of an inhuman *techne* that exceeds the causality of human reason. This means that the organism's teleological time is contaminated at its origin by a certain otherness. We can no longer think of organic life as the superior creation of a divine artificer that human *techne* imitates (the mimetic relationship between *physis* and *techne* in classical teleology and various forms of mechanism), nor model it after human artifice via the anthropomorphism of an original understanding (Kantian teleology). In both teleologies, the purposiveness of organic life is associated with an absolute presence that is the source of transcendence, whether this is a divine creator or human practical reason. The constitutive infection of organic life by *techne* in the general sense, however, keeps us mired in finitude. Hence, any attempt to incarnate freedom is inherently vulnerable to *techne* in the narrow sense, that is, subjective pragmatics and technics. Yet, paradoxically, this inhuman *techne* is also freedom's condition of possibility. As incarnational activity, moral reason is therefore constitutively subject to a strict law of contamination. This law can also be called the law of exappropriation, an appropriation or making proper that expropriates at one and the same time.[56]

As we have seen, the incarnational work of *Bildung* is an important aspect of the organismic metaphor and a crucial example of teleological time. In subsequent chapters, I explore how this power of remaking ourselves and the external world is contaminated by otherness. To anticipate, *Bildung* requires us to open ourselves to an ideal image, an other that we give to ourselves. Yet without our sheer exposure to alterity, without the inhuman other's *techne,* the teleological time of *Bildung* would not be possible in the first place. This exposure makes the appropriative activity of culture exappropriative or constitutively vulnerable. As the organismic metaphor takes on more determinate sociological shapes, the political ramifications of this contamination of organic life by death and *techne* will become more explicit. For Kant, culture is already the paradigmatic

---

56. See Jacques Derrida, "'Eating Well,' or the Calculation of the Subject," in *Who Comes After the Subject?* ed. Eduardo Cadava, Peter Connor, and Jean-Luc Nancy (New York: Routledge, 1991), p. 105: "The 'logic' of the trace or of *différance* determines this re-appropriation as an ex-appropriation. Re-appropriation necessarily produces the opposite of what it apparently aims for. Ex-appropriation is not what is proper to man."

relationship between the ideal state and its citizens. In the political topographies of Fichte and Hegel, culture's sheer exposure will signify vulnerability to state manipulation or national-cultural hegemonizing imperatives. I hasten to add that this susceptibility to contamination is not the consequence of unreason. The organismic metaphor is not inherently irrational. I am also not suggesting that the organismic metaphor's negative consequences follow from the aggrandization of a lower and inherently defective form of instrumental reason that can be purged or regulated by a higher, critical reason. My point is that the incarnation of rational ideals, which is the ontological paradigm of any normative political project, is constitutively susceptible to contamination because all incarnational activity occurs in finitude and is dependent on the absolutely contingent but necessary gift of time.

INCARNATIONS OF THE IDEAL:
NATION AND STATE IN FICHTE AND HEGEL

It was not enough to say that God was made man. . . . We must see how God has manifested himself in the man of every nation, how in the variety of national geniuses the Father has responded to the needs of his children. The unity that He ought to give us is not a monotonous unity, but a harmonious unity in which all varieties love one another. . . . Let them go on increasing in splendor to better enlighten the world. Let man be accustomed from childhood to recognize a living God in his native land!

—Jules Michelet

T his is the book's riskiest chapter. It gives the benefit of the doubt to what many regard as ethically indefensible: Fichte's nationalism and Hegel's statism.[1] It does so for three reasons: First, difficult as it is to imagine, the Germans were victims of foreign military oppression. The historical conditions for Fichte's and Hegel's political philosophy were Napoleon's defeat of Prussia at Jena, the occupation of Berlin and the dissolution of the Holy Roman Empire in 1806, and the incorporation of ceded Prussian territory into Westphalia and the Grand Duchy of Warsaw at the Peace of Tilsit (1807). Prior to this, Germany had lacked political unity. It was a cultural nation splintered into several territorial states. Napoleon dissolved the Holy Roman Empire, which loosely held these states together, and proceeded to incorporate part of Germany into the Confederation of the Rhine. The rational reforms that took place under his program to "enlighten" these conquered territories led to some erosion of

---

1. It is commonly suggested that Fichte's and Hegel's ideas were distorted and exploited by conservative political actors to justify the establishment of a coercive state or that they became attracted to cultural nationalism and abandoned their liberal and rationalist values or subordinated them to an authoritarian organic state. See Leonard Krieger, *The German Idea of Freedom: History of a Political Tradition* (Chicago: University of Chicago Press, 1957), p. 177. On Fichte's increasing conservatism, see Hans Kohn, "The Paradox of Fichte's Nationalism," *Journal of the History of Ideas* 10, no. 3 (June 1949): 319–43; and Krieger, pp. 191–92.

dynastic absolutism. This is the immediate occasion of the defiant nation-alism of Fichte's *Reden an die Deutsche Nation* (*Addresses to the German Nation,* 1808) and the catalyst of the emerging nationality principle in other parts of Europe that achieved its fullest flowering in 1848. Napoleon is also a source of inspiration for Hegelian statism. Meanwhile, Weimar classicism laid the ground for the exaltation of the German *Kulturnation* as the concrete embodiment of human freedom.

More importantly, Fichte and Hegel extend the connections between freedom, culture, and the political organism that Kant put into place. They regard culture as not merely the phenomenal analogue or simulacrum of freedom, but the incarnation of the ideal. They redefine freedom as the power to actualize ideas. Moral reason's vitality is the process of self-actualization by which it becomes objective, and this vitality is the *immanent work* of the political community, which strives to perpetuate its own life in the face of finitude. Fichte and Hegel articulate a discourse of exorcism aimed at Kant, whose ideas of the cosmopolitan federation and humanity they regard as phantoms that need to be concretely grounded or chased away. For Fichte, cosmopolitanism cannot be actual (*wirklich*) or effective unless it becomes a patriotism.[2] Hegel pointed to the deficiency of a cosmopoli-tanism opposed to "the concrete life of the state."[3] Hence, Kant's organis-mic vitalism assumes more concrete territorialized shapes: for Fichte, the German nation is a living community of language that can inspirit the dead mechanism of the state; for Hegel, the ideal state is the highest form of objective spirit because it regulates the selfish pursuit of individual interests within the machine of civil society. By emphasizing that the opposition between organism and machine derives from the more fundamental opposition between life and death, they introduce a thematic opposition central to subsequent nationalist and cosmopolitanist discourses: con-crete reality vs. empty phantasmatic form. Finally, the denunciation of these political organicisms as inevitably reactionary is precipitous because, through the mediation of Marxism, Fichte and Hegel provide two ideal types or practical logics for radical Third World decolonizing nationalism: a cultural nationalism that takes language as fundamental to the nation's

---

2. "Der Patriotismus, und sein Gegentheil," XI, 229.

3. *Grundlinien der Philosophie des Rechts* (in *Werke in zwanzig Bänden*), § 209A, 7:361; *Elements of the Philosophy of Right,* 240. Hereafter the work and its English translation are cited as *PR*.

definition and a political nationalism centered on patriotic love for the constitution.

However, the fact that their organismic ideas can so easily become a ghost of ideology or an instrument of the machine-state suggests that the rationality of life is constitutively infected by death. This internal disruption, which is similar to the infection of organic life by *techne* in Kant's Third Critique, is a haunting that inheres in incarnational activity. The border between life and death wavers because life necessarily opens itself to an other, which it has to pass through and overcome in order to be self-originating. This chapter explores how the ghostly possession of life assumes the determinate form of the hyphen joining "nation" to "state." Fichte and Hegel enable us to understand the living nation's capture by the machine-state or, conversely, the organic state's infection by the phantom nation as a process of original supplementation *internal* to the self-incarnational work of freedom.[4]

THE ORIGINAL PEOPLE: FICHTE'S *ADDRESSES* *TO THE GERMAN NATION*

The *Addresses to the German Nation* marks the point where the culture concept migrates from philosophy to politics, where it takes the form of the nation and has real efficacy.[5] As a cosmo-nationalism, Fichte's text also marks a moment when cosmopolitanism and nationalism are not quite distinct from each other because they originate from the same philosopheme of culture.[6] Fichte's demotic idea of the original living people is not an

---

4. The historical capture of German idealism by conservative political agents can, with further research into its history of reception, also be understood as a process of original supplementation rather than ideological mystification.

5. Leonard Krieger suggests that intellectuals like Fichte functioned as a two-way channel of communication between society and statesmen that impressed upon the statesmen the growing awareness of national values in society and communicated to society the statesmen's readiness to act on these values (See *The German Idea of Freedom*, 176).

6. See *Reden an die Deutsche Nation*, VII:456, 498; 187, 227, for the argument that the German people constitute an elect nation whose independence is crucial to the moral and spiritual regeneration of the human species. Hereafter cited as *RDN*. German culture is cosmopolitan and facilitates reciprocal exchange of culture (*Bildung*) and education between peoples that is beneficial to humanity's development (*Ausbildung*) (*RDN*, VII:471–72; 202). Cf. Friedrich Meinecke, *Cosmopolitanism and the National State*, trans. Robert B. Kimber (Princeton, N.J.: Princeton University Press, 1970), p. 94.

irrational sentiment. It reinscribes two themes that inform his entire corpus, whether he is a Jacobin or a nationalist, a rationalist or a religious mystic: the conceptualization of life as a spiritual activity that involves the positing and overcoming of borders and the understanding of culture as the incarnational work through which the moral actor remakes the external world according to ideas, thereby overcoming the border separating sensible and supersensible worlds.[7]

The Second Introduction of the 1794 *Wissenschaftslehre* clearly associates life with the self-positing *I*'s free self-activity (*Selbstthätigkeit*): "Whosoever ascribes an activity [*Thätigkeit*] to himself, appeals to this [intellectual] intuition [of self-consciousness]. The source of life is contained therein, and without it there is death."[8] For Fichte, life arises from intellectual intuition because the latter presupposes consciousness of the moral law. Through moral action, the *I*, as practically self-determining, is not a merely given entity or static object. It is a dynamic active being that is the source of its own life. It is self-giving and gives life to itself: "I am given to myself, by myself [*ich werde mir durch mich selbst . . . gegeben*], as something that is to be active in a certain fashion, and am thereby given to myself as active in general; I have life within me, and draw [*nehme*] it from myself" (*W*, I:466; 41). Fichte thus inherits Kant's association of freedom's auto-causality with life. He opposes freedom to "the dead persistency [*todten Beharrlichkeit*] of matter" and "the mechanism of Nature" (*W*, I:468; 42). But for Fichte, life is not just an analogue of freedom. It is a stage in the *I*'s self-positing activity. Awareness of life is a modality of the process of self-positing whose highest point is moral consciousness.[9]

Fichte's account of self-positing is a discourse of borders (*Grenzen*). As a finite being, the *I*'s action is limited (*begrenzt*) and opposed by something

---

7. Fichte's 1799 dismissal from Jena roughly coincides with the turning point in his thought. For a similar view that the conviction that the real is grounded in spiritual activity is continuous in Fichte's corpus, see Allen W. Wood, "Fichte's Philosophy of Right and Ethics," in *The Cambridge Companion to Fichte,* ed. Günter Zöller (New York: Cambridge University Press, forthcoming).

8. "Zweite Einleitung in die *WissenschaftsLehre* für Leser, die schon ein philosophisches System haben," I:463; *The Science of Knowledge,* 38. The 1794 *Wissenschaftslehre* and its English translation are cited hereafter as *W*.

9. Life is an inner force of a body that that body posits by and for itself. It is a form of auto-causality, a drive (*Trieb*) that the body feels as a force. See *W*, I:274; 241. Cf. I:293; 258: "The drive is an inner force, determining itself to causality. The inanimate [*leblose*] body has no causality whatever, save *outside* itself."

external. In its self-positing activity, it must therefore cross many borders, such as those between living and inanimate bodies and mere life (*bloßen Leben*) and intelligence.[10] The *I* transcends its finitude by overcoming these borders through appropriation and internalization. By seeing them as limits that it posits for itself, the *I* determines itself as a practical being that strives to make the external world conform to it.[11] By remaking the *not-I* through its self-activity, the *I* dissolves all limits to itself and grasps its own unlimited nature or infinitude, that is, freedom. Freedom thus involves working through finitude.[12] In Fichte's later writings, where the foundation of reality is the absolute spiritual principle of divine life, the organismic character of this discourse of borders is even more explicit. Death is an other that life opposes to itself in order to develop into a higher, more complete form:

> All death in nature is birth, and precisely in dying does the augmentation of life visibly appear. There is no killing principle in nature, for nature is throughout nothing but life. It is not death which kills, but rather a more living life [*das lebendigere Leben*] which, hidden behind the old life, begins and develops. Death and birth are only the struggle of life with itself in order to present itself more purely and more like itself. And how could *my* death be anything else? For I am not a mere representation and image [*Abbildung*] of life, but bear within me the original life which alone is true and essential. That nature might destroy a life which does not come from nature is not even a possible thought; nature, for whose sake I do not live, but which itself lives merely for my sake.[13]

For Fichte, culture is the paradigmatic case of finitude-transcending activity. It is a dynamic incarnational self-activity that serves freedom

---

10. See *W*, I:295–96; 259–60, and I:298; 262, respectively on the transition (*Uebergang*) from death to life and the leap (*Sprung*) from mere life to intelligence.

11. For a discussion of Fichte's attempted reconciliation of the absolute self-sufficiency (and infinity) of the *I* and its irreducible finitude or dependence on the *not-I* in the 1794 *Wissenschaftslehre*, see Frederick Neuhouser, *Fichte's Theory of Subjectivity* (Cambridge: Cambridge University Press, 1990), pp. 41–53.

12. "No infinity [*Unendlichkeit*], no bounding [*Begrenzung*]; no bounding, no infinity; infinity and *bounding are united in one and the same synthetic component*. . . . The activity of the *I* consists in unbounded self-assertion [*unbeschränkten Sichsetzen*]: to this there occurs a resistance. . . .—[I]f the *I* did not bound [*begrenzte*] itself, it would not be infinite.—The *I* is only what it posits itself to be" (*W*, I:214; 192).

13. *Die Bestimmung des Menschen*, II:317–18; *The Vocation of Man*, 122.

because it enables man to achieve complete harmony (*vollkommene Uebereinstimmung*) with himself as a rational being.[14] "Man's final end [*letzter Endzweck*] is to subordinate to himself all that is irrational, to master it freely and according to his own laws."[15] *Kultur* is the skill that enables us to restore "the original pure shape [*ursprüngliche reinen Gestalt*] of our I" (*Einige Vorlesungen*, VI:298; 150). Echoing Kant's distinction between skill and discipline, Fichte writes that culture is "in part the skill [*Geschicklichkeit*] to suppress and eradicate those erroneous inclinations which originate in us prior to the awakening of our reason and the sense of our own spontaneity [*Selbstthätigkeit*], and in part it is the skill to modify and alter external things in accordance with our concepts" (ibid.). He repeatedly figures culture as the giving of life to the external world, whether this occurs through the cognition of nature or through agricultural cultivation: "Into turmoil, man will bring order, and into universal devastation, design. Thanks to him, decay will create and death will summon to a new and splendid life."[16]

The *Addresses* reinscribes these two themes by identifying the German *Kulturnation* as the source of eternal life in the finite sensible world. The nation is therefore an organism whose life must be preserved. The fratricidal Wars of the Empire that led to its downfall are an example of a destructive self-seeking that has corrupted the member states (*Glieder*) of the national body, leading them to turn on each other and cut themselves off from this organic whole which gave them spiritual life, thereby making themselves and the now vivisected body vulnerable to ends imposed by an alien power (*fremde Gewalt*) (*RDN*, VII:271; 7–8). In Fichte's description of the nation's historical corruption and regeneration, Kant's organismic ontology is transposed into concrete political discourse. Kant's figure of the alien hand as a metaphor of heteronomy takes the historical shape of Napoleon.

This transposition is exemplary. It can be detected in one form or another in all nationalist discourse. Any historical appeal to the nation and any defence of national culture, no matter how mundane or concrete, will always be rooted in a traditional discourse of the transcendence of finitude.

---

14. See *Beitrag zur Berichtigung der Urtheile des Publikums über die französische Revolution*, VI:90.

15. *Einige Vorlesungen über die Bestimmung des Gelehrten*, VI:299; "Some Lectures Concerning the Scholar's Vocation," in *EPW*, 152.

16. *Über die Würde des Menschen*, I:413; "Concerning Human Dignity," in *EPW*, 84.

This means that every nationalism is essentially "philosophical" if by "philosophy" we mean "a discourse concerned with the ultimate nature of existence." Friedrich Meinecke confessed as much. However much he would have liked to make Fichte the first prophet of the German national state and national politics, he had to concede that "all his rather odd-looking positions on the state and the nation were but shifting deliberations about the most effective means for reaching his ultimate ideal goal of delivering humanity from the ban of material existence and raising it to a higher world of freedom and to its divine origin."[17] Fichte's views about the living nation are also exemplary for subsequent nationalist discourse, especially in decolonizing and postcolonial Africa and Asia, for three additional reasons. He emphasizes the importance of language in defining the nation, argues for the primacy of national culture in the struggle against foreign political domination, and, finally, figures the nation-people as a self-incarnating organism who must transform the state into an organ of its rational-purposive work.

THE NATION AS A COMMUNITY OF LANGUAGE
AND THE OVERCOMING OF DEATH

The *Addresses* defines the German nation as an original people, or *Urvolk*, a people in the higher meaning of the word, one "that has the right [*Recht*] to call itself simply *the* people [*das Volk*]" (*RDN*, VII:359; 92). The German people's original culture must be preserved and developed by a cultural-pedagogical project because it is the source of their freedom and is threatened with destruction by foreign occupation: "it is only by means of the common characteristic of German-ness [*Deutscheit*] that we can avert the downfall of our nation [*Nation*] which is threatened by its fusion with foreign peoples, and win back again a self that is self-supporting [*auf ihm selber ruhendes*] and quite incapable of dependence upon others" (*RDN*, VII:266; 3). The nation is thus an actually existing intellectual intuition, the self-positing *I* writ large as a collective cultural subject.[18]

---

17. *Cosmopolitanism and the National State*, p. 76.

18. There is an exact correspondence between the absolute *I*'s need to posit boundaries for itself and Fichte's argument that cosmopolitanism can only effectively pursue the final end of humanity by working through the limited form of the nation. See "Der Patriotismus, und sein Gegentheil,"

What Fichte adds to Kant's conceptualization of culture is the importance of rooting culture in a living language. For Fichte, language is not a mere tool of consciousness. Languages grow out of the shared life experiences of particular communities and are the *natural* metaphorical expressions of the supersensible world. A language is the basis of a nation's spiritual unity because it has a formative power in the constitution of a people's spiritual life:

> if we give the name of People to men whose organs of speech are influenced by the same external conditions, who live together and who develop their language in continuous communication with each other, then we must say: The language of this people is necessarily just what it is, and in reality this people does not express its knowledge, but its knowledge expresses itself out of the mouth of its people. (*RDN*, VII:315; 49)

A language's effectiveness as a medium for transmitting ideas to future generations will depend on how closely its designating system has remained in contact with the community's natural life. A living language, that is, a language that is rooted in the community's daily life and develops in concert with its changes, will continue to express the community's ideas clearly and remain the source of its *spiritual* life: "The words of such a language in all its parts are life and create life" (*RDN*, VII:319; 53). This is because a living language facilitates self-presence: the immediate and complete unity of thought and action, knowledge and practice, found in original creative activity. By bringing us into the closest proximity to ourselves, it enables pure thought to so completely stimulate and inspirit us in our capacity as moral actors that thought is itself action. Thought acts through us and becomes real and living:

XI:229: "[The will] can make advances only in the most proximate circumstance in which it lives immediately, by existing there as a living force. . . . [I]n whatever political state the will lives, these circumstances come under the control [*Wirkungsmöglichkeiten*] of that state, a state which separates itself off from the remaining world through its own organic unity. Thus the efficacy [*Wirksamkeit*] of that state, within itself, guides the good citizen, in its medium and after its laws. However, wherever the citizen separates himself from the environment, this efficacy sets itself forth against the barrier which regards itself as a unity. And so it is necessary that every cosmopolitan, by

Thought has by itself directly taken hold [*ergriffen*] of our self, and made it into itself; and through this actuality [*Wirklichkeit*] of thought for us, arising in this way, we obtain insight into its necessity. . . . [N]o freedom can forcibly bring about the latter consequence, which must be produced of itself, and thought itself must take hold of us and form [*bilden*] us according to itself.

Now this living effectiveness [*lebendige Wirksamkeit*] of thought is very much furthered and, indeed, where the thinking is of the proper depth and strength, even made inevitable, by thinking and designating in a living language. The sign in such a language is itself directly living and sensuous; it represents all life that is proper to/in possession of itself [*eigene Leben*] and so takes hold of and exerts an influence on life. To the possessor of such a language spirit [*Geist*] speaks directly and reveals itself as man [*Mann*] does to man.

(RDN, VII:331–32; 65–66)

We are formed into moral actors when we are grasped by the concepts (*Begriff*) of pure thought. This is most effective within a living language whose signs designate a life that is one's own and not an alien life. Our formative possession by thought would be a self-possession, where spirit speaks to us as one of us. In contradistinction, when a people give up their own language for a foreign language, such as some form of Latin (Fichte's typecase for the alien), they become possessed by ghosts. The new language is not a source of life for the community. It is a foreign, dead language cut off from everyday activity. Its meanings are arbitrary because its sensuous symbols derive from a foreign circle of observation. It cannot express supersensible ideas effectively because its concepts are equally foreign. It is a death-dealing force because it forms practical agents that lack the spontaneous unity of thought and action. This means that only the culture of a community bound together by a living language can effectively incarnate or actualize moral freedom. Such culture is itself spiritual life: "spiritual

---

means of his limitation [*Beschränkung*] through the nation, should be a patriot; and everyone who in his nation is the most powerful and active patriot, is by that very fact, also the most active citizen of the world, in which the ultimate end of all national education [*Nationalbildung*] is always that this education should spread itself across the species." My thanks to Paul Redding and Allen Wood for correcting my translation.

culture [*geistige Bildung*]—and here especially thinking in an original language [*Ursprache*] is meant—does not exert an influence on life; it is itself the life of him who thinks in this fashion. . . . [B]ecause that kind of thinking *is* life, it is felt by its possessor with inward pleasure in its vitalizing, transfiguring, and liberating power" (*RDN*, VII:333; 67).

Spiritual culture enables us to transcend our finitude because it is the quotidian matrix for incarnating what Fichte calls "divine life" (*göttliche Leben*): "when we speak here of life and of the influence exerted upon it by spiritual culture [*geistigen Bildung*], we must be understood to mean original life [*ursprünglichen Leben*] in its flow from the source of all spiritual life [*geistigen Lebens*], from God, the development [*Fortbildung*] of human relationships according to their archetype [*Urbilde*], and, therefore, the creation of a new life such as has never hitherto existed" (*RDN*, VII:329; 63). Divine life is Fichte's later way of overcoming Kant's infamous divide between the sensible and the supersensible. It is the eternal principle that generates all appearance. But unlike noumenality, it is not a fixed presence that is external and inaccessible to us, but a vital force animating the practical activity of all original beings.

The idea of divine life involves a remarkable discourse of borders. As the ever-renewing source of all appearance, divine life cannot be grasped as a bounded positive object. It "reveals itself never as a fixed [*stehendes*] and given entity [*gegebenes Sein*], but as something that is to be; and after it has become what it was to be, it will reveal itself again to all eternity as something that is to be. This divine life, then, never appears in the death of the fixed entity, but remains continually in the form of everflowing life" (*RDN*, VII:304–5; 38–39). Divine life is unboundedness or the movement of unbinding itself, a power that can cross through and remove all borders. The border between the sensible and supersensible worlds is removed because human practical activity reveals that divine life is immanent to actual existence. If the individual can recognize that he is a link within an eternal chain through the spiritual life of thought, he will be stimulated to original creative activity (*ursprünglich schöpferischer Tätigkeit*) that honors and participates fully *in* divine life. The individual will then exist in a world that is higher than mere mechanism, than "a world which is already given and existent [*eine schon gegebene und vorhandene Welt*], which can be accepted, indeed, merely passively just as it is" (*RDN*, VII:304; 38). He will be part of a living world that is infinitely in the process of becoming, where *freedom is actual.* Our original activity thus breathes life into dead mechanical nature. This life is the organism's purposive auto-causality raised to a higher spiritual plane. It annuls any limit that makes life finite and can even overcome the ultimate limit, death, because it gives us access to the eternal.

THE *KULTURNATION* AS SPIRITUAL ORGANISM

Fichte holds that the formation of spiritual culture is optimized in communities bound by a living language. For him, the German language is unique because of its organic continuity. Unlike the other Teutonic races, the Germans did not emigrate but "remained in the original [*ursprün-glichen*] dwelling places of the ancestral stock [*Stammvolks*]. . . . [They] retained and developed [*fortbildeten*] the original language . . . , whereas the latter adopted a foreign language and gradually reshaped it in a way of their own" (*RDN,* VII:313; 47). Consequently, "the German speaks a language which has been alive ever since it first issued from the force of nature, whereas the other Teutonic races speak a language which has movement on the surface only but is dead at the root. To this circumstance alone, to life [*die Lebendigkeit*] on the one hand and death on the other, we assign the difference. . . . *Between life and death there is no comparison; the former has infinitely more value than the latter.*" (*RDN,* VII:325; 58–59; emphasis added).

Fichte thus territorializes the key traits of freedom—purposive auto-causality, power of origination, and so on—in a specific national culture. Consequently, the border (*Grenze*) separating Germans from non-Germans is that between life and death. His argument that the German people are inherently predisposed to originality (*Ursprünglichkeit*) is, however, not an exclusionary chauvinism. The German nation is not a natural or biological community of blood, race or descent.[19] The Germans are unlike the other

---

19. Cf. Etienne Balibar, "Fichte and the Internal Border: On *Addresses to the German Nation,*" in *Masses, Classes, Ideas: Studies on Politics and Philosophy Before and After Marx,* trans. James Swenson (New York: Routledge, 1994), pp. 76–78. Note that Fichte does occasionally lapse into an argument about common descent because he defines the German language as living by recourse to a

branches of the Teutonic race. Because their power of origination stems from their living language, the Germans do not share an eternal essence. The original people is infinitely plastic and must continually give itself life and freely create itself through self-activity. This is why it is the bearer of freedom and spiritual life, which it will spread through all humanity.[20] As Jacques Derrida puts it, "the essence of the German is not to be confused with empirical factuality, with empirical belonging to the factual German nation, any more than empirical non-belonging to that German nation excludes the non-Germans from participation in some originary Germanity. . . . Whence this paradoxical consequence, which one can consider either as an expansion of generosity, or as the imperialist expansionism of a people sure of itself, and dominant: whoever shares in this originary philosophy— of originarity, of life, of creative freedom—is German, even if they apparently belong to another people."[21]

Thus, what makes the German people original is a certain boundlessness or infinity. "A people" in the higher meaning of the word, Fichte writes, is

> the whole of men continuing to live in society with each other and *continually creating themselves naturally and spiritually out of themselves* [*sich aus sich selbst immerfort natürlich und geistig erzeugenden*], a totality that arises out of the divine under a special law of divine development. *It is the subjection in common* [*Gemeinsamkeit*] *to this special law that unites* [*verbindet*] *this mass in the eternal world, and therefore in the temporal also, to a natural whole permeated by itself* [*von sich selbst durchdrungen*]. (*RDN*, VII:381; 115; emphasis added)

This characterization of the nation as a self-permeating organic whole indicates that originality is essentially one's ability to persistently deter-

---

myth of unique historical development: "Naturalness on the German side, arbitrariness and artificiality [*Willkürlichkeit und Künstelei*] on the foreign side, are the fundamental differences. . . . This unnaturalness comes of itself into the life of foreign countries, because their life deviated from nature originally and in a matter of the first importance" (*RDN*, VII:337; 71). Consequently he repeats many commonplaces in eighteenth- and nineteenth-century discourse about national character. On the other hand, this territorialization of the line between life and death may be a strategy for impressing the urgency of maintaining German freedom.

20. See *RDN*, VII:342; 76.

21. Jacques Derrida, "Onto-Theology of National-Humanism (Prolegomena to a Hypothesis)," *Oxford Literary Review* 14 (1992): pp. 12–13.

mine one's own limits or borders rather than be determined by externally imposed limits. This is not a simple assertion of political self-determination. The nation's borders are internal, spiritual borders more powerful than any physicoempirical territorial borders, which are simply their external retracings.

> The first, original, and truly natural boundaries of states are beyond doubt their internal boundaries [*innern Grenzen*]. Those who speak the same language are joined to each other by a multitude of invisible bonds by nature herself, long before any human art begins; they understand each other and have the power of continuing to make themselves understood more and more clearly; they belong together and are by nature one and an inseparable whole. . . . From this internal boundary, which is drawn by the spiritual nature of man himself, the marking of the external boundary by dwelling place results as a consequence; and in the natural view of things it is not because men dwell between certain mountains and rivers that they are a people, but on the contrary, men dwell together . . . because they were a people already by a law of nature which is much higher. (*RDN*, VII:460; 190–91)

The internal border is a spatioterritorial figure for the dynamic of internalization through which the *I* transcends its finitude by positing limits for itself. By affirming its internal border, the nation effectively interiorizes and overcomes the border between life and death. Death would be subsumed by life because it would no longer be an external limit to life, but a limit that life (qua patriotic individual) posits within itself (qua nation) through cultural work so that it can renew itself and live on. Life is nothing but this interiorization and self-positing. The internal border allows the nation, or life, to infinitely renew itself *in and for itself.*

The nation is, however, not a mystico-natural entity. It is persistently brought into being by rational-purposive activity. When individuals belong to a living national culture, Fichte argues, moral work immediately takes place as action in accordance with the spiritual law of the nation because the nation is immediately recognized as the sensible embodiment of an eternal order. Self-conscious moral work is thus always directed towards the nation. It immediately appears as national culture, as activity in the nation's service. At the same time, the nation also becomes imbued with and develops according to the divine life moral activity imparts.

Thus, the German nation is the territorialization of the power to overcome all borders. It is the binding of boundlessness itself. In contradistinction, the foreign spirit is a limited being who cannot transcend finitude because it confines existence according to limits. Ultimately, the foreigner is a creature *of* death because he defines life according to death.

> The inner being of non-German ways [*des Auslandes*], or of non-originality, is the belief in something that is final, fixed, and settled beyond the possibility of change, the belief in *a borderline* [*Grenze*], on the hither side of which free life may disport itself [*das freie Leben sein Spiel treibe*], but which it is never able to break through and dissolve by its own power, and which it can never make part of itself. *This impenetrable borderline* is, therefore, inevitably present to the eyes of foreigners at some place or other, and it is impossible for them to think or believe except with such a borderline as a presupposition, unless their whole being is to be transformed and their heart torn out of their body. *They inevitably believe in death as origin and end* [*das Ursprüngliche, und Letzte*], *the ultimate source of all things and, therefore, of life itself.*
>
> (*RDN*, VII:360–61; 93–94; emphasis added)[22]

Two crucial implications follow from Fichte's spiritualist definition of the nation: First, the true basis of political freedom is spiritual. When the nation's physical borders have been penetrated, it must preserve its invisible spiritual borders to avoid total destruction. The alien power may have overcome political borders, but as long as the cultural borders remain, the seeds of resistance are preserved. The German nation will not be vanquished, for it is first and foremost cultural. The cultural nation is therefore prior to the political nation. It is not excessive to say that for Fichte, the entire political crisis of Napoleon's invasion is an occasion for the German nation's *Bildung*, an incident that jolts it into self-activity. Foreign occupation is the nation's possession by a foreign spirit that is literally a specter because it is *of* death and threatens to infect the German people with death: "This belief in death, as contrasted with an original and living

---

22. Indeed, the non-German is that which is underwritten by foreign philosophy, a creed of death that regards the ground of appearances as an eternal essence that cannot be transformed by our activity (*RDN*, VII:361; 94).

people [*ursprünglich lebendige Volke*], we have called the foreign spirit [*Ausländerei*]. When once this foreign spirit is present among the Germans it will . . . reveal itself in their actual life also, a quiet resignation to what they deem the unalterable necessity of their existence, as the abandonment of all hope of improvement of ourselves or others by means of freedom" (*RDN*, VII:373; 106). The nation must recognize its internal border and decide whether it will act to preserve itself and strive to live or just die passively. Culture thus supplies the ontological paradigm for the political. It is more original, more powerful, anterior to, or more fundamental than politics proper because it is the power of origination or incarnational self-activity as such. A politics of culture is needed to lay the groundwork for political independence. Second, there is no reason why *Lebendigkeit* (vitality) needs to be unique to one particular language and the exclusive trait of one national culture. The line between life and death need not be drawn between an elect nation and what is foreign to it. It could arguably come into being whenever the free self-development of any language or national culture is threatened by external forces.

The above two points are key tenets of revolutionary decolonizing and postcolonial nationalism. Frantz Fanon and Amilcar Cabral make identical arguments about the importance of national culture to political liberation. Fichte's thematic oppositions of native/alien, natural/artificial, and life/death are fundamental to discussions about the politics of language in postcolonial national literatures. As we will see, Ngũgĩ wa Th'iong'o characterizes colonial and neocolonial literature produced in the alien languages of former colonizers as a form of mental alienation that serves foreign dead capital, and he argues for the necessity of popular radical African culture. All this attests to the emancipatory and revolutionary implications of Fichte's idea of the nation.

THE STATE AS INSTRUMENT OF THE PEOPLE: WHY NATIONAL *BILDUNG* IS NOT AN OFFICIAL IDEOLOGY

Just as the individual's sense of its own self-activity has to be awakened through training, and the vocational process of self-formation is a skill that has to be acquired, national culture needs to be pedagogically developed. The *Addresses* begins with the familiar nineteenth-century topoi of mass national education and the state's pedagogical function. The First Address speaks of national *Bildung* as "the only means [*Mittel*] left to a nation which has lost its independence and with it all influence over public fear and hope, of rising again into life from the destruction it has suffered" (VII:274; 10). The vocabulary is appropriately organismic. *Bildung* is the source of new life because it imparts a consciousness of organic form. It reorganizes the public by making the individual "conscious of itself only as part of the whole" and as capable of enduring "only when the whole is pleasing." (ibid.) "The new education . . . forms [*bilden*] the Germans into a corporate body [*Gesamtheit*], which shall be stimulated [*getrieben*] and animated [*belebt*] in all its individual members [*Gliedern*] by a common interest" (VII:276; 12). *Bildung* is the epigenesis of the nation. Patriotism, Fichte observes, has never been widespread in the German people and *Bildung* will make each individual "a universal and national self." The nation, "whose former life has died out and become the supplement of an alien life," will be educated "to a completely new life" (VII:274; 10–11).

Any mention of cultural pedagogy today inevitably leads to the commonplace charge that national *Bildung* entails the suppression of individuality through official indoctrination or, as the current argot has it, involves aesthetic ideology.[23] This is taken as confirmation that nationalism is an ideology the state uses to maintain its authority. The *Addresses* overturns all these conventional assumptions because it repeatedly foregrounds nationalism's demotic and dynamic character. In stark contrast to Hegelian statism, Fichte conceives of the state as an instrument of the nation and not vice versa. The territorial state and its institutions are an external mechanism of national culture that should be subsumed by the nation, infused with its vital spirit, and made to serve its work. Unless the state is rooted in the living nation, any plan to establish a perfect state will necessarily fail. It

---

23. Following Paul de Man, it is often argued that in the wake of the misreading of German idealism exemplified by Schiller, all culture is aesthetic and that the aesthetic is the paradigm of ideology. All nationalism, especially German philosophical nationalism, is then interpreted as a case of aesthetic ideology. See especially de Man, "Kant and Schiller," in *Aesthetic Ideology* (Minneapolis: University of Minnesota Press, 1996), 129–62. For a similar argument that proceeds from entirely different premises, see George Kelly's conclusions about Fichte's project of cultural education in *Idealism, Politics, and History: Sources of Hegelian Thought* (Cambridge: Cambridge University Press, 1969), 277–78.

will be an abstraction imposed on an aggregate of people from the outside and realized as a mechanical construction of parts that do not cohere. The most glaring example of this is the French Revolution's culmination in the Terror: "the state in accordance with reason [*vernunftgemäße Staat*] cannot be built up by artificial [*künstliche*] measures from whatever material may be at hand [*vorhandenen Stoffe*]; on the contrary, the nation must first be trained [*gebildet*] and educated [*herauferzogen*] up to it. Only the nation which has first solved in actual practice the problem of educating [*Erziehung*] perfect men will then solve the problem of the perfect state" (*RDN*, VII:353–54; 87).

The Seventh Address explicitly reinscribes this topographical subordination of state to nation in terms of the oppositions between organism and machine, life and death. The theory of the state as a perfect social machine established by an independent art (*freie Kunst*) with its own fixed rules, Fichte argues, attempts to produce the life of society out of dead mechanism.

> Undoubtedly it will be the art of finding a similarly fixed and dead order of things, *from which condition of death the living movement of society is to proceed,* and to proceed as this art intends. This intention is to make the whole of life in society into a large and ingeniously constructed clockwork pressure machine, in which every single part will be continually compelled [*genötigt*] by the whole to serve the whole. The intention is to do a sum in arithmetic with finite and given quantities, and produce from them an ascertainable result; and thus, on the assumption that everyone seeks his own well-being, to compel everyone against his wish and will to promote the general well-being.
>
> (*RDN,* VII:363; 96; emphasis added)

However, such mechanistic and utilitarian accounts of society must either assume an external energy source that sets the whole machine into motion or locate an animating principle within the machine, such as a soul, that cannot be explained according to mechanical principles. In contradistinction, a genuine (German) art of the state searches for regularity and independence from blind nature by beginning from the nation-people, where the spirit of life reposes:

> it does not seek a fixed and certain thing, as the first element, which will make the spirit, as the second element [*Glied*], certain; on the contrary, it seeks

from the very beginning, and as the first and only element, a firm and certain [*gewissen*] spirit. *This is for it the mainspring, whose life proceeds from itself, and which has perpetual motion; the mainspring which will regulate, and continuously keep in motion, the life of society.* (*RDN*, VII:365–66; 99; emphasis added)

We have seen a similar metaphor in Kant. For Fichte, an abstract state can only regulate its members through coercion because it sees its members as quantitative units whose interaction can be predicted in advance through mathematical computation. Its members do not form a cohesive self-regulating whole, an organism that is the source of its own movement and the maintenance of its own life. Hence, the state ought to be suffused by and rooted in the demotic communality of the nation because national culture, which has purposive auto-causality, can transform the political community from a mechanical assemblage into an actual operational whole with reciprocally interdependent parts.

This organismic metaphor is already present in the *Foundations of Natural Right* (1796–97), a text from Fichte's "rationalist" period, where it is the state formed from a civil contract that is organic. Fichte characterizes *techne* as heteronomous. It brings death to the organism's *Bildungstrieb*: "the product of artifice points to a creator outside itself, while the product of nature, by contrast, continually produces itself, and maintains itself precisely insofar as it produces itself."[24] Accordingly, he describes the civil contract (*Staatsbürgervertrag*) using Kant's elucidation of a tree's organismic causality. The organism, Fichte argues, is the most appropriate image for the civil condition (*bürgerliche Verhältniß*) as a whole.[25] The civil contract is an agreement through which "the individual becomes a part of an organized whole, and thus melts into one with the whole" (*GN*, III:204; 177). The state based on such a contract would not be an ideal aggregation (*Zusammenfassung*) of individuals, a collective united by an abstract concept, but a real unity, like the organism (*GN*, III:207; 180). Indeed, Fichte sees the constitution of humanity as identical to the constitution of organic nature.

---

24. *Grundlage des Naturrechts nach Principien der Wissenschaftslehre*, in III:78; *Foundations of Natural Right According to the Principles of the Wissenschaftslehre*, 73. Hereafter the German work and its English translation are cited as *GN*.

25. Fichte claims that his use of the organismic metaphor is original. It "has frequently been used in recent times to describe the unity of the different branches of public power, but . . . has not yet been used to explain the civil condition as a whole" (*GN*, III:208; 180–81).

In a product of nature, each part can be what it is only within this organic unity, and outside such unity, the part would not exist at all. Indeed, if there were no such organic unity, then absolutely nothing would exist, for without the reciprocal interaction of organic forces that keep each other in a state of equilibrium, there would be no enduring form [*bestehende Gestalt*] at all, but only an eternal struggle of being and not-being, a struggle that cannot even be thought. Similarly, it is only within the unity of the state that the human being attains a particular place [*bestimmten Stand*] in the scheme of things, a point of rest [*Ruhepunkt*] within nature; and each person maintains *this particular* place in relation to others and in relation to nature only by existing in *this particular* unity. . . . Nature constitutes herself by bringing all organic forces into a unity; humanity constitutes itself by bringing the free choice [*Willkühr*] of all individuals into a unity. (*GN*, III:208; 181)

Fichte likens the isolated and selfish human being to raw matter and the citizen who acts for the sake of others to organic matter. But although the state is an important step in achieving humanity because it brings about the political unity of individuals, he refuses to conflate state membership with morality or humanity. Political unity is not spiritual. It serves natural needs such as security and the protection of the political rights. Hence, unlike the ties that constitute the moral community of all human beings, those binding us to the state are not based in absolute freedom: "Humanity was divided into several independent members; the natural institution [*Naturveranstaltung*] of the state already cancels this independence provisionally and molds individual groups into a whole, until morality [*Sittlichkeit*] re-creates the entire species [*Geschlecht*] as one" (*GN*, III:203; 176).[26]

This means that a mediating form of organization is required to transform the civil contract and its state apparatus into a spiritual organism that incarnates reason. In the *Addresses,* the nation is given this task. The state is merely an instrument for fulfilling human needs. But it can be raised above finitude if it is inspirited by a higher power, namely, the nation as

---

26. On Fichte's separation of right from morality and personhood from moral autonomy, see Frederick Neuhouser, "Fichte and the Relationship between Right and Morality," in *Fichte: Historical Contexts/Contemporary Controversies,* ed. Daniel Breazeale and Tom Rockmore (New Jersey: Humanities Press, 1994), 158–80; and Luc Ferry, "The Distinction between Law and Ethics in the Early Philosophy of Fichte," *Philosophical Forum* 29, nos. 2–3 (winter/spring 1988): 182–96.

the vesture of divine life. Consequently, love of fatherland, and not the maintaining of peace, property, personal freedom, and well-being, must be the paramount political principle:

> People and fatherland in this sense, as a bearer and guarantee of eternity on earth and as that which can be eternal here below, far transcend the state in the ordinary sense of the word, viz. the social order as comprehended by mere intellectual conception and as established and maintained under the guidance of this conception. The aim of the state is positive right [*gewisses Recht*], internal peace, and a condition of affairs in which everyone may by diligence earn his daily bread and satisfy the needs of his sensuous existence, as long as God permits him to live. All this is only a means, a condition, and a framework for what love of fatherland really wants, viz., that the eternal and the divine may blossom in the world and never cease to become more and more pure, perfect and excellent. That is why this love of fatherland must itself govern the state and be the supreme, final and absolute authority. (*RDN*, VII:384; 118)

The nation is the sole terrain of moral action for humanity because individuals can only attain a certain life beyond death through it. The individual can participate in divine life through moral willing. But he is also a finite creature who demands that his moral faith in the permanence of his deeds be justified by the existence of an order of things that "is itself eternal and capable of taking up into itself that which is eternal" (*RDN*, VII:380; 114). The supersensible moral world needs to be incarnated in a sensible particular to secure the moral actor's faith. The nation is precisely such a universal particular. It is an organic and lawful substrate, a medium of subsistence for individual existence that precedes and surpasses the lives of individuals who play an active role in shaping it and who leave their marks encrypted in it for posterity. Such is the moral basis of patriotic sentiment: moral action finds its immediate "object" or destination in the nation. To die for one's nation is to sacrifice one's individual life for the preservation of one's permanent existence as a free moral being in the sensible world.

> [The noble-minded man's] belief and his striving to plant what is permanent, his conception in which he comprehends his own life as an eternal life, is the bond which unites first his own nation, and then, through his own nation, the whole human race, in a most intimate fashion with himself. . . . The divine

has appeared in it, and that which is original has deemed this people worthy to be made its vesture and its means of directly influencing the world. . . . Hence, the noble-minded man will be active [*tätig*] and effective [*wirksam*], and will sacrifice himself for his people. Life merely as such, the mere continuance of changing existence, has in any case never had any value for him; he has wished for it only as the source of what is permanent. But this permanence is promised to him only by the continuous and independent existence of his nation. In order to save his nation he must be ready even to die that it may live and that he may live in it the only life for which he has ever wished.

(*RDN*, VII:382–83; 116).

Nationalism also has an immediate political significance. However sophisticated, a constitution remains a mere mechanism for the regulation and fulfilment of finite needs. In times of crisis, it does not possess the absolute authority that can demand individuals to risk everything including their lives. This can only issue from "a truly original and primary life [*ursprüngliches und erstes Leben*]" (*RDN*, VII:386; 120). Love of the fatherland, which cannot be reduced to a citizen's love for the constitution and the laws of a polity, is such an authority. Hence, the external community of the political state must always be subsumed under the inner community of the cultural nation.

This equation of national culture with life and self-activity, and the association of the state with stasis, indicate that Fichte's cultural nationalism is not an official ideology. It continues the strong anarchistic streak of his earlier Jacobin writings, which insisted on the independence and superiority of society vis-à-vis the state by associating society in general with free purposive life and distinguishing it from "that particular, empirically conditioned type of society which we call 'the state'" (VI:306; *EPW*, 156). The state is only a means to a higher end, and it ought to wither away: "Life in the state is not one of man's absolute ends. The state is, instead, only a *means for establishing a perfect society*, a means which exists only under specific circumstances. Like all those human institutions which are mere means, the state aims at abolishing itself. *The end of government is to make government superfluous.* . . . [T]here will certainly be a point in the a priori foreordained career of the human species when all civic bonds will become superfluous" (ibid.). In the *Addresses*, the nation guarantees the freedom of citizens by limiting the state's measures at establishing internal peace. The most efficient means of establishing political order is to limit the freedom of citizens. But the nation, which is freedom itself, imposes a higher end on the state: "Freedom including freedom in the activities of external life, is the soil in which higher culture [*Bildung*] germinates; a legislation which keeps this higher culture in view will allow to freedom as wide a field as possible" (*RDN*, VII:385; 118–19). Hence, in stark contrast to Hegel, Fichte emphatically privileges cultural nationalism over constitutional patriotism.

But Fichte's project of national cultural pedagogy is not a form of *artificial* training that detracts from the people's spontaneous life. Organismic causality, to which national culture is likened, exhibits purposiveness and rational organization. The true spontaneity of life stems from its spirituality. It is not merely the unruly arbitrariness of instinct, but an activity that proceeds according to rules. Cultural education is likewise an active process. It attempts to bring out the subject's latent capacity for originality by encouraging active participation and stimulating its frequent exercise. Fichte points to the etymological link between *Bildung* and the imagination (*Einbildungskraft*), "the faculty to self-actively draw such images [*das Vermögen, selbsttätig dergleichen Bilder*], which are independent of reality [*Wirklichkeit*] and not copies [*Nachbilder*] of it, but rather its prototypes [*Vorbilder*]" (*RDN*, VII:284; 20). Not only must the *Bildung* of the human species take as its point of departure the imagination's capacity to generate these prefigurations of reality, but the pupil must be taught to create images by his own self-activity instead of being "merely capable of receiving passively the image presented to him by education, of understanding it sufficiently, and of reproducing it just as it is presented to him, as if it were a question simply of the existence of such an image" (VII:284–85; 20). This denunciation of rote learning and the passive assimilation of information is clearly inimical to indoctrination.

THE ORIGINARY INFECTION OF THE NATION-PEOPLE

I have argued that Fichte's nationalism is not a conservative, irrational mystification but a popular, radical political organicism in the Kantian tradition. Fichte refigures the border between life and death as the line between nation and state, and he argues for the national reinspiration of the state machine. His association of national culture with living self-activity and his subordination of the state to the nation are fundamental tenets of socialist decolonizing nationalism. However, given the repeated misprisions and historical deployment of organismic nationalist discourse for conservative purposes, we must ask whether any project of national *Bildung,* no matter how popular, radical, or rational and progressive in its original conception is somehow internally susceptible to ideologization and state manipulation. If the problem is merely formulated in terms of whether nationalism is an aesthetic ideology, the possibility of ideologization is only referred back to the category of the aesthetic. The question, however, needs to be posed at a more fundamental level because the possibility of ideologization is rooted in the organismic vitalism that underwrites the idea of *Bildung.*

Humanities scholars tend to privilege aesthetic culture. But it is only one among many forms of incarnation, culture being broader than the aesthetic since it includes the sciences as well as political and legal institutions. Fichte underscores this broader understanding of culture as the anthropologization of spontaneous incarnational activity by noting that the power of origination involves the active translation of ideational images into reality. We saw that in Kant's Third Critique, the teleological time of organismic causality was disrupted by an inhuman *techne.* This contamination inheres in every incarnational process because felicitous incarnation is always dependent on a radical alterity that exceeds the control of self-actualizing human reason even as it makes self-actualization possible. Any political project taking incarnational activity as its paradigm is subject to this contamination of which ideologization or state manipulation is a consequence. In the *Addresses,* this law of contamination is played out in the haunting of the living nation by the state.

As we know, according to Fichte, the living nation overcomes finitude by positing and internalizing death as its own limit. This internalized limit becomes the nation's internal border. But, for historical reasons, this insistence on the supreme authority of the internal border opens the nation up to *techne.* Because the German people has always been politically fragmented, its unity can only be maintained through literary *Bildung:* "The noblest privilege and the most sacred function of the man of letters is this: to assemble his nation and to take counsel with it about its important affairs. But especially in Germany this has always been the exclusive function of the man of letters, because Germany was split up into several separate states, and was held together as a common whole almost solely by the instrumentality [*Werkzeug*] of the man of letters, by speech and writing" (*RDN*, VII:454; 185). Such literary *techne* becomes all the more imperative because Napoleon has destroyed "the last external bond which united the Germans," the Holy Roman Empire (ibid.). Political independence is imperative because although the nation is prior to the state and may live for a period without its *own* state, its prolonged survival is endangered by foreign occupation. The nation's internal border must first be consolidated to lay the ground for liberation: "It is education [*Erziehung*] alone that can save us from all the ills that oppress us" (*RDN*, VII:433; 165).

However, this cultural project needs the state's mediation because it is a mechanism that can make education universal for all citizens (VII:434; 166). The state has an incentive to do this because education is the only remaining sphere (*Wirkungkreis*) where "it can act originally and independently like an actual [*wirklicher*] state and make decisions!" (VII:432; 164) The state has a right to compel its wards because such compulsion (*Zwang*), like Kant's discipline, is a means to rational self-determination. It "restores complete personal freedom when education is finished, and can have nothing but the most salutary results" (VII:436; 167). This means that although cultural *Bildung* is supposed to be prior to and more powerful than political *techne*, it *needs* to be supplemented by statecraft. Consequently, the nation's internal border becomes vulnerable to the state apparatus, which as mere mechanism is always on the side of death, and to official manipulation. This is especially dangerous when the nation is occupied by a foreign power. The public life of each occupied German state is subject to alien influence and is in danger of becoming a mere machine that can undermine the internal border's integrity. In these circumstances, literati who wish to influence public life may have to give up their own language and adopt a foreign one. As Fichte poignantly observes,

what sort of literature can that be, the literature of a people without political independence? . . . [A] sensible writer wants . . . nothing else but to influence public life, and to form [*gestalten*] and reshape [*umschaffen*] it according to his vision [*Bilde*]. . . . He wants to think originally and from the root of spiritual life for those who act just as originally [*ursprünglich wirken*], i.e., govern. He can, therefore, only write in a language in which the governors think, in a language in which the work of government is carried on, in the language of a people that forms an independent state. . . . [But] where a people has ceased to govern itself, it is equally bound to give up its language and to coalesce with its conquerors. (*RDN*, VII:452–53; 183–84)

Under foreign occupation, national *Bildung* itself goes awry and is infected by the state that was supposed to be the nation's means and instrument. The nation cannot safely internalize and annul the line that separates it from death. The internal border itself becomes contaminated and marks the unexpected eruption of death within the living nation.

Fichte tries to maintain the internal border's inviolability by arguing that the nation remains purely original. The living nation resists foreign influence because it is resolutely egalitarian and popular. The nation is led by the people (*Volk*), who are clearly not synonymous with the Third Estate, which includes the cultivated. It refers to the unprivileged rural and urban working masses who are the nation's original backbone. The nation-people is thus a collective sociopolitical subject who remains united despite social stratification. "In Germany," Fichte writes, "all culture [*Bildung*] has proceeded from the people" and the Reformation's success stems from popular participation (*RDN*, VII:355; 88). Indeed, the *Addresses* is framed by an acknowledgment of its own anomalous nature as a project of national *Bildung* initiated by the educated classes who will soon be absorbed by the people and become obsolete:

> Up to the present all human progress in the German nation has sprung from the people, and . . . to it, in the first instance, great national affairs have always been brought and by it, cared for and furthered. Now, for the first time, there-fore, it happens that the original reconstruction [*ursprüngliche Fortbildung*] of the nation is offered as a task to the educated classes [*gebildeten Ständen*]. . . . [T]hese classes cannot calculate how long it will still remain in their power to place themselves at the head of this movement, since it is now almost ready and ripe for proposal to the people, and is being practised by individuals from among the people; and the people will soon be able to help themselves without any assistance from us. . . . [T]he present educated classes and their descen-dants will become the people; while from among the present people another more highly educated class will arise. (*RDN*, VII:278–79; 14–15)

The *techne* of cultural pedagogy is a temporary measure that will, in due teleological time, be organicized into a popular self-incarnating whole where social stratification is irrelevant. Thus, Fichte always insists on the people's leading role in national development and on the fundamental unity between the masses and rulers who are genuinely German.[27] Social division in Germany, which led some German rulers to betray the nation, is an artificial and alien creation, an importation of "that gulf between the upper classes and the people which came about naturally in foreign countries" (*RDN*, VII:337; 71).

The problem, however, is that the people is *not* coextensive with the nation. The *Addresses* offers contradictory interpretations of German history that put the nation's organic unity into doubt. On the one hand, this postulated unity leads Fichte to absolve German rulers of any responsibility for the Holy Roman Empire's fall, which he views as the common fate of all German states.[28] On the other hand, however, when he describes Germany's collapse in the medieval period, he suggests that the princes are responsible and contrasts them to the ruling burgher class of the Hanseatic League who were part of the active and productive people.[29] The historical splintering of the original nation into several states loosely bound together by the Holy Roman Empire, the subsequent collapse of these states, and the nation's ensuing crisis need to be explained by pointing to a clearly determinable element within the nation that is infected by some outside influence. Pointing to uncontrollable external circumstances would consign the nation's freedom entirely to blind fate. This is why Fichte distinguishes the people as the nation's active part from other privileged strata, who are part of the diseased and now fallen German states, and intellectuals, who are influenced by non-German ideas of death. But this distinction undercuts the immediate spiritual unity that he repeatedly affirms as the living nation's defining feature. It suggests that the living nation is susceptible to contamination by *techne* from within itself, from other classes, especially the ruling class, which has demonstrated a historical affinity to death-dealing foreign ways.

---

27. "Though their princes, from love of foreign ways and the craving for brilliance and distinction, might at first separate themselves, as those did, from the nation and abandon or betray it, they were afterward easily swept into unanimity with the nation and took pity on their peoples" (*RDN*, VII:349; 82–83).

28. See *RDN*, VII:473–74; 204.

29. See *RDN*, VII:355–58; 89–91.

The lack of full coincidence between nation and people suggests the existence of some element in the living nation that facilitates its possession by the alien-occupied state, some internal member so hospitable to alien intrusion that it is indistinguishable from the foreign. The ambiguous relationship between people, nation, and state undoubtedly results from the lack of sociological analysis detailing the separation of state from national civil society in Fichte's text. Such ambiguous internal division may be a historical contingency that teleological time will overcome. But it also has a broader ontological import because the people incarnate divine life. It suggests that there may always already have been some indeterminable alien within life that cannot be expelled. There may always be some specter haunting the living nation that cannot be exorcised. This indeterminable form of death is not a limit to life that life can determine and subsume as its internal border. Or better yet, this limit to life is an internal border, but it would not belong to life as a manifestation of the infinite. It would proliferate itself uncontrollably within the living national body as the mark of a finitude that is so radical that it cannot be known and transcended by the national spirit qua purposive cultural work. The possibility of ideologization is inscribed here. What is put into question is precisely the organismic schema underwriting the conventional distinction between the nation-people and the state. Decolonizing nationalism will encounter exactly the same problem in postcoloniality, where it is haunted by the neocolonial state and the ambivalent role of the indigenous bourgeoisie, especially intellectuals.

THE ACTUALIZATION OF REASON: HEGEL'S ORGANIC STATE AND THE GHOST OF NATIONAL CULTURE

Hegel's definition of the ideal state as "the realm of actualized [*verwirklichten*] freedom, the world of spirit produced from itself as a second nature" involves a double territorialization of freedom (*PR,* § 4, 7:46; 35). In a sociopolitical register, freedom only attains self-conscious objective existence in the ideal territorial state. More importantly, freedom in the ontological sense of self-determination is the process of territorialization. It is the activity of remaining at home with oneself (*bei sich selbst zu bleiben*) in the subject's externalization as a second nature, a spiritual world in which it feels at home because it creates this nature out of and for itself. Hegel envisioned a form of constitutional patriotism that stressed the importance of individuality. It is closer to Montesquieu's idea of political culture than Herder's understanding of national culture as a genetic principle. Hegel was also a strong critic of the German nationalist movement and the project of establishing a united German state after Napoleon's defeat.[30] The state affirmed by the *Philosophy of Right* is emphatically not an absolutist machine-state, which the *Earliest System Programme* (written in Hegel's hand) had denounced, but a French-influenced modern constitutional state.[31] Nevertheless, Hegel's organic state is often accused of being authoritarian; an apologia for Prussian nationalism; and the intellectual progenitor of modern German totalitarian ethnonationalism.[32]

How can one account for this systematic equivocation between progressiveness and reaction that seems to be the fate of Hegel's political organicism? This perversion of Hegel's statism is especially significant because the principle of identity underwriting it concerns the elimination of errancy. As Shlomo Avineri notes, this identity is reason's ability to recognize and find itself in the external world: "modern man, who has found himself in his work, is in danger of losing himself again in his products; the political structure [the state], which reflects this knowledge of man as a subject, is aimed at overcoming this tension."[33] Following the Frankfurt School, we can interpret this overcoming of the difference between reason and its others as epitomizing reason's violent domination of nature. But Hegel also has a more radical view of freedom's actualization (*Verwirklichung*) that

---

30. This is conclusively argued in Shlomo Avineri, "Hegel and Nationalism," *The Review of Politics* 24 (1962): 461–82. In his 1816 essay on the constitutional struggle in Württemberg, Hegel writes: "The vain idea known as the German Reich has disappeared" (cited in Avineri, 462).

31. See Shlomo Avineri, *Hegel's Theory of the Modern State* (Cambridge: Cambridge University Press, 1972), pp. 70, 87. For a more detailed construction of historical context, see Eric Weil, *Hegel and the State*, trans. Mark A. Cohen (Baltimore: Johns Hopkins, 1998), chap. 1: and Z. A. Pelczynski, "Introduction" in *Hegel's Political Writings*, trans. T. M. Knox (Oxford: Clarendon, 1964), pp. 5–137.

32. For a good overview of the Anglophone pathologization of Hegel before and after the Second World War by Karl Popper, Sidney Hook, and others, see Walter Kaufmann, ed., *Hegel's Political Philosophy* (New York: Atherton, 1970). Ironically, Hegel was accused of antinationalism by German nationalists such as Rudolf Haym and Treitschke in the second half of the nineteenth century. See Shlomo Avineri, "Hegel and Nationalism," pp. 463–66.

33. *Hegel's Theory of the Modern State*, p. 112.

acknowledges that life is necessarily accompanied by its other, death. Unlike Fichte's formulation of effectivity (*Wirksamkeit*) as the *I*'s self-limitation through its positing of the *not-I,* Hegelian reason does not impose ideas onto an arational external reality. Reason's actualization is its necessary passage through otherness, its becoming an external object to itself, but with the crucial qualification that reason directs this entire process and *recognizes* itself in this other, thereby *returning to* and *becoming united* with itself even as it becomes objective existence. Hegel's radicality lies in his acknowledgment that reason can only actualize itself by opening itself up to alterity. It can only find itself by risking self-loss. This is the condition of possibility of its actuality and self-possession. His conservatism, which is not a simple political or ideological conservatism, is that he names this equivocation as a contradiction (*Widerspruch*) that can be resolved or sublated so that reason is always preserved in its exposure to alterity. Reason returns to itself because it recognizes that the other is nothing other than itself as substance.

The oscillation of Hegel's political organicism between progressiveness and reaction is rooted in this more primary equivocation in its ontological infrastructure. Insofar as the problematic of actualization underwrites all normative conceptions of politics, we cannot, I suggest, automatically dismiss his argument that political citizenship within the ideal state is the actualization of the rational as an authoritarian ideology, even though we may dispute the details of his political philosophy, such as his defense of monarchism, the status he grants to the bureaucracy, his criticisms of civil society, and so on. The more fundamental question is this: at what point and why do reason and freedom become something other in their process of actualization? How is this irreducible possibility of self-loss connected to the interpretation of Hegel's thought as a defense of totalitarianism and fundamentalist cultural nationalism?

By insisting that the topos of actualization is crucial to understanding the organic state, I am departing from the growing trend of historicist and nonmetaphysical interpretations of Hegel.[34] The *Philosophy of Right* is rich

---

34. This (generally historicist) occlusion can occur by way of a nonmetaphysical interpretation of Hegel, or by dissociating his "outmoded" metaphysics from his sociopolitical insights. See Robert Pippin, *Hegel's Idealism: The Satisfactions of Self-Consciousness* (Cambridge: Cambridge University Press, 1989); and Charles Taylor, *Hegel and Modern Society* (Cambridge: Cambridge University

in historical and sociological detail. It is rightfully praised for containing the first conceptual formulation of modern civil society and for narrating the liberation of the middle class, the stratification of society into economic classes, and the alienating impact of industrial modernity. But while Hegel's organic state is an institutional solution to the existential problems of modernity—the atomization of social life, increasing mechanization in industrialism, and so on—these disruptive forces are primarily symptoms of the finitude his philosophy attempts to overcome. The organic state is no mere metaphor. It is a spiritual *organism* that raises the dynamic of transcendence present in organic life to a higher level. Indeed, the very concept of the "concrete"—as in the idea of concrete (as opposed to abstract) political freedom guaranteed through legitimate institutions and economic freedom—is necessarily organismic. It belongs to the problematic of the actualization of freedom that Kant inaugurated. Instead of denouncing Hegel's organic state as a metaphysical mystification, we should ask whether the contamination of his political organicism is the irreducible fate of all post-Kantian, that is, organismic conceptions of freedom.

WIRKLICHKEIT AND THE IDEA OF THE STATE

The *idealism* which constitutes sovereignty is the same determination as that according to which the so-called *parts* of an animal organism are not parts, but members or organic moments whose isolation and separate existence [*Für-sich-Bestehen*] constitute disease. . . . It is the same principle which we encountered . . . as self-relating negativity, and hence as universality *determining itself to individuality*, in which all particularity and determinacy are superseded. . . . In order to grasp this, one must first have understood the whole conception of the substance and true subjectivity of the concept.

(*PR*, § 278A, 7:443; 315)

Press, 1979), respectively. Hegel, Pippin argues, does not appeal to natural teleology. His interest in organic life is a "preliminary metaphorical introduction," "simply the image by which Hegel introduces the basic idea of a historically determining subjectivity" (150). Taylor acknowledges that Hegel believed in a cosmic spirit and subscribed to an expressivist metaphysics, but anthropologizes spirit as humanity's creative potential, which becomes fully expressed in modern society (86–95; 140–41).

This passage, which specifies the connection between freedom and the animal organism, is the key to Hegel's theory of the organic state. For Hegel, freedom is the concept's self-determination, its teleological development to actuality in which it gives itself objective being while preserving itself. The ideal state is based on this principle of self-relation, that is, the concept's return to self from particularity and objective externality. The state's vitality must be rigorously distinguished from anything artificial or mechanical. For the principle of self-relation first becomes objectively present in the animal organism, which is the template for understanding the ideal state, the specification of its concrete institutions and their relations to each other, civil society, and individual citizens.

The *Philosophy of Right* is therefore an ontological argument and an argument about how the concept enters the realm of externality and finitude in its actualization through the human will, and how freedom achieves concrete existence in the modern state. The terms "actuality" and "concrete" are shorthand for the ontological argument, which is loosely mirrored by the anatomy of the ideal state's constitution and the relation between the state and its citizens.[35] For Hegel the organic state is literally the image (*Abbild*) or expression (*Ausdruck*) of reason, "a hieroglyph of reason which becomes manifest [*darstellt*] in actuality" (§ 279Z, 7:449; 321). It is the actualization of reason and freedom.[36] The idea of actuality expressly takes issue with Kant's definition of moral freedom as the causality of ideas. Causality is a transitive action upon a body by external forces. By defining freedom as the causality of ideas, Kant implies a prima facie separation between ideals and reality, possibility and actuality, which becomes insurmountable because of the finitude of human cognitive and practical powers. Hegel's cryptic dictum in the *Philosophy of Right*'s Preface—"What is rational is actual; and what is actual is rational [*Was vernünftig ist, das ist wirklich; und was wirklich ist, das ist vernünftig*]" (*PR,* 7:24; 20)—however,

---

35. The concept's inner self-determination is literally the origin (*Urprung*) of the state's constitutional powers, which correspond to the three propositions of a practical syllogism. See K.-H. Ilting, "Hegel on the State and Marx's Early Critique," in *The State and Civil Society: Studies in Hegel's Political Philosophy,* ed. Z. A. Pelczynski (Cambridge: Cambridge University Press, 1984), p. 109.

36. Cf: "the system of right is the realm of actualized freedom" (§ 4, 7:46; 35); the state is "reason as it actualizes itself in the element of self-consciousness" (Preface, 7:15; 12); and "the state is the actuality of the ethical Idea" (§ 257, 7:398; 275).

emphasizes that actuality is identical to reason. But this does not mean that *existing* reality is inherently rational.[37]

In Hegel's view, existence is being that has no absolute necessity or universal reason to be. What merely exists is not adequate to its underlying essence because as a form of being subject to external conditions, its essence is merely a possibility. This is why existence is contingent and transient. In the *Encyclopaedia Logic,* Hegel notes that "what is there [*Dasein*] is partly *appearance* and only partly actuality. . . . [A] contingent existence [*zufällige Existenz*] does not deserve to be called something-actual in the emphatic sense of the word; what contingently exists has no greater value than that which something-*possible* [*Möglichen*] has; it is an existence which (although it is) can just as well *not be* [*nicht sein*]."[38] Actuality, on the other hand, is existence united with its essence. It is objective being that is rationally necessary, that exists as it ought to. It is existence that *should be* what it *is* and is what it should be from a rational standpoint.

Reason's power to actualize itself removes the gulf between the rational and real.[39] Hegel writes, in clear rebuke of Kant:

The notion that ideas and ideals are nothing but chimeras, and that philosophy is a system of pure phantasms, sets itself at once against the *actuality of what is rational;* but conversely, the notion that ideas and ideals are something far too excellent to have actuality, or equally something too impotent to achieve actuality, is opposed to it as well. However, the severing of actuality from the Idea [*Idee*] is particularly dear to the understanding, which regards

---

37. Hegel's dictum is commonly misread as a totalitarian justification of existing political institutions as rational. For explications of the dictum's religious, ontological, and political meanings that summarize and reject previous right- and left-wing misunderstandings such as those of Haym, Rosenzweig, Marcuse, Popper, and so on, see, respectively, Emil Fackenheim, "Hegel on the Actuality of the Rational and the Rationality of the Actual," in *The God Within: Kant, Schelling, and Historicity* (Toronto: University of Toronto Press, 1996), 164–71; Yirmiyahu Yovel, "Hegel's Dictum That the Rational Is Actual and the Actual Is Rational," in *Konzepte der Dialektik,* ed. Werner Becker and Wilhelm K. Essler (Frankfurt: Klostermann, 1981), 111–27; and Robert Pippin, "Hegel's Political Argument and the Problem of *Verwirklichung,*" *Political Theory* 9, no. 4 (November 1981): 509–32.

38. *Enzyklopädie der philosophischen Wissenschaften I. Erster Teil: Die Wissenschaft der Logik,* § 6A, 8: 47–48; *The Encyclopaedia Logic,* part 1 of *The Encyclopaedia of the Philosophical Sciences,* 29. Hereafter the work and its English translation are cited as *EL.*

39. "*Wirklichkeit*" is derived from the verb "*wirken*" (to act).

its dreams (i.e., its abstractions) as something genuine, and is puffed up about the 'ought' [*Sollen*] that it likes to prescribe, especially in the political field— as if the world had had to wait for it, in order to learn how it ought to be, but is not. . . . [A philosophical] science deals only with the Idea—which is not so impotent that it merely ought to be, and is not actual—and further with an actuality of which those [trivial, external, and perishable] ob-jects, institutions, and situations [criticized by the understanding's 'ought to be'] are only the superficial outer rind. (*EL,* § 6A, 8:48; 30)

Actualization is the teleological self-development and explication of the concept (*Begriff*), the inner principle underlying existence, the "why" or "for the sake of which" any being *is.* The concept becomes concretized in an external shape through a process that unites subjective thought and the objectivity it determines such that rationality resides in the objective world. As Hegel puts it, "the actual is therefore manifestation; it is not drawn into the sphere of *alteration* by its externality, nor is it the *reflecting* of itself in *an other,* but it manifests itself; that is, in its externality it is *itself* and is *itself* in that alone, namely only as a self-distinguishing and self-determining movement."[40] Actualization is an incarnational activity linked to the absolute because it involves the overcoming of a being's finitude or limitation by another. Reason actualized is what Hegel calls the Idea.

the Idea is what is true *in and for itself, the absolute unity of Concept and objectivity.* Its ideal content is nothing but the Concept in its determinations; its real content is only the presentation [*Darstellung*] that the Concept gives itself in the form of external thereness [*Daseins*]; and since this figure [*Gestalt*] is included in the ideality of the Concept, or its might [*Macht*], the Concept preserves [*erhält*] itself in it. (*EL,* § 213, 8:367; 286)

The first clause of "what is rational is actual; and what is actual is rational" suggests that the concept contains within itself the power of determining itself as concrete, of giving itself external shape. Better yet, the rational is this process of self-actualization. It does not stand against and beyond reality as

---

40. *Wissenschaft der Logik II,* 6:201; *Hegel's Science of Logic,* 542. Hereafter the work and its English translation are cited as *WL.*

an alien understanding that can only guide reality through atemporal norms or regulative ideas that transcend the empirical world. As actuality, reason is immanent to reality. It determines or constitutes reality from within. The second clause states that what is actual or has attained actuality is not inert immediate being opposed to subjective thought, which lies waiting to be represented and cognized by abstract ideational forms. Instead, the actual is inherently rational because it is the unity or identity of the rational subject and the empirical object's structure.[41] For Hegel, the ideal state (the state as Idea) is reason and freedom in their objective dimensions just as the individual's legitimation of the state is reason and freedom in their subjective moments.

This is not a reactionary argument against critical resistance to state domination. Not all existing states are actual and inherently rational. Hegel repeatedly distinguishes between inadequate, deficient states, which merely exist because they are sunk in contingency and arbitrariness, and the ideal state, which has genuine actuality and is the vehicle of the infinite.

> A bad state is one which merely exists; a sick body also exists, but it has no true reality. A hand which has been cut off still looks like a hand and exists, but it has no actuality. . . . The state is indeed essentially secular and finite, and has particular ends and particular powers; but its secularity is only one of its aspects, and only a spiritless perception can regard it as merely finite. For the state has a soul which animates it [*belebende Seele*], and this animating soul is subjectivity, which creates distinctions on the one hand but preserves their unity on the other. . . . [To contend] that the secular spirit, i.e. the state, is purely finite is a one-sided view, for actuality is not irrational. A bad state, of course, is purely secular and finite, but the rational state is infinite within itself.
>
> (*PR*, § 270Z, 7:429; 302–3)

Regardless of the deficient shapes that the state assumes in finite existence, the infinite Idea of it remains.

> The state is not a work of art [*Kunstwerk*]; it exists in the world, and hence in the sphere of arbitrariness, contingency, and error, and bad behaviour may

---

41. My explication draws on Yovel, "Hegel's Dictum That the Rational Is Actual and the Actual Is Rational," pp. 120–21.

disfigure it in many respects. But the ugliest man, the criminal, the invalid, or the cripple is still a living human being; the affirmative aspect—life—survives [*besteht*] in spite of such deficiencies. (*PR*, § 258Z, 7:404; 279)

Hegel's account of the state therefore strikes a fine balance between prescription and affirmation. It acknowledges the deficiency of existing states, but insofar as the Idea of the state is present in them, he also cautions us from confusing our criticisms with a rejection of the state as such. For him, the state is the only way for freedom to be actualized. The noncorrespondence between its Idea and reality is eliminated in modernity, where the ideal state appears in external existence because the modern state achieves the unity of particularity and universality.

BECOMING OTHER WHILE STAYING AT HOME:
THE ANIMAL ORGANISM

In Hegel's view, the ideal state is an organism because the Idea first becomes objectively present in organic life. Life is external existence that conforms to the concept and the concept is the source of all vitality (*Lebendigkeit*).[42] The organism is "the first ideality of nature" and the actualized concept in immediate existence.[43] Hegel radicalizes Kant's characterization of the organism as an end in itself (*Selbstzweck*) and his elucidation of inner purposiveness.[44] He argues that although Kant broached the thought of the active concept or self-determining concrete universal, he shrank from the radical conclusion that the final end could be actualized (*EL*, § 55A, 8:140;

---

42. *Enzyklopädie der philosophischen Wissenschaften II. Zweiter Teil: Die Naturphilosophie*, § 251Z, 9:37; *Hegel's Philosophy of Nature*, part 2 of *The Encyclopaedia of the Philosophical Sciences* (1830), 25. Hereafter the work and its English translation are cited as *PN*. See also *EL*, § 160Z, 8:307; 236.

43. *PN*, § 337, 9:337; 273. Cf. *Vorlesungen über die Ästhetik I*, 13:163; *Aesthetics: Lectures on Fine Art*, 1:120: "This is the idealism of life [*der Lebendigkeit*]. . . . [N]ature as life [*Leben*], already makes matter of fact what idealist philosophy brings to completion in its own spiritual field"; and *EL*, § 216, 8:273; 291: "The *immediate* Idea is *life*. The concept is realised as soul, in a body." Hegel is referring specifically to the animal.

44. For Hegel, Kant's definition of the organism is the most important basis for grasping the concrete Idea and the concept's actuality since Aristotle. See *EL*, § 55–69, 8:139–47; 102–8; *PN*, § 337Z, 9:339–40; 275; § 360A, 9:473; 388–89.

102). Hence, Kant reduces the intuitive understanding to a mere regulative principle of reflective judgment instead of seeing it as immanent to nature and active in the organism. Hegel thus takes Kant's foreclosure of the heteronomy of organic life to human purposiveness to its logical extreme. Kant only draws an analogy between organic life and the human understanding. He accords a measure of alterity to nature by insisting that the intuitive understanding is a principle we project onto nature. Hegel obliterates this alterity by postulating an identity between nature and reason. The organism, he suggests, is developmentally continuous with our self-determining reason because it preserves itself in its relations to otherness. Human rational activity is the higher truth implicit in life. It raises the concept, which is immediately present in the organism, to the level of thought.

The animal organism has three fundamental traits that also characterize the ideal state. First, it is a self-organizing totality that concretely develops itself and is its own end.[45] As a determinate being made up of parts that are themselves concrete totalities and not mere qualities, the organism consists of relations to an other. But it preserves its identity in this otherness. Because both the individual parts and the external shape conform to and are united with its inner end, its objective existence is reflected back into itself. Hence, even in its determinateness, the organism is self-determining and not determined by another: its "*activity* as such is nothing but the pure essenceless form of its being-for-self, and its substance, . . . or its End, does not fall outside of it. It is an activity which spontaneously returns to itself, and is not turned back into itself by anything alien [*ein Fremdes*] to it" (*PG*, 3:202; 159). Organic nature thus mirrors self-consciousness, which sees itself in the shape of a thing when it observes life-forms (*PG*, 3:198; 156).

Second, for Hegel the animal's ability to remain at home with itself in externality epitomizes organismic self-relation. Unlike plants, the animal has this power because it has a nervous system and sensation and can distinguish between itself and the external world.[46] The animal does not lose

---

45. See PN, § 252Z, 9:39; 27. Cf. *Phänomenologie des Geistes*, 3:198; *Hegel's Phenomenology of Spirit*, 156. The latter work and its English translation are hereafter cited as PG.
46. See PN, § 344Z, 9:378; 309: "Only that which possesses sensation can tolerate [*ertragen*] itself as other, can, with the hardiness of individuality, assimilate it and venture into conflict with other

itself in its contact with the external world, which it assimilates, or its members, which are distinct individuals, because it can limit or check its relation to the other. Its subjectivity "consists in preserving itself in its corporeality and in its contact with an outer world and, as the universal, remaining at home with itself [*bei sich selbst zu bleiben*]" (*PN*, § 350Z, 9:430; 352). In the assimilative process, the animal's appetite may open and direct it to the outside, but it does so only to idealize objectivity, to purge external material of its foreignness so that it can be used to remedy a lack or defect within the animal, that is, satiating its appetite. "The animal is thus, in the negative, at the same time positively at home with itself [*bei sich*]; and this, too, is the privilege of higher natures, to exist as this contradiction [*Widerspruch*]. But equally, too, the animal restores its lost harmony and finds satisfaction within itself. Animal appetite is the idealism of objectivity [*Gegenständlichkeit*], so that the latter is no longer something alien to the animal" (*PN*, § 359Z, 9:472; 387–88).

"Remaining-at-home-with-oneself" is not a simple state of passive immobility. It is a process of active corporealization, where immediate existence is rendered fluid and dynamic by being incorporated into the subject (*PN*, § 350Z, 9:430; 352). As Hegel stresses, "in the animal, light has found itself, for the animal arrests [*hemmt*] its relationship to an other; it is the self which is for the self—the existing unity of distinct moments which are pervaded by it" (*PN*, § 350Z, 9:430; 351). The soul, which is the concept present in the body, enables the animal to return to itself from the other and be at home with itself (*PN*, § 350Z, 9:431; 352). It organizes the animal's parts into members of an articulated whole and maintains this unity against the external world, enabling the body to live instead of disintegrating. A detached finger, Hegel observes, quickly decomposes because it has been severed from the soul that gives it life. The *Philosophy of Right* uses the same Aristotelian metaphor of the dismembered limb to describe a state without actuality.

The capacity for self-perpetuation issues from the concept's ability to overcome otherness by containing it within itself. Such endurance of alterity

---

individualities." The plant's deficient form of self-preservation (its parts are not genuine members, it easily loses them, and the superficial unity of parts to whole) is characterized by impotence (*Ohnmacht*). See *PN*, § 337Z, 9:341–42; 276–77.

and contradiction is the organism's third characteristic. It reinscribes the topos of refusing to take from the other that marks Kant's idea of transcendental freedom and his philosopheme of culture. The organism takes from the other only because the other is the self externalized or externality made to conform to the image of the self. Better yet, it is only in taking from an other which is already itself that the organism can truly develop itself. The organism is therefore a process of self-limitation through an other that is *its* other, an other it has made its own or proper to itself. In Hegel's words, "since life, as Idea, is the movement of itself whereby it first makes itself subject, it converts itself into its other, into its own obverse; it gives itself the form of object in order to return into itself and to be the accomplished return-into-self [*um zu sich zurückgekehrt zu sein*]" (*PN*, § 337Z, 9:340; 275). The animal's assimilative processes—its practical appropriation of inorganic nature to satisfy its appetite and its adaptation of the external world into its habitat—are nothing other than the movements of reason's externalization in and conversion of otherness into itself.

This identification with otherness, which is the organism's *Bildungstrieb*, also involves the fashioning of mediating devices in the external world from the animal's secretions, for example, nests and shelters or instruments and weapons such as spider's webs or bee cells, that enable "the adaptation [*Umbildung*] of the non-organic to the ends [*Zweck*] of the living creature" (*PN*, § 357Z, 9:465; 381).[47] Such constructions (*Gebilde*) are analogous to the mediating devices binding the organic state, and they foreshadow culture's political vocation. As self-externalizations that impress the organism's form upon the world, they are an implicit form of *Bildung* before work (*Arbeit*) and cultural activity proper. "The living being," Hegel notes, "has this higher nature, to be the activity which fashions [*formiert*] the things outside of it, at the same time leaving them in their externality because, simply as purposive means, they have a connection with the concept" (*PN*, § 365Z, 9:495; 407). Human artifice is the animal's *Bildungstrieb*, or formative activity, raised to thematic consciousness.[48] The connection between *Bildung* and

---

47. Whereas Blumenbach only sees the *Bildungstrieb* as reproductive, for Hegel it as an objectivational artistic drive (*Kunsttrieb*) within the assimilative process.

48. See *PN*, § 365Z, 9:495; 407: "As *Kunsttrieb*, this concept is only the inner in-itself of the animal, only the non-conscious overseer; it is only in Thought, in the human artificer [*Künstler*], that the concept is for itself."

the transcendence of finitude is already in embryonic form. An animal's vital processes are the opposite of what happens in disease and its endpoint, death, where the organism loses its self and becomes part of the inorganic other, either through internal degeneration or susceptibility to external influences. Life processes are survival tactics that arrest death momentarily by limiting the organism's relation to alterity. Life is thus the subject's power to overcome its other by containing it within itself as a contradiction that can be sublated. This is its inherent rationality.

> The living creature is always exposed to danger, always bears within itself an other, but can endure [*verträgt*] this contradiction which the inorganic cannot. But life is also the resolving [*Auflösen*] of this contradiction; and it is in this that the speculative consists. . . . The perpetual action of life is thus Absolute Idealism; it becomes an other which, however, is always sublated. If life were a realist, it would have respect for the outer world; but it always inhibits the reality of the other and transforms it into its own self.
>
> (*PN*, § 337Z, 9:338; 274)

THE VITAL STATE AND THE MACHINE OF CIVIL SOCIETY

Hegel's definition of life leads to an organismic metaphor that is more detailed than Kant's or Fichte's in its specification of the ideal state's different constitutional powers and the political disposition of its subjects. The organic state is an internally articulated (*gliedert*) and organized totality, in which the parts are fully developed and united with the whole because they are differences that the whole qua concept has posited within itself. At the same time, these differences can only attain full development within the whole.[49] The state's life proceeds on two planes. The state organism refers to "the *political* state proper and *its constitution*," which is a fluid process that produces the members of the larger whole, the various institutional powers.[50] The constitution is "the organization of the state and the process of its organic life *with reference to itself* [*in Beziehung auf sich selbst*], in

---

49. *PR*, § 267Z, 7:413; 288.
50. *PR*, § 267, 7:413; 288.

which it differentiates its moments within itself and develops them to *established existence [Bestehen]*."⁵¹ Its goal is to preserve the state's *identity*.⁵² Referring to Livy's fable of the belly, Hegel notes that "it is in the nature of the organism that all its parts must perish if they do not achieve identity and if one of them seeks independence" (*PR*, § 269Z, 7:415; 290). The various powers have their specified functions, reinforce each other, and cannot subsist outside the larger whole, whose identity they also preserve.⁵³ But the state's life also depends on the rationality of its institutions, which induce individual subjects to actively recognize themselves in the state's substance. Such repeated rational *identification* constitutes the subjective ties of loyalty and obedience binding the individual to the state. It only occurs if the individual regards his membership in the political community as the necessary condition of the fullest development of his personality, so that his subjectivity willingly takes its content from state institutions (*PR*, § 269, 7:414; 290). Thus, the ideal state "is the spirit which knows and wills itself as having *passed through the form of Bildung*. . . . [It] knows what it wills, and knows it in its universality as something thought" (*PR*, § 270, 7:415; 290).

This unity between individual and state is emphatically not the passive compliance of ideological indoctrination. The modern state's defining feature is that its unity is a principle that has been internalized by and particularized in its citizens' subjectivities. The particular interests of individuals are reconciled with the state's universal interest because it guarantees concrete political liberties and welfare thereby enabling the complete development of individuality. This is the source of the modern state's strength vis-à-vis states of antiquity: the obedience it exacts is given freely and rationally. Its citizens are autonomous subjects who "knowingly and willingly acknowledge this universal even as their own substantial spirit, and actively pursue it as their ultimate end [*Endzweck*]" (*PR*, § 260, 7:406–7; 282). Thus, the modern state brings "the self-sufficient extreme of personal particularity" back to "substantial unity" and preserves its unity in the principle of subjectivity itself (*PR*, § 260, 7:407; 282). The free will is nothing else but the

---

51. *PR*, § 271, 7:431; 304.
52. *PR*, § 269–69Z, 7:414–15; 290.
53. *PR*, § 276–76Z, 7:441; 314. Cf. § 286, 7:456; 327.

will of a citizen because the individual will's freedom is constituted by the organic state and vice versa. This is why "the [modern] state is the actuality of concrete freedom" (*PR*, § 260, 7:406; 282). The Idea of the state was invisible in the states of antiquity because

> the particular determinations of this Idea have not yet reached free self-suffi-
> ciency. . . . [U]niversality was indeed already present, but particularity had
> not yet been released and set at liberty and brought back to universality, i.e. to
> the universal end of the whole. . . . [T]he universal must be activated, but sub-
> jectivity on the other hand must be developed as a living whole. Only when
> both moments are present [*bestehen*] in full measure can the state be regarded
> as articulated [*gegliederter*] and truly organized. (*PR*, § 260Z, 7:407; 282–83)

The metaphorical logic of Hegel's argument can be summarized as follows: the state form is an organism that derives its life from the dynamism of reason. The distinction between sick, bad, or contingent states and the good, healthy, or ideal state, with its nod to Aristotle, distinguishes between lower and higher forms of life. The ideal state is a spiritual organism that can overcome the vicissitudes of finitude. The imperfect state, however, is a deficient or disfigured body. As a lower form of organism, it is subject to disease and dismemberment and is like a cripple or invalid. What is coun-terposed to these higher and lower forms of organic life are bodies that have no life at all, phantom objects such as severed limbs. Whereas one can still catch glimmers of the Idea in the deficient state, the Idea is completely evacuated from what is dead. Inorganic objects are devoid of actuality. They are no better than specters because they exist as mere appearance or illusion.

The same organismic vitalism informs Hegel's critiques of the cos-mopolitan federation and civil society. Hegel's critiques foreshadow many contemporary debates about whether a cosmopolitan federation or the nation-state, a cultural community or a society formed by contract, is the best way to promote freedom. In his view, both the cosmopolitan federa-tion and civil society are devoid of life. Kant's project of perpetual peace is a phantom idea. International law "remains only an obligation [*Sollen*]" because it is not actualized in a universal supranational will (*PR*, § 333, 7:500; 368). A cosmopolitan federation will always "be tainted with contin-gency [*Zufälligkeit*]" because "based on moral, religious, or other grounds and considerations," it must presuppose an agreement between states that "would always be dependent on particular sovereign wills" (*PR*, § 333A, 7:500; 368).

The evils of civil society (*bürgerliche Gesellschaft*), the new private sphere of industrial modernity, stem from its ontological character as a lifeless machine.[54] Civil society is a social system for the organization of abstract labor. Its basic unit is the atomistic individual, and it is characterized by the egoistic pursuit of particularistic interests unleashed by the competitive institutions of capitalist exchange and production. Hegel describes civil society as the sphere of the mere appearance of ethical life. Civil society is composed from the mindless, entropic collision of self-sufficient atoms limited only by the abstract frame of a de facto universality. In civil society, the individual selfishly pursues particular interests and needs. Although their satisfaction occurs within a system, this unity is merely formal because it is limited to mutual self-interest. Universal and particular, "ought" and "is," are not actually united. A universal end is pursued only as the means to fulfill a particular end. Hence, civil society lacks actuality. Since "universality is present only as a formal *appearance* in the particular," civil society only exists at the level of semblance. It is characterized by contingent arbitrariness and subjective caprice, and experienced as "the loss of ethical life" (*PR*, § 181, 7:338; 219). Hence, it is devoid of the inner vitality of reason. Civil society is ethical life separated from its inner concept, alienated from itself and degraded by being externalized as "the world of appearance" (ibid.).[55] It is only "the *external state, the state of necessity* and *of the understanding* [*äußeren Staat, —Not- und Verstandesstaat*]," the state as it appears in the realm of necessity and to the mechanical, calculative understanding (*PR*, § 183, 7:340; 221).[56]

This ideational death is historically mirrored in the inhumanity of modern industrial life. "Civil society affords a spectacle of extravagance and misery

---

54. See *PR*, § 238, 7:386; 263. For more elaborate discussions of Hegel's account of civil society, see Andrew Arato, "A Reconstruction of Hegel's Theory of Civil Society," in *Hegel and Legal Theory*, ed. Drucilla Cornell, Michel Rosenfeld, and David Gray Carlson (New York: Routldege, 1991), pp. 301–20; and Pelczynski, ed., *The State and Civil Society*, esp., Pelczynski's "Introduction," pp. 1–13.
55. Cf. *PR*, § 184, 7:340; 221. Andrew Arato describes Hegel's conception of civil society as a *Gegen-* or *Antisittlichkeit*. See "A Reconstruction of Hegel's Theory of Civil Society," p. 304.
56. On the link between the calculative understanding and the satisfaction of needs, see *PR*, § 190Z, 7:348; 228–29.

as well as of physical and ethical corruption common to both" (*PR*, § 185, 7:341; 222). The subjective dehumanization suffered by the increasing number of paupers leads to the creation of a rabble (*PR*, § 244–45, 7:389–91; 266–67). The abstract nature of production in civil society leads to the substitution of man by machine (*PR*, § 198, 7:352–53; 232–33). Thus, Hegel's argument that civil society requires regulation by state authority is underwritten by the suggestion that the machine needs to be organicized and infused with a higher life.[57] His critiques of the social contract, popular sovereignty, and public opinion—civil society's three fundamental features—repeat this juxtaposition of the organic to the lifeless.

In his critique of instrumentalist-utilitarian and liberal theories that see the state as founded on a social contract designed to secure and protect property and personal freedom, Hegel argues that unless the state is regarded as an end in itself, political membership will be based on arbitrary choice because it is determined by common selfish interests (*PR*, § 258A, 7:399; 276). To transfer civil society structures onto the state is to treat the collective like a machine and deprive it of life. What is at stake is the ontological basis of the distinction between community (*Gemeinschaft*) and society (*Gesellschaft*) made famous by Ferdinand Tönnies. The Hegelian state is not a mere society, an aggregate of atomistic wills contractually bound to each other and mechanically related through common necessity and abstract dependence.[58] It is a spiritual organism, a living totality in which the parts are harmoniously related to the whole and each member is indivisibly united to the collective by rational necessity.

Hegel's critiques of popular sovereignty and public opinion also stress the phantasmatic nature of "the people" and "public opinion." Both are marked by indeterminate abstraction and nonactuality because they lack the rational organization that the state imparts. The people (*das Volk*),

---

57. The juxtaposition between the state as organism and machine is already found in *Differenz des Fichteschen und Schellingschen Systems der Philosophie* (1801). Hegel argues that the state in Fichte's *Foundations of Natural Right* "is not an organization at all, but a machine; and the people is not the organic body of a communal and rich life, but an atomistic life-impoverished multitude [*lebensarme Vielheit*]" (2:87; *The Difference Between Fichte's and Schelling's System of Philosophy*, 148–49).
58. See *PR*, § 75A, 75Z, 7:157–59; 105–6. Cf. Hegel's criticism of Rousseau for having confused the general or universal will with the common element arising out of the subjective individual will through contract instead of seeing it as an objective rational will in itself (*PR*, § 258A, 7:400; 277).

Hegel suggests, is a "garbled notion [*wüste Vorstellung*]" (*PR*, § 279A, 7:447; 319). Without the Estates and other institutions to act as mediating organs between it and the state, "the people" is simply "that category of citizens *who do not know what they will*" because they lack profound cognition and insight (*PR*, § 301A, 7:469; 340).

> *Without* its monarch and that *articulation* [*Gliederung*] of the whole which is necessarily and immediately associated with monarchy, *the* people is a form-less mass. . . . *[N]one* of those determinations which are encountered only in an *internally organized* whole . . . is applicable to it. (*PR*, § 279A, 7:447; 319)

In *Die Philosophie des Geistes* of his 1830 *Encyclopaedia,* Hegel suggests that an aggregate of private persons is no longer *populus,* but *vulgus.* It is characterized by self-destructive lawlessness, amorality (*Unsittlichkeit*), and unreason (*Unvernunft*). If such an aggregate determines the nation (*das Volk*), "it would only be a shapeless, wild, blind force." Hence, "it is the one sole end of the state that a nation should not come into existence, to power and action, as such an aggregate."[59] Similarly, public opinion is "the unorganized way in which the will and opinions of the people make themselves known" (*PR*, § 316Z, 7:483; 353). The mediatic devices of modern communications and the opinions they convey are subject to error, contingency, and perversion. They have no rational unity because unlike the forms of state mediation, they are not integrated organs of a rational whole. Public opinion is thus a mere subjectivism without substance that threatens to dissolve the state's existing life.[60]

The distinction between the organic state and civil society is essentially a distinction between two types of mediation. The state's mediations give life. They transform the mediated components into members because they are functions within an articulated whole. The types of mediation characterizing civil society are death dealing. They actively cause disunity because

---

59. *Enzyklopädie der philosophischen Wissenschaften III. Dritter Teil: Die Philosophie des Geistes,* § 544, 10:341; *Hegel's Philosophy of Mind,* part 3 of *The Encyclopaedia of the Philosophical Sciences* (1830), 272–73. This work and its English translation are hereafter cited as *EPG.*

60. See *PR*, § 316–20, 7:483–90; 353–59. For more detailed discussions of Hegel's critique of public opinion, see Jürgen Habermas, *The Structural Transformation of the Public Sphere: An Inquiry into a Category of Bourgeois Society,* trans. Thomas Burger (Cambridge: MIT Press, 1989), pp. 117–22; Eric Weil, *Hegel and the State,* p. 75; and Shlomo Avineri, *Hegel's Theory of the Modern State,* p. 174.

they are not rational functions and do not genuinely unite what they mediate. Left alone, civil society is inherently untenable. Its mediational structures corrode the ethical substance, siphon its life and subject it to outward dissipation. But civil society is also an essential moment of the organic state. It is a necessary point of transition to the self-conscious unity of particularity and universality, subjective and objective freedom, because it develops self-consciousness of individuality and generates new ties that bind particularistic needs into a formal system. Hence, these artificial mediational structures must be brought back to unity by the state, whose constitution organizes its constituents (individuals, the interests of the family, and civil society) as moments in a universal whole where they can fully develop their particular subjectivities and gain objective freedom. The individual must recognize the state as the ground and truth of civil society because its continued functioning can only be sustained by state organization.

Hegel's statism is decidedly quietistic in comparison to Kant's and Fichte's political organicisms. For Hegel, public opinion is not a phenomenal analogue of moral freedom—the scene of critical debate by citizens free from domination and power, and the exercise of enlightened reason that presses upon the state to transform it into a rational authority—as it was for Kant. Instead, the state must be protected from the errors and contingency of public opinion. Indeed, Hegel views the public sphere as an important means of the education (*Bildungsmittel*) of the people by the state, "a remedy [*Heilmittel*] for the self-conceit of individuals and of the mass" (*PR*, § 315, 7:482; 352). The direction of organicization has clearly been reversed. As Hegel's critique of popular sovereignty demonstrates, it is the people that ought to be defined by the state. It is not the absolutist mechanical state that needs to be organicized through public opinion, but mechanical civil society that should be organicized and subsumed by the ideal state.

Hegel's statism also differs from Fichte's nationalism in three respects. It contains a detailed sociological analysis that, for the first time in intellectual history, defines civil society as a private system of organized labor that is distinct from the state and which arises under the disruptive conditions of industrial modernity.[61] Second, Hegel regards the state as the

---

61. Before Hegel, civil society (*societas civilis*) referred to political or state-organized society that was distinguished from state-deficient, natural, or uncivil forms of collectivity. This usage spans the entire tradition of political metaphysics from Aristotle to Fichte. See Manfred Riedel, *Between*

vehicle for the transcendence of finitude and the actualization of freedom. A collective can only actualize the ethical Idea if its relation to the individual is based on reason, if there is a complete unity between individual and collective, where the universal end is only achieved within the satisfaction of particular interests and vice versa, and the identity of the whole is preserved through the individual's recognitive identification with the ethical substance. Thus, "the state is the actuality of the substantial *will*, an actuality which it possesses in the particular *self-consciousness* when this has been raised to its universality; as such, it is the *rational* in and for itself" (*PR*, § 258, 7:399; 275).

Oppositional forms of community such as "the people" or the public sphere of civil society do not possess universal rationality. But neither does a *Kulturnation* like Fichte's original people qua community of language. Such a community remains finite because it is formed from the contingency of birth within a linguistic group. For Hegel, the spirit of the constitution is the modern state's true foundation. It is the state that constitutes the nation and its culture, and not a prepolitical cultural nation that serves as a genetic matrix for the state.[62] Hence, the ties binding us to the organic state have a curious status. They are clearly not the artificial and mechanical ties of civil society. The constitution, Hegel stresses, is not an artifact, something that can be remade at will. But although the state is something we inherit, we are also not bound to it by the natural accidental ties of mother tongue, race, ethnicity, or culture. The modern state renders these irrelevant because its stability encourages the formation of culturally diverse, polyglot polities: "In our day the tie between members of a state in respect of customs [*Sitten*], culture [*Bildung*], language may be rather loose or even non-existent.

Tradition and Revolution: The Hegelian Transformation of Political Philosophy, trans. Walter Wright (Cambridge: Cambridge University Press, 1984), pp. 134–39, 147.

62. As Shlomo Avineri points out, Hegel is clearly critical of contemporary notions of nationalism that are based on ethnicity (*Hegel's Theory of the Modern State*, pp. 45–46). Cf. Z. A. Pelczynski's observation that in Hegel's view, the modern state does not rely on noninstitutional factors such as sentiment and character to bind the individual to the community. "Hegel's concept of nationhood, unlike that of the contemporary German Romantics, is thus heavily political in character. Pure culture or common ethnic and linguistic characteristics are not, in his view, sufficient by themselves to weld a large human group into a nation and to provide a firm focus of loyalty; only the possession of a common government and the tradition of political unity can do so." See "Nation, Civil Society, State: Hegelian Sources of the Marxian Non-Theory of Nationality," in Pelczynski, ed., *The State and Civil Society*, p. 266.

Identity in these matters, once the foundation of a people's union, is now to be reckoned amongst the accidents whose character does not hinder a mass from constituting a public authority. . . . [D]issimilarity in culture and customs is a necessary product as well as a necessary condition of the stability of modern states."[63]

Modern political ties are not constituted by passive immersion in natural immediacy nor the subjective will's arbitrary, particularistic activity. They are ties of universal reason actualized as an ethical substrate in which we subsist as rational individuals. Consequently, the paradigmatic relation between the individual and the organismic political body is that of civic patriotism or political nationalism, the exact opposite of what Fichte means by love of fatherland. It is not an affect aroused by belonging to a cultural community but a *political* sentiment that "is merely a consequence of the state's institutions within the state, a consequence in which rationality is *actually* present [*wirklich vorhanden*]" (*PR*, § 268, 7:413; 288). Patriotism is the rational glue holding the state together. "It is that disposition which, in the normal conditions and circumstances of life, habitually knows that the community is the substantial basis and end" (*PR*, § 268A, 7:413; 289). It explicitly expresses something that we take for granted, namely, that our daily existence depends on the smooth working of state institutions that have become "second nature" to us. Instead of leading to the exceptional heroism and sacrificial action of Fichte's nationalism, it fosters a habitual volition to obey the law. In turn, "rationality receives its practical application through action in conformity with the state's institutions" (*PR*, § 268, 7:413; 288).

BILDUNG AS THE PARADIGM OF SPIRITUAL WORK AND FREEDOM

The contrast between Hegel and Fichte indicates that the territorialization of freedom can take different sociological forms. Whereas Fichte saw the

---

63. *Die Verfassung Deutschlands*, 1:477–78; *Hegel's Political Writings*, 158. Language is also not a criterion in the definition of *Volksgeist* or an important component of national life in Hegel's philosophy of history. See *Vorlesungen über die Philosophie der Weltgeschichte. Band I: Die Vernunft in der Geschichte*, ed. Johannes Hoffmeister (Hamburg: Felix Meiner, 1955), p. 124; *Lectures on the Philosophy of World History: Introduction: Reason in History*, p. 104. Hereafter the work and its English translation are cited as *VPW*.

nation as the bearer of infinite life, for Hegel it is through the state that we transcend the finitude of civil society. But despite these differences, Hegel's organic state, like Fichte's *Kulturnation,* requires the formative work of *Bildung. Bildung* plays a fundamental role in binding the citizen to the state because it enables the individual to be "*at home* and *with itself* [*einheimisch und bei sich*] in this *externality* as such" (*PR,* § 187A, 7:344; 225). This power of self-actualization is already implicit in the self-perpetuating organism's ability to preserve its identity. But the organism is finite and can only arrest death temporarily. Only a being that transcends natural finitude can genuinely overcome death. Such a being would have an essence that is no longer at variance with its external shape because its concept is actualized in the universal form of a self-determining rational consciousness. Hegel calls this higher being "spirit [*Geist*]." Spirit has a higher life that endures beyond the death of immediate, sensuous existence because like the phoenix, it has emerged from the experience of death: "the life of Spirit is not the life that shrinks from death and keeps itself untouched by devastation, but rather the life that endures [*erträgt*] it and preserves itself in it. It wins its truth only when, in utter dismemberment [*Zerrissenheit*], it finds itself" (*PG,* 3:36; 19). Its infinite vitality is a magical power (*Zauberkraft*) that derives from its ability to linger (*verweilen*) with and borrow the negativity of death. It bears death within itself, surpasses it, and lives on.[64] Spiritual negativity has an affirmative dimension: it confers upon the particular a truth or spiritual meaning that transcends its immediate, transient and perishable existence.

Spirit belongs to the realm of freedom. As a self-moving being, an animal is an end for itself. However, because it does not possess self-consciousness, it cannot grasp this principle. Hence, an animal cannot produce the external conditions of its existence. It is not self-determining because the grounds

---

64. As Jean Hyppolite notes, human existence rises above animal life because "the animal is unconscious of the infinite totality of life in its wholeness, whereas man becomes the for-itself of that totality and internalizes death." See Hyppolite, "The Concept of Existence in the Hegelian Phenomenology," in *Studies on Marx and Hegel,* trans. John O'Neill (New York: Basic Books, 1969), p. 26. See also "The Concept of Life and Consciousness of Life in Hegel's Jena Philosophy," 3–21, in the same volume. The various figures for this internalization of death include the risking of life in the relation of lord to bondsman, spirit's willing submission to the promise of a beautiful death under the yoke of the law when confronted with meaningless death (the French Terror), and the willingness to sacrifice one's life to protect that of the state.

of its existence remain outside itself. In contradistinction, spirit is fully self-determining because it can take itself as the object of its own thought, grasp the grounds of its existence, and produce and transform them. Spirit persistently actualizes itself § through its own activity because it liberates itself from all externally imposed limits and conditions. As Hegel puts it, "its freedom does not consist in static being, but in a constant negation of all that threatens to destroy freedom. The business of spirit is to produce itself, to make itself its own object, and to gain knowledge of itself; in this way, to exist for itself. . . . The spirit produces and realises itself in the light of its knowledge of itself; it acts in such a way that all its knowledge of itself is also realised" (*VPW*, 55–56; 48).

Hegelian spirit is a more secure basis for joining organic life to culture than Kant's idea of a technic of nature. Spirit's self-actualization is the self-recursive externalization present in animal life raised to self-consciousness. This process is nothing other than *Bildung,* which is the self-conscious ability to remain at home with oneself in the other. This leitmotif governs the three modalities of Hegel's concept of *Bildung:* universal spirit's metaphysical self-formation; individual spirit's pedagogical education and cultivation and the work the individual engages in to satisfy his needs; and the collective anthropological processes of socialization and accession to political belonging.[65]

In its most basic meaning, *Bildung* is the formal aspect of thought that confers universal form onto particular material or given content, raising the latter to universality through negation.[66] This mental process is fundamental to the *Bildung* of universal spirit, understood as the entire historical development of the human species qua supranatural self-conscious being

---

65. As György Márkus notes, *Bildung* is an operational concept in Hegel's system. He uses the term in diverse ways, but does not give an analytical account of its different meanings and how they are connected. See "The Hegelian Concept of Culture," *Praxis International* 6, no. 2 (July 1986): 114–15, to which the following discussion is indebted. Hegel's main references to *Bildung* have been collected together in one volume with various critical commentaries by Hans-Georg Gadamer, Karl Löwith, Otto Pöggeler, and others in a companion volume. See Jürgen-Eckardt Pleines, ed., *Hegels Theorie der Bildung. Band I: Materialen zu ihrer Interpretation* and *Band II: Kommentare* (Hildesheim: Georg Olms, 1983, 1986).

66. See *VPW*, 65–66; 57: "[*Bildung*] is a formal category, and is always construed in terms of universal properties. . . . *Bildung* can . . . be defined quite simply as the imposition [*aufgeprägt*] of a universal quality upon a given content." Cf. *PR,* § 20, 7:71; 52: "The cultivation of the universality of thought is the absolute value of *Bildung.*" Theoretical *Bildung* is concerned with refining our ways of cognition. Practical *Bildung* is the purification of principles of action.

from natural immediacy to universality.⁶⁷ This power to reflect upon and regulate (*hemmen*) one's movement, to master one's natural immediacy through the mediation of thought, is not merely an attribute of subjective spirit. It is paradigmatic of spiritual activity as such, which consists of the ontological movement of turning in upon oneself: "This function of mediation [*Vermittelung*] is an essential moment of the spirit. Its activity consists in transcending and negating its immediate existence so as to turn in again upon itself [*die Rückher in sich*]; it has therefore made itself what it is by means of its own activity. Only if it is turned in upon itself [*Zurückgekehrte*] can a subject have real actuality [*reelle Wirklichkeit*]" (*VPW*, 57–58; 50).⁶⁸

From an anthropological viewpoint, *Bildung* is a type of spiritual work through which individuals can attain rational self-determination. Through the imprinting of universal form, a person can cast aside and raise up (sublate) his immediate natural existence and transfigure it into a second, spiritualized nature.⁶⁹ Thus, *Bildung* is associated with the purification of the crudity (*Roheit*) and barbarity of selfish drives through reflective comparison, dissection, and discipline.⁷⁰ It is the precondition of free ethical action because it enables us to see things from the multiple perspectives of others. It leads to the renunciation of one-sidedness and particularity, and to action in accordance with universal principles.⁷¹ More importantly, *Bildung* is also the purposive process of labor (*Arbeit*), where an idea is externalized and gains the shape of an object at the same time that the external world is appropriated and idealized by the subject.⁷² Labor is here a spiritual activity that forms (*bilden*) a second nature in which we recognize our reason.

---

67. The preface of *PG* describes the metaphysical process of *Bildung* in terms of the *Bildung* of the universal individual or self-conscious spirit (3:31; 16) and the history of the *Bildung* of the world (3:32; 16). *Bildung* takes on a specific *Gestalt* in each epoch of its history.

68. Cf. *PG*, 3:33; 16–17: "regarded from the side of universal Spirit as substance, *Bildung* is nothing but its own gift of self-consciousness, the bringing-about of its own becoming and reflection into itself."

69. See *VPW*, 58; 50–51: "Man can only fulfil himself through *Bildung* and discipline. . . . [He] must realise his potential through his own efforts, and must first acquire everything for himself, precisely because he is a spiritual being; in short, he must throw off all that is natural in him."

70. See *PR*, § 20, 7:71; 52.

71. See *VPW*, 66; 57: "The cultured [*gebildete*] man recognises the different facets of objects; all of them are present to him, and his fully developed [*gebildete*] powers of reflection have invested [*gegeben*] them with the form of universality. . . . [He] thus acts in a concrete manner; he is accustomed to act in the light of universal perspectives and ends."

72. As Hegel puts it, "(a) in laboring, I make myself immediately into the thing, a form which is *Being* [*Sein*]. (b) At the same time I externalize this existence of mine, making it something alien to

Hegel's conception of labor radicalizes the connection between culture and freedom. Kant had proscribed *techne* as a form of heteronomy, but had recuperated the higher technic of *Bildung* as a phenomenal analogue of freedom. Hegel makes *techne* integral to freedom by expanding *Bildung*'s self-recursive causality to include laboring activity. The products of labor are self-recursive mediating devices because the externalization is always already an appropriation.[73] As Manfred Riedel points out, Hegel dissolves the classical subordination of production (*poiesis*) to activity (*praxis*). The agent's activity (*energeia*) is not extinguished in the object, for it is not sundered from the agent. It is instead a form of support and an important means for the agent's self-preservation.[74] Labor is a concrete basis for actualizing freedom because formative activity, the laboring subject, and the product exist in a relation of ongoing reflexive interdependence and mutual feedback.

Hegel's integration of the sphere of labor into practical philosophy and his connection of moral freedom to the experience of modern industrial society consummate the implicit ontological presuppositions of earlier idealist claims that cultural work is the means for actualizing freedom. *Bildung* is not merely a simulacrum bridging sensible and supersensible worlds

---

myself and preserve myself therein. In the very same thing I see my being-recognized [*Anerkanntsein*], being as knowing [*Wissendes*]. . . . I therefore see my being-recognized as [my] existence [*Dasein*], and my will is this counting-for-something [*dies Gelten*]." *Jenaer Realphilosophie. Vorlesungmanuskripte zur Philosophie der Natur und des Geistes von 1805–1806*, ed. Johannes Hoffmeister (Hamburg: Felix Meiner, 1969), 217; *Hegel and the Human Spirit: A Translation of the Jena Lectures on the Philosophy of Spirit, 1805–6, with Commentary*. 13. Hereafterthe work and its English translation are cited as *JR*.

The section on lordship and bondage in *PG*, 3:153–55; 117–19, is the classical discussion of *Bildung* as objectivational work. Willy Moog suggests that a dialectical concept of work is already found in Hegel's *System der Sittlichkeit* (1802–3). See Moog, "Der Bildungsbegriff Hegels," in *Hegels Theorie der Bildung. Band II*, ed. Jurgen-Eckhart Pleines, p. 73. Cf. Karl Löwith's discussion of Hegel's concept of work in the Jena *Realphilosophie* in *From Hegel to Nietzsche: the Revolution in Nineteenth Century Thought*, trans. David E. Green (New York: Holt, Rinehart and Winston, 1964), pp. 265–270. This conception of labor is the basis of Hegel's pioneering incorporation of economic phenomena and social institutions as essential components of moral philosophy. See K.-H. Ilting, "The Structure of Hegel's 'Philosophy of Right'," in (ed.), *Hegel's Political Philosophy: Problems and Perspectives*, ed. Z. A. Pelczynski (Cambridge: Cambridge University Press, 1971), pp. 107–9; and Manfred Riedel, *Between Tradition and Revolution*, pp. 139–47.

73. *JR*, 218; 124: "I have accomplished something [and] have [thereby] externalized it from myself. This negation is positive; this externalization is an appropriation [*Erwerben*]."

74. *Between Tradition and Revolution*, pp. 8–9, 19–20.

(Kant's cosmopolitan society of culture), or the sensuous appearance of divine life (Fichte's *Kulturnation*). It is a fundamental moment of the concept's self-actualization, the precondition and ontological paradigm of *concrete* moral and political freedom: "*Bildung*, in its absolute determination, is therefore *liberation* [*Befreiung*] and *work* [*Arbeit*] towards a higher liberation; it is the absolute transition to the infinitely subjective substantiality of ethical life, which is no longer immediate and natural, but spiritual and at the same time raised to the shape [*Gestalt*] of universality. . . . *Bildung* is an immanent moment of the absolute, and . . . it has infinite value" (*PR*, § 187A, 7:344–45; 225–26).

Hegel's suggestion that culture is the paradigm of normative action (because action is the unity of an ideational moment and the process of actualization) may be his greatest legacy to practical thought. Henceforth, anyone who assumes a fundamental connection between culture and freedom is a Hegelian whether or not this inheritance is acknowledged. We have forgotten this connection because culture has been dissociated from its ontological roots and reduced to an educational or civilizing process or to a superstructure. Yet, all concrete activities such as political action, labor, and daily practice necessarily presuppose the ontological power to unify thought and reality that was culture's original preserve.

Hegelian *Bildung*, however, has decidedly quietistic implications. The various concrete historical shapes of universal spirit's *Bildung* necessarily involve alienation (*Entfremdung*), a form of externalization (*Entäußerung*) without return to self. The solution to alienation in modernity is to accept the ideal state's authority. Understood from an individualistic (and therefore limited and deficient) standpoint, *Bildung* is alienating because the subject transforms his natural self according to cultural norms issuing from a world (cultivated society) that appears to him as alien. The spiritual self formed from the subject's appropriation of the external world is therefore alien to his original self, which has to be cast off (*aufheben*).[75] Hegel stylizes the world of *Bildung* as the *modern* epoch of *self-alienated* spirit, where the subject cannot recognize itself in the external world, which it views as a corruption of nature.[76] The worker undergoes a related form of

---

75. See *PG*, 3:364; 298. Cf. Robert Bernasconi, "Comment on Religion and Culture in Hegel," in *Hegel's Philosophy of Action*, ed. Lawrence S. Stepelevich and David Lamb (Atlantic Highlands, N.J.: Humanities Press, 1983), pp. 117–18.

76. This epoch is epitomized by the Enlightenment and its critiques of religious faith, the vanity of the social world of the ancien regime, and the oppressiveness of its political institutions. It comes

degeneration in modern civil society, which is also based on nonselfrecursive forms of mediation, namely, the pursuit of particularistic needs and interests. In an instrumentalist, technological civilization with an entrenched division of labor, the worker's products are alienated from him and he lives in a condition of economic inequality.

For Hegel, the antidote to these evils can be found in a fuller understanding of *Bildung,* where the existing world is not viewed as opposed to individual spirit, but as the broader social and institutional context and substrate in which it develops itself and gains objective existence. If the subject can recognize the external world as its substance, the externalization that occurs in labor and cultivation will not be alienating. It will be spirit's actualization in the external world, its return to itself from objective reality. *Bildung* should therefore be understood as a socializing process. By interiorizing the standards and customs of civil society and, later, the political community, at the same time that he externalizes his ideals by participating in forms of ethical life in which they can be actualized, the individual becomes part of an existing articulated whole.

The *Philosophy of Spirit* in the 1830 *Encyclopaedia* glosses this with the generic narrative of the *Bildungsroman.*[77] Youth is a season of restless antithesis and anomie, typified by the struggle between subjective universality (youthful ideals, hopes, and ambitions) and immediate individuality (the inadequacy of the world to the ideal requirements of youth and the inadequacy of the youth to actualize his ideals). Hegel links youthful idealism to revolutionary ardor and enthusiasm. The youth is driven to transform (*umzugestalten*) the world, and to set it right where it has gone out of joint. But he is perpetually disappointed in the existing world, which he sees as contingent and accidental, because it is inadequate to the ideal:

The fact that the substantial universal contained in his ideal . . . has already succeeded in explicating [*Entwicklung*] and actualizing [*Verwirklichung*] itself, this is not perceived by the enthusiastic spirit [*schwärmenden Geiste*] of youth. To him the actualization of the universal seems a lapse from it. For this reason he feels that both his ideal and his own personality are not recognized by

to full crisis in the French Terror, where the world of *Bildung* itself cannot be sustained because all existing reality has been rejected as corrupt. See "Der sich entfremdete Geist. Die Bildung," *PG,* 3:359–441; 294–363.

77. The following paragraphs on youth are a gloss on *EPG,* §§396–396Z, 10:75–86; 55–64.

the world, and thus the youth, unlike the child, is no longer at peace with the world. (*EPG*, § 396Z, 10:83; 61–62)

Bildung teaches the youth to renounce his revolutionary enthusiasm and submit to the existing world by recognizing its actual rationality, its existence as the substrate of his rational activity and not its obstacle.[78] Instead of (unreasonably) demanding that the world recognize his ideals, the youth forms himself by adapting to temporal interests so that his ideals can be actualized. He yields his subjectivity to civil society's imperatives and develops the ability to undertake realistic economic activity by becoming practically acquainted with the material details of mundane life, such as daily labor and professional fulfilment, becoming an adult in the process.[79]

Bildung in this optimal sense is the individual's immersion and participation in objective spirit, that is, the shared customs and values, the ethical substance that enables meaningful reciprocal action in a collective setting. In the youth's passage to civil society, the ontological topos of being at home with oneself is literalized as habituation to and habitation within one's profession and enterprise.

With his entry now into practical life, the man may well be vexed and morose about the state of the world and lose hope of any improvement in it; but in spite of this he finds his place in the world of objective relationships and becomes habituated to it and to his work [*lebt in der Gewohnheit an dieselben und an seine Geschäfte*]. . . . [T]he longer the man is active in his work, the more does this universal rise into prominence out of the welters of particulars. In this way he gets to be completely at home in his profession [*in seinem Fache völlig zu Hause zu sein*] and grows thoroughly accustomed to his lot.

(*EPG*, § 396Z, 10:85; 63)

More importantly, *Bildung* also facilitates the passage from civil society to the state because "it is through this work [*Arbeit*] of *Bildung* that the subjective will attains *objectivity* even within itself, that objectivity in which alone it is for its part worthy and capable of being the *actuality* of the Idea"

---

78. See *EPG*, § 396Z, 10:84; 62.
79. See *EPG*, § 396Z, 10:85; 63: "*Bildung* alone is not enough to make him a complete, mature man; he becomes such only through his own intelligent concern for his temporal interests."

(*PR*, § 187A, 7:345; 225). *Bildung* enables the private individual to recognize that in modernity, the ideal state is the only political framework where the pursuit of particular interests can be united with the pursuit of universal ends.

The contrast between Hegel's quietism and Kant's populism or Fichte's radicalism is most pronounced here. As adaptation to existing social and political structures, *Bildung* leads to political realism. The mediation of corporations, official bodies and civil servants qua representatives of the executive is a crucial part of *Bildung*. Through the publicness (*Öffentlichkeit*) of the Estates Assembly's proceedings, the people become educated in and gain respect for the functions, abilities and virtues of official bodies and civil servants.[80] Conversely, the direct *Bildung* of civil servants in ethics and thought secures the rational identification of citizen and state because "the conduct and *Bildung* of the officials is the point at which the laws and decisions of the executive come into contact with individuals and are translated into actuality."[81] This seamless mediation between citizen and state remedies the defective forms of mediation found in civil society by returning them to spirit. *Bildung* thus affirms the state as the highest form of objective spirit in which alienation is overcome because the Idea is actualized.

VOLKSGEIST: THE APPARITIONAL SUPPLEMENT OF THE RATIONAL STATE

We should not be over-hasty in denouncing the statist tendency of Hegelian *Bildung*. It is a direct development of the organismic solution that Kant offered to solve the problem of freedom's actualization. It is arguable that in his definition of life as the concept's externalization through self-recursive mediation, Hegel revives preformationist ideas and deprives the organism of the epigenetic qualities Kant and Fichte attributed to it.[82] Consequently,

---

80. See *PR*, §§ 315–315Z, 7:482–83; 352. Publicness is a *Bildungsmittel*, the most important means for educating the people about the state's interests. The public assembly is a "great spectacle of outstanding educational value [*bildendes Schauspiel*] to the citizens."

81. See *PR*, §§ 295–96, 7:463–64; 334–35. The quotation is from § 295A.

82. Hegel reintroduces the Aristotelian idea of the soul as the principle of life that Kant rejected. Hence, in his view, the life process produces nothing *new* because everything is predetermined by the self-identical concept. See *PG*, 3:198; 156: "The organism does not produce something but only preserves itself; or, what is produced, is as much already present [*vorhanden*], as produced."

as a metaphor for the political relation, organic vitality does not refer to the individual's remaking of political conditions through the imprinting of ideal forms, but to the individual's articulation as a subjective moment within the self-preserving state-organism. Nevertheless, we must remember that a certain circularity is unavoidable in any argument that freedom's auto-causality is or can be actualized in an existing self-end or self-returning object such as the organism, culture, or the ideal political body. Such self-recursiveness is not inherently mystifying or totalitarian. It is the structure of self-determining reason itself. As Hegel repeatedly stresses, the organic state is reason in a concrete institutional shape. An oppressive state does not exhibit reason's organismic self-recursivity.

However, the ideal state also undergoes a form of self-alienation which suggests that reason's self-actualization is always haunted by the irreducible possibility of self-loss. For in its transition to world history, the organic state requires the supplementation of something other in order to be itself: *Volksgeist*. The *Volksgeist* appears on the scene to solve the problem of the state's ineluctable finitude. The ideal state may be infinite to its citizens, but it remains a finite particular vis-à-vis other states in the absence of efficacious international law. Hence, interstate relations are in a state of nature, and the norms of any state are infected by finitude, "the ceaseless turmoil not just of external contingency, but also of passions, interests, ends, talents and virtues, violence [*Gewalt*], wrongdoing, and vices in their inner particularity. In this turmoil, the ethical whole itself—the independence of the state—is exposed to contingency" (*PR*, § 340, 7:503; 371). Hegel attempts to affirm the ideal state's infinity by appealing to a higher teleological time: world history. The institutionalization of certain norms, he argues, coincides with the direction of world-historical progress. Although they can be modified, these norms cannot be revoked because they retain their universal validity in later stages of development. In any given epoch, the world spirit will be vested in one state, whose actions will have universal normative force. The eligibility of a given state to assume the mantle of world spirit depends on the character of its national spirit (*Volksgeist*), as manifested in the quality of its institutions. Hence, in world history, the ultimate measure of whether a state is the actualization of the Idea is the national community and all its spiritual products. Only something like "national culture" provides the strongest ties between individual and state, for it gives the state *absolute* legitimacy in its citizens' eyes. In modernity, the world spirit is vested in the (Prussian-led) German nation.

The fact that national culture is crucial to the smooth functioning of state institutions reaffirms *Bildung*'s fundamental connection to the ideal state. Just as a citizen undergoes *Bildung* in his identification with the state, the nation's spiritual activity also consists of "*Bildung*, over-development [*Überbildung*], and mal-development [*Verbildung*]" (*VPW*, 65; 56). The nation's *Bildung* is the concept in a self-consciously externalized shape.[83] Here, freedom takes the sensuous shape of objects that exemplify in themselves reason's self-incarnational power. These cultural objects are "the essentially necessary phenomena in which spirit appears as self-activating and self-determining" (*VPW*, 120; 101). Just as individual spirit recognizes itself in and as the product of its own labor and activity, culture is the mode and medium of the national spirit's self-particularization. A nation's various cultural products or spiritual powers (*Mächte*) are its self-determined activity in an objective shape: "its activity consists in making itself into an actual [*vorhandenen*] world which also has an existence in space. Its religion, ritual [*Kultus*], ethics, customs, art, constitution, and political laws—indeed the whole range of its institutions, events, and deeds—all of this is its own creation [*Werk*], and it is this which makes the nation what it is" (*VPW*, 67; 58). These powers are both the national spirit's content and the self-generated means enabling it to know its underlying principle. These media enable the nation to appear to itself and shape itself so that it can know and distinguish itself from other nations. The various branches of culture are thus means of national self-consciousness. They are "the spirit's relationships to itself," self-recursive mediatic devices that reflect the national spirit back into itself in its externalization (VPW, 122; 102).

More importantly, these cultural powers are also the *sensuous, affective* means for legitimating the state's role in world history. For Hegel, national culture enables a state's citizens to see and know the rational unity between their individual spirits and the national spirit. It infuses the citizen's identification with the state with such absolute conviction that the state becomes a second, infinite nature so inseparably fused to the citizen that it cannot

---

83. "The universal which emerges and becomes conscious within the state, the form to which everything in it is assimilated, is what we call in general the nation's *Bildung*" (*VPW*, 114; 96).

be transcended.[84] Its institutions, history, and cultural heritage, Hegel suggests, should be regarded as the property of every single citizen, "just as they are its property for it is their very substance and being. Their ideas are fulfilled within it, and their will affirms the laws of their fatherland. . . . The individuals belong to this spirit; each of them is the son of his nation. . . . The spiritual being is his being, and he is its representative; he arises out of it and exists within it. It is this which constitutes the objective element in all men, and everything else is purely formal" (*VPW*, 122; 103). Indeed, since the individual only achieves concrete existence by expressing the national spirit, anyone attempting to escape the national spirit must disintegrate in air, like a body trying to abandon the earth as its center of gravity (*VPW*, 95; 81)!

Hegel's conceptualization of the state undergoes a decisive mutation here. The *Volksgeist* introduces national-cultural ties into the identificatory or recognitive relation between individual and state that exceed the citizen's love for state institutions (constitutional patriotism). Hence, the state is no longer "the strictly political state" or even the broader ethical community formed from the organic unity of the three moments of modern *Sittlichkeit* (family, civil society, and state). It has a cultural dimension.

> The spiritual individual, the nation—in so far as it is internally articulated [*gegliedert*] so as to form an organic whole—is what we call the state. The term is ambiguous, however, for the state and the laws of the state, as distinct from religion, science, and art, usually have purely political associations. But in this context, the word 'state' is used in a more comprehensive sense, just as we use the word 'realm' to describe spiritual phenomena. A nation should therefore be regarded as a spiritual individual, and it is not primarily its external side that will be emphasised here, but rather what we have previously called the spirit of the nation, i.e. its self-consciousness in relation to its own truth and being, and what it recognises as truth in the absolute sense—in short, those spiritual powers which live within the nation and rule over it. . . . The actual state is animated by this spirit in all its particular transactions, wars, institutions, etc. This spiritual content is a firm and solid nucleus which is completely removed from the world of arbitrariness, particularities, caprices,

---

84. See *VPW*, 59–60; 52.

individuality, and contingency; whatever is subject to the latter is not part of the nation's character. (*VPW*, 114–15; 96–97)

This expanded definition of the state refers to the political state's embeddedness within the web of cultural relations that engenders it, enables it to function smoothly, and from which it derives its vital strength.[85] Hegel's idea of *Bildung* undergoes a related change. Previously, it did not refer to a people's *cultural identity,* but to the process whereby individuals recognize the state as the substrate for their pursuit of particular ends. Now, however, *Bildung* becomes *nationalized.* It is identified with a people's spirit. Because the citizens of a state embodying the world spirit become aware of their state's absolute right from its culture, the ethical substance that individuals must take over as their own through adaptation (*haben sich ihm anzubilden*) now includes a nation's state of knowledge and its arts and so on, in addition to the state's laws and social customs (*VPW*, 67; 58).

Hegel's *Volksgeist* is not a naturalistic, genetic principle like Herder's conception of national spirit. It is a minimal cultural identity, a self-consciousness that becomes aware of itself through its historical development as objective institutions and other cultural powers. Although it is an animating principle underlying the religion, knowledge, arts, and political institutions of a nation, it is shaped by and only becomes actual through these historical formations (*VPW*, 64–65; 56). Hegel emphasizes that the nation's spiritual activity and culture are not shaped by a primordial national identity: "the objective existence of this union [of the individual will and the universal substance of reason] is the state, which is accordingly the basis and focus [*Mittelpunkt*] of the other concrete aspects of national life—of art, justice, customs, religion, and science" (*VPW*, 124; 104). The branches of national culture necessarily take the state as their focal point because the state is self-determining reason or freedom in its concrete manifestation and culture is

---

85. Z. A. Pelczynski points to the shift in the basis of Hegel's definition of the state from *Sittlichkeit* to *Volksgeist.* See "Political Community and Individual Freedom in Hegel's Philosophy of State," in *The State and Civil Society,* ed. Pelczynski, pp. 56–57. The "expanded" state is anticipated in Hegel's suggestion that constitutions cannot be imposed from outside because they are shaped by the national spirit's character: "since the state, as the spirit of a nation, is both the law which *permeates all relations within it* and also the customs and consciousness of the individuals who belong to it, the constitution of a specific nation will in general depend on the nature and *Bildung* of its self-consciousness"(*PR*, § 274, 7:440; 312).

the means of reason's self-recursive externalization. The *Volksgeist* is the most spectacular example of the reversion of politics to culture we have seen so far. Culture and the state inhabit a relationship of organismic reciprocity or mutual feedback. The state as objective reason shapes the various cultural powers even as culture ensures the state's smooth functioning by giving sensuous proof of its rationality, thereby sublating and raising the merely political state into the infinity of the world spirit.

National culture's mediatic function is not per se ideological as long as it is coextensive with the self-recursivity of reason. We will see in the next chapter that the appeal to national culture is a pervasive theme of revolutionary decolonization in Asia and Africa. Ideally, national culture should enhance the unity of individual interests and the ideal political body's universal end. But we cannot assume this in Hegel's case. Despite his insistence that the state's constitution is the framework for individuals to develop themselves fully, his vagueness about how the organic state can give meaningful political expression to individual subjectivity indicates a structural instability in his theory.[86] Moreover, Hegel's state is a monarchy, where citizens live under the hegemony of an authoritarian bureaucratic elite. For state and individual to achieve genuine reconciliation, the civil service and the Estates should be mediating organs that impart rational universality to the particularity of the masses even as the state becomes an empirical universality in the subjective shape of a rational public consciousness. However, Hegel depicts an ethical whole split into two opposed collective subjects. Patriotism consists of two distinct components, which he ascribes to different social groups: habitual faith based on feeling and educated insight.[87] "The political *disposition*, i.e. *patriotism* in general, is certainly based on *truth* (whereas merely subjective certainty does not originate in *truth,* but is only opinion) and a volition which has become *habitual* [*Gewohnheit*]. . . . This disposition is in general one of *trust* (which may pass over into more or less educated [*gebildeter*] insight), or

---

86. Robert Pippin argues that Hegel's relative silence on what specific laws can meet the particular needs of citizens undermines the reconciliation of individual and state. See Pippin, "Hegel's Political Argument and the Problem of *Verwirklichung*," pp. 523–30. Cf. Raymond Plant, *Hegel* (Bloomington: Indiana University Press, 1973), p. 192.

87. My discussion relies on György Márkus, "Political Philosophy as Phenomenology: On the Method of Hegel's *Philosophy of Right*," *Thesis Eleven* 48 (February 1997): 1–19.

the consciousness that my substantial and particular interest is preserved and contained in the interest and end of an other (in this case, the state)" (*PR*, § 268, 7:413; 288).

Although *Bildung* can transform faith into insight, faith is only rational in a qualified sense. Hegel generally associates habit with the extinction of vitality in old age and death because it is unthinking.[88] He also distinguishes patriotism from merely subjective bonds of national belonging because the organic ties binding members of the modern state are secured by objective institutions: "such factors as the love of the people, character, oaths, coercion, etc. may be regarded as *subjective* guarantees; but when we are dealing with the *constitution,* we are concerned solely with *objective* guarantees or institutions, i.e. with organically linked and mutually conditioning moments" (*PR*, § 286A, 7:457; 328). And yet, the organic state *is* built on habitual sentiment. On the one hand, the middle class, which largely consists of the civil service and officialdom, embodies "the educated [*gebildetete*] intelligence and legal [*rechtliche*] consciousness of the mass of the people" (*PR*, § 297, 7:464; 335). It is the backbone of the state "as far as integrity [*Rechtlichkeit*] and intelligence are concerned" because it possesses "a political consciousness [*Bewußtsein des Staates*] and is the most conspicuously educated class" (*PR*, § 297Z, 7:464; 336). In stark contrast, "the people" refers to citizens who do not even know their own will because they lack insight and profound cognition. They must defer to officials who, by virtue of their "more profound and comprehensive insight into the nature of the state's institutions and needs," are better able to assist the Estates in providing universal welfare and public freedom (*PR* § 301A, 7:469–70; 340). Patriotic consciousness is thus irreparably split into two social subjects: the philosophically cultivated bureaucrat who belongs to the universal class and acts to further the universal good he grasps *objectively* as rational knowledge, and the mass citizen-subject who supports the state on merely *subjective* grounds, habitual trust formed from nonreflective emotional commitment.

This reliance on habitual trust suggests that the ideal state is not the source of eternal life, but disposed towards death. Its splitting reproduces internally the border between life and death. From this perspective, Hegel's

---

88. See *EPG*, § 396Z, 10:85–86; 63–64.

appeal to the *Volksgeist* as an absolute form of state legitimation is the ultimate *subjective* guarantee of political unity. The state can always deploy the nation's cultural powers to deepen the nonreflectiveness of popular patriotism. This degeneration of political feeling into a surrogate for religious belief is especially ironic given that Hegel initially distinguished the organic state from organized religion on the grounds that "the state possesses *knowledge*" because it is spirit that has passed through the universal form of *Bildung,* whereas Church doctrine appeals to faith, feeling, and subjective conviction (*PR,* § 270A, 7:425; 299). The *Volksgeist* can lead to blind cultural nationalism at this point, especially if we recall the quietism of Hegel's organismic metaphor, where the organicity of the political body does not refer to the people's self-organization, but to organization by the state, the articulation of the masses by the spread of knowledge from the top down to prevent the formation of a rebellious aggregate.

The important question is how we should understand this blindness. Hegel's quietism is customarily viewed as symptomatic of the historical limits of his political imagination, for instance, his deference to the reactionary Karlsbad decrees of the Restoration state. One might argue that because Hegel arrests the productive tension between statist and societalist elements in in favor of the former, the *Volksgeist* can easily become an official ideology.[89] The problem, however, goes beyond the historicist diagnosis of the limits of a given thinker. For what is undermined is precisely Hegel's conceptualization of freedom as the self-recursive externalization of reason. Despite Hegel's antipopulism and monarchism, his attempt to provide a concrete political medium for the actualization of freedom remains exemplary today. Its continuing legacy is twofold. First, Hegel defines freedom as the self-determination of reason, views *Bildung* as the paradigmatic activity for the actualization of freedom as a *concrete* state of existence, and models the incarnational process on organic life. Second, like Fichte, he territorializes culture in the nation-state. But something has gone awry with the ideal state. Instead of being the incarnation of self-determining reason, most of its members are alienated from its rationality because it demands habitual obedience and secures it through the subjective ties of national culture.

---

89. I am extending the thesis of Arato, "A Reconstruction of Hegel's Theory of Civil Society," to include the idea of *Volksgeist,* which he does not consider.

　　Hegel was undoubtedly wrong to think that freedom was actualized in the Prussian state. But can those who subscribe to the same topos of incarnation and view freedom as an ideal to be actualized say with indisputable conviction that freedom has been successfully actualized anywhere today? Instead of holding out for an ever-receding historical telos where freedom, unlike Beckett's Godot, will arrive, we might understand the ideal state's infection by the *Volksgeist* as an original or constitutive disruption of the teleological time of reason's self-incarnation. This haunting is not an external accident.[90] The cultural powers are mediations that originate from reason itself as part of its self-recursive externalization. To become actual, reason has to externalize itself. It has to open itself up to alterity. But in becoming other to itself, it risks losing itself in an other that is not simply *its* other, a mere foil for it to reflect back on and into itself. This radical contamination of teleological time marks all political organicisms. In Hegel's philosophy, alterity does not take the form of an inhuman technic of nature. It is a defective form of *techne* that cannot be organicized. Because Hegel tried to overcome the abstract nature of Kantian freedom under the rubric of *Verwirklichung,* the actualization of freedom is no longer dependent on a favor from nature. Human *techne* is not proscribed as long as these mediating devices are returned back to reason as their original source and final end. The possible use of national *Bildung* to reinforce alienation in the ethical whole is thus a nonrecursive form of technical mediation. It is a radical finitude that cannot be transcended by rational work because it inheres in the process of rational work itself and is the internal condition of possibility of ideologization. It is the condition of possibility of freedom's actualization *and* its condition of impossibility, a constitutive double bind that must be interminably negotiated.

　　Because the incarnational process is always figured in organismic terms, this internal possibility of failure is also an interminable dying, a haunting that cannot be exorcised. In territorial models of freedom, this haunting mainly occurs along the hyphen between nation and state. In constituting itself, the Hegelian state necessarily becomes vulnerable to a form of *techne*

---

90. This is the basic premise of historicism, which is essentially the belief that rational work can overcome historical limitations. Historicist critiques of Hegel should reckon with the fact that Hegel is an arch-historicist. He defines history as the process of reason's development and return to itself from the accidents of the external world.

that cannot be converted into life. Instead of being a spiritual organism and the Idea's highest objective incarnation in history, it can always become a nonactual, phantom body, possessed by the specter of *Volksgeist*. One can find other examples of contamination in Hegel's corpus. In military self-sacrifice, which "seems to be more mechanical and not so much the deed of a *particular* person as that of a *member* of a whole," the state also becomes a mindless machine, whose members are deprived of vital self-determination (*PR*, § 328A, 7:496; 365). The fact that this contamination moves in the opposite direction from Fichte's *Addresses*, where the living nation becomes corrupted by the mechanical state, indicates that regardless of whether the principle of eternal vitality is located in the nation or the state, life always bears within itself the shadow of death.

The next chapter explores the reemergence of these motifs in Marxist cosmopolitanism and socialist decolonization. Marx repeats Hegel's identification of concrete freedom with *Bildung* when he urges a return to the concrete reality of vital human labor. However, in his exorcism of the Hegelian state as a nonactual entity held together by the phantom bonds of nationalist ideology, he deterritorializes culture by projecting it into the cosmopolitan shape of a proletarian revolution. The persistence of the national question in Marxism, especially in decolonizing nationalism, is a reterritorialization of culture. Many theories of decolonizing nationalism rely on definitions of revolutionary national culture that are strikingly similar to Hegel's idea of *Volksgeist*. Because these practical discourses rehearse the Hegelian topos of actualization, they are afflicted by the same movement of becoming phantomatic that accompanies any attempt to incarnate freedom. We will be especially concerned with the becoming-phantomatic of the nation-form, which, despite its shortcomings, has historically become the most effective bearer of freedom in the postcolonial South. Decolonizing nationalism and radical popular postcolonial nationalism are the most urgent contemporary actualizations of the philosopheme of culture as actualization. Their vicissitudes perform its unraveling.

REVOLUTIONS THAT TAKE PLACE IN THE
HEAD: MARX AND THE NATIONAL QUESTION
IN SOCIALIST DECOLONIZATION

In the organism we have been following, the proletariat, Actuality is as plain as day to the dialectician. The movement of the proletariat, its seeking after the realization of its potentialities is plain. . . . But the bureaucracies, the organizations, the parties, these no longer express *the movement. . . . There is due now the total reorganization into something new. As Marcuse remarks in* Reason and Revolution, *the category of Actuality means merciless struggle.*

C. L. R. James, Notes on Dialectics: Hegel, Marx, Lenin

"**M**arx's philosophy of history," Jean Hyppolite once observed, "cannot be understood apart from the Hegelian philosophy which so strongly influenced it. . . . [I]t will not be possible to supersede Marxism until there has been a serious examination of the *philosophical presuppositions* and *structure* of the Marxian edifice."[1] This provocation is nowhere more apposite than in the case of Marx's views on the national question. Marx conceived of the proletarian revolution in incarnational terms from the beginning: "The emancipation of the German is the emancipation of man. The head of this emancipation is philosophy, its heart the proletariat. Philosophy cannot actualize [*verwirklichen*] itself without the sublation [*Aufhebung*] of the proletariat, and the proletariat cannot sublate itself without the actualization [*Verwirklichung*] of philosophy."[2] But despite all the energy expended in debates about what Marx meant by *nation,* and the appropriate place of nationalist movements in the proletarian revolution, the connection between his critique of nationalism and the organismic ontology he inherited from Hegel has never been explored.

---

1. Jean Hyppolite, "On the Structure and Presuppositions of Marx's *Capital,*" in *Studies on Marx and Hegel,* trans. John O'Neill (New York: Basic Books, 1969), pp. 148–49.
2. *Zur Kritik der Hegelschen Rechtsphilosophie. Einleitung,* I, 2:183; "A Contribution to the Critique of Hegel's Philosophy of Right: Introduction," *EW,* 257. Hereafter cited as "Hegel Critique I."

Marx's critique of nationalism is best expressed in the famous aphorism from the *Manifesto of the Communist Party* (1848): "The Communists are further reproached with desiring to abolish the fatherland and nationality. The working men have no fatherland. We cannot take from them what they have not got."[3] Elsewhere, he is even more acerbic: "The nationality of the worker is neither French, nor English, nor German, it is *labour, free slavery, self-huckstering*. His government is neither French, nor English, nor German, it is *capital*."[4] Yet, despite this emphatic deterritorialization of the proletarian movement, the wave of nationalist uprisings throughout Europe from the middle of the nineteenth century onward generated a series of qualifications, beginning with Marx's own reactions to Irish and Polish nationalism, that are subsumed under the rubric of "the national question in Marxism." After the breakup of the Second International, it is generally conceded that the national question became a major blind spot in socialist thought that urgently requires redressing if the proletarian movement is to remain an effective vehicle of freedom in the contemporary world. Indeed, by historical irony, the last major wave of socialism took the shape of national liberation movements in Asia and Africa. As E. J. Hobsbawm notes, "the general movement towards independence and decolonization, especially after 1945, was unquestionably identified with socialist/communist anti-imperialism, which is perhaps why so many decolonized and newly independent states, and by no means only those in which socialists and communists had played an important part in the struggles of liberation, declared themselves to be in some sense 'socialist.' National liberation had become a slogan of the left."[5]

This chapter examines Marx's determination of the nation-form as a phantomatic ideology that impedes the formation of cosmopolitan proletarian consciousness from a double perspective. It connects the problems

---

3. *Manifest der Kommunistischen Partei* (1848), 543; *Rev*, 84. Hereafter the work and its English translation are cited as *MKP*.

4. "Über Friedrich Lists Buch *Das nationale System der politischen Ökonomie*," *Beiträge zur Geschichte der Arbeiterbewegung*, no. 3 (1972): 437; "Draft of an Article on Friedrich List's Book *Das nationale System der politischen Ökonomie*," in Karl Marx and Friedrich Engels, *Collected Works*, vol. 4 (New York: International Publishers, 1975), 280. Hereafter cited as "List Critique."

5. E. J. Hobsbawm, *Nations and Nationalism Since 1870: Programme, Myth, Reality*, 2d ed. (Cambridge: Cambridge University Press, 1992), pp. 149–50.

of Marx's organismic vitalism to the persistence of the national question in Marxist debates, especially in socialist decolonization. These debates cast doubt on Marx's conviction that freedom is only actualizable in a deterritorialized community. The writings of Amilcar Cabral and Frantz Fanon are exemplary socialist attempts to reterritorialize freedom. They seek to reincarnate the nation Marx wished to exorcise by arguing that the decolonizing nation and its culture are the most effective vehicles for human emancipation because imperialism has transformed the contradiction between capital and labor into a geopolitical division between metropolitan nations and the colonized or neocolonized periphery. It is my contention that the failure of decolonization has broader implications for the incarnation of freedom as such.

THE WORLD COMMUNITY OF PRODUCTIVE LABORERS: MARX'S DETERRITORIALIZATION OF FREEDOM

In Marx's view, the material basis of proletarian cosmopolitanism has been laid by exploitation on a global scale through international commerce and the establishment of a global mode of production.

> The need of a constantly expanding market for its products chases the bourgeoisie over the whole surface of the globe. It must nestle everywhere, settle everywhere, establish connections everywhere.
>
> The bourgeoisie has through its exploitation of the world market given a *cosmopolitan* character [*kosmopolitisch gestaltet*] to production and consumption in every country [*Länder*]. To the great chagrin of reactionists, it has drawn from under the feet of industry the national ground on which it stood. All old-established national industries have been destroyed or are daily being destroyed. They are dislodged by new industries, whose introduction becomes a life and death question for all civilized nations, by industries that no longer work up indigenous raw material, but raw material drawn from the remotest zones; industries whose products are consumed, not only at home, but in every quarter of the globe. In place of the old wants, satisfied by the productions of the country, we find new wants, requiring for their satisfaction the products of distant lands and climes. In place of the old local and national seclusion and self-sufficiency, we have all-round intercourse [*Verkehr*], universal interdependence

of nations. And as in material, so also in spiritual [*geistigen*] production. The spiritual creations of individual nations become common property. National one-sidedness and narrow-mindedness [*Beschränktheit*] become more and more impossible, and from numerous national and local literatures, there arises a world literature.

. . . [The bourgeoisie] compels all nations, on pain of extinction, to adopt the bourgeois mode of production; it compels them . . . to become bourgeois themselves. In one word, it creates a world after its own image [*eigenen Bilde*].

(*MKP,* 529–30; 71)

In the mere fifty-three years between the materialist and idealist cosmopolitanisms of the *Manifesto* and Kant's *Perpetual Peace,* a sea change has occured. Nationality was not even an issue for Kant. Marx, however, characterizes the nation and its appendages—national economy, industry, and culture—in naturalistic, primordial terms and suggests that they are already being eroded by capitalist cosmopolitanism and its imminent successor, the proletarian world community!

The nation's imminent obsolescence is a necessary consequence of Marx's economistic definition. Nations are the subjective epiphenomena of the material boundaries of capitalist industry and the regulatory social, legal, and political forms required for their functioning. Their borders correspond to the territorial limits of production and consumption processes. They are neither ethnolinguistic communities nor communities of cultural descent, but political communities, where sovereignty is a superstructure of economic processes. Marx inherits this nonanthropological definition of the nation (already present in his presocialist writings) from Hegel's equation of nationality with political membership in a sovereign state.[6] After its augmentation with class analysis, the statist definition of the

6. In his early critique of Hegel, Marx dissociates the people (*Volk*) from the nation because nationality emanates solely from and is a function of the monarchical state. See *Zur Kritik der Hegelschen Rechtsphilosophie,* I, 2:39–40; "Critique of Hegel's Doctrine of the State," *EW,* 97. Hereafter cited as "Hegel Critique." This is why Marx describes the Jew as having a "chimerical nationality" as opposed to the "actual [*wirklichen*] nationality" of the (Christian) state. *Zur Judenfrage,* I, 2:142; "On the Jewish Question," *EW,* 213. For an incisive discussion of various misreadings of Marx's conception of the nation, see Roman Rosdolsky, "Worker and Fatherland: A Note on a Passage in the *Communist Manifesto,*" *Science and Society* 29, no. 3 (summer 1965): 330–37. Rosdolsky is unaware that this definition of the nation comes from Hegel. See Z. A. Pelczynski, "Nation,

nation becomes linked to modern capitalism. The nation is an epiphenomenon of a specific type of state. It corresponds to a *deficient* stage of
industrial production controlled by an underdeveloped bourgeoisie. The
German bourgeoisie is exemplary. Because it is weak, it is afraid of international competition and uses the nation as an ideological alibi to disguise its
interests as general interests that the political state should recognize.[7]
"[The German philistine] wants to be a *bourgeois,* an exploiter, inside
[*nach innen*], but he wants also not to be exploited outside [*nach außen*].
He puffs himself up into being the 'nation' in relation to the foreign [*nach
außen*] and says: I do not submit to the laws of competition; that is contrary to my national dignity; as the nation I am a being superior to huck-
stering. . . . [T]his commonality of interest [*Gemeinschaftlichkeit*], which is
directed against the proletariat inside, is directed against the bourgeois of
other nations outside. This the bourgeois calls his *nationality*" ("List Critique," 436–37; 280–81). The nation is thus not primordial. It is a phantasmatic fabulation of a retarded bourgeoisie, which arrests the cosmopolitan
tendencies of civil society by cathecting the accidental territorial limits of
production with a national identity. These limits are retraced as an existen-
tially meaningful inside and outside *of a nation,* when they are actually the
result of arbitrary territorial demarcations, industrial production being
spatially boundless.[8] The German nation's material backwardness makes it
the exemplary nation. Its *national* character is especially predisposed to
ideology.

Insofar as the nation belongs to the immediate stage of capitalist production, national chauvinism is an anachronistic form of ideological mystification akin to religious superstition and the sentimental ties of feudal
communality. It hearkens back to "natural" forms of exploitation that rely
on "intimate" interpersonal relations.

Civil Society, State: Hegelian Sources of the Marxian Non-Theory of Nationality," in *The State and
Civil Society: Studies in Hegel's Political Philosophy,* ed. Z. A. Pelczynski (Cambridge: Cambridge
University Press, 1984), pp. 262–78.
7. For a fuller discussion of Marx's critique of List, see Roman Szporluk, *Communism and Nationalism: Karl Marx versus Friedrich List* (Oxford: Oxford University Press, 1988), pp. 30–42.
8. The English translation obscures this point by supplying "inside" and "outside" with an object,
"the country" (*Land*). "Country," however, misleadingly suggests an emotional collective identity,
whereas Marx's point is that nationality does not have a primordial or "motivated" basis.

There is still the appearance of a relationship between owner and land which is based on something more intimate than mere *material* wealth. The land is individualized with the lord. . . . It appears as the inorganic body of its lord. . . . In the same way the rule of landed property does not appear directly as the rule of mere capital. Its relationship to those dependent on it is more like that of a fatherland. It is a sort of narrow nationality. . . . [The workers are partly linked to the lord] through a relationship based on respect, submissiveness and duty. His relation to them is therefore directly political, and even has a *cordial [gemüthliche]* aspect. Customs, character, etc. vary from one estate to another and appear to be one with their particular stretch of land; later, however, it is only a man's purse, and not his character or individuality, which ties him to the land.[9]

This analogy to the ties binding the worker to the feudal estate suggests that the nation has a weak ameliorative dimension. It provides the appearance of a natural collective-psychological or emotional barrier against the dehumanizing effects of capital. However, the sensuously seductive character of national ties also make it an ideological mask for bourgeois interests in less developed territories.

In Marx's view, the national state will inevitably disappear for two reasons. First, capital develops by denuding all illusions and shattering all barriers that mask and restrict it until it appears in its naked and universal form. Thus, universal competition gradually dissolves the territorial barriers that impede the global spread of commerce, and commercial, financial, and communicational networks will integrate the world into a monstrous totality, and so on. Large-scale industry "destroyed as far as possible ideology, religion, morality, etc., and where it could not do this, made them into a palpable lie. It produced world history for the first time, insofar as it made all civilised nations and every individual member of them dependent for the satisfaction of their needs on the whole world, thus destroying the former natural exclusiveness of separate nations."[10] The global totality that cosmopolitan bourgeois society builds in its own image may be more

---

9. *Ökonomisch-philosophische Manuskripte (Zweite Wiedergabe)*, I, 2:359–60; *Economic and Philosophical Manuscripts*, in *EW*, 318. Hereafter the work and its English translation are cited as *OPM*.
10. *Die Deutsche Ideologie*, 49–50; *The German Ideology*, 81. Hereafter the work and its English translation are cited as *DI*.

dehumanizing than national-statist forms of capital. But it is paradoxically also a more progressive stage in the unfolding of capital's true nature as a concrete universality. It is even a vital revolutionary force. As the negative mirror image of the world community of socialized labor, it is both the positive condition of revolution and also that which revolution should destroy.

Second, in the event that the nation's passing is not precipitous enough because of the tenacity of anachronistic national interests, universal exploitation also creates a universal class in advanced countries that has been dispossessed and freed of any illusory national identifications by utter immiseration. "Generally speaking, large-scale industry created every-where the same relations between the classes of society, and thus destroyed the particularity of the various nationalities. And finally, while the bour-geoisie of each nation still retained separate national interests, large-scale industry created a class which in all nations had the same interest and for which nationality is already dead; a class which is actually rid of all the old world and at the same time stands pitted against it" (*DI*, 50; 82). This is the proletariat.

The antagonism between proletarian cosmopolitanism and nationalism is thus premised on a collapsing of the nation into the state. Marx envi-sions a historical scenario in which national states are no longer able to command the loyalty of their proletariat. The masses are able to recognize the nation as a tool of oppression because the hyphen between nation and state has been rendered so tight that it has completely disappeared. Hence, Marx was more concerned about abolishing the state apparatus than the nation-form. National differences and antagonisms will automatically be eradicated with the end of class exploitation because they are merely its expressions. The phantom of a phantom (the abstract state), nationality was already becoming obsolete. Its dismantling would not require much effort: "In proportion as the exploitation of one individual by another is overcome [*aufgehoben*], the exploitation of one nation by another will also be overcome. In proportion as the antagonism between classes within the nation vanishes, the hostility of one nation to another will come to an end" (*MKP*, 543; 85).

Marx's deterritorialization of freedom can be summed up as follows. The presocialist Marx distinguished the people from the nation and located popular emancipation in civil society as the site of universal, democratic political participation. But he is not yet a cosmopolitanist because civil society is territorialized. He only becomes so after the introduction of class analysis. Because economic activity transcends territorial borders, modern civil society is inherently cosmopolitan: "It embraces the whole commercial and industrial life of a given stage and, insofar, transcends the state and the nation, though, on the other hand again, it must assert itself in its external relations as nationality and internally must organise [*gliedern*] itself as a state" (*DI*, 25–26; 98). The proletarian revolution must be directed against the national state because it contradicts the unbounded nature of civil society qua medium and form of economic activity.

Hence, Marx does much more than merely reverse Hegel's understanding of the state to civil society relation. He deterritorializes *Bildung* by redefining it as productive labor. But more importantly, he suggests that the proletarian revolution should also explode the cosmopolitan civil society he frees from the Hegelian state because it is a product of bourgeois life. One sees here the slender conceptual regard Marx held for the nation, its lack of thickness as an object. The proletarian movement is cosmopolitan not because it is primarily opposed to any positive content of the nation but because it originates from civil society and seeks to take over and destroy the state as the guarantor of private property and exploitation. The nation is only a revolutionary target because it is a secondary appendage of the political superstructure.[11] Marx's critique of nationalism is directed at national *states*. As Roman Rosdolsky points out, he did not intend to abolish "existing ethnic and linguistic communities . . . , but . . . the *political* delimitations of peoples."[12]

But precisely because Marx uses "nation," "nationality," and "national" to describe the characteristics that a sovereign state imposes on a people, he forecloses other possible political understandings of the nation, such as a bounded "national" form of civil society, or a popular "nation," a "non-traditional" demotic unity that occupies an oppositional stance vis-à-vis the state.[13] He excludes other anthropological bases for modern political

---

11. Cf. Ephraim Nimni, *Marxism and Nationalism: Theoretical Origins of a Political Crisis* (London: Pluto Press, 1991), p. 25. Indeed, Marx may not have arrived at his economistic characterization of the nation as a bourgeois ideology if he had not already reduced the nation to an expression of the state.
12. Rosdolsky, "Worker and Fatherland," p. 335.
13. Although Marx and Engels always use "nation" to refer to a people organized as a state, "nationality" is sometimes used (mostly by Engels) to refer to ethnic communities without states,

community that cannot be reduced to the state and, hence, to economic or class interests.[14] My point here is not that Marx fails to explain why cosmopolitan civil society must nevertheless "assert itself in its external relations as nationality and internally must organise [*gliedern*] itself as a state" (*DI*, 26; 98), or why "the bourgeoisie of each nation still retained separate national interests" even though their economic activity is cosmopolitan (*DI*, 50; 82). He attempted to explain bourgeois national chauvinism and the importance of fostering national antagonisms to further economic self-interest: the minimizing of competition from "foreign" industry, the attempt to control "domestic" markets, and the use of patriotism as an ideological tool to maintain hegemony over the proletariat.[15] These explanations may not convince all of us, but they were plausible in his time. Some of them still have credence today, for instance, in the subaltern-studies critique of Indian nationalism. My point is that Marx dismisses nationalism because he reduces the nation to an appendage of the bourgeois state.[16] He argued

---

"those numerous small relics of peoples which, after having figured for a longer or shorter period on the stage of history, were finally absorbed as integral portions into one or other of those more powerful nations whose greater vitality enabled them to overcome greater obstacles." Friedrich Engels, "What Have the Working Classes To Do with Poland?" (31 March 1866), *First International*, pp. 383–84. Engels explicitly distinguishes between the principle of nationality, the right of self-determination of ethnic communities, which he rejects, and the principle of nations, the right of national existence of the historic peoples of Europe (Poland, Italy, Germany, and Hungary), which he endorses because they are large and well-defined "national bodies of undoubted vitality" (ibid., 382). This idea of a historic people, which is clearly derived from Hegel's *Volksgeist*, is alien to Marx's conception of the nation. See Roman Rosdolsky, *Engels and the "Nonhistoric" Peoples: The National Question in the Revolution of 1848*, trans. John-Paul Himka, special issue of *Critique* 18–19 (Glasgow: Critique Books, 1986); Michael Löwy, *Fatherland or Mother Earth? Essays on the National Question* (London: Pluto Press, 1998), pp. 22–27; and Nimni, *Marxism and Nationalism*, pp. 26–42.

14. This is the central premise of Benedict Anderson's *Imagined Communities: Reflections on the Origin and Spread of Nationalism*, 2d ed. (London: Verso, 1991). Hereafter cited as *IC*.

15. Cf. Michael Löwy, "Marxists and the National Question," in *On Changing the World: Essays in Political Philosophy from Karl Marx to Walter Benjamin* (Atlantic Highlands, N.J.: Humanities Press, 1993), pp. 55–56.

16. There are also specific tactical reasons for Marx to hold these opinions during the period of the First International, such as his polemics against the appeal to nationalist mobilization in Europe by some of his socialist antagonists, most notably, Bakunin (democratic pan-Slavic national self-determination) and Lassalle (Prussian-led German nationalism), and his reservations about the movement for independent national socialist parties and union groups (although he finally favored a resolution endorsing this movement). In addition to delaying the class struggle, Marx regarded these as moves that would weaken the fragile international alliance of workers' unions, making them vulnerable to militarism and reformism within the ideological framework of the

that history was in the process of unmasking the economic truth behind the national illusion, and he interpreted the 1871 Prussian-French collaboration to crush the Paris Commune in the aftermath of the Franco-Prussian War as nationalism's death-knell: "Class rule is no longer able to disguise itself in a national uniform; the national governments are one as against the proletariat!"[17]

However, the Polish and Irish liberation struggles and the popular national uprisings of 1848 provided other historical signs that contradicted his narrow economistic and statist understanding of the nation. They led Marx to distinguish between the nationalism of developed bourgeois states and the nationalism of oppressed, colonized peoples, and he began to espouse tactical support for the latter. This modification is best indicated by his changing views on Poland and Ireland. In 1847, Marx saw the liberation of Ireland and other oppressed peoples as dependent on the victory of English Chartism, which he regarded as the most advanced proletarian movement: "The victory of the proletariat over the bourgeoisie," he pronounced, "also signifies the emancipation of all downtrodden nations. . . . Thus the victory of the English proletariat over the English bourgeoisie is of decisive importance for the victory of all oppressed peoples over their oppressors. Poland, therefore, must be freed, not in Poland, but in England."[18] In February 1848, he described the 1846 Cracow uprising as a model of socialist revolutionary nationalism for Switzerland, Italy, and Ireland: "The Cracow revolution has given all of Europe a magnificent example by identifying the cause of nationhood with the cause of democracy and the liberation of the oppressed class. . . . Poland . . . has taken the initiative . . . and from now on its liberation has become a point of honour for all the democrats in Europe."[19]

But Marx's most drastic reevaluation of the nationalism of oppressed peoples is his characterization of colonialism in Ireland as the most volatile form of exploitation because it is the exploitation of one people by

---

bourgeois democratic state (the subsequent reason for the breakup of the First International). For a fuller discussion, see Horace B. Davis, *Nationalism and Socialism: Marxist and Labor Theories of Nationalism to 1917* (New York: Monthly Review Press, 1967), chap. 2.

17. Marx, "The Civil War in France: Address to the General Council," *First International*, p. 232.

18. "Speech on Poland," (*Deutsche-Brüsseler Zeitung*, 9 December 1847), *Rev*, p. 100.

19. "Speech on Poland," (Brussels, 22 February 1848), in *Rev*, p. 105.

another: "The destruction of the English landed aristocracy in Ireland is an infinitely easier operation than in England itself . . . because it [the *land question*] is a question of existence, a *question of life and death* for the majority of the Irish people, because at the same time it is inseparable from the *national* question."[20] Instead of being dependent on the proletarian movement in the metropolitan center (England), Irish liberation is now a prerequisite and even the strategic catalyst of the English proletarian revolution. "The English working class will never achieve anything before it has got rid of Ireland," Marx wrote to Engels in 1869. "The lever must be applied in Ireland. This is why the Irish question is so important for the social movement in general."[21]

Marx's revised view of Irish independence articulates key principles that will be developed in the Marxist theory of national self-determination.[22] First, he suggests that proletarian emancipation necessarily involves the emancipation of oppressed peoples elsewhere because the exploitation of other peoples through colonization is intimately connected to the exploitation of workers within the "domestic" space of a colonial power. Both forms of exploitation are part of a system, and they have a common oppressor, the bourgeoisie. Second, imperial pride reinforces national chauvinism, the ideology by which bourgeois hegemony is maintained internally, by breeding hatred amongst the proletariat and preventing the formation of international solidarity: "this antagonism between the two groups of proletarians [Irish and English] within England itself is artificially kept in being and fostered by the bourgeoisie, who know well that this split is the real secret of preserving their own power."[23] The popular classes of a colonizing power perpetuate their own bondage by acquiescing to colonialism because "a people which subjugates another people forges its own chains."[24] Third, the emancipation of the proletariat within a colonizing nation must be coordinated with, and even take as its starting-point, the liberation of the oppressed nation because this will drain away the ideological, political, and

---

20. Marx to Meyer and Vogt (9 April 1870), in *First International*, p. 168.
21. Marx to Engels (10 December 1869), in *First International*, p. 167.
22. See Michael Löwy, "Marxists and the National Question," p. 57.
23. "The General Council to the Federal Council of French Switzerland" (1 January 1870), in *First International*, p. 117.
24. Ibid., p. 118.

economic strength of the dominating class in the oppressor nation. The English proletariat must work to end the enforced union between the two countries because it will lead to social revolution in Ireland and, subsequently, to emancipation in England.

In his reflections on the Irish question, Marx modifies his economistic understanding of the nation. He clearly distinguishes Irish nationalism from economic interests. But more importantly, where he earlier saw the nation as an ideological impediment to the worker's emancipation, he now sees anti-colonial national sentiment as a progressive subjective condition qualitatively distinct from the consciousness of economic exploitation. Indeed, national consciousness will accelerate the process of emancipation faster than the mere consciousness of economic suffering: "the overthrow of the landed aristocracy . . . will be infinitely easier . . . because in Ireland *it is not only a simple economic question* but at the same time a *national* question, because the landlords there are not, as in England, the traditional dignitaries and representatives of the nation but its mortally hated oppressors."[25] While this revised view of national consciousness may be specific to the Irish situation, it is provocative precisely because it resonates with Marx's unelaborated idea of the proletarian nation that occupies the interregnum between the bourgeois national state and the proletarian world community found in the *Manifesto,* which implies a nonbourgeois, nonstatist understanding of "nation": "Since the proletariat must acquire political supremacy, must rise to be the leading class of the nation, must constitute itself as the nation, it is, so far, itself national, though not in the bourgeois sense of the word" (*MKP,* 543; 84).

But this liberation of nationalism from economistic reductionism is immediately undercut by the fact that Marx's endorsement of the independence of oppressed peoples is the automatic corollary of his condemnation of "bad" oppressor nationalism. Nationalism is a by-product of the colonial shape taken by capitalist exploitation. It is not valuable in itself but only as a "lever" for overcoming the latter.[26] The value accorded to

25. Marx to Kugelmann (29 November 1869), in *First International,* p. 165. The emphasis on "national" is Marx's.

26. That Marx's endorsement of anticolonial movements only applies to European countries is further evidence of his economistic understanding of nationalism. Although he condemns British imperialism in India, he sees it as an unconscious tool of history that prepares Asia for social revolution by

'good' anti-colonial nationalism remains economically determined in the last instance because it is a moment within the process of capital's development and sublation by proletarian cosmopolitanism.

EPIGENESIS OF LABOR: THE *VERWIRKLICHUNG* OF HUMANITY AND THE PROLETARIAN REVOLUTION AS APPROPRIATION

The issue here is not simply that Marx failed to offer a progressive nonstatist or noneconomistic account of the nation as a viable communal form for the attainment of human freedom, but *why* he so adamantly refused to see nationalism otherwise despite evidence to the contrary. Why does Marx relentlessly refer all nationalisms back to either the bourgeois state or the overcoming of class oppression by proletarian cosmopolitanism? Why is the efficacy (or lack thereof) of any given nation for achieving freedom always subordinated to the class struggle? It is commonly argued that the persistence of the national question proves the myopia of Marx's interpretation of historical currents, especially industrialism. But Marx also insists on the national state's imminent demise because it fetters the *boundless* character of production. The national question is closely related to the organismic ontology informing his theory of labor, and a consideration of his inheritance from German idealism is necessary to the formulation of an adequate conceptual vocabulary for understanding the national question.

The labor process—the production of material objects for use and exchange—is colloquially more real than ideational activity because it concerns the mundane needs of human beings. Marx's argument, however, is not a vulgar realism. Production is intimately connected to freedom. It has finitude-transcending capacities essential to the formation of a genuinely universal community in which humanity can be actualized. For Marx,

---

shattering the foundations of Oriental despotism. See Marx, "The British Rule in India" (10 June 1853), in *Surveys from Exile*, vol. 2 of *Political Writings*, ed. David Fernbach (Harmondsworth, U.K.: Penguin, 1973), pp. 301–7. For discussions of Marx's Eurocentrism, see Nimni, *Marxism and Nationalism*, pp. 11–14; Löwy, *Fatherland or Mother Earth?* ch. 2; and Horace B. Davis, "Nations, Colonies and Social Classes: The Position of Marx and Engels," *Science and Society* 29, no. 1 (winter 1965): 26–43.

labor is a form of auto-causality, a process of self-actualization ontologically unique to humanity. Its defining feature is the ability to incarnate ideas and actualize the potentiality in nature and the human subject as part of nature: "What distinguishes the worst architect from the best of bees is that the architect builds the cell in his head [*in seinem Kopf*] before he constructs it in wax. At the end of every labour process, a result emerges which had already been conceived by [*in der Vorstellung*] the worker at the beginning, hence was already ideally present [*vorhanden*]. Man not only effects [*bewirkt*] a change of form in the materials of nature, he also actualizes [*verwirklicht*] his own end [*Zweck*] in those materials."[27] Hence, labor is the paradigm of our ability to produce the material conditions of life because through it we *rationally* produce our means of subsistence (*Lebensmittel*).

This understanding of labor as purposive self-actualizing activity hinges on the etymological and conceptual link between the actual (*wirklich*) and the ability of human beings to act (*wirken*) and create things to satisfy their needs. The entire arsenal of Marx's critical maneuvers—the characterization of the state and its political and legal institutions as superstructures of an economic base, the critiques of ideology, and fetishism as the mistaking of social relations for things—is etched in embryonic form here. "The social structure [*Gliederung*] and the state" are secondary entities that can be broken down and remade precisely because they "are continually evolving out of the life-process of definite individuals . . . as they actually [*wirklich*] are, i.e. as they act [*wirken*], produce materially, and hence as they work under definite material limits, presuppositions and conditions independent of their will" (*DI*, 15; 41).

The teleological conception of labor underwriting Marx's argument that humanity is actualized in proletarian cosmopolitanism is informed by German idealism's organismic ontology. Accordingly, labor is characterized by the epigenetic motifs of self-formation, growth and development, an organism's assimilation of the external world, and its reproduction as a species. Labor is an original ground in which consciousness and material activity are immediately united, just as the German idealists saw organic

---

27. *Das Kapital: Kritik der politischen Ökonomie, Erster Band* (Hamburg 1890), II, 10:162; *Capital: A Critique of Political Economy*, vol. 1, trans. Ben Fowkes (Harmondsworth, U.K.: Penguin, 1976), 284. Hereafter the work and its English translation are cited as *K1*.

life as the reconciliation of nature and rational purposiveness. "The production of ideas, of conceptions, of consciousness," Marx writes, "is at first directly interwoven with the material activity and the material intercourse of men—the language of actual life" (DI, 15; 42). Echoing Hegel's *Encyclopaedia*, Marx in his early writings described man as a finite being with species-life (*Gattungsleben*), a being that like all other animals physically needs to live from inorganic nature. However, as a universal being, man can assimilate the entire world external to its proper organic body. "[Man] makes the whole of nature his *inorganic* body [*unorganischen Körper*], (1) as a direct means of life and (2) as the matter, the object and the tool of his life activity. Nature is man's *inorganic body* [*Leib*], that is to say nature in so far as it is not the human body. Man *lives* from nature, i.e. nature is his *body,* and he must maintain a continuing dialogue with it if he is not to die. To say that man's physical and spiritual life is connected with nature simply means that nature is connected with itself, for man is part of nature" (OPM, I, 2:368–69; 328). Marx later figures this organic relationship to nature as a process of metabolism (*Stoffwechsel*), an ontological characteristic of our finite constitution, "the everlasting nature-imposed condition of human life" (K1, II, 10:167; 290).

But man has a unique place within nature. Unlike animals, human life is not merely blind or instinctive. Labor is not merely a means of life, but a self-conscious activity by which he rationally brings out and develops the true essence of his species in the objective world. Labor, as objectification, is thus at the same time, appropriation (*Aneignung*). In the later Marx's less metaphysical language, "the labour process . . . is purposive [*zweckmäßige*] activity aimed at the production of use-values. It is an appropriation of what exists in nature for the needs of man" (K1, II, 10:167; 290). Labor is

> a process by which man, through his own actions, mediates [*vermittelt*], regulates and controls the metabolism between himself and nature. He confronts the materials of nature as a force of nature. He sets in motion the natural forces which belong to his corporeality, his arms, legs, head and hands, in order to appropriate [*anzueignen*] the materials of nature in a form adapted to his own needs. Through this movement he acts upon [*wirkt*] external nature and changes it, and in this way he simultaneously changes his own nature. He develops the potentialities slumbering within nature, and subjects the play of its forces to his own sovereign power. (K1, II, 10:162; 283)

Because it bestows purposiveness and life to inanimate objects, labor is also a finitude-transcending activity. Labor is life insofar as it produces objects for consumption. But more importantly, it also gives life. Whatever is not infused by labor becomes infected by finitude, atrophies, and dies, whereas whatever retains its connection to labor lives infinitely.

> A machine which is not active in the labour process is useless. In addition, it falls prey to the destructive power of natural processes [*Stoffwechsels*]. Iron rusts; wood rots. Yarn with which we neither weave nor knit is cotton wasted. Living labour [*lebendige Arbeit*] must seize on these things, awaken them from the dead, change them from merely possible [*möglichen*] into real and effective [*wirkliche und wirkende*] use-values. Bathed in the fire of labour, appropriated as part of its organism [*als Leiber derselben angeeignet*], and inspirited with vital energy [*begeistet*] for the performance of the functions appropriate to their concept and to their vocation in the process, they are indeed consumed, but to some end [*zweckvoll*], as elements in the formation [*Bildungselemente*] of new use-values, new products, which are capable of entering into individual consumption as means of subsistence or into a new labour process as means of production. (*K1*, II, 10:166–67; 289–90)

The labor process is thus a form of self-generation. It exhibits a complete reciprocity of means and ends and a self-recursive causality. It produces to consume but consuming also serves future production and, therefore, it consumes and produces itself infinitely.[28]

More importantly, labor is also a form of social epigenesis. Because economic activity requires *social* cooperation, it transforms nature into *society*, an organic whole where humanity is the source of organization and center of reference. Unlike Hegel, Marx sees society as the rational essence of *human* existence.[29] Since society is the substrate for actualizing humanity

---

28. Cf. the discussion of the threefold identity between production and consumption as reciprocally means and ends of each other in *Grundrissen der Kritik der politischen Ökonomie*, II, 1.1:27–31; *Grundrisse: Foundations of the Critique of Political Economy*, trans. Martin Nicolaus (Harmondsworth, U.K.: Penguin, 1973), 90–94. Hereafter the work and its English translation are cited as *Grundrisse*.

29. See *OPM*, I, 2: 390; 349: "Activity and consumption, both in their content and in their *mode of existence*, are *social* activity and *social* consumption. The *human* essence of nature exists only for

in the realm of nature, the *social* individual is the ground of his own existence. Social labor is the epigenesis of humanity. Humanity incarnates/actualizes itself in genuine society by achieving freedom from the finitude of natural needs. This is why society is an organism. The early Marx defines society as a higher second nature conducive to rational ends: "*society* is . . . the perfected unity in essence of man with nature, the true resurrection of nature, the actualized [*durchgeführte*] naturalism of man and the actualized humanism of nature" (*OPM*, I, 2: 391; 349–50). The same idea of the organism as an end in itself underwrites the *Grundrisse*'s description of the production process as a social womb. Production, consumption, distribution and exchange exhibit the reciprocal means-ends relation of the parts of a self-relating organism: "they all form [*bilden*] the members [*Glieder*] of a totality, distinctions within a unity. . . . Mutual interaction [*Wechselwirkung*] takes place between the different moments. This is the case with every organic whole" (*Grundrisse*, II, 1.1: 35; 99–100). The production process is thus "the organic social body within which the individuals reproduce themselves as individuals, but as social individuals" (*Grundrisse*, II, 1.2: 698; 832).

This capacity for self-generation is crucial to the shaping of Marx's political imaginary. As the key premise of the infinite, exponential growth of productive forces, labor is the ontological source of historical dynamism, which culminates eschatologically in the proletarian revolution. The history of the class struggle is nothing other than the epigenesis of labor, its capacity for self-recursive mediation writ large and projected onto the historical plane of changing modes of production. Hence, contrary to the conventional view that it is governed by mechanical laws of motion, Marx's materialist teleology is organismic.[30] In his teleology of history, the two key moments of the organic labor process—externalization or objectification and appropriation—are magnified into labor's alienation and revolution against capital.

---

social man; for only here does nature exist for him as a *bond* with other *men*, as his existence for others and their existence for him, as the vital element of human actuality; only here does it exist as the *basis* of his own *human* existence."

30. As Shlomo Avineri observes, Marx's materialism, which takes Hegel's spiritualization of matter as its point of departure is sharply different from Engels's mechanistic materialism (later developed by Plekhanov, Kautsky, and Lenin), which deprives nature of the mediation of consciousness. See Avineri, *The Social and Political Thought of Karl Marx* (Cambridge: Cambridge University Press, 1968), pp. 65–77.

Marx's argument can be summarized as follows: the labor process is the immediate example and paradigm of human self-actualization. But the historical actualization of humanity is a collective process that requires the development of productive forces through rational social cooperation so that we can satisfy our infinitely proliferating human needs and attain higher standards of life. Hence, each stage in the development of productive forces has its own corresponding social form for the regulation of production, distribution and consumption. But the efficient development of productive forces, which reaches its highest point in large-scale industry, is necessarily premised on the division of labor, which is first manifested in the separation of intellectual and material labor. This is the primary diremption of the original unity of human activity. It leads to the alienation of the products of human activity such that they are seen as autonomous entities opposed to their producers.

The generation of self-valorizing capital through the extraction of surplus labor is likewise understood under the philosophical sign of alienation. Because all previous historical social forms belong to various stages of capital's appearance, their corresponding political and legal superstructures, and the varieties of fetishism and ideology sustaining them are marked by and perpetuate inequality. The primary diremption of human activity is thus expressed in a series of historical contradictions (*Widersprüche*), the most important of which is the contradiction between the infinitely expanding capacity of productive forces and the different social relations in each stage that impose artificial limitations upon these forces. In the capitalist mode of production, this contradiction reaches catastrophic proportions as a result of the stark juxtaposition of the abundant resources modern industry creates to satisfy human needs with the immiseration resulting from their limited distribution and consumption. Because capitalist society itself now impedes the development of productive forces, it will inevitably be overthrown by the proletarian revolution.[31] The proletarian revolution thus sublates all contradictions and diremptions. It overcomes the contradiction between society and the economic base and restores the original unity of consciousness and material activity by establishing a truly

---

31. See *Das Kapital* (*Ökonomische Manuskript 1863–1865*), *Drittes Buch*, II, 4.2:324; *Capital: A Critique of Political Economy*, vol. 3, trans. David Fernbach (Harmondsworth, U.K.: Penguin, 1981), 358: "The true barrier [*Schranke*] to capitalist production is *capital itself*." Hereafter the work and its English translation are cited as *K3*.

universal and rational form of social regulation in which labor is no longer alienated and all social inequalities are abolished. This is socialism, society in its true shape just as capitalism is capital in its naked form.

What is important for us is that just as Fichte's and Hegel's political topographies were governed by the border between life and death, Marx also figures the conflict between labor and capital as a struggle between the actual and living and the nonactual, dead, phantom, monstrous, or magical. Marx's poignant analysis of alienated labor (*Entfremdete Arbeit*) articulates six important vitalistic themes: First, the commodification of labor separates the worker from the products of his living activity, which become autonomized. As the property of an other, these products constitute an alien and hostile second nature that dominates their producer like a monstrous power (*OPM*, I, 2:365; 324). Second, the worker's subjectivity is depleted by wage-labor. Instead of being a form of *Bildung* that adds greater meaning to his life, labor is a heteronomous activity that miscultivates or deforms his inner being: "the more values he creates, the more worthless he becomes; the more his product is shaped [*geformter*], the more misshapen [*mißförmiger*] the worker; the more civilized his object, the more barbarous the worker" (*OPM*, I, 2:366; 325). Because his life activity has been reduced to a mere means of subsistence and he can no longer recognize his species-being in it or in his relations with others, the worker is eventually robbed of his humanity. Heteronomous labor undermines the Hegelian motif of being-at-home-with-oneself. The worker "does not confirm [*bejaht*] himself in his work. . . . Hence . . . [he] feels himself only when he is not working. . . . He is at home [*Zu Hause*] when he is not working, and not at home when he is working. . . . [His labor] is therefore not the satisfaction of a need but a mere *means* to satisfy needs outside itself" (*OPM*, I, 2:367; 326).

Third, capital, the spawn of alienated labor, is demonic and vampiric. It is a nonactual sensuous shape, a ghost whose source of movement lies outside itself. But it has reversed the direction of living labor's appropriation of the external world and appropriated the source of life: "by incorporating living labour into [the] dead objectivity [of commodities], the capitalist simultaneously transforms value, i.e. past labour in its objectified and dead form, into capital, value which can perform its own valorization process, an animated monster [*beseeltes Ungeheuer*] which begins to 'work', 'as if its body were by love possessed'" (*K1*, II, 10:177; 302). By parasitically draining the life from labor, the circuit of commodification and the money form transmute capital into a vital being that endlessly augments its own value such that the metabolism with nature now "appears . . . as the metabolism of capital; as the existence of circulating capital" (*Grundrisse*, II, 1.2:577; 701). However, this vitality is a form of demonic possession and the automatism of a machine.[32] Fourth, although the use of machines is not inherently dehumanizing, the division and commodification of labor has degraded it into a meaningless, mechanical process, which enables the machine to usurp the human worker in industrial production: "Since the worker has been reduced to a machine, the machine can confront him as a competitor" (*OPM*, I, 2:330; 286).

Fifth, Marx's base-superstructure (*Basis-Ueberbau*) model is a topographical projection of living labor's relation to its products.[33] The superstructure grows out of and is determined by the economic base, just as any product is produced according to the form and end prescribed to it in the true labor process. It is dependent on the base just as the product of true labor is not an autonomous object. Hence, when it or its ideological forms are perceived under alienated conditions as determining material life, they have to be recognized as prostheses devoid of actuality, re-embedded in the social relations from which they originate by immanent critique, and destroyed by social revolution. Finally, the capitalist mode of production is the furthest development of a magicized (*verzauberte*), inverted world where capital is a mystical being attributed with the productive powers of social labor (*K3*, II, 4.2:849; 966). The confusion of specifically capitalist social relations with material relations of production conjures up "the bewitched, distorted and upside-down [*auf den Kopf gestellte*] world haunted by Monsieur le Capital and Madame la Terre, who are at the same time social characters and mere things" (*K3*, II, 4.2:852; 969). Capital's magic is best exemplified by money, which is a sensuously appearing prosthetic God who can supplement all natural human deficiencies and transcend finitude. Money usurps the human power of actualization itself to the point where it can actualize the humanly impossible! It has made the

---

32. See *Grundrisse*, II, 1.2:580; 704.

33. The economic base consists of material forces of production that are articulated into a functional whole by relations of production (society), and the epiphenomenal superstructure consists of legal and political institutions and their corresponding forms of consciousness. See preface to *Zur Kritik der politischen Ökonomie*, II, 2:100–101; *EW*, 425–26.

whole of reality prosthetic and phantasmatic, so that it is virtually impossible to distinguish material life from the mystical, and the actual from the impossible.

> [Money] is the visible divinity, the transformation of all human and natural qualities into their opposites, the universal confusion and inversion of things; it brings together impossibilities [*Unmöglichkeiten*]. . . . *Money*, which is the external, universal *means* and *ability* [*Vermögen*] . . . to turn *notions* [*Vorstellung*] *into actuality* and *actuality into mere notions,* similarly turns *actual human and essential powers* into purely abstract representations, and therefore *imperfections* and tormenting phantoms [*Hirngespinste*], just as it turns *actual imperfections and phantoms*—actually impotent powers which exist only in the individual's imagination—into *actual essential powers* and *abilities.*
>
> (*OPM*, I, 2:437–38; 377–78)

It is important to emphasize that capital's phantomatic and demonic nature does not merely refer to its illusory or religious character. Capital is *of* death. It deprives the worker of any meaningful life because it is cut off from living labor and devoid of actuality. But the ghost is not simply what is dead. It is *apparitional.* It is the dead that takes on a sensuous shape and, in appearing to live, mystifies the true origin of life. In contradistinction, the proletarian revolution is living labor's return to itself. It is an organismic process of *appropriation,* where the alienated totality of productive forces is restored to individuals as social beings. Appropriation in the sociopolitical sense is the reincarnation and magnification of appropriative labor into a world historical movement against capital. It accomplishes the actualization of humanity by restoring the individual's social being and self-activity.[34]

We can see from the above that despite the notorious anticulturalism of Marx's base-superstructure model and his denunciation of spiritual products as ideologemes of the dominant class, he retains the lineaments of culture as the actualization of freedom. Proletarian appropriation is structurally identical to the organic process of *Bildung,* which Hegel elevated into the paradigm of spiritual activity. Even as he exorcises spiritual culture, Marx generalizes *Bildung*'s essential features into a model for sensuous

---

34. See *OPM*, I, 2:389; 348; *DI*, 57; 96.

transformative action.[35] The *Manifesto* describes the globalization of capital as a form of bourgeois *Bildung* that makes the world into a materially interconnected whole. But this totality is an inhuman machine that is alienated from living labor. Genuine organicization will only be achieved by the proletarian revolution, which transforms the world into a rationally organized totality of human producers. By seeking to actualize humanity in every aspect of mundane life, Marxist appropriation goes further than Hegelian spirit. Total appropriation involves the rational control and mastery of the forces and means of production in their entirety through the *incarnation* of rational consciousness as the whole material world. Through universal social intercourse, *material* productive forces, which have developed exponentially under industrialization, must be imparted with the *form* of a global totality.[36] In *Capital*, the rational takes the shape of the *social* sphere, the site of co-operative decision-making and social accounting, where "socialized man, the associated producers, govern the human metabolism with nature in a rational way, bringing it under their collective [*gemeinschaftliche*] control instead of being dominated by it as a blind power; accomplishing it with the least expenditure of energy and in conditions most worthy and adequate to their human nature" (*K3*, II, 4.2: 838; 959). In decolonization, this hidden trace of *Bildung* returns as revolutionary *national culture*. The activist literature of Pramoedya and Ngũgĩ, examples of revolutionary postcolonial nationalist discourse to be discussed later, will be informed by Marx's vitalist themes.

GHOSTLY CONSCIOUSNESS, HAUNTED ACTUALITY

I have argued that Marx's political thought is irrigated by the same organismic vitalism and philosopheme of *Bildung* found in German idealism.

---

35. On the similarities between Marx's and Hegel's understandings of actualization, see Jean Hyppolite, "Marx and Philosophy," in *Studies on Marx and Hegel*, pp. 93–105; and Karl Löwith, *Meaning in History* (Chicago: University of Chicago Press, 1949), pp. 33–51. Cf. Hannah Arendt's criticism that Marx reduced all creative work to material labor. See Arendt, *The Human Condition* (Chicago: University of Chicago Press, 1958).

36. For the argument that labor and social relations are respectively the material and formal aspects of production, which is the unity of *praxis* (social forms of interaction) and *poiesis* (labor), see György Márkus, "Praxis and Poeisis: Beyond the Dichotomy," *Thesis Eleven* no. 15 (1986): 39–40.

Unlike contemporary sociocultural constructionism and performativity theory, which are too timid to touch the substance and matter of the real, Marx's transformational sense of actuality broaches the active unity of ideality and matter itself. He dissolves objectivity into human activity and abolishes the distinction between them. As the first thesis on Feuerbach puts it, "the chief defect of all hitherto materialism . . . is that . . . actuality, sensuousness, is conceived only in the form of the *object, or of contemplation* [*Anschauung*], but not as *sensuous human activity* [*Tätigkeit*], praxis."³⁷ The revolutionary implications of this conviction that the world can and must be transformed by human activity remain important today although the proletarian revolution is no longer feasible. Ernest Mandel succinctly captures Marx's organismic view of politics as an organizational activity that actualizes the rational: "whether the potential [to bring about world socialism] will actually be realized will depend, in the last analysis, upon the conscious efforts of organized revolutionary Marxists, integrating themselves with the spontaneous periodic striving of the proletariat to reorganize society along socialist lines, and leading it to precise goals: the conquest of state power and radical social revolution."³⁸ This has become axiomatic to our understanding of normative political causality. All of us who hold on to the admirable hope that freedom can be actualized are vitalists for whom culture is the paradigm of the political.³⁹

But the empiricist and teleological grounding of Marx's materialism is inherently unstable. Despite the "epistemological break" between the pre-1845 writings, which are still concerned with the philosophical critique of ideological philosophy, and the later dialectical materialist view of history sanctioned by the aura of "science," Marx's corpus retains the Hegelian concept of actualization even as he discards its *original philosophical form* after he denigrates philosophical conceptuality as the inverted ideological reflection of material conditions.⁴⁰

---

37. "Marx über Feuerbach," 533; "Concerning Feuerbach," in *EW,* 421.
38. Ernest Mandel, introduction to *Capital,* vol. 3, pp. 89–90.
39. A similar vitalism informs Michael Hardt and Antonio Negri, *Empire* (Cambridge: Harvard University Press, 2000), which relies on the Marxist concept of reappropriation.
40. Marx situates the turn in *The German Ideology,* which he describes as a critique of "the ideological [conception] . . . of German philosophy" that is intended "to settle accounts with our former philosophical conscience" (preface to *Zur Kritik der politischen Ökonomie* (1859), II, 2:101–2; preface

My dialectical method is, in its foundations, not only different from the Hegelian, but exactly opposite to it. For Hegel, the process of thinking, which he even transforms into an independent subject, under the name of 'the Idea', is the creator of the actual world [*des Wirklichen*], which is only the external appearance of the idea. With me the reverse is true: the ideal is nothing but the material world reflected in the head of man, and translated into forms of thought [*im Menschenkopf ungesetzte und übersetzte*]. . . . With him it [the dialectic] is standing on its head [*auf dem Kopf*]. It must be inverted, in order to discover the rational kernel within the mystical shell. (*K1*, II, 10:17; 102–3)

Marx's inversion does not destroy the Hegelian topos of actualization as self-recursive *externalization*. He only corrects Hegel's understanding of externality (*Äusserlichkeit*) as alien to human essence so that *material* labor's paramount role in human self-actualization can be recognized. He praises Hegel for understanding "the self-production of man as a process, objectification [*Vergegenständlichung*] as loss of object [*Entgegenständlichung*], as externalization [*Entäusserung*] and as sublation of this externalization" (*OPM*, I, 2:404; 386).[41] For Marx, labor is also the process of "man's coming to be for himself within externalization or as an externalized [*entäusserter*] man," which Hegel grasps when he "conceives objective man—true, because actual man—as the result of his *own labour*" (*OPM*, I, 2:404–5; 386). But because Hegel defines human activity in spiritual terms, he sees the material world as the concretization of thought, its becoming-other in externality through self-conscious activity. Hence, his actuality is an inverted, ghostly actuality made up of abstract thought forms.

For Marx, the objective world is not alien to humanity because our corporeal nature consists of material activity.

---

to *A Contribution to the Critique of Political Economy*, in *EW*, 427). The phrase, "epistemological break," is Louis Althusser's. "Introduction—Today," in *For Marx*, trans. Ben Brewster (London: Verso, 1990), pp. 33–38.

41. Hegel distinguishes between *Entfremdung* (alienation) and *Entäusserung* (externalization). *Entfremdung* refers to a defective or nonrecursive form of *Entäusserung*. Although Marx radically distinguishes *Vergegenständlichung* (objectification) from *Entfremdung*, he sees *Entfremdung* as synonymous with *Entäusserung*. In *EW*, *Entfremdung* is translated as "estrangement" and *Entäusserung* as "alienation." To preserve the Hegelian origin of these terms, I have translated these words as "alienation" and "externalization" respectively. Marx's understanding of Hegel's conception of labor is based on the *Phenomenology* and not the earlier unpublished Jena philosophy of spirit.

When actual, corporeal *man*, his feet firmly planted on the solid earth and breathing all the powers of nature, posits [*setz*] his actual, objective *essential powers* as alien [*fremde*] objects by externalization, it is not the [ideational act of] *positing* [*Setzen*] which is subject; it is the subjectivity of *objective* essential powers whose action must therefore be an *objective* one. An objective being acts [*wirkt*] objectively, and it would not act objectively if objectivity were not an inherent part of its essential nature. It creates and posits only objects because it is posited by objects, because it is at home in *nature* [*von Haus aus Natur ist*]. . . . [I]ts *objective* product simply confirms its *objective* activity, its activity as the activity of an objective, natural being. (*OPM*, I, 2:407–8; 389)

By redefining actuality as objective activity, Marx acknowledges that externality is an essential aspect of human nature. Whereas for Hegel spirit's freedom derives from the fact that it contains its essence within itself, Marx recognizes the *irreducible* heteronomy of human existence, the fact that as finite, corporeal creatures, we are part of the sphere of necessity. We suffer and are susceptible to passions because we are exposed to externality in our ontological constitution.

As a natural, corporeal, sensuous, objective being [man] is a *suffering*, conditioned and limited being, like animals and plants. That is to say, the *objects* of his drives exist outside him as *objects* independent of him; but these objects are objects of his *need*, essential objects, indispensable to the exercise and confirmation of his essential powers. . . . *Hunger* is the acknowledged need of my body for an *object* which exists outside [*ausser*] itself and which is indispensable to its integration and to the expression of its essential nature [*Wesensäusserung*]. . . . A being which does not have its nature outside itself is not a natural being and plays no part in the system of nature. . . . [A] non-objective being is a non-actual, non-sensuous, merely thought, i.e. merely conceived being, a being of abstraction. (*OPM*, I, 2:408–9; 390)

However, this irreducible opening-up is held in check. Human labor differs from animal production because we have consciousness. Animal production is instinctual and occurs in immediate response to the compulsion of physical needs. Human labor, however, is characterized by *mediation*, which enables the human being to step back from, reflect upon, and regulate his activity according to rational ends that he prescribes.

Man is not only a natural being; he is a *human* natural being; i.e. he is a being for himself [*für sich selbst seiendes Wesen*] and hence a *species-being*, as which he must confirm and actualize [*bethätigen*] himself both in his being [*Sein*] and in his knowing. Consequently, *human* objects are not natural objects as they immediately present themselves, nor is *human sense*, in its immediate and objective existence, *human* sensibility and human objectivity. Neither objective nor subjective nature is immediately present in a form adequate to the *human* being. And as everything natural must *come into being*, so man also has his process of origin in *history*. But for him history is a conscious process, and hence one which consciously sublates itself. (*OPM*, I, 2:409; 391)

The practical production of an *objective world*, the *fashioning* [*Bearbeitung*] of inorganic nature, is proof that man is a conscious species-being, i.e. a being which treats the species as its own essential being or itself as a species-being. . . . Such production is his active species-life. Through it nature appears as *his* work and his actuality. The object of labor is therefore the *objectification of the species-life of man:* for man duplicates [*verdoppelt*] himself not only intellectually, in his consciousness, but actively and actually, and he can therefore contemplate himself in a world he himself has created. (*OPM*, I, 2:369–70; 328–29)

This is the same gesture Hegel used to foreclose human finitude. Human nature transcends mere nature because our rational consciousness enables us to alter given external conditions through purposive activity. The human actor's relation to externality is such that he always returns to himself. He recognizes himself in the world because he remakes it according to his ends. Hence, externality is reduced to a moment of our self-objectifying activity, to a stimulus prompting our appropriation of the world to satisfy our needs.

But for this very reason, material activity and actuality are irreducibly haunted by the apparitions of consciousness Marx tried to exorcise. We see this most clearly in his equivocal use of the phrases "in the head" and "on its head." Ideology makes "men and their relations appear upside-down [*auf den Kopf gestellt,* placed on their head] as in a *camera obscura*" (*DI*, 15; 42). For the Germans, whose economic backwardness led to a compensatory hypertrophy of philosophical consciousness at the expense of practical action, revolution only takes place *in the head:* "the Germans have *thought* in politics what other nations have *done*. . . . The abstraction and arrogance of Germany's thought always kept pace with the one-sided and stunted character of their actuality. . . . Germany's *revolutionary* past, in the form of the *Reformation,* is also theoretical. Just as it was then the *monk,* so it is now the *philosopher* in whose brain the revolution begins" ("Hegel Critique I," I, 2:176–77; 251). The critique of such alienated ideas must stand the misperception that actuality originates from the head on *its* head. It repatriates the phantom formations (*Nebelbildungen*) of national sentiment, morality, religion, and metaphysics to their true source, "actual, active [*wirklichen, wirkenden*] men, as they are conditioned by a definite development of their productive forces and of the intercourse corresponding to these" (*DI,* 15; 42). However, because Marx reduces externality to a moment within the process of human self-objectification, appropriative labor—the origin of actuality and revolutionary dynamism—is itself a teleological process that begins from within the head! With a conception (*Vorstellung*)! Hegel coined the term *alienation* to describe a nonself-returning form of mediation, a defective form of externalization that does not lead to spirit's self-actualization. The difference between Marxist alienation and appropriation is essentially the difference between two types of *Vorstellung.* Whereas appropriation involves the deployment of the good type of *Vorstellung,* which is inner-directed and returns to the human self in its externalization (either as a use-value/actualized end or as control of the forces of production), alienation involves a type of *Vorstellung* that does not return to the self and is autonomized as an alien being.

One can also understand this as a distinction between two types of prosthesis. One enhances the actualization process because it is integrated into the proper organic body and remains in the service of the living source of movement. The other perverts the course of actualization because it substitutes a phantomatic body (itself) for the true source of life, thereby infecting and usurping the organic whole. What is at stake is precisely the problem of *techne.* Marx's proletarian cosmopolitanism is premised on the technological development of productive forces. Just as Hegel does not proscribe *techne,* Marx argues that technology is crucial to humanity's self-actualization because it is an organic, self-recursive form of mediation. As the means for transforming the raw materials nature gives us, labor is already a technical activity. More complex forms of production interpose technical instruments (*Arbeitsmittel*) between the worker and the object to facilitate the labor process (*K1,* II, 10:163; 285). Such instruments are prostheses analogous to our bodily organs: "nature becomes one of the organs of his activity, which he annexes to his own bodily organs, adding stature to himself [*seine natürliche Gestalt verlängernd*—extending his natural shape] in spite of the Bible. . . . [T]he earth . . . is his original toolhouse" (*K1*, II, 10:163; 285). Hence, although *techne* entails the denaturing of nonhuman nature, it is organic to humans as tool-making animals.

By arguing that nature itself becomes technical in the labor process, Marx literalizes the Aristotelian interplay between *physis* and *techne*. By inverting Hegel, he also revives and concretizes Kant's idea of the technic of nature. Nature does not only supply raw materials. She literally lends the worker a helping hand! In more advanced stages of production, the entire earth (the sum of all objective conditions necessary for the labor process) is a "universal instrument [*Arbeitsmittel*]" because it is a material infrastructure labor has constructed (*K1*, II, 10:164; 286). Thus, although technology's alienated form leads to the worker's enslavement by the machine, it can be reorganicized, brought back within the epigenesis of labor through appropriation. The *Grundrisse* figures machines as technological *organisms* that overcome the diremption of manual and intellectual labor. "They are *organs of the human brain, created by the human hand;* the power of knowledge objectified. . . . [They indicate t]o what degree the powers of social production have been produced . . . as immediate organs of social praxis, of the real life process" (II, 1.2:582–83; 706). What is important here is not technology per se but its status as an external device that originates from the mediational power of human consciousness, a prosthesis serving freedom's self-actualization, the complete rational mastery over nature through the spiritual or material remaking of this inorganic body in humanity's image.

But like all political organicisms, Marx's socialist vision is afflicted by a radical heteronomy. His confidence in the eventual return of all prostheses to humanity is premised on consciousness's ability to regulate externality. Yet, he suggests despite himself that the possibility of malignant prostheses is originally inscribed in our mediational activity. The products of animals "belong immediately to their physical bodies, while man freely confronts his own product" (*OPM*, I, 2:370; 329). But our ability to relate to our products through the mediation of consciousness is both a gift and a curse. On the one hand, it is the precondition of appropriative labor and human self-objectification. Consciousness distances itself from the world to grasp it as an object and transform it. But this distancing from nature is also the original possibility of alienation before social alienation. Consciousness is the first tear in the fabric of human life, the sundering of the immediate self-proximity of the human individual to itself and its original unity with its environment. The generation of *Vorstellung* is the first technical and prosthetic activity, the first movement of autonomization, which social alienation merely repeats: "in tearing away the object of his production from man, alienated labor therefore tears away from his species-life, his actual species-objectivity, and transforms his advantage over animals into the disadvantage that his inorganic body, nature, is taken from him" (ibid.).

Simply put, the original possibility of alienation inheres in the incarnational process itself, which is thereby always haunted. Although idealization is essential to human freedom, this does not mean that we can always reappropriate our alienated forms. To the contrary, the mediation of consciousness is what is most inhuman because it opens us up to radical heteronomy. A conception is a double-edged tool. Its use is dependent on its permanence as an ideal, its persistence in time. But time is what we do not have. We cannot possess or control time because it is given (to us) by something radically inhuman. This inhuman gift necessarily shadows and disrupts any process of self-actualization or, which is the same thing, the self-recursivity of any organic body. My point should be rigorously distinguished from both the "postmodern" attempt to overthrow the modern subject's tyranny over nature by "dissolving" it *and* the Frankfurt School's demonization of instrumental reason. Adorno and Horkheimer acknowledge that the rational regulation of natural forces is necessary to the actualization of freedom, but criticize systemic Marxism by connecting its evils to the failure to regulate instrumental reason. But the distinction they draw between instrumental and critical reason (the power of critical reflection on our reflective powers so that our technical ability to control nature does not degenerate into domination) is decidedly organismic.[42] Like Marx, they assume that the generation of *Vorstellung,* our first prostheses, can be fully controlled by us because it is the same process of negativity that enables humanity to transcend finitude. Habermas's distinctions between communicative action and instrumental reason, life-world and system-world are governed by the

---

42. Max Horkheimer and Theodor W. Adorno, *Dialectic of Enlightenment,* trans. John Cumming (New York: Continuum, 1994).

same organismic vitalism.[43] I am suggesting, however, that creative labor's teleological time is always disruptible because what makes it possible also makes it impossible. This does not mean that the project of actualizing ideals must be renounced as utopian. It is only that actuality is inherently unstable because the incarnational process is always shadowed by the inhuman other. We have yet to come to terms with the ethicopolitical implications of this haunting.

ACTS OF CULTURE: THE RETURN OF THE NATION-PEOPLE IN SOCIALIST DECOLONIZATION

The political opposition between proletarian cosmopolitanism and idealist national statism is a schism within organismic ontology. The disagreement is only that Marx denounces what Hegel regards as actual (the ideal state) as a mystification of what he thinks is really actual: laboring activity for the fulfillment of needs and its social(ist) regulation. Thus, whereas Hegel consigns cosmopolitan civil society to the realm of accidentality and appearance and finds its substantial truth in the state, Marx sees the former as the more actual sociopolitical form because it is the objective result of living labor's self-actualizing dynamism. The national state is a fictitious entity, a malignant prosthesis that obstructs the limitless expansion of productive forces that will lead to the humanization or organicization of the material world. It elevates itself into a self-supporting being although the source of its existence lies in the society of organized labor.[44] Hence, the state must be reabsorbed into civil society and dissolved by political revolution. The phantomatic nation must be exorcised because it stifles the development of proletarian cosmopolitanism.

From this perspective, nationalism's disruption of proletarian cosmopolitanism is a historical example of the usurpation of labor's organic

---

43. Jürgen Habermas, *Theory and Practice*, trans. John Viertel (Boston: Beacon, 1974), pp. 168–69.

44. See "Hegel Critique," I, 2:124; 184: "[Hegel's organic state] is not actualized power. It is *supported* impotence; it represents not power over these supports but the power of these supports. The power lies in the supports." Pramoedya and Ngũgĩ will reverse Marx's quasi-Hegelian understanding of fiction as mere existence without actuality by giving fiction the power to incarnate freedom.

body by a bad prosthesis. The persistence of the national question signifies the infection of the *proletarian* actualization of freedom by a form of non-recursive externalization that leads to irretrievable self-loss. But in fact, the nation's continuing tenacity both affirms and undoes political organicism. For the persistence of progressive national movements from Marx's time to the postcolonial present are also reassertions of national culture's vitality and *Wirklichkeit*. Arguments about the emergence of a revolutionary national culture from anticolonial resistance, or the formation of popular nations that are irreducible to the state by print capitalism all attempt to reincarnate the ghosts of culture and the nation that Marx tried to exorcise. The nation moves back to the side of life. But in the contemporary world, where nationalisms in the postcolonial South are not unequivocal actualizations of freedom, the nation hovers between the actual and the phantasmatic, life and death, like a ghost that cannot be contained within the organismic ontology informing our thinking of freedom. This is the theoretical work the national question in socialist decolonization performs: it indicates that the teleological time of freedom's self-actualization is always haunted.

Marx's suggestion that the global emancipation of the proletariat requires the united action of "the leading civilized countries" already intimates an affinity between popular nationalism and socialism (*MKP*, 543; 85). Within the context of capital's uneven globalization, where the exploitation of one nation by another is intensified, Marx's unelaborated idea of a proletarian nation gains greater cogency. For instead of leading to the withering of the state, *colonial* and *neocolonial* global capitalism consolidates the state form because it requires strong colonial states or a global hierarchy of states divided between North and South. In such scenarios, where an emergent popular nation rises against the colonial state, or the postcolonial nation seeks to reappropriate the neocolonial state that has been alienated from it, the nation becomes a more efficacious vehicle for actualizing freedom than proletarian cosmopolitanism.

Significantly, the most important revaluation of the national question since the Second International's breakup was a response to anticolonial struggles. In 1907, Otto Bauer tried to rescue the nation from orthodox Marxist ideology critique. He reasserted its actuality by dissociating it from national spiritualism. The nation, he argued, is a community of character that has evolved epigenetically from a community of fate. It is "situated within the overall chain of events in which every cause is itself understood as an effect and everything that was initially an effect itself becomes a cause."[45] Unlike Hegel's *Volksgeist,* the modern nation is actual because it emerges with the development of productive forces and technological progress.[46] Although prosperity is important to binding a people into a nation, the nation is not an epiphenomenon of capitalism. It can only be fully actualized under socialism. "Only socialism can integrate the broad mass of the working people into the national community of culture," confer self-determination to the nation, and free it from alienation.[47]

Lenin dismissed Bauer's ideas of national unity and cultural autonomy as a "false phantom" that divides the proletariat and a fraudulent petit bourgeois ideology. But in his polemic against Rosa Luxemburg, he championed the idea of the *political* self-determination of oppressed nations.[48] Lenin formalized Marx's ad hoc views on Irish and Polish nationalism into a distinction between two successive stages of capitalism: a stage where national state formation is the norm because the nation is the condition for the intense growth of capitalist industry and bourgeois society's political victory over feudalism and absolutism, and an advanced stage where national barriers are eroded by the growth of international intercourse and the transition to socialism is imminent.[49] Contra Luxemburg's argument that national self-determination was necessarily based on metaphysical principles, he argued that it was derived from the historical experience of national movements throughout the world from the period of the formation of the bourgeois democratic state. In this form, "the national movements for the first time become mass movements and in one way or another draw all classes of the population . . . through the press, participation in

---

45. Bauer, *The Question of Nationalities and Social Democracy,* ed. Ephraim Nimni, trans. Joseph O'Donnell (Minneapolis: University of Minnesota Press, 2000), p. 31. For a fuller discussion of Bauer, see Nimni, *Marxism and Nationalism,* pp. 119–84; and Michael Löwy, "The Nation as Common Fate: Otto Bauer Today," *Fatherland or Mother Earth?* pp. 45–50.

46. Ibid., p. 85.

47. Ibid., pp. 94, 96.

48. V. I. Lenin, "Draft Platform for the Fourth Congress of Social-Democrats in the Latvian Area," in *Collected Works,* vol. 19 (Moscow: Foreign Languages Publishing House, 1963), p. 117. For a fuller discussion of Lenin's position on nationalism, see Horace Davis, *Nationalism and Socialism,* pp. 185–214; Alfred D. Low, *Lenin on the Question of Nationality* (New York: Bookman, 1958); Ronaldo Munck, *The Difficult Dialogue: Marxism and Nationalism* (London: Zed, 1986), pp. 69–87.

49. Lenin, "Critical Remarks on the National Question," *Collected Works,* vol. 20 (Moscow: Progress Publishers, 1964), p. 27.

representative institutions etc." into the struggle for political liberty and the rights of the nation.[50] This type of nationalism has actuality because of its *economic* foundations. National unity and a national language, Lenin argued, "are the most important conditions for genuinely free and extensive commerce on a scale commensurate with modern capitalism, for a free and broad grouping of the population in all its various classes and, lastly, for the establishment of a close connection."[51] "The most profound economic factors drive towards [the formation of national states] . . . , and, . . . for the entire civilised world, the national state is typical and normal for the capitalist period."[52]

Because progressive nationalism has already run its course in the period between 1789 and 1871, Western European nationalism is now reactionary and marked by the absence of mass democratic movements. But whenever the struggle for self-determination by oppressed nations occurs in the rest of world, the proletarian movement should support it because political democracy is a step closer to socialism. At the same time, this "good nationalism" should not be confused with the "bad cultural nationalism" of the bourgeoisie of oppressed nations and the chauvinistic nationalism of oppressor nations. Keeping socialism's internationalist aspirations in mind at every moment, the proletarian movement must tentatively embrace the nation, but curtail the modulation from its benign face to its evil face, especially any talk of national culture.

To throw off the feudal yoke, all national oppression, and all privileges enjoyed by any particular nation or language is the imperative duty of the proletariat as a democratic force, and is certainly in the interests of the proletarian class struggle, which is obscured and retarded by bickering on the national question. But to go beyond these strictly limited and definite historical limits in helping bourgeois nationalism means betraying the proletariat and siding with the bourgeoisie. There is a border-line here, which is often very slight.[53]

---

50. Lenin, "The Right of Nations to Self-Determination," *Collected Works*, vol. 20, p. 401.
51. Ibid., pp. 396–97.
52. Ibid., p. 397.
53. "Critical Remarks on the National Question," p. 35.

Insofar as the bourgeoisie of the oppressed nation fights the oppressor, we are always, in every case, and more strongly than anyone else, *in favour*. . . . But insofar as the bourgeoisie of the oppressed nation stands for *its own* bourgeois nationalism, we stand against. We fight against the privileges and violence of the oppressor nation, and do not in any way condone the strivings for privileges on the part of the oppressed nation. . . . The bourgeois nationalism of *any* oppressed nation has a general democratic content that is directed *against* oppression, and it is this content that we *unconditionally* support. At the same time we strictly distinguish it from the tendency towards national exclusiveness[.][54]

(As we will see, the postcolonial problem is that the slight border between progressive and oppressive nationalism, actuality and phantoms, is impossible to police.)

Because Lenin's defense of national self-determination relies on the national awakenings and anti-imperialist struggles for democracy in Asia, Africa, and other colonies after 1905 as crucial examples of progressive nationalism, these national awakenings have the same vitality as living labor. "*Hundreds* of millions of people are awakening to life, light and freedom. What delight this world movement is arousing in the hearts of all class-conscious workers. . . . [A]ll young Asia . . . has a reliable ally in the proletariat of all civilised countries."[55] Lenin thus widens the small foothold opened by Marx's tactical support for nationalism. Decolonizing nationalisms flourish in this opening. They seize this precarious foothold and augment Lenin's culturally thin notion of political nationalism with positive cultural content, in some cases even going as far as reinventing Marx's phrase, "the proletarian nation," to describe the paramount revolutionary potential of colonized nations.[56] A detailed comparative study of this

---

54. "The Right of Nations to Self-Determination," pp. 411–12.

55. Lenin, "Backward Europe and Advanced Asia," in *Collected Works*, vol. 19 (Moscow: Foreign Languages Publishing House, 1963), p. 100. See also "The Revolutionary Proletariat and the Right of Nations to Self-Determination," in *Collected Works*, vol. 21 (Moscow: Progress Publishers, 1964), pp. 407–8; "The Awakening of Asia," in *Collected Works*, vol. 19 (Moscow: Foreign Languages Publishing House, 1963), pp. 85–86; and "The Socialist Revolution and the Right of Nations to Self-Determination," in *Collected Works*, vol. 22 (Moscow: Progress Publishers, 1964), pp. 150–52.

56. For instance, by using the phrase "proletarian nation" to describe the advantages of China's backwardness for the development of socialism, Li Dazhao fused Marxism with Chinese nationalism. See Maurice Meisner, *Li Ta-chao and the Origins of Chinese Marxism* (Cambridge: Harvard

wave of revolutionary nationalisms stretching across Asia, Latin America, and Africa up to the 1970s as exemplified by China, Cuba, Algeria, Vietnam, and so on, and their shifting relations to communist internationalism is beyond the scope of this book.[57] The important point is that it gives rise to a new strain of Marxism that questions the Eurocentrism of mainstream Marxism. Instead of regarding anticolonial movements in the Third World as belated derivations of Western European bourgeois nationalism, Third World Marxist discourse privileges these nationalisms as the new bearers of socialist universalism. Moreover, because they are responses to the Eurocentrism of Western imperialism and mainstream Marxism and are produced by the interaction between indigenous religious cultural ethics and the shock of colonial capitalist exploitation and uneven development, Third World Marxisms invariably emphasized the *cultural specificity* of non-Western experiences of nationalism.

Decolonizing nationalist discourse bears two striking resemblances to German idealist nationalism. First, there is a strong sociological parallel between the important role ascribed to radical popular national culture in the anti-imperialist struggle and the general project of building a vernacular universal German culture in the eighteenth and early nineteenth centuries as an antidote to French cultural and military imperialism, and the atomizing forces of modern industrial capitalism. Second, these theories of revolutionary national culture are irrigated by the same vitalist ontology. One sees here the same organismic metaphor of the national body, the same affinity between national culture and organic life found in German idealist nationalisms. These appeals to national culture are emphatically not irrational or mystical. They do not fetishize ancient traditions, but privilege the living culture of workers and peasants in their ongoing struggle to reappropriate

---

University Press, 1967), pp. 47–48; Germaine A. Hoston, *The State, Identity, and the National Question in China and Japan* (Princeton, N.J.: Princeton University Press, 1994), pp. 195–203.

57. For accounts of the Eurocentrism of Lenin's position on non-European nationalism, his support for a tactical concilation with bourgeois nationalism, dissenting voices in the Comintern (Third International) meetings by M. N. Roy and others who favored a more revolutionary form of nationalism, the growing independence of Chinese communism under Mao from Soviet-style internationalism, and the relationship between communism and nationalism in Latin America and Africa, see Hélène Carrère d'Encausse and Stuart R. Schram, eds. *Marxism and Asia* (London: Allen Lane, Penguin Press: 1969); Horace B. Davis, *Toward a Marxist Theory of Nationalism* (New York: Monthly Review Press, 1978), pp. 165–246; and Ronaldo Munck, *The Difficult Dialogue*, pp. 88–125.

what has been alienated from the people by (neo)colonialism. Thus, the national culture Lenin rejected is radicalized and invested with the power to actualize proletarian freedom. Here, the political reverts to its original paradigm, culture, which Marxist anticulturalism had obscured.

Amilcar Cabral's and Frantz Fanon's exemplary theories of decolonizing nationalism continue this legacy. Notwithstanding his insistence on the primacy of reality over theory and the need to adapt political struggles to the specific conditions of a given society, Cabral's analyses of social stratification in Portugese Guinea and his political strategies are framed by a theory of revolutionary struggle as the overcoming of finitude. Struggle is "a normal condition of all living creatures in the world."[58] Every organism struggles to maintain its life against external forces that limit it. Such forces range from the ravages of time to active opposition and oppression from other objects. "Plants, like animals . . . contain struggle within, and there may be thousands of such struggles. But the fundamental struggle is between the capacity for preservation and the destruction which time brings to things. . . . [T]he passage of time is written on things, from man to the most trifling thing."[59] The struggle against colonial oppression is a people's self-preservation on the international political stage. "The Portugese colonialists have taken our land, as foreigners and as occupiers, and have exerted a force on our society, on our people. The force has operated so that they should take our destiny into their hands, has operated so that they should halt our history for us to remain tied to the history of Portugal, as if we were a wagon on their train."[60]

Cabral's tactical suggestions for the nationalist movement reinscribe the Leninist idea of party organization with a populist organismic twist. Because revolutionary consciousness "is not and never was spontaneous in any part of the world," the success of the nationalist struggle depends on organization, the *rational* articulation of the people into an organic unity, and its mobilization as a revolutionary force by a vanguard Party.[61] The

---

58. Amilcar Cabral, "Unity and Struggle," in *Unity and Struggle: Speeches and Writings,* trans. Michael Wolfers (New York: Monthly Review Press , 1979), p. 31. Unless otherwise noted, all quotations of Cabral's speeches come from this volume.

59. Cabral, "Not Everyone is of the Party," p. 83.

60. "Unity and Struggle," p. 32.

61. Cabral, "Presuppositions and Objectives of National Liberation in Relation to Social Structure," p. 120.

Party is therefore "a base instrument, the mother instrument. Or if we like, the principal means which creates other means linked to it. It is the root and the trunk which produce other branches for the development of our struggle."[62] Although the Party begins as the chief organ of the popular organism, it must *reciprocally* become infused by the people because it is the substrate in which the nationalist struggle thrives and its principle strength.[63] As the struggle develops and gathers momentum, the Party becomes composed only of those possessing exemplary moral conduct who serve the people. It is transformed into "a broad national liberation movement" that encompasses the mass of the people, "not a movement in name, but the hard fact of struggle, as an entirety of folk in movement against Portugese colonialism."[64] The people is therefore a *causa sui,* life itself pitted against imperialist forces and their agents, which are viruses infecting the popular organism. This organismic schema is exemplary for decolonizing nationalism and its revolutionary successors in postcoloniality. Although the schema is directly inherited from Marxism, it modifies Marx's thesis that the chief motor of history is class struggle. The fact of imperialism implies that the primary shaper of struggle for the (neo)colonized peoples that make up the mass of the world's population is not socioeconomic class, but nationalism.

Cabral argues that living labor and freedom are necessarily territorialized in a people's culture. Following Lenin, he defines imperialism as the globalization of capitalist accumulation under monopolistic finance capital. Imperialist capital exploits nations rather than classes, which are not yet developed in Asia and Africa. It vitiates a people's historical personality by violently taking away its economic freedom. Since national integrity is crucial to an effective economic whole, the fettering of productive forces occurs at the *national* level. "When they underwent imperialist domination, the historical process of each of our peoples (or of the human groups of which each is composed) was subjected to the violent action of an external factor. This action . . . could not fail to influence the process of development of the productive forces of our countries and the social structures of our

---

62. "Not Everyone," p. 85.
63. Cabral, "Struggle of the People, by the People, for the People," p. 77.
64. "Not Everyone," p. 85.

peoples."[65] To achieve optimum development, the Marxist topos of reappropriation needs to be reformulated to include the reappropriation of the historical personality negated by imperialism. This is precisely how Cabral defines national liberation: it "is the phenomenon in which a socio-economic whole rejects the denial of its historical process. . . . [T]he national liberation of a people is the regaining of the historical personality of that people, it is their return to history through the destruction of the imperialist domination."[66] Cultural autonomy is a corollary of "the inalienable right of every people to have their own history," which imperialism has violently usurped.[67]

In arguing that the nation is actual because it is integral to the development of productive forces, Cabral's materialist nationalism seems opposed to Fichte's idealist nationalism. However, in "National Liberation and Culture" (1970), Cabral gives culture a paramount role in labor's struggle for freedom. Culture is not only the fundamental precondition of the reappropriative process, it is the original source of resistance to colonial domination and precedes and lays the ground for political, economic, and social liberation.

> Whatever the conditions of subjection of a people to foreign domination and the influence of economic, political and social factors in the exercise of this domination, it is generally within the cultural factor that we find the germ of challenge which leads to the structuring and development of the liberation movement. . . . A people who free themselves from foreign domination will not be culturally free unless . . . they return to the upwards paths of their own culture. The latter is nourished by the living reality of the environment and rejects harmful influences as much as any kind of subjection to foreign cultures. . . . [I]f imperialist domination has the vital need to practise cultural oppression, national liberation is necessarily an *act of culture*. (143)

Precisely because he views culture as the paradigm and true end of political struggle, Cabral repeats the idealist philosopheme of culture as the power of human self-actualization and overturns Marx's denigration of culture as a phantomatic superstructure. Culture is the product and self-conscious reflection of a society's life, its economic and political activities,

---

65. "Presuppositions," p. 126.
66. "Presuppositions," p. 130.
67. Ibid.

and, more generally, the metabolic relations between humanity and nature. It is the source of a people's life because as an objective form of social self-consciousness, it enables a society to rationally grasp and regulate its own historical progress: "culture, whatever the ideological or idealist characteristics of its expression, is . . . an essential element in the history of a people. . . . Culture plunges its roots into the humus of the material reality of the environment in which it develops, and it reflects the organic nature of the society, which may be more or less influenced by external factors. . . . [It] enables us to know what dynamic syntheses have been formed and set by social awareness in order to resolve these [economic, political, and social] conflicts at each stage of evolution of that society, in the search for survival and progress" (142).

Hence, like Fichte, Cabral argues that culture is an indestructible refuge because it is the *Bildungstrieb* of a people's historical personality, its principle of self-preservation. He likens culture to a flower with the capacity for forming and fertilizing the germ that ensures the prospects for social evolution and progress. As long as a people continues to exist, culture survives and in turn revitalizes this people in the face of death: "as long as part of that people can have a cultural life, foreign domination cannot be sure of its perpetuation. At any given moment, . . . cultural resistance (indestructible) may take on new (political, economic and armed) forms, in order fully to contest foreign domination" (140). Because it "acts as a bulwark" that preserves a people's identity, culture safeguards the future possibility of freedom. Indeed, "the people are only able to create and develop the liberation movement because they keep their culture alive despite continual and organized repression of their cultural life and because they continue to resist culturally even when their politico-military resistance is destroyed."[68]

Fanon's definition of national consciousness in *The Wretched of the Earth* is similarly organismic. National culture is the symbolic expression of revolutionary consciousness, a form of praxis that violently negates the existing colonial framework.[69] Since individual wills are united into a

---

68. "Identity and Dignity in the Context of the National Liberation Struggle," in *Return to the Source: Selected Speeches by Amilcar Cabral,* ed. African Information Society (New York: Monthly Review Press, 1973), pp. 61, 60.

69. Fanon, *The Wretched of the Earth,* trans. Constance Farrington (New York: Grove Weidenfeld, 1963), p. 93. Hereafter cited as *WE.*

national will by revolutionary action, the nation is not a preexisting entity but something persistently reformulated by the experience of the masses in their ongoing struggle. The Mau Mau uprising in Kenya is an epigenetic process: "Every native who takes up arms is a part of the nation which from henceforward will spring to life. . . . [T]he national cause goes on progressing and becomes the cause of each and all. . . . Everywhere, we find a national authority. Each man or woman brings the nation to life by his or her action, and is pledged to ensure its triumph in their locality" (*WE*, 131–32). As the eternal source of ever-present life, the people is a self-causing absolute being that can transcend all limitations. It "legislates, finds itself, and wills itself into sovereignty. In every corner that is thus awakened from colonial slumber, life is lived at an impossibly high temperature. There is a permanent outpouring in all the villages of spectacular generosity, of disarming kindness, and willingness . . . to die for the 'cause'" (*WE*, 132).

But unorganized political spontaneity alone is insufficient. For peasant revolt to become a revolutionary war that has an enduring impact on social and political institutions, "the political education of the masses is . . . a political necessity" (*WE*, 138).[70] Hence, revolutionary action must assume an objective form that can educate mass consciousness about the aims of struggle even as this form remains capable of dynamic evolution according to the people's changing needs. This is the function of national culture. It

> is not a folklore, nor an abstract populism that believes it can discover the people's true nature. It is not made up of the inert dregs of gratuitous actions, that is to say actions which are less and less attached to the ever-present reality of the people. *A national culture is the whole body of efforts made by a people in the sphere of thought to describe, justify and praise the action through which that people has created itself and keeps itself in existence.*
>
> (*WE*, 233, emphasis added)

Fanon's Hegelian view of culture as the objectification of a people's living activity into a self-recursive mediating device, a spiritual medium that enables it to know and return to itself, also rejects the Marxist repudiation

---

70. For a fuller discussion of Fanon's argument that unorganized peasant outbursts need to be transformed into organized revolutionary violence, see B. Marie Perinbaum, "Fanon and the Revolutionary Peasantry—The Algerian Case," *The Journal of Modern African Studies* 11, no. 3 (1973): 427–45.

of culture. For Fanon, culture is a causal force in the struggle for political freedom because it gives rational organization to popular spontaneity: "the conscious and organized undertaking by a colonized people to re-establish the sovereignty of that nation constitutes the most complete and obvious cultural manifestation that exists" (*WE*, 245). Indeed, because he views the state as the product of a secondary supplementary incarnation of the people's activity, Fanon departs from Hegel. Like Fichte, he argues that national culture is the primary objectification of the national spirit. "Culture is first the expression of a nation, the expression of its preferences, of its taboos and of its patterns. . . . A national culture is the sum total of all these appraisals; it is a result of internal and external tensions exerted over society as a whole and also at every level of that society" (*WE*, 244). In contradistinction, political nationalism and the state are only the nation's secondary institutional instruments. Such institutional support becomes necessary when culture is in danger of extermination because colonial domination puts the nation itself under threat. The reappropriation of the state through national liberation is then crucial to culture's survival: "the first necessity is the re-establishment of the nation in order to give life to national culture in the strictly biological sense of the phrase" (*WE*, 245).

Fanon's biogenetic schema has the virtue of underscoring the organismic character of the sociological opposition between decolonizing nation and state. The state is the national spirit's carnal body. Both it and the political party from which it is formed are mere matter or mechanism, and their animation comes from the people: "the party is not an authority, but an organism through which they as the people exercise their authority and express their will" (*WE*, 185). A true nation-state is popular and national. States are living wholes only when they exhibit a rational unity of the government, the people, and the task of nation building. As in the political organicisms of Kant and Fichte, for Fanon and Cabral, culture is also the means by which the people organicizes the state-machine so that it is no longer a foreign body that divides the popular organism and perpetuates its alienation. Such revolutionary *Bildung* thus inherits the universal vocation of modern *Bildung*, which European colonialism has betrayed.

As a process that organicizes alien elements *within* native society, revolutionary culture has very precise sociological contours. Cabral associates it with a peasantry intimately tied to the land. In colonial Africa, the forced migration of parts of the peasantry to urban centers created a new social stratum comprising salaried workers, civil servants, and people in commerce or the liberal professions. A revolutionary vanguard arises from this urban petit bourgeoisie, who will guide the economically and socially backward peasantry.[71] But because the petit bourgeoisie is a culturally alienated stratum that has assimilated the colonizer's culture and identifies with its mentality, the vanguard must be brought back in touch with the people's culture through a process of *Bildung*. Cabral takes the Cuban revolution as a model. "A spiritual reconversion—of mentalities—is . . . vital for their true integration in the liberation movement. Such reconversion—*re-Africanization* in our case—may take place before the struggle, but is completed only during the course of the struggle, through daily contact with the mass of the people and the communion of sacrifices which the struggle demands."[72]

Such popular nationalist *Bildung* is even more urgent in the postindependence period, where the existence of a national state run by indigenous elements gives the illusion that there has been a national reappropriation of productive forces. The indigenous bourgeoisie has the ability to transform the state apparatus left by the departing colonial power in the image of the masses' aspirations. But to be revolutionary, it must renounce its objective class tendency to maintain its newly found political power and betray the revolution. In Cabral's famous words, which uncannily echo the sublative reincarnation of the Hegelian phoenix, "the revolutionary petty bourgeoisie must be capable of committing *suicide* as a class, to be restored to life in the condition of a revolutionary worker identified with the deepest aspirations of the people to which he belongs."[73] *Bildung* is the indispensable condition for this *Aufhebung:* "if national liberation is essentially a political question, the conditions for its development stamp on it certain characteristics that belong to the sphere of morals."[74] *Bildung* should be a mass-based undertaking that culminates in the "constant raising of the

---

71. The section of the urban population consisting of jobless people from the country who live in the city at the expense of relatives is especially important here. They are intermediaries between city and country because they have experienced colonial oppression but are also in touch with rural life.

72. Cabral, "National Liberation," p. 145.

73. "Presuppositions," p. 136.

74. Ibid.

political and moral awareness of the people (of all social categories) and of *patriotism,* spirit of sacrifice and devotion to the cause of independence, justice and progress."[75]

Because national reappropriation is a form of reason's self-actualization and not a mystifying nativism, modern *techne* is indispensable to the nation's incarnation. In an essay on the radio's role in the Algerian struggle, Fanon analyzes how the resistance movement adapts this foreign technical instrument to its ends. Before 1954, radio ownership was negligible among the native population because it was seen as irrelevant to native life, especially in rural areas. Indeed, the radio was an emblem of colonial power that purveyed content proscribed by traditional familial taboos. However, "after 1954, the radio assumed totally new meanings. The phenomena of the wireless and the receiver set lost their coefficient of hostility, were stripped of their character of extraneousness, and became part of the coherent order of the nation in battle."[76] The intermittent messages transmitted by the Voice of Algeria, which were often blocked by the colonial authorities, were repeated and circulated amongst the masses by those who were able to receive them. This circulation conjured up the revolutionary struggle for the masses, changed their consciousness, and united them into a nation. This means that the decolonizing nation is not a primordial traditional community, but the product of rational *Bildung.* Modern *techne* plays a crucial role in its repeated actualization. The nation assimilates foreign *techne* and shapes it into an extension of its organic body: "the foreign technique, which had been 'digested' in connection with the national struggle, had become a fighting instrument for the people and a protective organ against anxiety" (*DC,* 89). Thus, modern technomediation incorporates the nation and is incorporated into the life of the nation: "the Voice of Algeria, created out of nothing, brought the nation to life and endowed every citizen with new status, telling him so explicitly" (*DC,* 96). This assimilative process remains crucial for the unfinished task of postcolonial nation building. "This voice, often absent, physically inaudible, which each one felt welling up within himself, founded on an inner perception of the Fatherland, became materialized in an irrefutable way. . . . The nature of

---

75. "National Liberation," p. 153.
76. "This is the Voice of Algeria," in *A Dying Colonialism,* trans. Haakon Chevalier (New York: Grove Press, 1967), p. 89. Hereafter cited as *DC.*

this voice recalled in more than one way that of the Revolution: present 'in the air' in isolated pieces but not exactly" (DC, 87).

As opposed to this form of self-recursive mediation, both Fanon and Cabral characterize the decolonized nation's fall into neocolonialism as the national body's infection by a nonrecursive form of *techne*. For Fanon, nationalism's teleological time goes awry when the people's true destiny undergoes a contingent diversion, detour, or deferral because of the intrusion of an intermediary term. Examples of this corrupting intermediary include the commercial and liberal professional middle class that mediates between the colonial bourgeoisie and the natives; leaders of nationalist political parties who are out of touch with the masses' needs and pacify them by invoking a nostalgia for the days of the liberation movement; and the postcolonial national bourgeoisie, a comprador class serving as a transmission line between the nation and global capitalism.[77] But the paradigmatic example of the perverting prosthetic foreign body is the native intellectual who possesses a retrograde consciousness as "the result of the intellectual laziness of the national middle class [of underdeveloped countries], of its spiritual penury, and of the profoundly cosmopolitan mold that its mind is set in" (WE, 149). In the initial anticolonial phase, the intellectual reacts against his ideological victimage by projecting a sterile nativism, a superstitious return to tradition. Likewise, bourgeois nationalism and political institutions that mask their inability to express popular social consciousness with spurious nativism are merely "the hollow shell of nationality" (WE, 159). Nativism is a form of national consciousness that lacks real life.

> The bourgeois leaders of underdeveloped countries imprison national consciousness in sterile formalism. It is only when men and women are included on a vast scale in enlightened and fruitful work that form and body are given to [national] consciousness. Then the flag and the palace where sits the government ceases to be symbols of the nation. The nation deserts these brightly lit empty shells and takes shelter in the country, where it is given life and dynamic power. (WE, 204)

Cabral expresses identical reservations about the indigenous petit bourgeoisie and nativism, although he sees them as quite distinct. The bourgeoisie

---

77. See WE, 152, 168–69, 175–76.

is characterized by vacillation and indeterminacy. A product of colonialism, it is an externally introduced technical instrument. Although "the first important steps towards mobilizing and organizing the masses for the struggle against the colonial power" arises from the petit bourgeoisie, this revolutionary vanguard constitutes only a very small minority.[78] Other members of the class assume "the identity of the foreign dominant class, while the silent majority is trapped in indecision."[79] But Cabral is just as critical of the unassimilated tribal chief. He cautions us from confusing revolutionary culture with ossified indigenous traditions. The latter is complicit with colonialism. In situations of negligible cultural assimilation, where the traditional vertical social structures of certain ethnic groups remain intact, colonial regimes exploit the cultural authority of tribal leaders. During the liberation struggle and in postcoloniality, such indigenous culture resurfaces as opportunistic tribalism. It is merely a particularistic ideology that enables traditional and religious leaders to reestablish their precolonial cultural and political domination over the people. Such culture is as inorganic to the living people as the culturally assimilated petit bourgeoisie. Both are artificial contraptions the colonial power uses to divide the people and divert it from its final end of true freedom. The national struggle's success depends on the popular organism's ability to eradicate these prostheses, or to appropriate them so that they can be put in the service of its life.

Because they see revolutionary national culture as the means for transcending finitude and the ontological basis of liberation from all internal and external forms of domination, neither Cabral nor Fanon doubt the eventual overcoming of neocolonialism. Fanon's famous announcement of a new humanism that sublates the European project of modernity that closes *The Wretched of the Earth* exemplifies this confidence in revolutionary nationalism's teleological time:

It is a question of the Third World starting a new history of Man, a history which will have regard to the sometimes prodigious theses which Europe has put forward, but which will also not forget Europe's crimes. . . . For Europe,

<hr />

78. "Identity and Dignity," in *Return to the Source*, p. 69.
79. Ibid., p. 67.

for ourselves, and for humanity, comrades, we must turn over a new leaf, we must work out new concepts, and try to set afoot a new man. (315–16)

Today, we routinely dismiss such eschatological visions as revolutionary romanticism or idealist utopianism. Fanon, one commentator observes, "puts his trust in the revolutionary impact of awakening consciousness to such an extent that he fails to specify the economic conditions of such a development and to give any thought to the opposing forces which get mobilized at the slightest sign of incipient processes of liberation."[80] But such criticisms obscure what is truly at stake. Because they oppose the ideal to material reality, they overlook the fact that any project of emancipation however rational and realistic, including Marxist materialism itself, necessarily presupposes the ability to incarnate ideals in the external world. Such incarnation is unfailingly associated with organic life and culture. This is precisely why Cabral's and Fanon's nationalisms are exemplary constellations of Marxist materialism with national culture.

Indeed, almost all contemporary discourses about postcolonial nationalism are organismic, especially radical theories that see a national culture of resistance as the source of collective life that ensures a colonized people's survival through the continued expression of its enduring spirit. In such accounts, the neocolonial state is death dealing. It cripples and deforms a people's culture by subordinating it to the dictates of global capitalist accumulation. It must be appropriated because it is an alien mechanism in which the nation-people cannot recognize itself. This juxtaposition of the living dynamism of resisting peoples and their institutional capture by the *techne* of reactionary class and state apparatuses has many different sociological permutations. Its ubiquity in theories of postcolonial nationalism indicates that the fundamental issue of postcolonial nationalism is identical to the problem endemic to all political organicisms: Can the social or political body transcend finitude and assimilate the artificial prostheses that threaten to contaminate it, or is it irreducibly exposed to an inhuman and nonorganicizable *techne*? This is certainly the problematic animating two currently influential theories that have gone beyond the euphoria of

---

80. Renate Zahar, *Colonialism and Alienation: Concerning Frantz Fanon's Political Theory*, trans. Willfried F. Feuser (Benin City, Nigeria: Ethiope Publishing, 1974), p. 108.

Cabral's and Fanon's early nationalist ardour: Benedict Anderson's well-known defense of the nation as an imagined political community and Partha Chatterjee's neo-Marxist critique of Indian nationalism as a statist ideology.

In *Nationalist Thought and the Colonial World,* Chatterjee sketches a topography wherein populist dynamism is subsumed by the nation-form and captured by the bourgeois state qua instrument of capitalist development. Drawing on Gramsci's theory of passive revolution, he argues that Third World anticolonial cultural nationalism is the ideological discourse that a weak indigenous bourgeoisie uses to bar the masses from direct participation in the governance of the postcolonial state even as they are co-opted into its struggle to wrest hegemony from the colonial regime.[81] Postcolonial nationalism and national culture thus constitute a false resolution of the contradiction between the people and capital. Indeed, Chatterjee even proposes that the opposition between state and civil society should be replaced by that between capital and community because it inevitably confines radical political action to the debilitating nation-state form.[82] But whether we see the fundamental contradiction of social life as that of civil society or the people vs. the state, or community vs. capital, the opposition is always between popular vitality and its ideological manipulation.

Benedict Anderson's *Imagined Communities* is of the same organismic persuasion. Anderson defends nationalism against Marxist critiques by means of a historicist argument that the nation is the most effective vehicle for the incarnation of freedom. In its initial emergence, the nation is a mass-based political community induced by a constellation of historical forces in the late eighteenth and early nineteenth centuries, such as the technological innovations of print capitalism and a new mode of homogeneous empty time. To this pioneering style of emancipatory popular national consciousness, he counterposes the reactionary official nationalism deployed by European dynastic states to naturalize themselves in response to popular nationalist challenges (*IC*, 86). The problems of postcolonial nationalism, he suggests, need to be understood as a Janus-like modulation between

---

81. Partha Chatterjee, *Nationalist Thought and the Colonial World: A Derivative Discourse?* (London: Zed, 1986). Hereafter cited as *NT*.
82. Partha Chatterjee, *The Nation and its Fragments: Colonial and Postcolonial Histories* (Princeton, N.J.: Princeton University Press, 1993), pp. 235–36.

good and bad, popular and statist models of nationalism adopted by each decolonizing nation after it achieves statehood.

Both accounts of postcolonial nationalism thus insist on a strict demarcation between organic spontaneity and artificial and technical manipulation: between the nation-people and the state (Anderson), or between the people/community and capital (Chatterjee). This distinction ultimately turns out to be the line between life and death. For Chatterjee, the nation is an ideological extension of the bourgeois state, a tool of dead capital. Conversely, Anderson characterizes the nation as a sociological organism and describes the vicissitudes of postcolonial nationalism in terms of the contamination of life by manipulative technomediation. "Often," he writes,

> in the nation-building policies of the new states, one sees both a *genuine* popular nationalist *enthusiasm* and a *systematic, even Machiavellian,* instilling of nationalist ideology through the mass media, the educational system, administrative regulations, and so forth. . . . One can think of many of these nations as projects the achievements of which are still in progress, yet projects conceived more in the spirit of Mazzini than that of Uvarov.
>
> (*IC,* 113–14; emphasis added)

Decolonizing nationalism is an organismic process of becoming that is perverted in the aftermath of independence when the postcolonial nation becomes possessed by the state it thinks it controls. Anderson evokes this possession and stultification of the living national body by official nationalism via images of the ghostly technical infrastructure of a house and suffocating anachronistic garb that are reminiscent of Fanon's images of the palace as a brightly lit empty shell and the flag as a hollow symbol of the nation.

> The model of official nationalism assumes its relevance above all at the moment when revolutionaries successfully take control of the state, and are for the first time in a position to use the state in pursuit of their visions. . . . [E]ven the most determinedly radical revolutionaries always, to some degree inherit the state from the fallen regime. . . . Like the complex electrical system in any large mansion when the owner has fled, the state awaits the new owner's hand at the switch to be very much its old brilliant self again.
>
> One should therefore not be much surprised if revolutionary *leaderships,* consciously or unconsciously, come to play lord of the manor. . . . Out of this

accommodation comes invariably that 'state' Machiavellism which is so striking a feature of post-revolutionary regimes in contrast to revolutionary nationalist movements. The more the ancient dynastic state is naturalized, the more its antique finery can be wrapped around revolutionary shoulders.

(*IC*, 159–60)

Hence, whether one regards the nation as an ideological phantasm or as a dynamic growing body, one is always on the side of the open-ended becoming of the people (conceived as a community of language or the collective agent of class struggle), and against the territorial state qua artificially bounded entity that imposes stasis on the people's dynamism by diverting it to serve dead capital. Anderson and Chatterjee are in agreement on this fundamental point: the living people possesses a transfigurative power, and *techne* must either be made part of its self-actualizing organic body, or expunged.

In attempting to reconcile and subordinate the artificial to the organic, death to life, neither author relies on the catastrophism of a Marx or a Fanon. Whereas Fanon sees the state as a phantomatic edifice that will be reinspirited by the nation-people because it is the latter's alienated work, Chatterjee concedes that in its malignant turn against its creator, the state has become a more tenacious external fixture that may have completely escaped its creator's grasp. At the very least, its exorcism is not possible in the present. Anderson goes even further. He suggests that the state is utterly alien to the nation-people. It is an evil foreign body that cannot be reappropriated without contaminating progressive nationalism. By acknowledging the historical predicament of the nation's or people's actualization as a free collective subject, Anderson and Chatterjee go some way towards uncovering the irreducible susceptibility of life to *techne* that afflicts political organicism. However, they fail to locate the problem within the idea of freedom as self-actualization itself. In the final analysis, all obstacles remain external to the process of freedom's actualization in and by a collective body, which aims to remove such impediments to its life. Anderson's figuring of the relation between nation and state via a simile of the possession of the human occupant by the ghostly infrastructure of the house may be a despairing view of the transfigurative power of the people. But it is nevertheless a pessimism that tries to hold this power of becoming in reserve as a future horizon. A revolutionary *leadership*, he notes, may inherit the second-hand switchboards and palaces of the previous state but *people* are *never* the beneficiaries of this spectral legacy (*IC,* 161). The living people never willingly receives the ghost of *techne* into its home.

The vicissitudes of postcolonial nationalism and its enduring imperativity in the current global conjuncture, however, render untenable this belief in the people as an organismic power of self-origination that is uncompromised by *techne.* On the one hand, contra Chatterjee, political love for the nation cannot be reduced to an ideological mystification the state inculcates in its citizens' minds. Marx failed to foresee nationalism's tenacity because he hastily determined it as a statist ideology and foreclosed its popular and emancipatory face. This face, which revolutionary decolonization exemplifies, is especially important given the uneven globalization of capital. But on the other hand, contra Anderson, there cannot be an absolute qualitative difference between a popular nationalism that is completely free of the state and an official nationalism. In Asian and African decolonization, the line between state and nation-people is especially fuzzy. Because the bounded national community is arbitrarily generated from colonial state frontiers, popular national consciousness is initially weak and needs to be actively fostered through political-organizational techniques, which the state can always monitor. Furthermore, the patriarchal nature of revolutionary nationalist movements such as the FLN in the Algerian liberation struggle indicates that popular nationalism is not a purely egalitarian force.[83] The technical state apparatus is not the sole source of postcolonial oppression. Any analytical separation between an oppressive, hierarchical nationalism and a good, demotic nationalism needs to account for the common element between them. This continuity allows nationalism to modulate between its good and bad faces without any sharp transition.

My point is that although the decolonizing nation has crossed over to the side of life, its status as a mediator between the masses and the state is

---

83. See, for instance, Marnia Lazreg, *The Eloquence of Silence: Algerian Women in Question* (New York: Routledge, 1994); Marie-Aimée Hélie-Lucas, "Women, Nationalism and Religion in the Algerian Liberation Struggle," in *Opening the Gates: A Century of Arab Feminist Writing,* ed. Margot Badran and Miriam Cooke (Bloomington: Indiana University Press, 1990), 104–114; Cherifa Bouatta, "Feminine Militancy: *Moujahidates* During and After the Algerian War," and Doria Cherifati-Merabtine, "Algeria at a Crossroads: National Liberation, Islamization, and Women," both in *Gender and National Identity: Women and Politics in Muslim Societies,* ed. Valentine Moghadam (London: Zed, 1994) 18–39 and 40–62, respectively.

always fundamentally ambiguous. If it is captured by the state it hopes to inspirit, it will fall back onto the side of death. Instead of expressing the people's spirit, national culture will degenerate into an ideological state apparatus. The problem can be formalized as follows: Postcolonial political domination and economic exploitation under the sign of capital and the capture of the people's dynamism by neocolonial state manipulation signal the return of death. The task of the unfinished project of radical nationalism is to overcome this finitude. But revolutionary national culture's ability to check or transcend this finitude is precisely what is put into radical doubt. The living people and its culture need the state as a necessary supplement to survive. But the state exists within a capitalist world order the transcendence of which is not in sight. Hence, the people's contamination by the postcolonial nation-state (Chatterjee) or the nation's infection by the neocolonial bourgeois state (Cabral, Fanon, Anderson) is not the perverse diversion or deferral of a spiritual organism's true becoming by a contingent intruding foreign body that can be sublated or permanently removed. It is a more original susceptibility, the people's a priori receptability, its opening out onto what is other to it, the welcoming of an other that dislocates even as it constitutes the people's self-identity.

The living people's vulnerability is precisely the aporia of *techne* and *physis* afflicting Kant's inaugural explanation of organic life as the technic of nature. Because it describes a form of *techne* that cannot be reduced to human purposiveness, Kant's formulation points to a radical heteronomy, a nontranscendable death that is constitutively inscribed within the teleological time of life. I have attempted to trace how subsequent political organicisms—cosmopolitanist, nationalist, or statist, and those of republican and monarchist persuasions—are marked by this aporia. We saw how Fichte's living nation was opened up to the state-machine, and Hegel's ideal state to the supplement of the *Volksgeist*. These are consequences of the fundamental dependence of freedom's actualization on an inhuman *techne* that cannot be fully assimilated into the political organism's proper body. The interruption of Marx's proletarian cosmopolitanism by the national question is a historical performance of the same aporia. Postcolonial nationalism's haunting by the bourgeois neocolonial state belongs to the same problematic.

Political organicism is extremely widespread. It is not confined to the German philosophical tradition as is commonly assumed. It would not be excessive to say that organicism is the unacknowledged frame guiding contemporary social, political, and historical research. Today, we invariably associate freedom with life. This is why we speak of "liberation *movements*" or "new social *movements*." Organicist thematic oppositions between empty form and concrete actuality, death and life, resurface with great ubiquity and frequency across all disciplines in the humanities and the social sciences. Sociological oppositions such as the state and the nation or civil society, the proletariat and capital, the party leadership and the common masses, the indigenous urban bourgeoisie and the rural peasantry, the city and the country, saturate the entire discursive field of the social sciences. We take these categories as positive facts when we study empirical social phenomena, but they are constitutively imbued with values derived from organismic ontology. This understanding of freedom as the transcendence of finitude and its association with organic life and culture needs to be reassessed today along with the analytical categories that organismic vitalism informs.

In the second half of the book, I explore such issues by focusing on the vicissitudes of postcolonial nationalism. Revolutionary nationalism in the South is arguably the final persuasive example of philosophical modernity's grand narrative of freedom. It is a response to the failure of what Samir Amin has called (after the 1955 Bandung Conference) the Bandung project: the attempt at accelerated modernization and industrialization in Asia, Africa, and Latin America through state-regulated negotiations with global capital in the four decades after the Second World War.[84] The catchphrases of Bandung were "national development" and "non-alignment." Although developmentalist ideology was used to legitimize bourgeois statist intervention and management of society, the Bandung spirit also had a popular and radical dimension. It was able to draw on the revolutionary ideas of Cabral and Fanon because the desire to increase the nation's material welfare and strengthen its geopolitical position through economic development grew out of anti-imperialist struggle. It shared the same organismic

---

84. See Samir Amin, *Re-Reading the Postwar Period: An Intellectual Itinerary*, trans. Michael Wolfers (New York: Monthly Review Press, 1994), chap. 5; *Delinking: Towards a Polycentric World* (London: Zed, 1990), pp. 15–16 (hereafter cited as *D*), and "The Social Movements in the Periphery: An End to National Liberation?," in *Transforming the Revolution: Social Movements and the World-System*, ed. Samir Amin, Giovanni Arrighi, et al. (New York: Monthly Review Press, 1990), pp. 112–13 (hereafter cited as "SM").

metaphor of the nation-people as a living body striving to maximize its capacity for self-preservation and autonomy. However, as Amin observes, with the possible exception of East Asia and parts of Southeast Asia, the national bourgeoisies who assumed state power after formal decolonization were incapable of autonomous economic accumulation. The international division of labor inevitably causes the global capitalist system's diremption into center and periphery. Hence, the bourgeoisies either form comprador states "which purely and simply accept transnationalization and merely try to integrate according to their 'comparative advantage'" by accepting "specialization in agricultural and mining exports and/or export industries founded on cheap manpower" (a fate Cabral and Fanon diagnosed), or attempt to construct an independent capitalist national economy only to end up undergoing dependent industrialization and coerced structural adjustment according to the dictates of transnational capital (*D*, 139).

Despite the contemporary rise of quasi-legal human rights instruments at the transnational level, cosmopolitanism is not an effective vehicle for the actualization of freedom for the peripheral majority of the world's population. Transnational instruments are necessarily imbricated with the spread of flexible global capitalist accumulation. But more importantly, they are ineffective with respect to nonexceptional everyday situations of exploitation and oppression.[85] Socialist internationalism and cosmopolitanism have also collapsed. In the developed center, Marxism is "tending to become an academic current without the power of transforming reality" because the general standard of living has increased (*D*, 160). Hence, the revolutionary project of the working class has become, in Amin's words, an Asian and African vocation.[86] Such is the predicament and challenge of

---

85. I have argued this in "Given Culture: Rethinking Cosmopolitical Freedom in Transnationalism," *Boundary* 2 24, no. 2 (summer 1997): 157–97; "The Cosmopolitical—Today," in *Cosmopolitics: Thinking and Feeling Beyond the Nation*, ed. Pheng Cheah and Bruce Robbins (Minneapolis: University of Minnesota Press, 1998), 20–41; and "Posit(ion)ing Human Rights in the Current Global Conjuncture," *Public Culture* 9, no. 2 (winter 1997): 233–66. Arguments about the rise of a transnational political order are generally utopian. Antonio Negri and Michael Hardt anchor their thesis of the rise of a global multitude against empire in the demand for global citizenship based on labor, and fail to take into account the necessarily truncated nature of transnational labor flows. See *Empire*, pp. 396–400.

86. See *D*, chap. 4. For a related account of Thai and Indonesian communism, see Benedict Anderson, "Radicalism after Communism," in *The Spectre of Comparisons: Nationalism, Southeast Asia, and the World* (London: Verso, 1998), 285–98.

postcoloniality in contemporary globalization: "the global outlook . . . is of compradorization of the Third World national bourgeoisie, and its subjection to transnationalization. This process creates the very conditions for a new revolutionary wave in Asia and Africa, where the conditions of the exploited popular masses are not only deplorable but are worsening day by day" (*D*, 141). Amin argues that polycentric regionalism is a transition towards socialist universalism. However, he concedes that popular national movements are at present the first step in the teleology of freedom. "There is no alternative to popular national transformation in the societies of the periphery" ("SM," 124). "These people's movements [are] . . . the principal determinant of the evolution of the world-system toward a transcending of capitalism in its double dimension, pushing into the background (very gradually) the effects of the world polarization peculiar to capitalism . . . , and encouraging (equally not without contradiction) the social forces that aspire to abolish capitalist exploitation" ("SM," 115).

We are concerned with the broader theoretical significance of this continuing struggle. In the current conjuncture, postcolonial nationalism consummates the series of territorializations and deterritorializations of freedom punctuating the historical development of political organicism. However, its haunted and troubled life, "contradictory and ambivalent," and not "a guaranteed transition towards the abolition of class," makes it exemplary as a persistent undoing of the grand narrative of freedom and its philosophemes of culture and organic life.[87] It is not a matter of transcending finitude, but of mere surviving.

---

87. *D*, p. 160.

PART 2

Surviving (Postcoloniality)

NOVEL NATION: THE *BILDUNG* OF THE POSTCOLONIAL NATION AS SOCIOLOGICAL ORGANISM

I have argued that in modernity a philosopheme of culture as incarnational work supplies the ontological paradigm for the political. This politics of culture has three main traits: First, it involves a traditional discourse of human finitude that emphasizes the limited intellectual and practical capabilities of the sensuous human creature. Second, as the power of human self-actualization, culture in the broader sense of rational-purposive collective work is the means for transcending finitude and realizing freedom. Third, the imagistic and specular dimension of culture qua self-recursive mediating device is associated with the organism as a self-perpetuating being. The concepts of culture and organism are integral parts of a vitalist ontology. This discourse of exorcism that subordinates death to life governs the sociological topographies of various modern forms of political community, which primarily differ in terms of what is seen as the best way of arresting death.

Culture's political vocation lies in its ability to articulate society into an organic community, to transform the masses into a dynamic self-generating whole that approximates or actualizes the ideal of freedom. However, just as decolonizing nationalism has inherited the task of bringing the grand narrative of freedom to fruition, the most cogent examples of culture's political vocation today also seem to come from postcolonial space. In the North Atlantic, the demystification of culture's celebrated autonomy has followed from the Marxist critique of the free human subject as bourgeois property owner. The following remark by Horkheimer and Adorno on aesthetic culture is indicative: "even as the negation of that social purposiveness which is spreading through the market, its freedom remains essentially bound up with the premise of a commodity economy. Pure works of art which deny the commodity society by the very fact that they obey their own law were always wares all the same."[1] With the unfolding of its true nature as commodity, culture loses its organicizing powers. In its intensified commodification (the "culture industry"), culture retains a semblance of its redemptive dimension as high culture. But this is cut off from the masses' everyday life, which is shaped by mass culture. The unifying function of industrialized culture is a perverse mockery of *Bildung*. "Culture now impresses the same stamp on everything," but the totality it generates is not a genuine organism.[2] There is no dynamic integration of parts into a whole that embodies universal reason, but merely a bland, mindless uniformity: "The whole and parts are alike; there is no antithesis and no connection. Their prearranged harmony is a mockery of what had to be striven after in the great bourgeois works of art."[3]

This perversion of culture is a manifestation of the aporia between *techne* and organic life. Organismic culture itself has degenerated into a nonrecursive form of mediation and a technique of domination. The question is whether this degeneration is reversible. Horkheimer and Adorno attempt to quarantine culture's vitality from the vicissitudes of commodification by preserving it in critical thought and the artistic avant-garde.[4] In contradistinction, contemporary cultural studies has willfully refused a pessimistic interpretation of mass culture. Echoing Walter Benjamin's suggestion that industrial mediatic techniques are the material means of the democratization and proletarianization of culture, cultural studies has extended culture's vocational dimension to popular consumer culture, which is given a dynamism that resists authority and domination.

---

1. Max Horkheimer and Theodor W. Adorno, *Dialectic of Enlightenment*, trans. John Cumming (New York: Continuum, 1994) p. 157.

2. Ibid., 120.

3. Ibid., 126.

4. Max Horkheimer, "Art and Mass Culture," in *Critical Theory: Selected Essays* (New York: Continuum, 1995), pp. 273–90; and Theodor Adorno, "Culture Industry Reconsidered," *New German Critique*, no. 6 (fall 1975): 12–19.

Postcoloniality may be a more apposite test case for assessing culture's fate and future. The postcolonial condition emphatically underscores the point that culture is the paradigm for the political. Cabral and Fanon attach paramount importance to cultural resistance because culture is the most cogent example of freedom's self-actualization and our capacity to transcend finitude. Samir Amin likewise suggests that the Third World intelligentsia is a crucial social force in national *Bildung*. It is fundamental to the construction of a popular alliance and the formulation of a popular national project that can rebuild the state and arbitrate conflicts between the socialist, capitalist, and statist elements.[5] Culture is therefore integral to the living people's oppositional relation to the bourgeois postcolonial state. Examples of national *Bildung* include the opening up of the people's proper body to *techne* as instantiated by the formative roles of modern knowledge, technomediation, and organization in the nation's genesis and ongoing development; the importance of culture in the narrow sense as image-creating phenomena in the formation of a national public sphere; and the penetration of the state by the light of public reason. Conversely, the nation's exposure by the same formative technics to monitoring and manipulation by the neocolonial state as a servant of dead capital, and the stifling of the national will's attempt to overcome the current world order by the global circulation of neocolonial images are forms of miscultivation or deformation.

My conceptualization of radical postcolonial nationalism as a process of *Bildung* echoes Hegel's characterization of the state as a spiritual individual and his extended analogy between the *Bildung* of universal spirit and the development of an individual person to maturity and meaningful membership in collective life.[6] More recent arguments by Jürgen Habermas and Benedict Anderson confirm the connections between culture, organic life,

---

5. Samir Amin, *Capitalism in the Age of Globalization: The Management of Contemporary Society* (London: Zed, 1997), chap. 7.

6. For Hegel, pedagogical education and cultivation are the objective correlatives of universal *Bildung* seen from the individual's subjective standpoint. "The task of leading the individual from his uneducated [*ungebildeten*] standpoint to knowledge had to be seen in its universal sense, just as it were the universal individual, self-conscious Spirit, whose *Bildung* had to be studied" (Hegel, *Phänomenologie des Geistes*, 3:31; *Phenomenology of Spirit*, 16). "[I]n the child's pedagogical progress, we shall recognize the history of the *Bildung* of the world traced, as it were, in a silhouette" (*PG*, 3:32; 16).

238 SURVIVING (POSTCOLONIALITY)

and the institutional realization of freedom. I have already discussed Anderson's account of how the nation is imagined as "a sociological organism . . . moving steadily down (or up) history."[7] Although the nation is imagined within the mechanical "meanwhile" of homogeneous empty time, Anderson's understanding of it as an interconnected totality "gliding endlessly towards a limitless future" necessarily implies a teleological notion of time, that of the purposive interdependence of parts and whole that enables the organism to perpetuate itself to infinity.[8] For Anderson, the source of this organismic causality is the technomediation of print. Habermas's well-known characterization of *Öffentlichkeit* as a sphere of the private realm that presses upon public political authority, mediating between the state and social needs and making demands upon the state in the name of critical reason also emphasizes its self-determining, self-generating nature and its ability to organicize the state. The public sphere "is capable of assuming a political function only to the extent to which it enables participants in the economy, via their status as citizens, to mutually accommodate or generalize their interests and to assert them effectively *that state power is transformed into the fluid medium of society's self-organization.* This is what the young Marx had in mind when he spoke of the reabsorption of the state into society that has become political in itself."[9] For Habermas, the mediating device through which society can return to and organize itself is likewise public communication, which organizes individual reason into collective reason because it entails universal access and participation.[10]

Habermas and Anderson both emphasize the importance of literary *Bildung* in a people's epigenesis. For Anderson, the novel is an analogue of the nation that maps its social space for readers: "the novelty of the novel as a literary form lay in its capacity to represent synchronically this bounded, intrahistorical society-with-a-future."[11] Habermas also notes the

---

7. Benedict Anderson, *Imagined Communities: Reflections on the Origin and Spread of Nationalism,* 2d ed. (London: Verso, 1991), p. 26.

8. Benedict Anderson, "El Malhadado País," in *The Spectre of Comparisons: Nationalism, Southeast Asia, and the World* (London: Verso, 1998), p. 334.

9. Jürgen Habermas, "Further Reflections on the Public Sphere," trans. Thomas Burger, in *Habermas and the Public Sphere,* ed. Craig Calhoun (Cambridge: MIT Press, 1992), p. 431, emphasis added.

10. Jürgen Habermas, *The Structural Transformation of the Public Sphere: An Inquiry into a Category of Bourgeois Society,* trans. Thomas Burger (Cambridge: MIT Press, 1989), p. 37.

11. Anderson, "El Malhadado País" p. 334.

self-recursive causality of the eighteenth-century public sphere of letters: "The privatized individuals coming together to form a public also reflected critically and in public on what they had read, thus contributing to the process of enlightenment which they together promoted. . . . [Institutions such as coffee houses, salons, and so on that are] now held together through the medium of the press and its professional criticism . . . formed the public sphere of a rational-critical debate in the world of letters within which the subjectivity originating in the interiority of the conjugal family, by communicating with itself, attained clarity about itself."[12] This emphasis on literature helps us understand the remarkable affinity between decolonizing and radical postcolonial nationalism and the novelistic genre, the bildungsroman.

As exemplified by José Rizal's *Noli Me Tangere,* the novel of early or decolonizing nationalism almost invariably figured the emergent nation-people as a living organism suffering from the chronic malaise of colonialism. The remedy to this disease was always a form of *Bildung,* a concerted effort at reaching out to the colonized masses, educating and raising their awareness so that they might rationally organize themselves into a people who can overcome the distance between itself and the colonial state and appropriate this foreign prosthesis to form a united whole.[13] As Elías puts it in *Noli Me Tangere,* "the treatment [the measures of colonial authority to curb unrest] applied to the evils of the country is so destructive as to affect even a sound organism, whose vitality weakens and conditions it for evil. Would it not be more reasonable to strengthen the sick body and lessen somewhat the violence of the treatment?"[14] This exemplary lesson about the imperativity of national *Bildung* was invariably personified in the novel's protagonist whose formation or *Bildung* parallels and symbolizes that of the emergent nation because he is its first patriot and ideal citizen.[15] This affinity

---

12. Habermas, *Structural Transformation,* p. 51.

13. These themes can be found especially in chap. 50 of *Noli Me Tangere,* trans. Ma. Soledad Lacson-Locsin (Honolulu: University of Hawaii Press, 1997). For a brilliant discussion of the *Noli* as a nationalist novel, and also its deep ambivalence, see Caroline Hau, *Necessary Fictions: Philippine Literature and the Nation, 1946–1980* (Manila: Ateneo de Manila University Press, 2000), chap. 2.

14. *Noli,* p. 325.

15. The first biography of Rizal by León Ma. Guerrero, his first English translator, was entitled *The First Filipino* (Manila: Guerrero Publishing, 1998). But literature is always more complicated. In Rizal's novel, Ibarra, the *ilustrado* protagonist, is not the ideal patriot. The ideal patriot seems to be

between activist nationalist literature and the bildungsroman seems to have been heightened after formal independence. It is true that many postindependence novels from Asian and African countries such as Ayi Kwei Armah's *The Beautyful Ones are Not Yet Born* (Ghana), Nuruddin Farah's *Maps* (Somalia), and Ninotchka Rosca's *The State of War* (the Philippines) are concerned with the violence of national identity or the betrayal of the nationalist movement's ideals by the neocolonial state's political leaders and the indigenous bourgeoisie. They are marked by despair or at least a greater awareness of the vicissitudes of the protagonist's *Bildung,* which often ends tragically. Yet, they remain novels of nationalist *Bildung,* where their protagonists' lives parallel the history of their respective nations.

More significantly, such novels do not only reflect or thematize the nation's *Bildung.* They are themselves intended to be part of it. They are meant to have an active causal role in the nation's genesis insofar as they supply the occasion and catalyst for their implied reader's *Bildung* as a patriotic subject. Certainly, Rizal's *Noli* played an important role in the history of Philippines nationalism.[16] In the spirit of Habermas and Anderson's arguments, one can say that activist postcolonial nationalist novels are conceived as a means for generating a reading public that can be a renewing basis of the nation-people, the medium and substrate in which it can regenerate itself by reflecting upon and knowing itself. Hence, in postcoloniality, the political vocation of culture finds its exemplary performance in and as activist nationalist literature, especially in and as the novelistic genre of the bildungsroman. In the remaining chapters of this book, I explore the continuing viability of *Bildung*'s sociopolitical vocation and the organismic metaphor of the social and political body by assessing the impact of Pramoedya Ananta Toer's and Ngũgĩ wa Th'iong'o's late nationalist novels on the radical *Bildung* of their respective nations.

Such a focus may encounter at least three different objections. The most obvious ones arise from literary theory. First, in presupposing that the plot

---

a composite that emerges from the dialectical tension between Ibarra and Elías, a self-identified *indio.* For a fuller discussion of Elías's patriotism, see Hau, *Necessary Fictions,* pp. 86–88.

16. On *Noli*'s historical impact on Philippines nationalism, see John N. Schumacher, S.J., *The Propaganda Movement, 1880–1895: The Creation of a Filipino Consciousness, the Making of the Revolution* (Manila: Ateneo de Manila University Press, 1997), and *The Making of a Nation: Essays on Nineteenth-Century Filipino Nationalism* (Manila: Ateneo de Manila University Press, 1991), chap. 6.

of a type of novel instantiates the concept of *Bildung,* am I not positing an artificial continuity between *Bildung* and the bildungsroman? Second, even if this continuity is assumed, it has been repeatedly pointed out that the genre itself is so phantasmatic that even the novel widely considered as its original model, Goethe's *Wilhelm Meisters Lehrjahre,* may not in fact be a bildungsroman.[17] How can I be sure that the novels I examine are indeed *Bildungsromane?* In this situation, I am fortunate enough to be able to have recourse to the fiction of "authorial intention." Both Pramoedya and Ngũgĩ also produced theories of literature as *Bildung* and they saw their novels, which have the shape of the narrative of formation, as examples of these theories. But then is the importance I accord to the bildungsroman in national *Bildung* an extravagant literary theoretical proposition that pays no heed to historico-empirical forces? This is by far the most troubling objection.

One needs however to recall again the remarkable historical affinity between the novel form, the nation, and the concepts of culture and organism. The last two concepts were formulated to describe rationally meaningful forms of natural and social existence in the wake of the displacement of a cosmological worldview by an anthropologistic and mechanistic modern worldview. The organism was ascribed a teleological causality by being characterized as a totality in which parts and whole derive their significance from each other because they are reciprocally the means and ends of each other. Culture was understood as a higher second nature, a spiritual totality that alleviated the atomistic pursuit of self-interest in modern industrial society. Similarly, the novel's emergence is frequently related to the modern demagicking (*Entzauberung*) of the world.[18] It is argued, by Benjamin and Lukács for instance, that the purging of the world of sacredness and mystery by science and technology dissolved the preestablished harmony and inherent meaningfulness of the unmediated communal

---

17. For careful discussions summarizing previous literature on the issue, see, for instance, Martin Swales, *The German Bildungsroman from Wieland to Hesse* (Princeton: Princeton University Press, 1978); Jeffrey L. Sammons, "The Mystery of the Missing Bildungsroman, or What Happened to Wilhelm Meister's Legacy?" *Genre* 14 (summer 1981): 229–46; and Marc Redfield, *Phantom Formations: Aesthetic Ideology and the Bildungsroman* (Ithaca: Cornell University Press, 1996).

18. "*Entzauberung*" is Max Weber's word. See "Science as Vocation," in *From Max Weber: Essays in Sociology,* ed. H. H. Gerth and C. Wright Mills (New York: Routlege, 1991), pp. 129–156.

Greek world and led to the rise of a new form of literature that could express the *created* and, hence, imperfect unity appropriate to modern social life. In Lukács's famous definition, "the novel is the epic of an age in which the extensive totality of life is no longer directly given, in which the immanence of meaning in life has become a problem, yet which still thinks in terms of totality."[19]

The novel is the magical glue that symbolically holds together a demagicked world. But the newly generated totality is merely a rational construct: "a new perspective of life is reached on an entirely new basis—that of the indissoluble connection between the relative independence of the parts and their attachment to the whole. But the parts, despite this attachment, can never lose their inexorable, abstract self-dependence: and their relationship to the totality, although it approximates as closely as possible to an organic one, is nevertheless not a true-born organic relationship but a conceptual one which is abolished again and again."[20] Lukács's description of the Greek community as organic is, however, anachronistic. It overlooks the organism's modernity. It is the novel's totality that is properly organismic because it is a rational-purposive form of organization.[21] Likewise, in Anderson's account, the imagined community of the nation is a new form of purposiveness within the mechanical ticking of clock and calendar. It replaces the religious communities of the premodern era as a way of giving meaningful organization to modernity's atomizing forces. "It is the magic of nationalism," Anderson notes, "to turn chance into destiny," and this magic finds a precise analogue in the novel.[22]

This conceptual contiguity or proximity of nation, novel, culture, and organism helps elucidate why the bildungsroman is so widely deployed in the activist literary *Bildung* of the postcolonial or decolonizing nation. For the nation qua predominant form of modern community lacks immediate unity. It is not merely a given, but a habitat one has to seek and affirm as one's proper home through rational effort. The bildungsroman is the most appropriate symbolic expression of this search because its fundamental

---

19. Georg Lukács, *The Theory of the Novel: A Historico-Philosophical Essay on the Forms of Great Epic Literature*, trans. Anna Bostock (Cambridge: MIT Press, 1971).
20. Ibid., pp. 75–76.
21. Note that in Dilthey's classical definition, the bildungsroman is organic not because of the continuous development of a preformed germ, but because of the dynamic interconnection between parts and whole that is achieved at the end of the process, which is always subject to chance.
22. *Imagined Communities*, p. 12.

premise is a self that is alienated from the world, a condition of "transcendental homelessness—the homelessness of an action in the human order of social relations," where meaning is no longer immanent but must be rationally posited by the seeker for himself.[23] The bildungsroman provides the symbolic resolution to this homelessness. Just as the genre charts the progress from the anomie of youth to a meaningful life, first in civil society and then the state, the nation-state also offers an antidote to modernity's upheaval.

The resolution is, however, necessarily more problematic in colonial space, where the entropy of modernity is experienced as the shattering of traditional forms of community by colonialism. *Bildung* in general, and in Hegel's understanding in particular, involves accommodation to the existing state and social world. But the predicament of decolonization is that there is no preexisting community for the individual to be reconciled to. The colonial state and society that have replaced the traditional world are emphatically not comfortable habitats since they are themselves the sources of alienation. Thus, a home that is an antidote to colonialism has to be conjured up or created anew. But this home—the nation—cannot just be a revival of precolonial indigenous traditions, even though it may draw on progressive elements from such traditions, such as communalism or oral culture, as resources for sustenance. Little wonder then that many early nationalist *Bildungsromane* from these spaces could not espouse a quietistic accommodation to existing society. They were not ideological means of socialization, but called for the radical transformation of society.[24]

Such novels clearly give the lie to the common interpretation of *Bildung* as an apolitical subjectivism, a psychologistic process typified by introspection and inwardness.[25] What they emphasize is precisely the process of incarnation, objectivation, or actualization of universal ethical and political ideals as a second nature. They also caution us from hastily reducing the bildungsroman to a product of the educated bourgeoisie and an ideological

23. Lukács, *Theory of the Novel*, p. 61.
24. In Franco Moretti's taxonomy, the principle of transformation is stronger than the principle of classification in these novels. See Moretti, *The Way of the World: The Bildungsroman in European Culture* (London: Verso, 1987), p. 7.
25. Thomas Mann's comments on *Bildung*, especially his 1923 lecture, "Geist und Wesen der deutschen Republik," are often cited as evidence of its apolitical nature. See W. H. Bruford, *The German Tradition of Self-Cultivation: "Bildung" from Humboldt to Thomas Mann* (Cambridge: Cambridge University Press, 1975), vii.

superstructure of capitalism and its mythology of individualism. They undo the distinction between the bildungsroman's individualistic psychologism and the social novel's realism and panoramic view of society precisely because their protagonists' *Bildung* must involve the interiorization of viewpoints from different social classes and religious groups.[26] These protagonists must undertake a cognitive mapping of the boundaries, strata, and contents of the entire social world to qualify as model protonational subjects, and the novels seem to invite their implied addressees to do the same through specular identification with the protagonists.[27] They therefore retain the original dual sense of *Bildung* that Karl Morgensten attributed to the bildungsroman when he coined the term in 1819: "It could well be called the *Bildungsroman,* first and foremost because of its content, because it presents the hero's *Bildung* from its inception and continuation until a certain stage of completion; secondly, however, because precisely through this presentation it encourages the cultivation of the reader more fully than any other type of novel."[28]

As I mentioned above, the affinity between activist literature and progressive nationalism seems to have become stronger but also more troubled in postcoloniality. The ideal emancipatory projects of revolutionary nationalism in the Third World attempted to mold the newly independent states so that the people's interests could be better expressed in the economic, political, and cultural spheres. However, once the initial euphoria of inde-

---

26. For contrasting views on whether or not the bildungsroman should be rigorously distinguished from the social-realistic novel, see Marianne Hirsch, "The Novel of Formation as Genre: Between Great Expectations and Lost Illusions," *Genre* 12 (fall 1979): 297; Jeffrey L. Sammons, "The Mystery of the Missing Bildungsroman"; and Harmut Steinecke, "The Novel and the Individual: The Significance of Goethe's *Wilhelm Meister* in the Debate about the Bildungsroman," in *Reflection and Action: Essays on the Bildungsroman,* ed. James Hardin (Columbia, S.C.: University of South Carolina Press, 1991), pp. 94–95; and Ferenc Fehér, "Is the Novel Problematic? A Contribution to the Theory of the Novel," *Telos* 15 (spring 1973): 47–74. Steinecke and Fehér both insist on the social-political vocation of the bildungsroman.

27. This is why the *Noli* or Pramoedya's Buru Quartet, for instance, are full of didactic Socratic dialogues between characters from different social locations about how to remedy colonial oppression.

28. Morgenstern, "Über das Wesen des Bildungsromans," *Inländisches Museum* 1, no. 2 (1820): 50, cited in Fritz Martini, "Bildungsroman—Term and Theory," in *Reflection and Action,* ed. James Hardin, p. 18. For discussions of the reader's *Bildung,* see Harmut Steinecke, "The Novel and the Individual" and Dennis F. Mahoney, "The Apprenticeship of the Reader: The Bildungsroman of the 'Age of Goethe,'" in the Hardin volume, op. cit., pp. 69–96 and 97–117, respectively.

pendence subsided in the late 1960s and the early 1970s, there was a gradual tightening of control over the economic and political spheres by an indigenous bourgeois elite, often in collaboration with transnational capital. This continuing situation of neocolonial globalization has attenuated nationalism as a popular emancipatory project led by progressive intellectuals. Especially in countries with authoritarian governments or oppressive military regimes, radical nationalist projects have been increasingly confined to the sphere of culture, limited to the contestation of sociocultural consensus or hegemony. The rearticulation of the nation-people has primarily become a cultural project because the possibility of immediately penetrating and transforming the political and economic spheres has become so slight.

This scenario seems to repeat Amilcar Cabral's dictum that "national liberation is necessarily an act of culture," but with a melancholy irony. Cabral saw culture as the germ of challenge to foreign domination, a seed that would inevitably develop *in due time* into political liberation and structural transformation. In neocolonial globalization, however, the cultural project of emancipatory nationalism can only posit the telos of radical transformation as a utopian horizon in which the malaise of the neocolonial present will be transcended. Radical literary projects of national *Bildung* remain cases of political organicism. They still endorse the idea that a radical national culture of the people contains the seeds for the reappropriation and transformation of the neocolonial state. But they no longer possess the same confidence in the inevitable progress of history, the unfaltering consciousness of time characterizing the organism's self-recursive causality.

Armah's *The Beautyful Ones are Not Yet Born* succinctly describes this wavering of the teleological time of self-actualizing reason as a nostalgic yearning for an unfulfilled promise that had existed in the past present. The promise (of decolonizing nationalism) was corrupted. And yet, it did exist in the past and has left a historical trace.

> The promise was so beautiful. Even those who were too young to understand it all knew that at last something good was being born. It was there. We were not deceived about that. How could such a thing turn so completely into this other thing? Could there have been no other way?[29]

---

29. Ayi Kwei Armah, *The Beautyful Ones are Not Yet Born* (Portsmouth, N.H.: Heinemann, 1988), p. 85.

And yet, we also cannot be certain that this promise will be realized in a future present. On hearing about a coup against the Nkrumah government, a revolutionary regime that had become a corrupt totalitarian state, the novel's protagonist doubts that anything new has occurred.

> He was not burdened with any hopes that new things, really new things, were as yet ready to come out. Someday in the long future a new life would maybe flower in the country, but when it came, it would not choose as its instruments the same people who had made a habit of killing new flowers. The future goodness may come eventually, but before then where were the things in the present which would prepare the way for it?[30]

The frustration of teleological time, with its accompanying despair, is here explicitly linked to instruments or prostheses that are death dealing because they are not self-recursive. The paradigm of such prostheses is clearly the neocolonial state.

In Pramoedya's and Ngũgĩ's attempts to narrate the nation, the interruption of organismic causality is indicated by an uncontrollable recurrence of ghosts and prostheses that possess or invade the nation's proper organic body. A ghost is that which traverses the border between life and death. The wavering of organic life is quite literally the becoming-indeterminate of this border. The failure of their literary projects of radical nationalist *Bildung* to organicize the foreign prosthesis of the neocolonial state and, therefore, to make the nation-people fully self-organizing, points to a certain ghostliness within the living national body. This haunting of the nation in the very process of its *Bildung* implies a critique of political organicism that strikes at the heart of vitalist ontology. As a defective form of mediation that does not return to and augment the nation's proper body, as the invasion of life by *techne*, this ghostliness does more than question the philosophemes of culture and organic life as the incarnations of freedom. What is ultimately broached is the realization of freedom itself, of freedom as the self-directed actualization of ideals and the transcendence of finitude. This haunting, which disrupts the teleological time of reason's self-actualization, is a type of finitude that blocks transcendence through

---

30. Ibid., pp. 159–60.

rational work. This questioning of the modern philosopheme of freedom is, however, emphatically not a form of postmodern pessimism or nihilism. For the point is not that ideals cannot be incarnated, that one should therefore dismiss efforts toward transcendence as senseless and futile. It is rather that what makes incarnation possible—a ghostliness linked to the gift of time—also makes it impossible. This ghostliness both enables and impedes the living nation's self-perpetuation because it is the condition of (im)possibility of the epigenesis of life itself. It makes the homeland *unheimlich*.

THE HAUNTING OF THE PEOPLE:
THE SPECTRAL PUBLIC SPHERE IN
PRAMOEDYA ANANTA TOER'S BURU QUARTET

6

Pramoedya Ananta Toer and Ngũgĩ wa Thiong'o come from very different national milieus. Indonesia is densely populated, multiethnic, and polyglot, with a strong Islamic heritage and a complex history of Dutch and Japanese colonization. The former British colony of Kenya is, on the other hand, small and dominated by Christians. These differences have marked their language choices. Pramoedya, who is Javanese, writes in Malay, the Indonesian lingua franca, whereas Ngũgĩ (initially James Ngũgĩ), wrote in English before switching to his mother tongue, Gikuyu, the language of the dominant Kenyan tribe. Yet both authors recall culture's original sociopolitical vocation by granting radical literature a crucial role in their peoples' ongoing struggles against neocolonialism. Their belief in culture's incarnational power attests to the strength of organismic vitalism, which both authors inherit from Leninism. They are also exemplars of the Third World intellectual, to whom Samir Amin entrusts the task of popular national *Bildung*. Hence, the success of their literary projects has a decisive bearing on culture's ability to incarnate freedom in contemporary globalization.

———◆———

Born in Blora, Java, in 1925, Pramoedya Ananta Toer has experienced the iron fist of both the Dutch colonial regime and the neocolonial New Order

Indonesian state at first hand.[1] A revolutionary youth (*pemuda*) during the Japanese occupation and the ensuing four years of revolution against the returning Dutch colonial state (1945–49), he was imprisoned by the Dutch from 23 July 1947 to 18 December 1949. He achieved renown for his fictional portrayal of resistance to the Japanese occupation in the years immediately following the Dutch cession of sovereignty and played an important role in Indonesian literature and cultural politics from 1950 to 1965, especially in his capacity, from 1962 to 1965, as the editor of *Lentera*, the weekly cultural supplement to *Bintang Timur*, the socialist daily linked to Lekra (the Institute of People's Culture), the cultural arm of the PKI (the Indonesian Communist Party). In the period between 13 October 1965 and 20 December 1979, Pramoedya was arrested, imprisoned, and exiled to various places including the notorious Buru gulag (August 1969–November 1979) by the postcolonial Indonesian government.[2] He was released at the end of 1979, but his books were banned and he lived under city arrest in Jakarta until Suharto's downfall.

Pramoedya's understanding of the genesis of Indies national consciousness and its subsequent arrested development in postcolonial Indonesia is resolutely dialectical in a Hegelian and Marxist sense. For him, the initial rise of national consciousness obeys a teleology of history.[3] National consciousness (*kesadaran bernasion*), the awareness of belonging to a homeland (*bertanahair*), Pramoedya suggests, is distinct from merely instinctual territorial consciousness (*kesadaran berwilayah*). A historically inevitable consequence of international and internal processes, its constitutive precondition is the consciousness of negation under colonialism: "National Awakening is . . . a process of emergence, growth and development; the awareness of having a nation and a homeland as the result of the awareness

---

1. For a brief autobiographical sketch up to 1982, see Pramoedya Ananta Toer, "*Perburuan* 1950 and *Keluarga Gerilya* 1950," trans. Benedict Anderson, *Indonesia*, no. 36 (1983): 43–44. For a detailed biographical survey up to the 1960s, see A. Teeuw, *Modern Indonesian Literature*, 3rd ed., vol. 1, (Dordrecht: Foris Publications, 1986), pp. 163–80.

2. Pramoedya's memoirs of his Buru years are published as *Nyanyi Sunyi Seorang Bisu. Catatan-catatan dari Pulau Buru* (Kuala Lumpur: Wira Karya, 1995); *The Mute's Soliloquy*, trans. Willem Samuels (New York: Penguin, 2000). See Rudolf Mrázek's account in *Engineers of Happy Land: Technology and Nationalism in a Colony* (Princeton, N.J.: Princeton University Press, 2002), pp. 193–233.

3. See Pramoedya Ananta Toer, *Sang Pemula* (Jakarta: Hasta Mitra, 1985), pp. 141–42. Hereafter cited as *SP*; all English translations are mine.

that there is a foreign nation and homeland, and more saliently, that there is a people who rules and peoples who are dominated" (*SP*, 141). The Indies awakening occurred after the geographical territory was given a political name, Indonesia, that contested its colonial name, the Dutch Indies. Indeed, Pramoedya suggests that the homeland itself is an imaginary entity formed in this renaming. The nation figures forth in the performative summoning of Indonesia:

> With the use of the ethnographic-ethnological name *Indonesia* as a political name . . . we can say that the political struggle to recognize [*menemukan*] the motherland has been successful. . . . Theoretically speaking, the Epoch of National Awakening can be said to have been completed in 1917 with the discovery of the homeland that is named Indonesia. (*SP*, 142)

However, the analytical distinction between the (Indonesian) nation and the (Dutch colonial) territorial state implies that although the nation exists in the imagination of native intellectuals, it needs to appropriate the existing territorial unit before it can achieve freedom and become a concrete actuality. It remains an incomplete project and requires full *institutional* actualization. Decolonization is clearly an important moment in the Indonesian nation's progression toward freedom. But the process is far from over. The repressive neocolonial New Order state, transnational capital's accomplice, represents another moment of negation within the dialectical process: "Nationalism has no priority for the current regime in Indonesia. Their concern today is how to get money. Everything revolves around multinational capitalism. . . . The Indonesian nation is still not free. The aims of the revolution have not been achieved."[4] The national process is an "unfinished business":

> as a person and a writer who shares in bearing the burden of change, I look at it [the New Order] according to national criteria. The era of Soekarno and the Trisakti doctrine was nothing but a sort of thesis. The New Order, an antithesis.

---

4. Chris GoGwilt, "Pramoedya's Fiction and History: An Interview with Pramoedya Ananta Toer, January 16, 1995, Jakarta, Indonesia," *Kabar Seberang*, nos. 24/25 (Special double issue: Essays to Honour Pramoedya Ananta Toer's Seventieth Year) (1995): 12, 16.

> Therefore, for me, it is something that in fact cannot be written about yet, a process that cannot yet be written as literature, that does not yet constitute a national process in its totality, because it is still heading for its synthesis.[5]

For Pramoedya, the nation has the same ontological status as for Cabral and Fanon. It is an organism striving to maximize its capacity for life. It is a principle of vitality and the animating force of history. Its struggles against the colonial and neocolonial states are life's struggles against all that negates and obstructs its dynamism and causes its stagnation. Pramoedya ascribes to culture, especially literary culture, a fundamental causal power in the dialectical process of national becoming because he sees it as the highest expression and embodiment of vitality. This conception of national culture rearticulates the philosopheme of culture as freedom within two related political contexts: the reclamation of the colonial state by native intellectuals through conscientious cultural critique, and the penetration of the post-independence state by a culture of the people. I read Pramoedya's Buru Quartet with two questions in mind: First, in view of the failure of Sukarno's attempt to complete the National Revolution, the seeming stability of the New Order regime, and its tenacious legacies after its collapse on 21 May 1998, how plausible is Pramoedya's organismic schema for understanding the relationship between the state and the nation?[6] More importantly, what does the living people's failure to inspirit the state say about the philosopheme of culture itself, from which this schema is derived? The answers are not to be found solely in philosophical inquiry or political history, for these questions concern the historical performance of the philosophemes of freedom, culture, and organic life, how they are contaminated and transformed by their incarnation in history or by their finitude. There is a certain aporetic doubling in these questions. Freedom is human self-actualization, the incarnation of human ideals, and we are concerned here with the less-than-ideal incarnation of freedom itself, the incarnation of incarnation gone awry.

---

5. Pramoedya Ananta Toer, "My Apologies, in the Name of Experience," trans. Alex G. Bardsley, *Indonesia*, no. 61 (1996): 8. The phrase "unfinished business" comes from p. 12.
6. For various assessments of the New Order's collapse, see the contributions by John Sidel, Vedi Hadiz, and James Siegel in *Indonesia*, no. 66 (October 1998). See also Benedict Anderson, "Indonesian Nationalism Today and in the Future," *New Left Review*, no. 235 (1999): 3–17.

THE BURU QUARTET'S FUNCTION: REANIMATING A CRITICAL
PUBLIC SPHERE IN NEW ORDER INDONESIA

The Buru Quartet attempts to construct an archive or cultural memorial, a truthful historical record that would preserve the events surrounding the birth of revolutionary national consciousness at the turn of the century. This memorial is intended for present and future Indonesians who are unaware of their origins as a people and the historical forces that have produced their present because of historiographical distortions based on Dutch colonial archives and the collective amnesia actively enforced by President Suharto's New Order government.[7] But the quartet also has a normative task beyond its historiographical function. Written *after* the onset of despair at the betrayal of the Indonesian people by the elites who run the postcolonial state, Pramoedya looks back into the history of Indies nationalism in order to go forward.[8] "The New Order," he observes, "is born from stone, without any history. The old order, by contrast, was historical. The New Order is simply the New Order, victimizing millions of people."[9] Historical fiction has the didactic purpose of pointing the nation beyond its neocolonial present. Pramoedya wishes to retrieve the forgotten ideals of a revolutionary past that had somehow taken a wrong turn in

---

7. See GoGwilt, "Interview," pp. 10–11. This historiographical turn is a new phase in Pramoedya's writing. The works of this phase include *Sang Pemula*, the biography of Tirto Adhi Soerjo, the historical figure on which Minke, the quartet's protagonist is based, a study of Kartini, and the maritime epic, *Arus Balik*, which is set in the immediate pre-Dutch era.

The quartet consists of the following volumes: *Bumi Manusia* (Kuala Lumpur: Wira Karya, 1981); *Anak Semua Bangsa* (Kuala Lumpur: Wira Karya, 1982); *Jejak Langkah* (Kuala Lumpur: Wira Karya, 1986); *Rumah Kaca* (Kuala Lumpur: Wira Karya, 1988). These are cited hereafter as *BM*, *ASB*, *JL*, and *RK*, respectively. The English translations by Max Lane are *This Earth of Mankind* (New York: Penguin, 1996); *Child of All Nations* (New York: Penguin, 1996); *Footsteps* (Victoria: Penguin Australia, 1990); *House of Glass* (Victoria: Penguin Australia, 1992). Lane has omitted sentences and sometimes entire paragraphs from his translations. Since it is not possible to assume that these omissions are always of no significance, I will be quoting from the Malay edition and providing corresponding page references to the English edition, following a semicolon. Benedict Anderson and I collaborated on the translations.

8. Pramoedya's writings in the mid-1950s, such as *Tjerita dari Djakarta* and *Korupsi*, offer savagely ironic portrayals of the moral corruption of the postcolonial middle-class elite, who are condemned as betrayers of the nation (identified with the working people). See Keith Foulcher, "In Search of the Postcolonial in Indonesian Literature," *Sojourn* 10 (1995): 147–71.

9. GoGwilt, "Interview," p. 14.

political history—a past summoned up again in images, reincarnated through narrative fiction—and to implant seeds of change in the minds of his readers in the hope of reorienting the nation on its rightful path.

> I began deliberately with the theme of Indonesia's National Awakening— which, while limited regionally and nationally, nonetheless remains part of the world and of humanity. Step by step I am writing [my way] to the roots of its history. . . . In this way, I have tried to answer: why did my people get to be like this, like that?[10]

Indeed, because Pramoedya regards the colonial state as the New Order's predecessor, the colonial state the Buru Quartet potrays is an allegorical stand-in for the latter. His criticisms of the colonial regime are also directed at the policies of Suharto's postcolonial regime. In the 1955 short story, "*Machluk Dibelakang Rumah*" (Creatures behind the house), Pramoedya had already drawn a parallel between the feudal mentality of the *priyayi* caste (the lower-level Javanese aristocracy that supplied native officials for the colonial bureaucracy) and the ethos of inherited superiority used by the parasitic bureaucratic middle class in postcolonial Jakarta to justify their exploitation of the productive labor of others.[11] The Buru Quartet offers more elaborate condemnations of the complicitous role of Javanism, the indigenous cultural source of the *priyayi* attitude, in ensuring native subservience to colonialism. More significantly, in the historically anachronistic figure of Pangemanann, a high-ranking native civil servant who claims to be the brains behind Rinkes, the head of the colonial secret police, Pramoedya personifies the native element within the colonial state that will later take over the state apparatus from the Dutch. "Pangemanann" embodies the New Order state's values and interests.[12]

---

10. "My Apologies," p. 4. Cf. Pramoedya, "Literature, Censorship and the State: How Dangerous are Stories?" *Kabar Seberang,* nos. 24/25 (1995): 100

11. See *Tjerita dari Djakarta: Sekumpulan Karikatur Keadaan dan Manusianja* (Djakarta: Grafica, 1957), pp. 121–22; English translation, *Tales from Djakarta: Caricatures of Circumstances and Their Human Beings* (Ithaca, N.Y.: Southeast Asia Program Publications, Cornell University, 1999), p. 106.

12. Other significant parallels between the quartet's events and contemporary Indonesian politics include the similarities between Pramoedya's persecution by the Suharto regime and Minke's/Tirto Adhi Soerjo's plight, whose achievements colonial historiography attempts to erase from public memory, and the official instigation of anti-Chinese feeling that led to the 1921 boycotts and riots,

But in terms of sociological agency, what adversarial role can radical literature have vis-à-vis the state? How can it transform political reality? Pramoedya's conception of interventionist literary *Bildung* is informed by an unelaborated theory of the public sphere that is similar to Habermas's theory of *Öffentlichkeit*. He opposes the national awakening's egalitarian populist spirit to the rationality of the New Order regime, the genealogical heir of the Dutch colonial state. For Pramoedya, the national spirit achieved institutional embodiment in Sukarno's Old Order. But it was negated by the New Order and awaits reincarnation. This distinction between the national spirit and the state corresponds precisely to the sociological topography of civil society and state. Benedict Anderson has proposed an identical account of the nation/state distinction that clarifies the political pertinence of literary culture. In his view, the nation pursues popular-representational or participatory interests whereas the administrative state is an institution concerned with self-preservation and political and territorial aggrandisement, sometimes regardless of considerations of commercial advantage.[13] In Indonesian political history, Anderson suggests, the colonial era (in which the state's functions under the Ethical Policy proliferate to include education, religion, irrigation, agricultural improvements, hygiene, and political surveillance) typifies a situation where the state apparatus extends deeply into native society, while Old Order Indonesia (where an initial period of parliamentary democracy is followed by Guided Democracy under which Sukarno tries to remobilize extra-state popular organizations) exemplifies a situation where the state is weak and vulnerable to penetration by society. However, under the New Order military regime, this national-popular penetration of the state is reversed. Strengthened by military support, the state begins to repenetrate society:

---

and the state-fostered racial enmity that eventually led to the riots of 1998. For a discussion of Pramoedya's position on Chinese contributions to Indies nationalism, see Ben Abel, "Beholding a Landmark of Guilt: Pramoedya in the Early 1960s and the Current Regime," *Indonesia*, no. 64 (October 1997): 25–26. The New Order actively fostered the retreat of the economically powerful Chinese from the political public sphere to prevent challenges to its hegemony. See Benedict Anderson, "Old State, New Society: Indonesia's New Order in Comparative Historical Perspective," in *Language and Power: Exploring Political Cultures in Indonesia* (Ithaca, N.Y.: Cornell University Press, 1990), p. 116; and James Mackie, "Towkays and Tycoons: The Chinese in Indonesian Economic Life in the 1920s and 1980s," *Indonesia* (1991): 83–96.

13. Anderson, "Old State, New Society," pp. 94–96.

the New Order state is best understood as the resurrection of the state and its triumph vis-à-vis society and nation. The basis for this triumph was laid in the physical annihilation of the PKI and its allies, the suppression of popular movements, sweeping purges of the state apparatus, and the removal of President Sukarno as an effective political force—all achieved between October 1965 and April 1966.[14]

Sukarno's Old Order regime thus represents what a democratic nation-state ought to be, a formation where popular penetration of the state is at its highest. Pramoedya wishes to resurrect this optimal condition. The nation, which is here defined in terms of popular movements and radical political parties instead of race, ethnicity, or cultural tradition, is precisely the public sphere of civil society, a collective ethical agent that presses against the state and makes demands on it in the name of the masses. Indeed, the nation and the public sphere are mutually constitutive. For it is only through public activity such as political organization that the masses become united into a totality, the nation or the people, at the same time that the public sphere's legitimacy derives from its ability to represent the masses' collective interests, which it also actively shapes.

The national public sphere is thus a self-generating and self-causing phenomenon. It is an organism capable of incarnating itself perpetually. Showing itself through the light of publicness, it does nothing less than give phenomenality and, therefore, life, to itself. Indeed, since the national public sphere is the condition of possibility of its own appearing, it may even be phenomenality itself (self-)incarnated as a phenomenon. Hence, although the term "public sphere" originates from positivist sociology, the transformative agency ascribed to it is actually a species of vitalism. This is why Pramoedya characterizes the nation-people as the source of life and the state-institution as an inorganic body or machine, an inanimate apparatus that needs to be imbued with the people's life. Otherwise, as in the New Order, the state will be an instrument of death that stultifies the people's dynamism.

This understanding of political domination as the stultification of life's dynamism is rooted in post-1945 Indonesian cultural politics. It is the

---

14. Ibid., p. 109

direct heir of Chairil Anwar's universal-humanistic understanding of human freedom as vitality, which can be traced back to European philosophical and aesthetic ideals via the "democratic-socialist nationalism" of the Sjahrir circle.[15] As Professor Teeuw observes,

> closely associated with the passion for universality and humanity is an emphasis on Hidup (Life). For Chairil and his contemporaries it was as if the generation before them had not lived; at best they had vegetated in what was, after all, with its bars, a sheltered colonial imprisonment. But the contemporary generation had no excuse any longer for not living life to the full, and passing on their experiences by incorporating them in their creative work. . . . Intensity of living is a criterion of true art.[16]

Lekra, the cultural arm of the Indonesian Communist Party (PKI) to which Pramoedya belonged in the mid-1950s, gave this vitalism a radical cultural nationalist interpretation.[17] Lekra was founded in response to the disappointment with the failure of the 1945 Revolution to achieve a people's democracy. This was coded as the failure to establish a people's culture that could stimulate the masses to become agents of revolutionary struggle.[18]

---

15. The Sjahrir circle was interested in European literature from the romantics to the moderns (mostly Dutch, but also French, German, and English), which, along with philosophy and politics, constituted a source for their ideas. See Keith Foulcher, "Literature, Cultural Politics, and the Indonesian Revolution," in *Text/Politics in Island Southeast Asia: Essays in Interpretation*, ed. D. M. Roskies (Athens, Ohio: Ohio University Center for International Studies, 1993), pp. 228–29.

16. A. Teeuw, *Modern Indonesian Literature*, 1:124–25. In the section entitled "The Angkatan 45: Chairil Anwar and Vitalism," Teeuw suggests that Anwar was inspired by the Dutch poet Marsman's veneration of intensity and the primeval strength of life.

17. After independence, the Gelanggang group of intellectuals sought to claim the Angkatan 45 as the precursor of its ideology of universal humanism and disinterested aestheticism, which it opposed to Lekra's cultural nationalism. For a more elaborate account of the polemics between Gelanggang and Lekra, and Pramoedya's connection to Lekra, see Foulcher, "Literature, Cultural Politics, and the Indonesian Revolution;" Martina Heinschke, "Between Gelanggang and Lekra: Pramoedya's Developing Literary Concepts," *Indonesia*, no. 61 (1996): 145–69; and Hendrik Maier, "Chairil Anwar's Heritage: The Fear of Stultification—Another Side of Modern Indonesian Literature," *Indonesia*, no. 43 (1987): 1–29.

18. Lekra's "Mukadimah" (manifesto) states that "the failure of the Revolution of August 1945 also means the failure of the cultural workers to destroy colonial culture and replace it by a democratic culture, a People's culture." A People's culture "should be the stimulus of the masses, the source that incessantly creates enthusiasm and revolutionary fire that can not be extinguished. . . . People's

Lekra's vitalist and materialist discourse offers to Indonesian politics the felicitous schema of a people's culture penetrating the weak body of the postindependence state to breathe life into it, to inspirit and reinvigorate it, thereby transforming it into a popular-democratic nation-state. This schema was especially appropriate to the political situation in 1960–1961, when Sukarno, whose power was increasingly challenged by the army, forged an alliance with the PKI to strengthen his position through the use of the PKI's popular base. Lekra played an essential part in consolidating Sukarno's hegemony because its discourse about creating a "People's culture" helped extend the PKI's mass base.[19] This alliance is precisely the penetration of a weak state by extrastate elements, society galvanised by the cultural intelligentsia.

Herein lies the connection that Pramoedya, Ngũgĩ, and other theorists of postcolonial nationalism have made between radical literature and the transformation of political reality: radical literature plays an important role in creating a critical public sphere. If we scratch this commonsensical answer for its underlying ontological presuppositions, we see that for Pramoedya, literature can catalyze the negation of the New Order in the dialectic of Indonesian nationalism because it is the quintessential expression of life's vitality and the paradigmatic example of the power of actualizing ideals. For Pramoedya, a radical culture that is rooted in the Indonesian people's daily lives is the best expression of life's vitality and human freedom.[20] Through aesthetic representation, literary culture can conjure up and reincarnate

---

culture is obliged to teach and instruct the People to become the hero of its own struggle" (quoted in Hendrik Maier, "Chairil Anwar's Heritage," 4–5).

19. Sukarno attended Lekra's first National Congress in 1959 and praised it for making an important contribution to the mental revolution of the Indonesian people, the necessary precondition of the political and social revolution he intended to take place (Hendrik Maier, "Chairil Anwar's Heritage," 12).

20. Pramoedya was a marginal member of Gelanggang until the mid-1950s when he became disaffected with universal humanism. In his Magsaysay speech, "Literature, Censorship, and the State," he refers to Anwar's poem, "Aku," as a unique example of avant-garde literature that constitutes an act of rebellion against (Japanese) military oppression (100). He transposes Anwar's individualistic definition of the free person of modernity as "an ego . . . cast out from its community" into a national communitarianism: "Indonesia can also grow strong by creating strong individuals, who . . . will be able to say *I am an integral member of the whole community*," a community founded on and supported by the principles of Pancasila" (Pramoedya, "The Role and Attitude of Intellectuals in the Third World," *Kabar Seberang*, nos. 24/25 [1995]: 118).

the national spirit. By giving this spirit sensuous form, the radical writer implants in his society an embyro from which will spring forth an organis- mic, dynamic, national public sphere that can transform the state.

Pramoedya's idea of a revolutionary people's culture thus fuses Anwar's vitalism with that of a Hegelian-Marxist discourse. This reaffirmation of the view that culture is the ontological basis of political freedom is essential to the Buru Quartet's conception. The quartet is neither straight historiog- raphy (like *Sang Pemula*), nor a political treatise on Dutch colonialism. However, the events and characters portrayed in the books are also not merely imaginary. The events are fictive and contain a kernel of historical fact; the characters have names that are slightly different from their histori- cal counterparts.[21] Alloys of fact and imagination, these altered names are synecdoches for the dialectical relation between literature and historical reality at the quartet's heart. The characters are not faithful reflections of individuals in Indonesian political history, but ideal historical types in the Weberian sense, a logically precise conception constructed by abstraction from historical reality, a pure or extreme case that does not exist histori- cally.[22] However, an ideal type is not an imaginative invention without any connection to reality. It is abstracted from historical material. Similarly, for Pramoedya, literature is neither just a more truthful reflection of his- torical reality, a rote recounting, nor the expression of utopian ideals that

---

21. Minke, the narrator, refuses to disclose his name and is only identified by Tirto's initials in the last volume. Other characters have names that are not quite identical to the historical figures they are based on but easily allow one to infer who they are. Douwes Dekker becomes Edu Douwager and Soewardi Soerjaningrat becomes Wardi; Marco becomes Marko, and so on. Minke's personal life is part fact, part fiction. Tirto really does marry a Princess of Bacan, but he never had a Chinese wife. He is exiled for six months, not six years.

22. See Max Weber, "The Social Psychology of the World Religions," in *From Max Weber: Essays in Sociology*, ed. H. H. Gerth and C. Wright Mills (London: Routledge, 1991), p. 294. A cursory read- ing of an earlier version of the quartet's final volume, *Di Atas Lumpur* (unpublished manuscript, n.d., John M. Echols Collection on Southeast Asia, Kroch Asia Library, Cornell University), is instructive because the characters retain their true historical names and the narrator of *Jejak Langkah* is explicitly Tirto Ardhi Soerjo, and not Minke, whereas Pramoedya retains the narrator- ial persona throughout the published version of the quartet. Cf. *Di Atas Lumpur,* 140; *RK,* 193. One might surmise that Pramoedya decided to retain Minke throughout the quartet to emphasize that its protagonist is an ideal type. He confirms this view by having Pangemanann observe that in his narrative, Minke is primarily a witness to social conditions of his time and places more importance on them than on faithful self-portrayal (*RK,* 193; cf. *Di Atas Lumpur,* 140).

are completely divorced from real existence.[23] It is a different way of seeing the past that can intervene as an event to change the tide of history.

In a 1992 essay, Pramoedya uses the metaphor of the ebb and flow of a stream to characterize literature's formative force or causality:

> it is not the materials of history that I examine but its *spirit*. This I began with the tetralogy *Bumi Manusia*, particularly working on the currents that ebbed and flowed during the period of Indonesia's National Awakening. *And so there came to be a new reality, that is, a literary reality,* a downstream reality, whose origin was an upstream reality, that is, a historical reality. A literary reality that contains within it a reorientation and evaluation of civilization and culture, which is precisely not contained in the historical reality. So it is that *the literary work is a sort of thesis,* an infant that on its own begins to grow in the superstructure of the life of its readers' society. It is the same with new discoveries in every field, that carry society a step forward.[24]

The use of "spirit" and "thesis" in Pramoedya's idea of "literary reality" reveals a dialectical understanding of the historical process and literature's role within it. The quartet's primary function is not to portray "what really happened" in the past ("the materials of history"), but to examine *why* history happened the way it did. As something spiritual, history is more than mere facticity. It is also the realm of possibility. It is the product not only of accidentality and blind chance, but also of rational actions. Because it is spiritual, its path is open to the possibility of ethical transformation. Literature can play a fundamental role in reorienting Indonesian political history

---

23. Pramoedya views the relationship between literature and reality as one of dialectical causality. I depart from Wim Wertheim's and Hendrik Maier's views of the quartet's status. Wertheim sees the quartet as an example of historical fiction. It is identical in function to the revisionist historiographical *Sang Pemula*. In this view, fiction is secondary to and derived from reality, which it aims to faithfully represent. Its historiographical value is lower than that of historical research because it is less true. See "Pramoedya as Historian," *Kabar Seberang,* nos. 24/25 (1995): 82–83. In contradistinction, Maier suggests that for Pramoedya, literature is the free play of the signifier, and it constructs an imaginary domain by reshaping historical facts according to literary criteria to provide temporary relief from the vicissitudes of history. Literature is a realm of ideals that is separate from reality and can be used to evaluate the latter. See "The Dream of Reality—The Writing of 'Blora,'" *Kabar Seberang,* nos. 24/25 (1995): 69. Both views miss the point that Pramoedya attributes to literature a causal power over reality.

24. Pramoedya, "My Apologies," p. 4; emphasis added.

because it can return to the source of history by retracing its upstream movement and capture the original ground or essential spirit underlying the contingencies of factical existence.

What this retracing creates is a "literary reality," which ought to be understood as *Wirklichkeit* in the Hegelian sense. Literary reality is not an escapist fantasy without any relation to banal existence. Paradoxically, it is truer, more *wirklich*, than historical reality because it is the truth of history, the purposiveness of history's unfolding, incarnated in the sensuous shape of literature. For Pramoedya, the spiritual truth of Indonesian political history is, of course, the nation-people. The personal experience of writers is, he observes, "also the experience of their people, and the experience of their people is also their personal experience. A part of this experience, small or large or the whole lot, will erupt in their writings, and will return to the people in the form of new realities, literary realities. *That is why the truth of fiction is also the truth of history.*"[25] The dialectic between fiction and reality is part of the larger dialectic of the Indonesian nation's epigenesis. The quartet offers a prescriptive patterning to Indonesian political history, projecting and opening up a future beyond the New Order from the detritus it retrieves from a past when the nation was in the process of being born and its political history was still full of possibility.[26]

Literature is thus a form of *Bildung*. It attempts to actualize the spiritual truth of history, to give it flesh as a recharged national public sphere. In a 1983 essay on the creative process, Pramoedya echoes the modern philosopheme of culture by suggesting that literature is the paradigmatic example of freedom understood as a creative power that cobelongs with the human faculty of reason. Drawing an extended analogy between the creation of the natural world by an absolute Creator and the creation of human works of art, he suggests that artistic creativity originates from a mystical fusion of the writer's self with an Absolute Creator. Instead of a moment in which the identity of the writer is lost in a delirious, orgiastic synthesis with the divine other (such as in "traditional-pagan" mysticism), this fusion, which Pramoedya calls the "*mysticum*," is a moment of ascesis in which the "I"

---

25. Ibid., pp. 8–9; emphasis added.
26. Ibid., p. 12: "[The task of literature is] not to mirror or reflect events, because the task of literature is not to take pictures, but to change upstream realities to become a literary reality, that will carry its readers further forward than the established order."

finds itself secreted, or secretes itself, as an absolute self-identity outside of empirical space-time. Pramoedya figures this insularity from the outside as "liberation, a total freedom to survive as a self, intense, immune to all political, military, social, and economic power in no matter what system— a sanctuary of meditation."[27]

This is precisely the auto-causality of Kantian transcendental freedom. The creative process is a crystallization of humanity's freedom from mechanistic laws: "courage, determination, discipline, faith, responsibility and awareness [*kesedaran*] . . . lead [man] to take initiatives of his own without being commanded" ("*Perburuan* 1950 and *Keluarga Gerilya* 1950," 28). What is crucial is the creative process's autonomy, its ability to raise itself to the level of an absolute authority independent from all external influences: "this *mysticum,* a condensed personal freedom, . . . liberates the I from the world outside it and places the I beyond the reach of the power of Time. . . . [T]his experience is so individual in character, it needs no validation by anyone else" (ibid., 28). As the self's ability to extract itself from the causal chain determining past and present events, freedom is the sheer power of initiation, the ability to bring into existence what does not yet exist. Just as the absolute Creator is revealed to humanity as life's inexhaustible capacity to perpetuate itself infinitely through the incarnation of natural beings, human creativity, which involves the materialization of ideal forms, is the trace of the absolute in us: "creative work means honoring that Lord who brings all to life, it means giving birth to a new entity, which then lives on outside time" (ibid., 27). Hence, the work of art is an *attunement* to life's vitality: "literary works function effectively to stimulate rational and emotional awareness and responsibility towards the infinite variety of life" (ibid., 28), and "the problematic of literature is the problematic of man in his living existence" (ibid., 40).

This organismic idea of freedom underwrites Pramoedya's socialist conception of committed literature in the same way that the German idealist conception of freedom informs Marxist materialism. The first step to achieving concrete freedoms is enlightenment, the ability to free oneself from traditional sociopolitical structures through rational critique. For Pramoedya, enlightenment is identical to transcendence through creativity:

---

27. "*Perburuan* 1950 and *Keluarga Gerilya* 1950," p. 26.

"the pattern of 'kampung' civilization and culture, that self-same vicious circle . . . can only be broken by a reevaluation of it, *Verlichting, Aufklaerung,* that produces the creativity to break through its own ceiling."[28] Indeed, the isomorphism between the living integrity of the Indonesian people qua critical public and the personal dignity of an individual means that national culture is the paradigmatic case of genuine creative endeavor. One sees here the strong affinity between culture, organic life, freedom, and the nation-form. Pramoedya repeatedly suggests that each socially engaged literary work is a contribution to the nation's epigenetic struggle against the New Order state. Intellectual work should be a form of national *Bildung,* evolving according to national needs and playing a crucial role in developing the nation and securing its future. The writer is not a propagandist, but the nation's conscience. "The work of the intellect is not simply a social attribute but is spontaneous, purposeful, and a natural mode of thought and ethics for the whole nation."[29] Because it is attuned to life's vitality, committed literature can revive the national public sphere. Conversely, genuine literature is national in vocation because the nation is the medium in which individuals can achieve autonomy. Thus, genuine literature can incarnate "the spirit of the Third World, what was once known as the spirit of Afro-Asia, and then, the spirit of Asia, Africa and Latin America."[30]

Pramoedya counterposes the New Order ideology of universal humanism and detached aestheticism to popular radical nationalist or internationalist culture. This official ideology is a form of spiritual death. Its widespread acceptance would put an end to the committed literary culture that can incarnate the national spirit. Hence, this deadly ideology is satanic. It is opposed to spiritual objects (*benda rohani*) and actuality and brings about orgiastic delirium and self-loss: "what is produced, either without, or in rejection of, awareness and responsibility—such as trance or "possession" [*kesetanan*]—not only is not art, but is what one can call anti-culture."[31] A detached humanism can only engender an anticulture consisting of nonactual phantomatic objects because it is not rooted in the Indonesian people's

---

28. "My Apologies," p. 7. The image of breaking through a circle echoes the motif of breaking through the circle of time in the 1983 essay.
29. "The Role and Attitude of Intellectuals," pp. 117–18.
30. Ibid., p. 118.
31. "*Perburuan 1950* and *Keluarga Gerilya 1950*," p. 28.

concrete life: "No matter how wonderful our ideas are, if we make no attempt to realise them physically they remain as mere wandering spirits—evil spirits whose only purpose is to lead mankind astray."[32]

Pramoedya's commentators have largely deferred to the weight of his authorial intention. They have read the Buru Quartet as an incarnation of the Indonesian national spirit and mostly devoted themselves to a sociological reconstruction of his polemical ideas. Instead of *reading* the quartet, they have regarded it as an example of or illustrative footnote to Pramoedya's theory of national *Bildung*. But since we cannot take for granted the successful incarnation of a national spirit that transcends the New Order state, we cannot dogmatically assume that the quartet is a successful incarnation of Pramoedya's ideas about literature. The quartet puts the idea of incarnation itself at stake. It tries to reincarnate the spirit of the national awakening as a historical sign of the past existence and future possibility of freedom for the Indonesian people. But, as we will see, this reincarnation goes awry because the national spirit is infected with a certain ghostliness, which the neocolonial state embodies, sometimes to the point where nation and state are no longer distinct entities. This constitutive haunting of the living nation by the death-dealing state—from which Pramoedya tries to guard it—puts into question the organismic-vitalist philosopheme of culture as the power of human self-actualization.

THE BIRTH AND ARRESTED LIFE OF THE INDONESIAN NATION CIRCA 1900

Pramoedya's decision to write a tetralogy charting the birth of a proto-Indonesian national consciousness hearkens back to a point when literary culture, in the form of an emerging native press, played an important role in the performative constitution of an Indies-wide native public sphere that challenged the colonial state. Here, organismic vitalism is performed in/as history in that not so far-flung corner of the world where Ludwig Fischer, Hegel's illegitimate son by his landlady in Jena, died on 28 August 1831. It is experienced and inflected in the lives of early Indies nationalists.

---

32. "The Role and Attitude of Intellectuals," p. 118.

This emergent public is the nation in embryo. Born from modern, rational forms of political organization and technomediation, the nation-people is an instance of the successful incarnation of life's spirit. The quartet is its reincarnation, where the bildungsroman becomes a means of the nation's *Bildung*.

The quartet recounts the nation's birth and predicts the imminent arrestation of its growth and its afterlife. The books follow the life and demise of Minke, the protagonist and narrator of the first three volumes— *Bumi Manusia* (This earth of humankind), *Anak Semua Bangsa* (Child of all nations) and *Jejak Langkah* (Footsteps)—and his nemesis, Pangemanann, the high-level native official of the Dutch colonial regime who is responsible for Minke's death, who narrates the final installment, *Rumah Kaca* (Glass house). Based on the historical figure Tirto Adhi Soerjo, whom Pramoedya regards as the initiator of the national awakening and the father of the national press, Minke personifies the nation. Pangemanann personifies the colonial and neocolonial states.

The first two volumes focus on how Minke, a Dutch-educated Javanese youth of aristocratic descent, develops into a moral personality under the maternal wing of Nyai Ontosoroh, a native woman who was sold into concubinage as a teenager to a Dutch factory administrator but later becomes a wealthy independent businesswoman. Minke's maturation takes place in the turn-of-the-century era of rapid technological and geopolitical change that saw the spectacular modernization of Japan, the rise of a modernizing Chinese Youth movement, and the Filipino revolution against Spain. The third book chronicles Minke's life in Batavia, the capital of Dutch Indies colonial power. Unlike other natives of his social caste, he chooses to devote his life to the betterment of his people, eschewing the wealth and status of official service in the native arm of the Dutch colonial bureaucracy. *Jejak Langkah* also documents how Minke, influenced by the Chinese republican movement, becomes a nationalist who founds the first modern native political organization in the Indies, the Sarekat Islam, his establishment of the first native-owned Malay newspaper, and his subsequent exile and fall. The final volume recounts the life of the native awakening, or *pergerakan*, in the years of its founder's exile and Minke's return and ignominious death from the perspective of the colonial state. Simply put, the quartet's didactic message is that if Minke's death and the Sarekat Islam's stagnation allegorize the nation's obstruction by the New Order state, the subsequent haunting of his destroyer, Pangemanann, by Minke's spiritual offspring (his ideals and his followers in the *pergerakan*) allegorizes the nation's afterlife as an inexorcisable specter that haunts the state.

As radical literary culture, the quartet continues this haunting of the contemporary Indonesian state. It is an active example of the nationalist project. It does not only reflect the birth of nationalism as a past event, but aims to revive the nation by jogging Indonesian public memory. An example of literature as a modality of the power of incarnation, the quartet has the status of an event. It summons a forgotten specter of Indonesian history into the present to bring it back to life and give it flesh. Indeed, as censored literature, the quartet had the shadowy existence of a specter in New Order Indonesia. Therefore, one specter refers back to another in order to reincarnate the other and itself as an actual and concrete living force, the national public sphere that can penetrate and transform the neocolonial state. This is precisely the sense in which Marx spoke of the proletarian movement as the incarnation of the specter of communism in Europe by modern capitalist forces circa 1848. For Pramoedya, the nation is what the proletariat was for Marx, a living collective body that is the best vehicle for actualizing freedom. Hence, like Cabral, Fanon, and other theorists of decolonizing nationalism, Pramoedya also formulates the class struggle in national terms. The nation is the spirit of Indonesian political history and not an atavistic ideological formation of the bourgeois state. Far from being based on traditional feudal ties or those of culture and blood, Indonesian national consciousness was based on political, legal, and economic necessity in its inception. It is an organism, the product of modern forms of rational organization that give shape to public opinion and disseminate a democratic spirit that opposes the colonial state. The press especially "became not merely an instrument of the national struggle, but also an instrument for uniting the nation."[33]

Pramoedya's organismic nationalism has clear affinities with both Habermas's theory of the public sphere and Benedict Anderson's conception of the nation as an imagined political community. For him, print epitomizes the light of modern reason and has the power to shape the public and unite

---

33. *SP*, p. 147.

the nation. This is a valuable alternative to the contemporary dismissal of nationalism in postcolonial criticism as a pathological ideology that underwrites fundamentalist identity politics in the South. The postcolonial critique repeats the conventional critique of nationalism. However, it identifies postcolonial nationalism's pathological nature not with irrationality, but with the European Enlightenment itself. The Enlightenment's drive for mastery and domination of the external world, it is suggested, has been bequeathed to the Third World through colonialist discourse's *rational will* to totalitarianism. Partha Chatterjee's formulation is exemplary:

> If nationalism expresses itself in a frenzy of irrational passion, it does so *because* it seeks to represent itself in the image of the Enlightenment and *fails* to do so. For Enlightenment itself, to assert its sovereignty as the universal ideal, needs its Other, if it could ever actualize itself in the real world as the truly universal, it would in fact destroy itself. No matter how much the liberal-rationalist may wonder, the Cunning of Reason has not met its match in nationalism. On the contrary, it has seduced, apprehended and imprisoned it [nationalism].[34]

Pramoedya is an interesting counterexample of a radical intellectual in the postcolonial South because he defends nationalism and insists on the importance of modern reason as the basis of national consciousness. He implicitly questions the plausibility of dismissing postcolonial nationalism's emancipatory potential simply because it is based on modern reason. In the first place, arguments such as Chatterjee's subscribe to an idealistic understanding of the genesis of national consciousness. Instead of attending to the material upheaval that accompanies modernity and how these changes are fundamental conditions of the emergence of national consciousness, they focus on the reception of European Enlightenment *ideas* by native intellectuals. Second, and more importantly, postcolonial critics almost always confuse the instrumental rationality of the historical Enlightenment with modern reason per se and construct a monolithic bogeyman. They

---

34. Partha Chatterjee, *Nationalist Thought and the Colonial World: A Derivative Discourse?* (London: Zed, 1986), p. 17.

seem unaware that the English did not have an Enlightenment and fail to differentiate between the Scottish, French, or German Enlightenments, or the latter from the German idealist legacy.[35] These postcolonialist arguments also do not emphasize the heterogeneity of reason—for instance, the Frankfurt School's distinction between instrumental and critical reason. As we will see, Pramoedya associates colonialism with instrumental reason. But unlike Chatterjee, he does not think that nationalism has the same origins because it emerges from the self-recursivity of rational organization. In his view, vernacular print is the necessary condition for the development of a modern consciousness in a relatively large number of natives who did not have a formal Dutch education. The modern ethos is not a gift of the Dutch *ethici*. It is induced by material conditions that include the dissemination of print technology. Pramoedya's understanding of modernity is therefore resolutely materialist. For him, modernity refers to a constellation of sociological conditions that generate the spirit conventionally identified as modern. Minke does not learn this ethos from his school lessons although their content goes under the name of "Enlightenment." For enlightenment is not a body of knowledge disseminated in colonial schools to be learnt by rote, but the attitude of self-questioning that allows one to escape self-incurred tutelage (à la Kant).

My analysis of Pramoedya's affirmation of Indonesian national consciousness will involve a critique of the modern philosophemes of freedom, organic life, and culture. But unlike the general thrust of postcolonial theory, I will not paint nationalism as an ideology of modern reason or a statist ideology against which one opposes the real masses. To believe that one can leave modern reason behind through critique is precisely to endorse it since it is to believe that one can rationally *free* oneself of modern reason. Indeed, as I argued in chapter 4, the thought of freedom as the self-determination of a collective body (the proletariat, the masses, the nation, and so on) necessarily implies the organismic self-recursivity that defines reason. But conversely, although its radical potential needs to be affirmed, postcolonial nationalism is also not the vehicle in which the freedom of the

---

35. Chatterjee's primary target is English utilitarianism and liberalism. He seems unaware of the distinction between the understanding and reason in idealist philosophy. Yet, as I pointed out in chapter 4, his solution to postcolonial nationalism's impasse is organismic. It relies on the self-recursivity of reason.

Indonesian masses can be fully incarnated. The Buru Quartet's textual conduct indicates that even though the nation cannot be reduced to an ideological epiphenomenon or insubstantial ghostly reflection of the state, it is also not the effectively actual progressive force or living incarnation of modern freedom that Pramoedya would like it to be because it is haunted by the state apparatus it wishes to inspirit and transform. The task is to examine how the very structures of national consciousness are at one and the same time both the condition of possibility and impossibility of (its own) freedom. Since freedom is coextensive with the vitality and incarnational power of human reason, it is also to attend to the specter that constitutively inhabits reason and to grasp the nation as a case of spectrality, precariously hovering between the actual and the ideological.

THE MODERNITY OF NATIONAL CONSCIOUSNESS: THE SPECTRAL WORLD OF MODERN KNOWLEDGE

Why is national consciousness a case of modern reason? For Pramoedya, national consciousness is not rooted in traditional mystical forms of rationality. Its historical conditions are the material forces of upheaval that irreparably change the native world after its encounter with modernity. In the quartet, the national awakening (even before it is named) takes the form of Minke's development of a modern rationality as a result of his access to enlightened education and the gradual demagicking of the traditional world of the Indies natives by modern technoscientific progress. The first three volumes are a "phenomenology" of the genesis of national consciousness. They show us that national consciousness has the traits of modern reason's two fundamental structures: a perception that has been deepened by scientific knowledge of the objective/empirical world and technomediation, and a capacity for self-reflection that enables a consciousness to view itself not only as a subject, but also as an object within the larger objective world so that it can transform itself and its external surroundings.

The second chapter of *Bumi Manusia* (This earth of humankind) begins with a eulogy to modern scientific knowledge. "Scientific knowledge," the young Minke observes, "has already bestowed upon me a blessing that is of unlimited beauty" (2; 16). This gift or present should be understood in the most literal sense. Modern learning bestows to the youth the world as a complex object of empirical knowledge. The modern positivist conception of the natural world as the totality of objects that are governed by immutable laws and have scientifically verifiable qualities deepens and widens the realm of the visible—the field of perceptual experience—because it replaces the mere beliefs of a cosmological worldview with certainties that can be witnessed and verified. As Minke notes, "I place greater trust in scientific knowledge, reason. At least with them, there are certainties that one can hold on to." (*BM*, 5; 19) What is intoxicating about modern knowledge is not only the demystification of the world into a cognizable object: more importantly, as an object for the knowing subject, the external world has become an objective ideality. Its individual contents are not isolated entities we apprehend with our naked eye but objects we can insert into a larger web of relations by virtue of knowledge, even if we have never had any immediate experience of them.

Because it frees the subject from being tethered to the object's immediate presence, modern knowledge deepens human vision and extends its reach beyond the field of immediate experience and face-to-face contact. One can know the truth about something without ever having seen it because the knowledge obtained from reading was originally empirically verified. Reading deepens how we see because concrete reality becomes penetrated or suffused by absence and the insubstantial, the spectrality of modern science and *techne*. Nothing evokes this deepening of visibility by *techne* more eerily than photography, especially in its intersection with modern print technology. Photography uncannily extends the field of presence and experience by allowing people to see a world that they cannot immediately apprehend. As Minke observes, the printed photograph captures reality in its entirety, unlike premodern block and lithographic prints: "pictures of landscapes, august and important people, new machines, American skyscrapers, everything and from all over the world—I can now witness for myself on these sheets of printed paper" (*BM*, 2; 17).

This deepening of perception by the spectrality of modern knowledge and technomediation brings the world closer to us and allows us to place ourselves within a larger totality. It achieves at the level of subjective consciousness the shrinking of the world that technological progress inevitably brings about: the annihilation of spatial distance by the rail tracks that connect the whole of Java and the telegraph cables that connect the Indies to the larger world. The specters of modern knowledge and technomedia are thus not opposed to actuality. They represent a historically new type of effectivity or productive force (*kekuatan*) that is more powerful in its capacity to transform physical reality than merely physical force. This is the incarnational power of practical reason, humanity's power to make its ideas actual through the formation of nature as material and the technical harnessing and redirection of natural forces according to rationally self-prescribed ends, using screws and nuts and so on.

The internalization of humanity's perceived mastery over nature leads to the emergence of a self-reflective consciousness that can map its place within the external world and situate itself in relation to the cultural ties and social norms governing the surroundings in which it finds itself. For a self-reflective consciousness, such ties and norms are no longer quasi-natural, inherited characteristics of one's makeup, but objects of thematic understanding. This is why modernity gives rise to national consciousness. Minke begins to take meticulous notes about his experiences because life experience is the source of knowledge that can be accumulated and set aside for future use. He sees his scribbling as a sign of his modernity, his alienation from his traditional Javanese heritage:

> The science and knowledge that I received from school and the truth of which I witnessed in life made my personality [*pribadiku*] very different from that of my people [*sebangsaku*] in general. Whether or not it violated my existence as a Javanese person, I do not know. And so it is that my life experience as a European-educated Javanese determined my fondness for making notes. One day, they would be of use to me, like they are now [the moment of the narration].
>
> (*BM*, 2; 16–17)

This propensity for note taking indicates that the self-reflective consciousness of a modern personality is a narrative consciousness, one that can produce public narratives with a general validity beyond the self-interested private individual who is their origin. National consciousness develops from this narrative responsibility to a public. Minke first begins to make notes after his second visit to Buitenzorg, the home of his future mentor and symbolic mother, Nyai Ontosoroh.

> I entered the room, opened up my notebook and began writing about this strange and frightening family that, by sheer accident, had now involved me

too in its affairs. Who knows, I thought, some day in the future I may be able to produce stories like "When Roses Wilt," the remarkable serial by Hertog Lamoye? Yes, who knows? So far I've only written advertisements and short articles for the auction papers. Who could tell? With my own byline and read by the public? Who could tell? (*BM*, 60–61; 68)

Minke's consciousness sees itself as persisting through linear time. It signs a pact or contract with its future self who is an unknowable other, the "who" of the unforeseeable future, to whom he feels himself accountable, who surges up to question and judge his present actions. I must take notes now because who can tell, who knows whether they will be useful in the future. If I do not take notes now, I will have failed this other who is my vocation, my future self. As the passage progresses, this "who" opens up into a public when Minke contemplates the possibility that he could be a public persona, a writer for a public. Here, an accountability to a collective body begins to take shape. My actions in the present are *destined* for the collective body of posterity that exceeds the spatiotemporal boundaries of *my* individual body and mind located in *this* space and *this* present time. This implicit sense of responsibility to a yet-undefined collective body takes shape precisely because Minke is developing a modern consciousness capable of internalizing his experiences of the external world, rationally integrating them into its stream so that these voices become an interior debate within what has now become an enlarged, worldly consciousness.

This worldly consciousness has no essential substance. It develops epigenetically and changes depending on how it decides to respond to external events, the collective vocation it prescribes for itself, and the collective identifications it makes. This collective interiority that develops from the capacity to narrate is the basis of the nation-people. Minke distinguishes it from the immediate unity of self and collectivity in traditional communities: "the generation before me has been deprived indeed—a generation that is satisfied with the sum of its own footsteps in the lanes of its villages" (*BM*, 2–3; 17). A traditional consciousness is complacent and satisfied with the narrow ambit of *kampung* (parochial) life, the limits of which it cannot perceive. By sundering all immediate affective ties, modern knowledge gives us a larger field of possibilities from which we can choose how best to develop ourselves. Hence, a modern person is bound by affiliations that he chooses for intelligent reasons. That Minke can even contemplate being alienated from his Javanese heritage means his being-Javanese, and, indeed, Javanese culture as a whole, have become topoi for him, matters of thematic knowledge. Modern knowledge has enabled him to imaginatively step out of his factically given position so that he can view himself as a *factum* from the outside, so to speak, thereby allowing him to see himself as a Javanese and choose whether he wishes to *be* Javanese.[36]

THE COMPARATIVE GAZE AND THE DESIRE FOR NATIONAL *BILDUNG*

A modern consciousness that can free itself from heteronomous determinations is not yet national. It can become so because the world of print also engenders a comparative gaze that stimulates the desire for collective progress and national self-determination by enabling the native subject to cognitively map his geographical position within the larger world. The dedication in *Anak Semua Bangsa* (Child of all nations) refers to this comparative gaze as a crucial stage of *Bildung*, the inner-directed shaping of the self through the internalization of an image (*Bild*) of an ideal personality prescribed by communal norms: "It is tiresome and tedious to follow every single step of any person in the process of finding his place within the world and his society, so as to become himself [as a full personality]." Contrary to the conventional understanding of the bildungsroman as a linear narrative of progress toward an ideal goal, the process of *Bildung* is inherently unstable. For the moral personality that is its prescribed telos cannot be taken for granted. Since it is formed by the ingestion of an image by rational consciousness, it is marked by an a priori vulnerability, the a priori opening-out of itself onto something other (here, the image). This becoming-open to alterity must be constitutive of rational consciousness if it is to receive and internalize an image, even a self-prescribed one. As we will see, the national organism will always be susceptible to *techne* because the incarnation of national consciousness is marked by this a priori vulnerability to otherness.

---

36. This projection in advance of oneself is also an ability to see oneself as a third person ("you as someone else, as a question . . . as an actor, as somebody else that you see in the mirror") so that one can solve one's problems rationally. See *BM*, 249; 256.

Minke's consciousness is riddled with uncertainty. The older Minke, the narrator who recounts material from notes he made earlier, does not know where he is heading because he is not sure if these past events lead to something meaningful. In the opening of chapter 1, the narrative of events following Annelies's (his wife, Nyai Ontosoroh's daughter) enforced departure for the Netherlands is framed by a meditation on the contingency and finitude of human existence and knowledge, and immediately preceded by an admission that the narrative has no rationally justifiable origin or intentional design: "I do not really know whether this is an appropriate beginning for this narrative [*catatan*]. At the very least everything must have a beginning. And this is the beginning of my narrative" (*ASB*, 2; 14). It is as if Minke were saying "do what you may with my notes." Here, these are my notes, even though this may not be a proper origin and I cannot justify that it is the proper way to begin. Everything must have an origin somewhere, and so here they are, take them as you find them. He makes a similar admission about the notes of his encounter with Ter Haar, a radical pro-native Dutch journalist:

> (I myself had doubts at the time of writing this whether or not it would be appropriate to include all that follows, especially since I was not able to fathom all that he said). But it would also not be right not to write it down: Ter Haar took me into other continents that never came up in my geography lessons. So if these notes read like a pamphlet—yes, that was the situation I had entered. *The ship, the ocean, the past, Surabaya and Wonokromo back there—uh, they also became pages of a pamphlet. Fragments of meaning that were incomplete.* (*ASB*, 260; 259; emphasis added)

Hence, the constitution of Minke's personality as a committed social and political consciousness does not occur during his intense experience of events. It occurs belatedly, when he sits down to arrange (*susun*) these experiences. In themselves, these events are fragments that do not make a whole. Their significance does not exist prior to the act of rearrangement by attentive rereading. Similarly, since Minke only becomes a full personality after he grasps and interiorizes the significance of these events, the constitution of his personality occurs only through, and as a result of, an extended scene of reading and rereading his own notes of what has occurred to him—this makes up the first three books. This reading gives place to his personality; he reads himself into place. Ideally, the quartet's putative Indonesian reader is also supposed to read himself into (national) place in a similar process of *Bildung*.[37]

The mapping of a self in terms of its place within the chain of links that make up society or the world at large, a mapping which produces a social consciousness, is first of all a revisionary act of thematization. To position or place oneself is also to posit oneself within a chain of events. Indeed, many significant events in Minke's *Bildung* are *events of reading*. Reading is an event because it is an important means of receiving information about the larger world. The extension and supplementation of the field of immediate apprehension by this new global space opened up by writing and print also makes the formation of Minke's personality a process of national *Bildung*. The initial sequence in chapter 3 consists of Minke's summaries of newspaper reports and editorial discussions on the Dutch colonial government's granting of European status to the Japanese in the Indies at the end of the nineteenth century. It evokes a consciousness, inundated by too many different sources of information, trying to organize this sometimes conflicting information so that he can better position himself within this global space:

I returned to my old activities again: reading newspapers, certain magazines, books and letters, writing notes and articles. . . . All this reading taught me a great deal about myself, about my place within my immediate surroundings [*di tengah-tengah linkunganku*], the world at large, and the relentless march of time. Looking at all this as in a mirror, I felt myself afloat in the wind without a place on earth where I could stand [*melayang-layang tanpa bumi tempat berpijak*] (ASB, 38; 47).

This larger world is a mirror that allows Minke to stand outside of himself and observe himself as a being in the world. He draws on his previous notes on Japan's invasion of China to make things less confusing and to help him arrange this new information into a meaningful account:

---

37. This is similar to Fredric Jameson's idea of "cognitive mapping." See "Cognitive Mapping," in *Marxism and the Interpretation of Culture,* ed. Cary Nelson and Lawrence Grossberg (Urbana, Ill.: University of Illinois Press, 1988) 347–60; and *Postmodernism, or the Cultural Logic of Late Capitalism* (Durham: Duke University Press, 1991).

The story reads like this if I arrange it in my own way. . . . In my old notes I read. . . . Three years ago, a history book said, a treaty was signed between the Netherlands Indies and Japan. Japan again! In it: the Netherlands Indies have the right to look upon Japanese residents in the Indies as having the status of Orientals [*Timur Asing*]. That was three years ago. A year after the treaty: the Indies government hurriedly drafted a new law that grants the same legal status to Japanese in the Indies as to Europeans. And now, the time that I write, Japanese residents in the Indies have the same status as European residents.

(*ASB*, 38–39; 47–48)

What is important is not the informational content but the emergence of a consciousness that is essentially comparative. Print communications gives rise to a phantom public world where one "sees" what happens in other "territorial communities" (*bangsa*) and assumes that one can be seen in return as a member of a territorial community by those "others." Strictly speaking, this is not perception, but only representation. As Minke notes, Japan is "something abstract and my admiration for her was an admiration of an abstraction. In my mind, I could not yet feel Japan as something concretely existing [*wujud*]" (*ASB*, 44; 53). Yet, modern knowledge allows Minke to see what the naked eye of uneducated native peasants cannot see:

I know these notes won't be of much interest to anyone. But I have no choice but to include them. Why? Because they have become a concrete part of my everyday surroundings [*termasuk ruang lingkup kehidupanku sendiri*—literally, have entered or penetrated the space]. Ai, knowledge: Trunodongso never knew this world [*dunia*] had a neighboring country called the Philippines. And knowledge, the fruit of reading, made the Philippines a part of my world. Even though only in my thoughts. The magic [*Keajaiban*] of knowledge: without their eyes seeing the world, it enables people to know the expanse of the world: its richness, its depth. (*ASB*, 276; 274)

Through modern knowledge, one begins to see oneself as being part of this "objective" world of public others, fixing oneself as an object by means of this comparative public gaze. This comparative perception is cartographic. News cables conjure up and place one upon a global stage where "the entire world can now observe the activities of a single individual. And an individual can observe the activities of the entire world" (*BM*, 316; 321).

This mapping induces (in the sense of inference, but also in the sense of bringing about artificially) the interiority of a people or nation, the feeling that there is this people or nation and that one belongs to it. Thus, Minke places Japan on a spectrum with other civilizations and peoples, behind Europe but ahead of the Chinese, the Indians, the Arabs, and the Turks (*ASB*, 40; 49). He can proudly identify with this ideal of Asian modernity as "an Asian" at the same time as he is humbled by its might when he compares it to the backwardness of "his people," the colonized Javanese.

This comparative perception begins to penetrate Minke's everyday life. It influences how he views his personal tragedy and his daily activities. This inspiriting of everyday reality by the spectrality of print, or—which amounts to the same thing—Minke's internalization of this phantom public gaze, makes him identify with the frustrations of the Chinese youth movement: "[The backwardness of my people was] Shameful. But not only that. I became incensed because of my powerless awareness [*kesadaran yang tidak berdaya*]. . . . And Maarten Nijman wrote: 'The Chinese Young Generation of intellectuals are envious of Japan's progress. . . . Envious! Also furious and incensed because they are aware but powerless.' *Just like me.*" (*ASB*, 46; 55–56; emphasis added).

But at this point, Minke's consciousness is not yet national. It takes the form of a universal humanism registered in the second novel's title, *Child of All Nations*. The process of becoming national involves a series of discussions with teacher figures such as Jean Marais, Khouw Ah Soe, Kommer, and Ter Haar, which extend the spectral world opened up by technomediation. By amplifying the news information, Minke's interlocutors present this spectral world of print through a speaking face. They make it immediately human and concrete by giving it an intersubjective dimension. In discursive space, one sees oneself as an object amidst worldly connections not by induction, but through the eyes of an other. In the various scenes of instruction, Minke is repeatedly told about the ideals and responsibilities that accompany his social position. He only attains self-reflexivity as a social and political being when he assimilates into his consciousness this discursive structure in which he is addressed and questioned or put into question by another, literally placed in the accusative.

Minke's incorporation as a national consciousness, his *Bildung* as a socially responsible person, is characterized by a discursive structure where he addresses himself as a second person in free indirect speech, exhorting himself to know his people. These exhortations concern his duty to know his people so that he can understand and serve the needs of native society. For instance, the suggestion that Minke is ignorant about native peasants becomes lodged in his consciousness as a repeated self-accusation: "Do not know their own people [*bangsa*]! The judgment went too far and injured, like a blow from a blunt axe. It hurt even more that it originated from people who weren't Natives: an Indo and a Frenchman. In their eyes, I did not know my own people. Me!" (*ASB*, 106; 113) The accusation haunts him throughout his train ride to Tulangan until he promises to remedy this defect: "As we moved onto the main road, my serene mood began to change. You don't know your own people! Now there was an additional accusation: you don't know your own country [*negerimu*]! Yes, I did not know my people and my country. The shame I felt was not undeserved. I will redeem myself from these irrefutable accusations" (*ASB*, 110; 117). He is similarly reprimanded in his encounter with an oppressed peasant, Pak Trunodongso, when he feels offended because he is addressed in low Javanese (*ngoko*) instead of the high Javanese befitting his caste: "He was truly a peasant who had transcended his caste. So why should I treat him so well? But you have resolved to know your own people! You must understand their hardship. He is one of your own people about whom you know nothing, your own people about whom you wish to write once you have begun to understand them!" (*ASB*, 157; 162). Later, Minke repeatedly questions his own motives for writing in Dutch, and not Malay. He accuses himself of not giving up his traditional privileges:

> If you are truly an admirer of the French Revolution, why are you offended when a peasant, like Trunodongso, speaks in Low Javanese to you. . . . You have betrayed the ideals of Freedom, Equality and Fraternity of the French Revolution for your hereditary privileges. You are only inspired by the ideal of Freedom, and then it is nothing more than freedom for yourself. Are you not ashamed when you declare yourself to be an admirer of the French Revolution? . . . You are not honest as an educated person should be, Minke. . . . You have still not learnt enough about justice [*adil*] nor practiced it until it has become part of your character. . . . You have begun to learn to understand your people. You now have a little knowledge about them: how through the Javanese language you yourself actually continue to enslave your people

[*memperbudak bangsamu*]. And you pretend that you want to defend Trunodongso through your newspaper articles. (*ASB*, 183–84; 186–87)

This exhortatory structure is also at work when the implied Indonesian reader reads the quartet, which is intended to enable its addressee to step outside himself to gain a fuller knowledge of his social situation. It introduces a gap or dehiscence within the private self that enables it to gradually expand into a national consciousness. The special affinity between the nation-form and modern consciousness is determined by the foundational role of discourse and technomediation in the latter's formation. Although modern consciousness may initially appear as a universal humanism or cosmopolitanism (which Minke espouses in the first two books), it generally becomes a national consciousness or universal particular because the global reach of its vision is attained through comparative activity. This is especially so in colonized territories where the comparative gaze inevitably instills in the educated native an anxious restlessness. He is aware that his people have been subjected to a foreign people because of their comparative backwardness. Because ancestral culture is viewed as the cause of stagnation, the people's uplifting is inevitably a spiritual affair involving the formation of a vital, modern, *national* spirit. This poignant (if condescending) comparison between the dynamism of his will to organize and the stagnant tranquillity and childlike ignorance of "traditional" communal life pushes Minke to begin organizational activity in chapter 7 of *Jejak Langkah*.

I began to observe more closely the life of the village. I clearly could not ask its inhabitants to discuss the issue of modern organization. They did not possess any knowledge of their own country. Most probably, they rarely left their own village.

. . . A large number of them [the small children playing] will die due to a parasitical disease. . . . And if they survive, if they manage to overcome the parasitical diseases, is their condition any better than the time of their childhood? They will continue to live within their narrow destiny. Without ever having any comparison. Happy are those who know nothing. Knowledge, comparison, makes people aware of their own situation, and the situation of others, there is dissatisfied restlessness in the world of comparison [*gelisah dalam alam perbandingan*].

... The people around me have never known what I know. ... They do not know anything except how to make a living and reproduce themselves. Oh, creatures like herded cattle! They do not even know how lowly their lives are. Nor do they know of the monstrous forces [*kekuatan raksasa*] in the wider world, which grow and expand, gradually swallowing everything in their way, without being satiated. Even if they knew, they would not pay any heed.

Within these surroundings, I felt like an All-Knowing god, who also knew their fate. They would become the prey of both criminals and imperialists. Something had to be done [*harus dikerjakan*]. Was organizing the only way?

(*JL*, 170–71; 132–33)

Minke connects modern organization to the *Bildung* of the Indies people as an organism striving to maximize its own capacity for life. Throughout the quartet, he draws extended analogies between biological germs and imperialism; the human body and the body of the people; and the doctor and the activist-intellectual. Minke is a medical student who is impressed by the fact that Sun Yat-Sen, the father of modern China, and José Rizal, who influenced the Filipino revolution, were both doctors. Knowledge is the blood and life force of the nation as a rationally integrated body or organized/organic whole. It is the animus of the collective effort, work, and action (*usaha, kerja,* and so on) through which a people determines its own destiny in the same way that an organism contains a drive towards self-preservation: "In the end, a progressive people can also look after its own welfare, no matter how small in number or in geographical size it is. The Dutch Indies government has an interest in limiting the access of Natives to science and knowledge. Natives must work [*berusaha*] to further their own interests" (*JL*, 173; 132–33).

Pramoedya's organismic conception of the nation, which aligns the nation with modern reason, should therefore be rigorously distinguished from liberal and Marxist myths of nationalism as the anachronistic residue of a premodern form of community in a disenchanted anthropocentric world. But his position should also be distinguished from most of contemporary postcolonial theory. For Pramoedya, the decolonizing or postcolonial nation is not congenitally infected by a colonialist will to domination because he does not regard modernity and enlightenment as Europe's exclusive property. Let us situate his position more carefully.

FREEDOM THROUGH THE NATION: THE CRITIQUE
OF COLONIALIST INSTRUMENTAL REASON AS THE
REENCHANTMENT OF THE WORLD

In the first two volumes, Minke mainly identifies modernity with his European education, and he oscillates between identification with Javanese culture and his modern education. However, by the third volume, his intense personal experiences of the arbitrary oppressiveness of Dutch colonial law and his realization that colonial exploitation actively prolongs the backwardness of the Indies cause his disillusionment with European modernity. Shedding his identification with both Europe and the ethnocultural entity "Java," he embraces "the Indies natives" as his people.

The genesis of Minke's national consciousness is typical of the dilemma of the colonized native intelligentsia whose encounter with modernity is marked by an ambivalent relationship to Europe as both teacher and oppressor. However, Pramoedya's conception of national consciousness cannot be contained within a Weberian typology of traditional and modern rationality. The modern drive towards secularization and demystification creates an earth of mankind (as opposed to a cosmic world of deities) in which traditional forms of domination based on mystical authority are delegitimized. This anthropologistic conception of the world, Pramoedya suggests, is a necessary condition of freedom. Minke rejects the *priyayi* world of rank, position, salary, and embezzlement in favor of "this earth of mankind with all its problems" (*BM*, 120; 125). He tells his mother, "I want only to be a free person [*manusia bebas*], ruled by no one and ruling no one" (*BM*, 123; 128). Pramoedya's scathing critique of traditionalism is elaborated in the fourth volume by a Javanologist official, Meneer L., who uses a Weberian typology to differentiate European modernity from Javanese tradition.[38] Javanism is a stagnant premodern culture of death that cannot be the bearer of world-historical progress because it espouses an ethos where the self seeks accommodation to the external world instead of viewing it as an

---

38. For a discussion of the different types of practical ethics or paths of rationalization, see Max Weber, "The Social Psychology of the World Religions." See also Weber, *Economy and Society: An Outline of Interpretive Sociology* (Berkeley: University of California Press, 1978), 1:24–25.

object to be conquered and shaped in the image of humanity's own ideal purposes (*RK*, 177; 166). Hence, Javanese culture is primarily an adaptive, passive, or submissive practical ethics that accepts outside influences by seeking similarities between the foreign (initially Islam and, later, European colonialism) and the indigenous (*RK*, 69, 71; 67–68).

Javanism is responsible for the political degeneration of the great Majapahit maritime empire and the subsequent military defeat of the Javanese by the Dutch. Instead of trying to learn from European knowledge, Javanese rulers escape from the reality of defeat by means of a web of mystifications: the poetic illusions and dreams woven by celebratory court chronicles such as the *Babad Tanah Jawi,* and superstitious belief in the power of magic spells (*RK*, 115; 109). Hence, the Javanese have been left behind in the march of world history. They cannot arrive at modernity because no modern spirit can grow in this shadowplay (*wayang*) world of escapism and illusion (*RK*, 78–79; 74–75). All that remains is a culture of compromise that is too weak to free itself from its own defeat and can never hope to progress until it learns the trick of modernity from its European conquerors.

But notwithstanding his preference for modern rationality, Pramoedya also suggests, in a way reminiscent of Adorno and Horkheimer, that the purely instrumental aspect of modern knowledge can easily lead to a remythologization where enlightenment or technological progress itself reverts to myth. The colonial state apparatus's arbitrary power is the paradigmatic embodiment of the remythologization of the world. Despite the colonial regime's pretensions to be the bearer of light and modern knowledge, it is fundamentally complicit with the Javanism of the traditional rulers it supplants. Colonial hegemony depends on the support of a group of native leaders. As Pangemanann observes in an apostrophe to Minke, "the Government needs their illusions, it does not need people who have no illusions such as you" (*RK*, 310; 293). Part of the quartet's brilliance lies in its vivid portrait of how the colonial state and colonial society are part of the same premodern world of illusions that the colonial regime denounces. As we will see, the character of Pangemanann illustrates that the native bureaucrat who is totally consumed by his official status (*jabatan*) is a hybrid product of colonial society's antimodern structures of governance and the *priyayi* caste's traditional ethos. Indeed, the colonialist ethos (*watak* or *wajah*) is figured as contaminating mud (*lumpur kolonial*) that soils most Europeans in the Indies, causing them to mimic the despotism of native rulers. The murky colonial world is the dark underside of modernity, the place where modernity becomes estranged from itself in such a way that the opposition between European enlightenment and native darkness that props up the colonial state's civilizing face breaks down.

But Pramoedya's critique of colonialist instrumental reason does not lead to an antimodern denunciation of the nation-form as the offspring of colonialist discourse, nor to a theory of postcolonial countermodernity that proposes alternative descriptions of modernity resolutely opposed to the nation-form. For unlike the South Asian subcontinent that is the unspoken geographical provenance of most postcolonial theory, Indonesia has a more tenacious history of popular radical nationalism because it was not the product of negotiated independence.[39] Indeed, Pramoedya suggests that Indonesian nationalism may have an enduring world-historical significance. The proclamation of the Republic of Indonesia on 17 August 1945 was the snapping of the weakest link in the chain of imperialism. "A few days later Vietnam took the same step. Once the first links had been broken, others soon followed. The movement spread to the Asian mainland, then to Africa, and later to Latin America."[40] This historical vocation was reaffirmed in the Bandung Conference of April 1955, where Sukarno's speech, "Let a New Asia and Africa be Born," "made him the Father of the Third World."

Pramoedya's faith in the popular radical dimension of the modern nation-form stands in stark contrast to subaltern studies, whose similar critique of the "classicization of tradition" by hegemonic historiography leads to a search for an ineffable noncolonized subaltern consciousness manifested in fragmented resistance to the hegemonic project of nationalist modernity.[41] In Pramoedya's view, although secularization sunders affective ties based on inherited myth and tradition, the danger of a remythologization

39. See Takashi Shiraishi, *An Age in Motion: Popular Radicalism in Java, 1912–1916* (Ithaca: Cornell University Press, 1990).
40. This and the following quotation is from Pramoedya, "The Role and Attitude of Intellectuals," p. 115.
41. For instance, Chatterjee's positive definition of collective peasant consciousness in terms of the "extraordinary, apocalyptic, timeless moment of a world turned upside down" that allows us to "glimpse . . . that undominated region in peasant consciousness" reads like Beckett's Godot arrived on a bus (*The Nation and its Fragments*, p. 171).

of life under modern technocratic capitalism becomes greater in a demag-icked world of atomistic beings unrelentingly pursuing their self-interest because there is no collective agency that can curtail the instrumental use of reason in the sphere of economic production or act as a buffer between individuals and a bureaucratic system of domination. This danger is exac-erbated in colonial space by the state's practices of co-opting the ruling strata of native society and reshaping their traditional authority to facilitate colonial domination. Pramoedya shows us how this vicious colonial sym-biosis of premodern and modern forms of domination results in horren-dous forms of destruction and exploitation of natives by foreign-owned big capital.

But modernity succors even as it destroys. Modern knowledge and tech-nological advances also generate new ties that can replace the traditional ones torn apart by modernity's arrival. They create a novel type of com-munity, the popular nation, that can better shelter the modern native from colonial capitalism and can lead ultimately to political freedom. Indeed, we can even say that as a phenomenon of modernity's progressive face, the nation-people embodies the critical reason that can check colonialist instrumental reason. The quartet stages this argument in Minke's gradual transformation from an atomistic individual without any ties into a responsible consciousness who realizes that his freedom is inseparably bound to that of the Indies-wide community of natives in which he is con-cretely embedded. This is also a graduation from the negative notion of freedom ("freedom from") implied by instrumental reason's desire for mastery over nature to a positive notion of freedom entailing reciprocal responsibilities.

Jejak Langkah opens with Minke's arrival in Batavia, where he feels that he has truly become a free modern person because he is no longer over-shadowed by Nyai Ontosoroh's forceful personality. The free self is a monad who does not require the help of others because such reliance means dependency on the outside. But because freedom requires the stripping of external trappings that encumber the self such as traditional kinship ties, the autonomous being of modernity also suffers the solitude of an orphan: "modernity is also the solitude [*kesunyian*] of orphaned humanity, impelled to free itself from all contingent ties [*ikatan yang tidak diperlukan*]: custom, blood, even the earth, and if need be, from others of its kind. . . . Those who need help place themselves in a situation of subjection in which they are dependent on others" (*JL*, 1; 1). Pramoedya suggests that this solipsistic definition of freedom as the feeling of being without responsibilities other than the responsibility for one's own actions and a freedom from reliance on others (for instance, independence from the economic need to sell one's services to live) is limited and limiting. Freedom in this sense is primarily contemplative and does not require action arising out of responsibility towards others. It has no concrete political objectives or a larger plan. The two characters who offer an alternative model of freedom for emulation are Khouw Ah Soe and his fiancée, Ang San Mei, who later marries Minke. They are Chinese nationalist activists who are persecuted by the Ching state and have left their homeland to spread Republicanist ideals to the Indies Chinese diaspora.

When Minke tells Mei of his ambition to be a free person, she cautions him from mistaking selfish arbitrary action for freedom. She reminds him that as an educated Asian native, his primary responsibility is to his people:

> Do not misunderstand what is meant by liberty in the slogan of the French Revolution. . . . Even some of the French have interpreted this to mean that they are free to steal and free of responsibilities [*bebas tak berkewajiban*] towards anyone, with the result that they start to act completely arbitrarily. They are only after greatness for themselves in their own country! In their freedom, all educated natives of Asia have an interminable responsibility to awaken their own peoples. Otherwise, Europe will colonize Asia. (*JL*, 66; 52)

Minke rejects this false sense of freedom after Mei's death, when her exhortation to him to begin organizing to awaken his people returns to haunt him as a voice lodged within his consciousness. As before, Minke is moved to action by being put in the accusative by a spectral voice that addresses him, summoning him to response/responsibility:

> The narrow-slit eyes of my wife on the wall, eyes that would never blink again, stared at me. But even so, I felt them shining strongly in my heart, like the first time that she urged me to start organizing.
>
> Will you let your people stay bent under the yoke of their ignorance? Who will begin if you don't?
>
> I reflected again on all that she had stood for, her efforts, her sacrifices. She had never spoken of what she had achieved. She only spoke about the Young

Generation and its dynamic spirit, its goals and its concerns. She had spoken about them all–the bacteria that was British imperialism, its twin, Japanese imperialism, the Empress Ye Si, who was another kind of bacteria.

(*JL*, 152–53; 119)

The educated native initially seemed a hybrid creature caught between European and native worlds, passively consuming modern European knowledge. This shift from liberal individualism to a concrete notion of freedom that entails a collective responsibility towards one's people is a more active form of absorption. The emerging national bodies of decolonizing Asia figure forth as sublations that retain what is valuable in the European individualist determination of freedom, at the same time that its limitations (existential solitude and the atomistic pursuit of self-interest) are annulled in a new community, the modern nation, that rises from the ashes of the traditional native cosmos. Notwithstanding the quartet's repeated references to the French Revolution, Minke is also made aware through the printed page and discussions with Khouw Ah Soe and Ter Haar of non-European models of modernity: imperialist Japan and also anti-imperial China and the decolonizing Philippines. These examples form a chain of events. Their restless energy is now felt in the Indies and stimulates Minke's desire for modernity. These repeated juxtapositions and comparisons cumulatively suggest that the newly born nations of decolonizing Asia, and not the colonial state or the Dutch liberals, are the true heirs of the world-historical spirit of freedom.

Throughout the quartet, Pramoedya repeatedly associates the instrumental reason of the colonial state with the satanic and distinguishes this bad, remythologizing magic from the good magic that incarnates the decolonizing nation as the bearer of critical reason and an organism capable of absorbing and appropriating European influences. Khouw Ah Soe, who offers a vision of modernity critical of Europe and America, teaches Minke that modern knowledge is not good in and of itself. Because it expresses and instills in mankind the insatiable desire to control the external world, scientific knowledge can also intensify human oppression. European colonialism exemplifies the instrumentality of modern knowledge run riot. Nyai Ontosoroh points out to Minke that even modern juridical institutions can be objects of use, "exploited by the wicked for their own purposes" (*ASB*, 69; 76). European colonialism's boundless appetite for power and control, she cautions, is the manifestation of the satanic: "Don't idolize Europe as a totality. . . . Only one thing never changes, my child, and is eternal: the colonialist is always a devil [or colonialism is always devil's work—*yang kolonial, dia selalu iblis*]. . . . [T]he colonialist will be a devil till the end of time" (*ASB*, 75; 82).

For Pramoedya, inhuman capital's relentless expansion epitomizes satanic possession. In her letter to Minke, Miriam de la Croix, the daughter of a liberal colonial official, suggests that capital's restless invisible power induces the frenzied desire for innovation and the endless proliferation of new needs and desires. Human beings become demonically possessed and dehumanized, subsumed by the statistics of capitalist production:

> It seems that the fever for the pursuit of novelty and novel instruments makes it impossible for men to be content with what they already have. They are possessed [*keranjingan*] by anything and everything new, new etiquettes, new ways of behaving. . . . *How easily men are lulled into unawareness that behind all the appeals, enticements, and obsessions [kegilaan] with the new there stands a spectral power [kekuatan gaib—magical force, powerful specter] with gaping jaws and an unappeasable hunger for victims [mangsa—prey]. This spectral power is the array of protozoa—numbers—whose name is Capital.*
>
> (*ASB*, 95; 102; emphasis added)

After his visit to Tulangan, Minke begins to see sugar capital as a parasitic vampire. It thrives on coerced economic exploitation that sucks the natives dry. Despite a smallpox epidemic which kills many villagers, vampirelike capital lives on eternally, with greater command over all living things, even as humans, left untended, die: "Tulangan itself has never been burned down. . . . The giant sugar-centrals can not be permitted to be destroyed by smallpox. It is necessary that capital survive [*hidup*] and grow [*berkembang*]. As for human beings, let them die. . . . And the Tulangan sugar-central continues its majestic domination and surveillance over the whole of Tulangan: over its human beings, over its animals, and over its crops" (*ASB*, 151–52; 156–57).

These oppositions between the living human and the satanic or ghostly power of modern capital mark out the discursive field of Pramoedya's affirmation of the decolonizing nation. The nation lies on the side of life and the colonial state, a servant of capital, is unequivocally an agent of death. Minke learns that even institutions of enlightenment, such as schooling, agricultural innovation, medicine and law, and, indeed, the Liberal Policy itself, are part of an economic infrastructure. They function as necessary cogs for the smooth running of the capitalist machine (*ASB*, 272–73; 271). Ter Haar points out that "that which is called the modern age is really the age of capital's triumph. Every person in the modern age is ruled by big capital, even the education that you received at the HBS was arranged in accordance with its needs and not your personal needs. The same goes for newspapers. Everything is arranged by it, including morality, law, truth and knowledge." (*ASB*, 260; 259) Thus, the magic of modern knowledge is continuous with capital, which Ter Haar describes (by paraphrasing the *Communist Manifesto*) as "something efficacious, abstract, with an invisible/spectral power over material objects [*kekuasaan gaib atas benda-benda nyata*]. . . . A new Divinity [*Dewa*] that holds the whole world in its fist" (*ASB*, 261; 259).

These figural and thematic oppositions between the living human and the satanic power of modern capital, the concretely actual and the invisible and ghostly, indicate that Pramoedya divides the spectral conjurations of modern knowledge (*keajaiban pengetahuan*) into a good and bad component. On the one hand, in a more or less Marxist manner similar to the Frankfurt School argument about the culture industry and Habermas's denunciation of bad publicity, Pramoedya regards instrumental forms of knowledge and technomediatic apparatuses as ideological epiphenomena of capital's supernatural power, the *kekuatan gaib* of *sang modal*. On the other hand, as an emerging native press run by progressive members of the native intelligentsia, the good magic of modern knowledge incarnates an Indies-wide native public sphere that can truly express the Indies people's living needs and true interests.[42] The emerging nation-people is clearly the embodiment of critical reason. As Khouw Ah Soe puts it, "there is no power that can arrest this lust for domination except science itself, in a higher form, in the hands of men of higher morality" (*ASB*, 83; 90).

---

42. For a historical account, see Ahmat B. Adam, *The Vernacular Press and the Emergence of Modern Indonesian Consciousness, 1855–1913*), Studies in Southeast Asia no. 17 (Ithaca, N.Y.: Southeast Asia Program, Cornell University, 1995).

It should also be clear that Pramoedya's affirmation of the decolonizing or postcolonial nation as the paradigmatic incarnation of critical reason is resolutely organismic. The phantomatic is always subordinated to life. Pramoedya's distinction between good and bad spectrality presupposes that the spectral is a secondary or subordinate phenomenon that either derives or deviates from a more actual and original living ground. In the final instance, the spectrality of modern knowledge becomes converted into living effectivity and the concretely actual, the vital national body, even though the nation's self-proximity is a moment that has to be deferred in the present. The modern nation is distinguished from illusory communities of premodern faith precisely because it is the process and product of reason's self-actualization. Following Marx, Pramoedya suggests that capital is a monstrous phantom totality that needs to be exorcised because it is the inverted form of the system of needs generated by living labor where labor becomes alienated and estranged from itself. In contradistinction, good spectrality refers to the generation of a critical native public sphere out of spontaneous market forces, the functioning of which requires a vernacular press. The Indies people would then be the originators of the native press's power, which is the means for rearticulating the nation-people, for imagining new political solidarities that can resist and ultimately transcend the colonial state and even the circuit of global capital. In other words, the quartet envisions the springing forth of a concretely living collective agent, the national public sphere, that can exorcise the various phantoms of capital and remove them forever from the Indies people's lives. This act of exorcism is also the political event that founds and inaugurates the decolonizing nation as the bearer of freedom and keeps the postcolonial nation alive in neocolonial globalization.

CONJURING THE PEOPLE, GIVING LIFE TO THE NATIONAL BODY: ORGANIZATION AS VITAL MOVEMENT AND POWER

We can only properly understand the philosophical basis of Pramoedya's affirmation of the nation by recalling the stakes of political organicism of which it is a case. In Pramoedya's view, modern organization and print can conjure up to the proto-Indonesian nation-people and give it life because the decolonizing nation is a modern community held together by ties that are paradoxically neither merely natural nor technical and artificial. The Weberian typological distinction between modern and traditional rationality he uses to characterize European and native worlds also implies a distinction between the meaningful causality of a cosmos where every entity has a preordained place in the world according to divine natural law, and the mechanical causality that governs the world as a scientific object. As I argued in the first part of the book, the concepts of organic life and culture and the organismic metaphor of the social and political body were formulated to introduce rational organization and purposive order into blind mechanical nature. As analogues of the auto-causality of transcendental freedom, they indicated that freedom could be actualized in this world. In contradistinction, the satanic is linked to the mechanical as a form of automatism devoid of reason and freedom.

The opposition between critical and instrumental reason that Pramoedya uses to further distinguish the decolonizing nation from the modern colonial state extends the machine/organism distinction into the sphere of human purposiveness. Because it embodies critical reason, the nation has the same ontological status as the organism. Unlike primordial forms of community, its life derives from the technic of modern organization. However, it is also a means of defense against the technical rationality of capitalism, of which the colonial state is an agent. To afford shelter from capitalism's atomizing forces, the affiliative ties of nationhood must be as strong as the ties of kinship and custom modernity destroyed. They should not be easily repudiated even though they are not primordially given. The nation's stability derives from the fact that it is a self-articulating, self-organizing whole brought into being and maintained by the repeated rational affirmation of its members. Since its organization comes from within itself, this form of *techne* is not merely artificial. The nation is an organism. Even though it is patently the product of modern techomediation, the technical has been subordinated by and made into an integral moment of the people's life process.

The decolonizing nation thus sublates both the European liberal individualist determination of modern freedom and the stable bonds of the traditional native world. It preserves the meaningful stability associated with a cosmos because it is rooted in the Indies people's everyday culture. One ought to understand the nation as artifacticity, as *techne* that has become incarnated as a second nature, where nature is now an inherently intelligible world governed by human reason instead of divine will. "Birth" is the most apposite metaphor for the emergence of the Indies people because it suggests the creation of something completely new through an organic process, which includes colonialism and market imperatives as important moments.

Unless we grasp the nation's ontological status as an organism, a higher purposive nature that reconciles *physis* and *techne,* we will not be able to understand how the artifice of modern organization can incarnate an organic community. Before the third volume's full exploration of the counterintuitive link between the national organism and organization, Minke's fumbling search for a referent for "the people" in the second volume already intimates this coimplication of the technical and the organic. To the extent that he becomes aware of the people primarily as the victims of state subjection and the subject in need of awakening, Minke's consciousness of the people is coextensive with the colonial state's gradual appearance in more and more concrete shape. The spectrality of modern knowledge and technomediation makes the colonial state and "the people" appear as mutually implicated entities, the ground and figure for each other.

At this stage, it is far from clear to Minke what constitutes "the people," who remain a contentless form defined in solely negative terms as the object of colonial oppression. Much of *Jejak Langkah* will be concerned with finding the basis for a modern association that can best serve the people's interests. The second volume shows how modern knowledge imparts a minimal referential content to the empty national form induced by the comparative gaze. By comparing his meeting with Pak Truno's family to Columbus's discovery of a new continent, Minke suggests that the people is a preexisting entity awaiting for him to discover (*ASB*, 162; 167). However, this discovery of the native world is in fact a performative constitution, the saturation of the field of perception by the spectrality of European knowledge. Minke's seeing is already a reading because what he sees is "read" as a verification of an anonymous pamphlet about Javanese peasants his teacher, Magda Peters, gave him. His apprehension turns out to be a rereading of the pamphlet: "This pamphlet is really brilliant. Its author is a European. He knows all about the Javanese peasantry, whereas I myself have only just discovered this continent. And truthfully, I now really know the inner core of their lives: its names are fear and suspicion" (*ASB*, 164;

168). Indeed, Minke considers the spectral world that knowledge confers to him to be truer than the peasants' intuitive experience of their own immediate world and even their own thoughts: "It's obvious that the peasantry has no knowledge of itself as such. But on the other side of the world, in the Netherlands, people do have such knowledge, and it is a true knowledge. Indeed they know the essence of the peasantry as a social group. . . . It is only through Europe that you will be able to get to know your own people" (*ASB*, 164; 169). This is, of course, the discourse of the consciousness raising of the masses through intellectual knowledge. A similar spectral production of the people occurs when Minke describes the social gap between himself, as a Europeanized native, and the Trunodongso family, representatives of the uneducated masses who need to be awakened: "This perhaps was what *my old history teacher had once said:* social distance can also become historical distance" (*ASB*, 239; 239; emphasis added). These acts of reading-seeing conjure up the spectral body of "the people," giving what is mere form some concrete content.

Other conjurations occur when "the people" is brought into motion by modern organization and the public sphere of Malay print. "Organization" is used for the first time in *Jejak Langkah* to refer to the creation of the Tiong Hoa Hwee Koan (Chinese Association) in 1900, the first legally registered social association in the Indies (*JL*, 59; 47). But organizing far exceeds the Hwee Koan's immediate activity of establishing Chinese schools with a non-Dutch curriculum to educate modern Chinese people. As Ang San Mei explains, organization involves the bringing together of individuals to create a new entity more powerful than the sum of its parts. Instead of a mere aggregate of microforces, organization creates a totality or system of interdependent parts and generates an entirely new life force:

> By organizing themselves, becoming comrades, associates, a multitude of men, dozens, hundreds, even hundreds of thousands in number, become an invisible giant [*raksasa gaib*], with a strength far greater and wider than that of its individual members . . . [w]ith colossal [*raksasa*] hands, colossal legs, and a giant's vision and power of endurance. (*JL, 97; 75*)

The adjective repeatedly used to describe this totality is "*raksasa,*" "gigantic" or "colossal." As a noun, "*raksasa*" is a mythical giant. But although it is described in anthropomorphic terms as having legs, hands, and vision, its force is not available to phenomenality because it is a "*raksasa gaib*," that is, invisible or supernatural. Hence, unlike a machine, its power (*kekuatan*) is not reducible to mechanical calculation or the adding up of the forces of its component parts. What organization engenders is a self-generating organism. Techniques of organization are thus instances of the magic of modern reason. We have already seen the words "*raksasa*" and "*gaib*" used to describe the bad spectrality of capital, represented in the Indies by the Sugar Syndicate. They translate what Marx, following Adam Smith, called the invisible hand of capital. When these words are used to describe the good spectrality of modern organization, they refer to the organicizing power generated by organization, which exceeds mechanism even though the modern world is desacralized and devoid of divinity.

The process by which modern organizations give rise to the living body of the Indonesian nation-people is marked by the aporetic interplay between *physis* and *techne* in Kant's idea of the technic of nature that I discussed in chapter 2. A modern native organization is a legal body or corporation (*badan hukum*) constituted through state recognition (*JL*, 118; 92). Its members have certain rights they do not possess in their individual capacity because it has the same status before the law as a European individual. Such native organizations are the embryos of the native social body because they represent and defend native interests before the law. They also educate children and prepare them for life in the modern age (*JL*, 119–20; 93). They thus give more elaborate shape to the *form* of the nation that was delineated through comparative cognitive mapping. They situate this form within sociological space by creating a public space through technomediatic means in which "the people" will come to be. As a form of legal personality that can address and make demands of the colonial state, they also introduce natives to the idea of rights, allowing them to think of themselves as an integrated social body with legitimate proprietorial claims on the Indies earth that the colonial state should recognize. In Minke's words, "it was as though . . . I was no longer treading on colonial ground, and as though I had become with my countrymen a rightful owner of this land. Experience, knowledge, wisdom, but most importantly the spirit of life develops the individual into a giant. With a strength that is greater than the sum of its parts" (*JL*, 190; 148).

An artificial body or prosthesis is thus a necessary supplement to the Indies people's genesis and continuing life. Although organizations are meant to awaken the people from slumber, the people is not a preexistent entity, but something organization conjures up. Firstly, organization confers on individuals a modern form of sociality that is new to the traditional native world. Secondly, by claiming to represent the people's interests before the law, it induces the people insofar as it only becomes graspable or cognizable as an entity deserving the political recognition of the colonial state through the legal and artificial body that claims to be its representative. An organization's claim to represent the Indies natives is therefore a performative rather than a constative utterance. Yet, the legitimacy of the organization depends on taking this performative utterance as a constatation. Indeed, the nation-people must itself take this performative as a constative.

This conjuring of the people through the prosthetic technics of organization is not a species of ideology. It is not the distortion of an actual concretely living body by the supervention of an obfuscatory, mystifying ideational film. The living national body did not exist prior to organizational fabulation because the people did not know itself as such before organization. Indies national consciousness is not a false collective consciousness to be rejected for a truer consciousness such as proletarian class consciousness. For Pramoedya, national consciousness is a fundamental moment in the genesis of radical proletarian consciousness in the Indies because there was no other preexisting form of rational political consciousness that national consciousness distorted and obstructed. The conjuration of the people is better understood as the becoming-*physis* of *techne* in exactly the same way that Kant spoke of the technic of political organization as an analogue of the technic of nature. The decolonizing nation is the counterpart of organic/organized nature in the sphere of human sociality. It transcends mechanical causality because as a modern community held together by meaningful rational ties, it is an antidote to the instrumental behavior of the atomistic individual. It is important to recall that political organicism is a response to human finitude. It suggests that individuals willingly bind themselves to a political body because it is a lawful substrate that enables one to prolong the effects of human moral endeavor beyond a finite lifespan. In contradistinction, the mechanical is synonymous with the permanent death and meaningless anonymity of the merely given. The technic of political organization is an exorcism of death because it imbues mere matter with an inner vitality. Instead of opening up organic life to the irreducible contamination of artifice, it subordinates *techne* and makes it work in the service of life. By supplementing organic nature and becoming an indistinguishable part of the life process, organization extends organismic causality to the social sphere.

In the quartet, this economy of life is expressed by a medical figural logic that views a healthy social body as the necessary precondition of a healthy human body. An old Javanese doctor tells Minke that as an educated person, a native doctor has the same onerous responsibilities as a social worker: "what a pity it is if . . . his service fails to give his people some surplus value. A doctor doesn't simply cure the body of disease, he also awakens his people's spirit [*jiwa*], which is intoxicated by ignorance. . . . The task of a Native doctor is not simply to heal wounds and cure their illnesses, . . . but also to care for his patients' souls [*jiwa*], and their future" (*JL*, 120–21, 123; 94, 96). Thus, colonialism is repeatedly figured as syphilitic bacteria that eats away at the national body, whereas Mei's chain letters, which shape public opinion, are a good form of bacteria, an antibiotic: "Public opinion will get formed. This is also a microbe, but not a malignant protozoa, in fact it will resist the gonococcus and the teponema pallidium" (*JL*, 136; 106). Indeed, Pramoedya suggests that social organizations are sublimations of familial belonging. Mei's revolutionary fervor is related to the fact that she is an orphan. Much is made of the fact that Minke is sterile. In *Rumah Kaca*, Minke's newspaper and his organization are described as his progeny.

On her deathbed, Mei makes Minke promise that he will become a doctor. Just as a doctor cures and strengthens a human body by understanding it as a complex organism that interacts with the outside world, political organization infuses the social body with vital movement. What is crucial is the importance of modern knowledge to the nation's epigenesis. The people can only change oppressive reality if it can understand how this reality results from a connected chain of events. Organization is the act of connecting various things to bring about a certain purpose. It increases a social body's ability to survive by teaching its members that they are an organized entity, a complex totality of interdependent parts within this larger network of connections. Thus, organization is the ability to imaginatively connect oneself to others to form a collective agent that can negate and change the existing totality of oppressive external conditions.

Minke's desire to arrange (*menyusun*) disparate pieces of information into a meaningful whole is already an embryonic form of the will to organize, the logical endpoint of a modern consciousness. When Minke decides to begin organizing, his first act is to reread all his previous jottings and newspaper clippings to gain a clearer picture of the totality of past events that have led to the present. This information, Ter Haar's letters about the war in Bali which remind him that "the Balinese people are also your people" (*JL*, 161; 126), and all his previous conversations cumulatively become a chorus that gives birth to a national consciousness:

> What must I do now? Struggle [*perjuangan*] in the modern era . . . demands modern methods: organization. Become a giant, the retired Java-Doctor had said. Mei too. With limbs more powerful than those of the human beings amassed within it. Start organizing! (*JL*, 164; 128)

"LANDASAN [YANG] LEBIH MENGIKAT": WHAT BINDS A HEALTHY NATION-PEOPLE TOGETHER

At this point, national consciousness is only the will to organize. What is needed is a basis of organization, a common source of strength, power, or life, a common goal that will override the private interests of individuals and integrate or unite them into a totality. This basis gives determinate *content* to organizational activity. This distinction between the form and content of the national body is essentially the difference between the means and the animating principles of organization. To take Minke's newspaper, *Medan,* as an example, the native press as means of organization opens up a new ideational communicative space for natives to learn more about themselves, to see themselves as an organic unity, a collective agent who can own things, and to elaborate their interests and voice them to the Malay reading public in colonial society. The press forms a collective native consciousness and life-world without necessarily specifying its content. *Medan* first arose as an organ of the Sarekat Priyayi (SP), the first modern native organization, but outlived it.[43] The paper is also a forum (*"medan"* means "arena") for publicizing and discussing the competing views of Boedi Oetomo (BO) and the Sarekat Dagang Islam (SDI) on what

---

43. Pramoedya abbreviates the title of Tirto's newspaper, *Medan Priyayi.*

constitutes the people. These competing views concern the content of the nation. A native organization aspiring to be the embryo of a new community should be more than a mere gathering of individuals around a provisional interest. Its animating principle must be most proper to the Indies people, must best reflect its true essence, for only then will it be able to exert the strongest ties (*ikatan*) over the maximum number of individuals. Thamrin observes that "*Sarekat*" (league) is a better term than "organization," "association" (*perkumpulan*) or "alliance" (*persekutuan*) because it is derived from "*ikat*" (tie), and means an alliance and association *for a common interest* (*JL*, 184; 143).[44]

In *Jejak Langkah*, Pramoedya explores the concrete content of "the people" through an elaborate reconstruction of Indies political history. This exploration is informed by the same organismic vitalism that subordinates *techne* to life. The distinction between form and content is figured as heterosexual reproduction: the forum of print is the womb for the gestation of modern native society. The differing ideas about the nature of this society are the active seed that inseminate the passive receptacle. They grow into different organizations, embryos that have the potential of becoming the national body. The animating principle that is the best basis for organizing/giving birth to the nation-people is that which can produce the strongest, healthiest child.

Minke is the mouthpiece for Pramoedya's conclusions. In his view, the animating principles of SP and BO are deformed and infected by death from the start because they espouse the ideal of stasis (*kebekuan*). Their stultifying spirit derives from the connections they wish to establish with the colonial state. The SP is named after the *priyayi*, the scribe caste or educated sector of Javanese society. It is a restrictive association that excludes the lower classes as well as traders. But more importantly, the *priyayi* ethos of passively imitating the behavior of superiors stifles any responsible thought.[45] It is a congenital disease that deforms the infant

---

44. "*Syarikat*" is the Arabic-Malay form, "*sarekat*," the Javanized form.

45. The relevant passage has been excised from the translation. "In fact of course, the Bupati [Regent] simply imitates the manners of his Dutch superior, the Resident. Imitating one's superiors is their standard of good behavior. They couldn't care less if that superior is an unregistered devil or spook from hell. After all, the more one imitates one's superiors, the less one's personal responsibility" (*JL*, 191).

organization, stultifying its life from the start and making its death inevitable. *Priyayi*-ness is continuous with the habitual submissive ethos bred by bureaucratic service: "In search of the masses, I had looked in the wrong direction. Its members were all *priyayi*–static, without initiative, without vitality, wishing only to finish their lives in peace in government service" (*JL*, 230; 179). BO is similarly fated to die. Its organizational efforts are limited to the building of Dutch schools with a Government curriculum designed to create more educated natives to fill the *priyayi* ranks, "Government officials, salary-eaters [*pemakan gaji*], servants" (*JL*, 249; 194). BO is the prototype of official nationalism and is quickly taken over by princes and bupatis. It becomes an extension of the stagnant, traditional world of old men, a world tethered to the colonial state.

These oppositions of stasis/dynamism, life/death associate freedom and life with youthful ideals that are free from state diktat. But the state is not the only source of death. The hierarchical, recidivist, and fossilizing ethos of Javanism (which is part of BO's charter) is also an unhealthy basis for a modern national community. First, it cannot reflect the complex composition of Indies society, which contains many peoples (*berbangsa ganda*). Javanism can only lead to divisiveness amongst the various Indies *bangsa* because it is a cultural and linguistic chauvinism that celebrates Javanese superiority (*JL*, 251; 196). Javanism is perfectly suited to the colonial policy of divide and rule, whereby different *bangsa* are used to fight each other in colonial wars of conquest. Second, Javanism is inimical to the formation of a democratic society because it originates from a hierarchical culture and fosters a sense of innate superiority in the arrogant *priyayi*. The *priyayi* are integral to the colonial state's functioning. They secure colonial hegemony because their divinely ordained hierarchy maps neatly onto bureaucratic hierarchy.

Minke's attempt to free the Indies from Java's unhealthy cultural dominance is an exorcism. Javanism represents two different types of ghosts. It is a devil that alienates human beings from each other. Because it stands in the way of humane friendship and fraternity, Java is the enemy of modern democracy: "Alas, between us stands the Javanese devil/demon [*iblis*]. An omnipresent devil: a devil of social hierarchy, lord of a no man's land, divider of one Javanese from all, all Javanese from one, and one Javanese from another. . . . Satanic power of the Javanese devil, begone!" (*JL*, 259; 202). But more importantly, Javanism is also a mystification that facilitates the reification of exploitative colonial capitalist socioeconomic relations. Its superstitious illusions are major obstacles to the people's progress towards freedom and self-determination because it encourages human subservience to external supernatural forces. Pramoedya points to the historical convergence of religious and commodity fetishism in the colonial Indies. The Javanese belief that words (such as mantras) have a supernatural power over human beings leads to apathy and the abdication of responsibility in the face of colonial domination: "all of this has a single origin: a denial of reality, a refusal to think—in the manner of Cashier Sastro who in the face of his endless difficulties, surrendered everything, without any resistance, to the supernatural [*kegaiban*]" (*JL*, 373; 295). Javanism is associated with the familiar word, "*gaib*." But this now connotes the exact opposite of the life-giving, nation-gestating spectrality of modern knowledge. It describes mystical (*gaib*) acronyms detached from concrete life—hollow and floating phantom signifiers sundered from semantics, etymology, and all sociohistorical significance—as well as slavish submission to invisible forces. "Reason that has been pawned and given over to the grip of a spectral hand [*tangan yang gaib*] will certainly not wear out, like false teeth" (*JL*, 373; 295). Bad spectrality is a form of *techne* that cannot be converted and returned back to life. It is the mummification of human reason, as false as artificial teeth.

To this bad spectrality, Pramoedya/Minke counterposes a native organization formed by modern knowledge that is attuned to life and rooted to the earth through concrete experience. This organization strives to actualize the common goals that give it unity. Its composition and aims must be based on two principles, which are its source of vitality and actuality. First, because colonialism has created a territorial body made up of many *bangsa*, any Indies-wide organization must be open to this actually existing diversity if it aims to be true to historical reality. An organization will not flourish unless it is multi-*bangsa* (*JL*, 251–52; 196–97). The nation envisioned here is clearly not based on cultural chauvinism. Second, to remain young and vital, the organization must also consist of people free from the state's stultifying influence. The state is the harbinger of death and is associated with old age. Nationalism is here coextensive with a radical popular vision of civil society that is the reverse of Kant's enlightened civil servant. For Pramoedya, an organization led by officials in their private capacity will invariably be shaped by state imperatives because persons dependent on the state for their livelihood and social status are subject to official pressure. But more importantly, the organization's life would be constricted from the moment of its birth because the complacency accompanying the social and financial stability of official position also stifles dynamism.

What is crucial here is that life, freedom's phenomenal analogue, explicitly takes on a sociological shape in Pramoedya's reinscription of civil society in the Indies. The organization that qualifies as the healthiest embryo of the Indonesian people and the best basis for the evolution of national unity should be formed from natives in their capacity as free individuals, what Minke calls a *"kaum merdeka,"* an independent or liberated class. This is a transformative reinscription of the Dutch *Vrije Burgers*. This class is the repository of liberation and life in a concrete manner. Its members are economically independent, not only in the sense of autonomy from state bureaucratic norms, but in the more exacting sense of earning their living through concrete work. Taking as his point of departure the laissez-faire argument that the dynamic activity of trading (*perdagangan*) is a country's life and soul (*jiwa negeri*), a democratizing force, and the source of freedom, Minke redefines the trader (*pedagang*) to include anyone who makes a living from one's own ability (*JL*, 334; 264). Workers and peasants can also trade. They market their own labor and its products. An organization of traders would not be limited to merchants, but would include all who achieve freedom through their ability to trade. Because the movement of trade and its products penetrate every sphere of life and every level of colonial government, a social organization based on trade can exert immense political power through boycott and strikes (*JL*, 335–36; 264–65). Indeed, Pramoedya even suggests that trading is the source of life as such: "everything can come to life if it is touched by trade" (*JL*, 339; 268).

But Pramoedya's Marxist inflection of bourgeois free-trade ideology and the categories of the burgher and civil society is also not entirely faithful to European Marxist teleology. Echoing the Asian Marxist idea of the proletarian nation, he envisions an emerging Indies native civil society that is already, fundamentally, a society of productive laborers. Over and above the intelligentsia and the emerging petit-bourgeois and trading class, this civil society already includes workers and peasants in its moment of inception. Moreover, Pramoedya suggests that trading is an Islamic tradition, which is a crucial part of everyday Indies culture. Hence, "the middling sort of Native who determines the everyday life of the Indies, Islam as a foundation for solidarity, and free endeavor and trade as the basis for collective life" would be the most practical or realistic basis for nationalism (*JL,* 447; 354). This is the animating principle of Minke's organization, the SDI. It is more inclusive than the Indisch (Indies-wide) political identity proposed by Douwager, the leader of the Indische Partij (IP).[46] The latter only leads to a privative nationalism modelled after the oligarchic Creole nationalism of the South African Dutch because it regards independent Indos (Dutch Indies Eurasians) and educated natives as the core of native civil society. Indisch political identity is another illusory specter to be exorcised. It is an intellectual abstraction that lacks actuality and effectivity: "Islam and trade have a broader and more binding foundation than Indies-ness. . . . The latter has no grounding . . . it's an ideal, not a reality. It's true that ideals can one day become reality, but their basis must still be the social reality of our time" (*JL,* 337; 266).

The SDI is also the repository of life because the language of its organizational activity is Malay, not Dutch. Malay is the lingua franca of the Indies, the language for communication across different *bangsa.*[47] Its democratic nature (vis-à-vis Javanese) and its wider reach as a language of native journalism (vis-à-vis Dutch) were discussed in the second volume. Jean Marais and Kommer had pointed out that Minke could disseminate modern knowledge further and understand his people better if he addressed the natives in Malay. Minke had acknowledged that Malay is the best language for understanding his people because unlike Javanese, which has a hierarchical structure of address, Malay fulfils the ideals of liberty, equality, and fraternity. It can bring equality into existence because it creates a community of equals through its form of address. In *Jejak Langkah,* Malay is affirmed as the language of native civil society, freedom, and life because, as the language

---

46. Douwager is the fictional version of Douwes Dekker. Minke articulates the SDI's doctrinal basis as a result of his disagreements with him. The polemic clearly differentiates Minke's radical popular nationalism from Douwager's top-down Creole nationalism, which is masterminded by political parties and privileges the Dutch language.

47. Ironically, Malay originated as the language of colonial administration. The Malay that Pramoedya regards as the language of freedom and life is not formal administrative Malay, but "Market Malay," the language of trade, commerce, and exchange. For a fascinating discussion of the history of Indies Malay and its role in "generating an organized self-awareness among the indigenous people of themselves as 'Indonesians,'" see John Hoffman, "A Foreign Investment: Indies Malay to 1901," *Indonesia,* no. 27 (1979): 65–92.

of trade and commerce (*bahasa pasaran,* or market language), it encourages the widest forms of sociality. It is a living language (*bahasa hidup*) that is forever evolving because it is rooted in the daily lives of the entire Indies population, educated and uneducated, native, Chinese, and Indo alike. As one character puts it, "Malay is . . . a language of extraordinary freeness/freedom [*luarbiasa bebasnya*], which can be used in any situation whatever, in any atmosphere, milieu, or environment, without anyone feeling that they have lost their dignity or honor" (*JL,* 278; 218).

———◆———

We can distil the organismic logic of Pramoedya's account of Indies nationalism into five propositions: First, as a creature of good spectrality, the desacralizing incarnational magic of modern knowledge (native civil society formed by market forces and the Malay print world), the living nation is a product of modernity that is radically discontinuous with traditional forms of community. Second, the colonial state is an agent of death that exemplifies the instrumental aspect of modern knowledge. By co-opting the illusions and specters of Javanism, it effects a remythologization or reenchantment of the native world under capitalism. These are bad forms of spectrality that need to be exorcised. Third, spectrality is necessary but also necessarily subordinate. Although the bad spectrality of instrumental reason is an inevitable trait of enlightenment, it is merely a degraded or lapsed state of reason that can be corrected by final recourse to the light of self-recursive, organismic critical reason. Instrumentality is merely an accident that befalls reason, a removable stain external to reason in the final instance, because it is a consequence of how reason is used.

Fourth, as a modern community held together by bonds that keep instrumental reason in check, the nation is the reconciliation of *techne* and *physis.* National consciousness is neither an ideological illusion of the European Enlightenment nor the artificial product of machines. The nation is not assembled from completely foreign parts brought to the Indies by colonialism. It grows organically out of the legacy of precolonial Islamic trading activity and the interests of the peasant masses as they interact with and are shaped by modern technomediation and market forces. Fifth, although Pramoedya emphasizes that good spectrality in the form of modern organizational knowledge and the native press has a constitutive role in the formation of the national organism, he views it in instrumentalist terms. It is an organ that can be used by native organizations as collective rational subjects to shape public opinion (*pendapat umum*). By being harnessed to maximize the vitality of the Indies national body, *techne* becomes organicized.

There is much to recommend Pramoedya's affirmation of the decolonizing nation as the incarnation of freedom. Given the territorial state's tenacity, dismissing the nation's radical potential for transformatively mediating between the masses' needs and the state leads either to the ludicrous celebration of the transnational migrant's resistant hybridity, or the utopian characterization of subaltern politics as a subversive negativity that disrupts institutional practices. Hybrid resistance is only feasible for arriviste formerly colonial academics. The latter, more serious alternative, which almost always takes the form of fragmented resistances to the hegemonic project of nationalist modernity, is marked by a certain idealism that is best evidenced by Partha Chatterjee's belief that "the imaginative possibilities afforded by the fuzziness of the community" can be an inexhaustible resource for the overcoming of capital.[48] This may perhaps be the only avenue remaining for followers of the orthodox Marxist critique of nationalism.

I want to outline a different critique of Pramoedya's affirmation of nationalism that the next chapter will develop. In my view, the last proposition of Pramoedya's organismic logic threatens to unravel the entire set of axioms it is supposed to complete because it alerts us to a constitutive spectrality that gives birth to the nation. For if this gestating spectrality always carries the risk of being infected from the start by instrumentality in such a way that we cannot distinguish the good specter from the bad specter, then the living nation will always be haunted by ghosts that cannot be exorcised, even, or better yet, especially, after formal independence, in postcoloniality. The living nation would be nothing but this haunting. This haunting should also be understood in terms of *Bildung*. Because the ability to step outside oneself that typifies a modern practical consciousness is premised upon the intrusion of the ghostly world of writing, print, and discursive space in the very heart of consciousness, a radical alterity

---

48. *The Nation and its Fragments*, p. 225.

always insists in the self-reflective act of national *Bildung* regardless of the self-presence implied by concrete action, work, decisiveness, and other values of a self-determining free being. This dehiscence or inadequation means that a certain ghostliness is constitutive of revolutionary nationalism even as the popular nation is viewed as the repository of life.

This ghostliness, which renders the line between life and death unpoliceable and opens the living nation-people up to the state, is a version of the radical heteronomy that afflicts Kant's conceptualization of organic life and all other political organicisms following from it. Because *techne* is the paradigm of heteronomy, the organism is our most apposite analogue of freedom. Yet organic life is itself inconceivable without some recourse to *techne*. This does not mean that the living postcolonial nation is merely a reflection of the neocolonial state and an ideological superstructure of capital. However, the *possibility* of becoming-ideology irreducibly marks the nation from within. This haunting of the nation-people succinctly captures the experience of freedom that characterizes the postcolonial nation in a conjuncture where the transcendence of global capital is not in sight. This makes nationalism neither the political telos of modernity's unfinished project nor its betrayal, as its defenders and opponents want to believe, but instead the political aporia of modern freedom.

Although Pramoedya wishes to bequeath a deferred telos of redemptive incarnation to his readers, we already glimpse this aporia in the final chapters of *Jejak Langkah*. When Minke explains his vision of national unity to the masses during his trip to Solo, we see the national organism animated through modern organization: "I saw their shining eyes beaming with idealism, as though they wanted to convince me that they understood the meaning of these words: the State will surrender [*tunduk*] to us without our needing to take up arms. . . . Unity will suffice, a rock-solid and mighty Islamic Trading League will suffice" (*JL*, 449; 355). The native world set in motion by print exemplifies the infinite epigenesis of life itself: "For me the world has now begun to become open, and all impediments remove themselves, fleeing in shame. Just look! *Medan*'s newspaper and magazines are circulating ever more widely, penetrating the heads and hearts of their readers, and implanting there seeds which in time will bloom" (*JL*, 422; 334). But the nation's life is forcefully truncated. At the very moment that Minke sees a new world opening up above the colonial earth as the result of his endeavors, he feels the colonial state's iron hand. It takes his life away from him without warning. He is evicted from his offices and exiled to Ambon for six years, a symbolic death that does not end with his return to Batavia in the quartet's final volume. Life, or the national body, has come face to face with death in the shape of the colonial state and finds its path blocked. But death is not a mere obstacle that can be transcended, removed, and subsumed by life. It is a radical finitude that contaminates the national organism from within as its constitutive possibility.

AFTERLIVES: THE MUTUAL HAUNTING OF STATE AND NATION

THE NEGATION OF LIFE: THE STATE AS THE AGENT OF DEATH

What kind of sociological figure does death cut? How does it appear to life? In *Jejak Langkah,* the haunting of the native *pergerakan* by the colonial state is personified by a mysterious figure, Jacques Pangemanann. At the end of the novel, at the point that Minke feels the native world is in optimal motion, something else sets off a chain of events that leads to the resignation of SDI central leadership members, the loosening of control over local branches, and the anti-Chinese boycott in Solo. This suggests the intentionality of another consciousness at work, whose designs are unknown to Minke. With the first page of *Rumah Kaca* (Glass house), we step abruptly into the murky world of the colonial state-machine, witnessing its ethos of death from the inside. *Rumah Kaca* is part investigative archive and part memoir. It is narrated by Pangemanann, whose identity is now revealed to be that of a highly placed Sorbonne-educated Menadonese official responsible for native affairs in the General Secretariat of the Dutch colonial state.

The novel's first chapter evokes the thriving activity of two emergent nationalisms in the Indies, Chinese and native, at the time of Governor-General Idenburg's appointment. It recapitulates some events portrayed in the previous novel from the state's perspective. A critical native public sphere and a new democratic spirit have arisen to publicize (*mengu-mumkan*) native dissatisfaction and challenge state authority. This new power, the power of modern knowledge and communications, cannot be destroyed because it is the inevitable product of the sociological structures and material changes accompanying modernity. "The rise of nationalism," Pangemanann notes, "is essentially a product of the modern age itself" (*RK,* 3; 3). Caught between these two waves of awakening, the colonial state tries to channel them into a path that is less threatening to it. By attempting to co-opt and give these nationalisms a reactionary shape, the state reveals itself as the agent of lies and ignorance.

Corroborating Minke's views about nationalism, Pangemanann repeatedly emphasizes that national unity is a modern form of solidarity different from traditional communal ties: "Over the entirety of the past hundred years there has never been a Native like him, who by the force of his personality, good will, and knowledge, has been able to unite thousands of people without recourse to the authority of kings, prophets, *wayang* heroes or devils [*iblis*]" (*RK,* 7; 7). The colonial state is an agent of death because it stultifies the vitality that the national awakening embodies. As we have seen, this stultification is primarily manifested in the state's betrayal of Enlightenment ideals despite its claim to be the bringer of progress and light; and the suffocation of a native's love for his or her people by official position. *Rumah Kaca* brilliantly portrays this work of death as a process of degeneration and miscultivation, an anti-*Bildung* that kills the promise of a future life.

The estrangement of modernity's ideals is strikingly evidenced by the illegality and criminality of the state's activities towards the native awakening. Although the *pergerakan* is a competing source of power that challenges the government's authority and seeks to bend it to the native people's will, it acts within the bounds of colonial law. It is the normativity of publicness itself that presses against the state. This is an inevitable consequence of the spread of European education in the colonies. It is the progress of the law of reason itself. No legitimate government can stop it without invoking emergency powers that endanger the state's own legitimate existence. Colonialism thus contains the seeds of its own downfall. As Pangemanann observes,

> European education and instruction in every colony bear the same fruit: difficulties for the colonial state. And as the people it colonizes become more

enlightened [*cerah*], so the State must itself become more enlightened/transparent, for the force of progress can not be held back by power [*kekuatan*]. Once a colonized people becomes enlightened, even if the State tries to restrict its development, it will seek its own path and will be successful in finding it. With or without the State. To ignore this law of development [*hukum perkembangan*] is unwise, stupid. (*RK*, 8; 8–9)

This account of nationalism's inevitability, which echoes Fanon's Manicheanism, is derived from Marx's argument that capitalism generates the proletariat as its own negation. The people exhibit the epigenetic capabilities of an organism. It develops according to inner rational laws and purposes, which are juxtaposed to the colonial state's brute force and might and the empty legality of its laws. Because it obstructs progress, the state's authority is shown to be as unreasonable as traditional despotism. It loses its right and is confronted by the victimized *pergerakan* as the true bearer of modern reason and progress. This confrontation is the Hegelian-Marxist dialectical moment of the negation of the negation in decolonizing space. It is figured as a haunting of the state.

The Dutch Indies state has become the inverted monstrous double of European democracy. In Pangemanann's words, "the Indies isn't a European state, it is merely a colonial state. Here, there is no parliament to channel the existing social forces. . . . The foundations of its strength are weaker than those of the democratic states of Europe" (*RK*, 8; 8). Ruling by arbitrary military force and the loyalty of a small stratum of native officials, the colonial state exercises domination without hegemony and social consensus. It is democracy alienated from itself through colonialism. The stain that colonialism makes on modern reason and the European moral conscience is evoked by recurring imagery of the sterile mud of a marshy swamp. This *lumpur kolonial,* which nourishes dead capital, is contrasted with the fertile living soil of the peasants (*RK*, 19; 18). The colonialist sinks in this mud and drowns, his conscience suffocated. This muck contaminates the native servants of the colonial state who implement its orders to murder and oppress.

Pangemanann is especially well placed to witness the Enlightenment's murky side. As a high-ranking *native* official, he is especially subject to colonial intrigue. Pangemanann develops a nervous hiss. His European colleagues attribute it to his residual native savagery, but it is in fact a symptom of the colonial state's cruelty. Because the colonial state also contains a rational moment, its victims haunt it. They leave contaminating marks on the colonial archive's pristine sheets and become invisible ghosts that cause Pangemanann's hiss:

> The moral face of Europe must be kept pure and clean, and to this end I must use, and am licensed to use, the vilest, filthiest methods.
>
> I am fully aware that I am the plaything of a spectral power [*kekuatan gaib*] born almost a century ago, of spectres [*roh-roh gaib*] whose shape I can not grasp, and whose traces I can only track in the clean pages of the archives, and in the filthinesses of life in the colony, the life of my own time—today.
>
> And to whom should I appeal? In my era, it is colonial power that triumphs. Everything non-colonial is its adversary. I myself am a colonial agent/tool. In their elegant language the professors recount the world's enlightenment beginning with the Renaissance, the *Aufklärung*, the rise of humanism, the shifts in class [hegemony] from the feudal nobility to the bourgeoisie that commenced with the French Revolution—in this way peddling their allegiance to the progressiveness of History. And here I am drowning in this kind of colonial muck. (*RK*, 46; 44)

Pangemanann sketches a psychological portrait of the colonialist as an inhuman species. The drive to possess colonies, which is likened to the polygamist's lust for secondary wives, arises from the desire for self-aggrandisement and not economic profit (*RK*, 65–66; 62–63). Colonialist thought is also characterized by hypocritical moralism and a disavowal of colonial rule's true basis in arbitrary might. The individual colonialist abuses official power to impose his will on others. The colonial character is therefore intrinsically cruel and oppressive. It finds self-importance in the obstruction and humiliation of others. This character is institutionally entrenched in hierarchical social customs (*adat*) that govern the lives of natives and Europeans alike. Finally, the colonial way is an infectious vapor that causes Europeans to ironically mime the despotic and pagan behaviour of native rulers Christian morality prohibits, such as the provision of native women for visiting officials.

The colonial state is also the agent of a subtler, more horrifying kind of death: the sentence of moral death that the lure of office imposes on native civil servants. This lure is deadly because someone possessed by desire for official status abdicates his autonomy or capacity for rational self-determination and allows himself to be determined by an external fetish. The desire for office is thus an instance of the mechanical or demonic. It is worse than physical death because it erodes the self-reflective consciousness that is freedom's basis. More concretely, an individual's identification with official position obstructs the attainment of political freedom because it undermines identification with the Indies people. Pramoedya characterizes this as a deformation or derangement of moral personality (*kepribadian*). It is *Mißbildung*, or even anti-*Bildung;* the opposite of national *Bildung,* the formation of a member of the decolonizing nation. Shackled to the colonial state by this spectral identity which he takes on as his real body, the civil servant becomes a zombie or automaton of the state-machine, his actions harnessed in the service of its work of death, and against the national organism's vital becoming. This spectral incorporation is all the more horrifying because the educated native could be a valuable member in the national process.

Pangemanann personifies this spectral incorporation. Educated at the Sorbonne and married to a Frenchwoman, he sees himself as a product of French Revolutionary ideals. But as a native totally consumed by his official status, he is a hybrid product of the colonial state's antimodern structures of governance and the *priyayi* mentality, even though he is Menadonese. He is the representative of death because he willingly stifles the development of a modern native conscience and works to dam the tide of the emerging national consciousness. Pramoedya shows this gradual corrosion of Pangemanann's conscience by his office. It is initially imposed on him by the outside, but he *decides* to surrender and accept it as a mystical power that dictates all his actions:

> It looks as if I have no way out. I'll remain mired in my abasement. Yes, Lord, *how terribly Office has changed the inner self/humanity of a person of this type. . . .*
>
> People say that when one reaches fifty, one begins to achieve firmness of character. One's attitude to life becomes stable, and one's treasury of experience grows ever richer. But with me, it's the opposite. Now that I'm on the verge of fifty, it's exactly my treasury of experience that has become chaotic, and I've lost any stance towards life. *And what's still worse: I know exactly why this has happened, and I don't have the courage to resist.*
>
> (*RK,* 40; 38–39; emphasis added)

Pangemanann compares himself to a wire bent beyond repair:

> Once the course of my life had no twists, it ran straight as a taut wire. It was only after I was assigned to destroy the remnants of the Pitung Gang that the wire was never again straight—not simply bent here and there, but an utter tangle. And I can see no way of straightening this tangle out again. *An external power called Office every day tightens its stranglehold round my neck.*
>
> (*RK*, 53; 50–51; emphasis added)

The official mindset is an atavistic and fundamentally immoral ethos that demands the abdication of personal responsibility for one's own moral *Bildung*. More importantly, it is the direct negation of life. It prevents the formation of a collective solidarity (national consciousness) through which individuals can transcend their finitude in collective moral work that will overcome the antihuman totalitarian state, which dominates natives through arational fiat. As Pangemanann observes,

> As an official, I too have the character of an official: anything and everything opposed to the principle of good 'Indies subject-hood' I ban, I denounce as immoral, and I anathematize. People must be submissive and obedient to the State as a power legitimated by God the Father. Were it not so, this State would have collapsed long ago. Nonetheless, I often can't help feeling tempted by the human thought that this abstract State whose effects can only be sensed, is simply the highest manifestation of human power; and human error is also a feature of its flawedness. (*RK*, 286; 271)

THE NEGATION OF DEATH

But how can the negation of life, that is, the (colonial and neocolonial) state and everything it represents be negated in turn? The above passage already intimates Pramoedya's solution. The abstract state is alienated from living human work. It can be reappropriated and its violent consequences, the effects of alienation, can be rectified. There are once again two sorts of ghosts, two forms of magic. The colonial state is satanic. But precisely because it is a defective by-product of modern knowledge's life-producing magic, it is haunted by a second ghost, the native awakening.

The latter can be converted into flesh (the nation) and will exorcise the first ghost.

This dialectical structure is indicated by the cloying proximity between the metaphor of the glass house and modern knowledge. *Rumah Kaca* is not only the title of Pangemanann's notes bound in book form. It also denotes the domain of his surveillance activity. The phrase is repeated many times and it is almost always italicized and capitalized to indicate the proper name of a technical apparatus that he wields to further the work of death.

> In both my functions, as Inspector and as Police Commissioner, my job is simply to exercise the tightest possible surveillance over my people in the interest of the well-being and long-term survival of the State. I have put, and will continue to put, all the Natives—and especially these modern Pitungs who disturb the ease of the State—into a Glass House placed on my desk. Every single thing they do will become fully visible. And that's my job: surveillance over every activity going on in this Glass House. This is also what the Governor-General desires. The Indies cannot be permitted to change—it must stay forever as it is. So that if I can manage to keep these notes in safety, and they eventually reach your hands, I'd like to ask you to title these notes of mine *Glass House*. (*RK*, 56; 54)

This Benthamite or Foucauldian image of the glass house links the gaze of surveillance, modern scientific observation, instrumentality, and the modern will to knowledge. It refers to the files Pangemanann keeps on the educated natives. But it also evokes the controlled environment of a hothouse in which plants can flourish. Even more to the point, the emphasis on observation and surveillance (*mengawasi*) evokes the lens of a microscope focused on organisms that breed in a laboratory petrie dish.

This recurring motif of scientific observation indicates that Pangemanann sees himself as a scholar and budding social scientist. He claims to be a practitioner of modern sociology and a specialist on colonial society who is compelled by a strong will to truth because he keeps jottings that are separate from the official colonial archive. The objects of his science are the emerging modern native organizations:

> My job is a special, not a public one. . . . This makes for interesting experiences. *So I ought to write everything down—who knows, one day it may come in*

handy. I'll begin from the angle of education, because this is what makes the eye see, listen, and evaluate events taking place far away, outside one's own country; it is what makes one look at one's self in the mirror and weigh one's self, and finally recognize/understand how long is the road before one, and how far along it one presently stands. (*RK*, 3; 3; emphasis added)

Pangemanann's will to truth is surprisingly close to modern science. It is not reducible to colonial domination although it shades into sadistic surveillance and is always susceptible to capture by the colonial state. For instance, Pangemanann regrets the likelihood that Siti Soendari, the first native woman activist, will be destroyed by his efforts because he is interested in her as a scientific specimen and an ethical exemplar.[1]

The gaze of surveillance that grasps and surreptitiously interns its objects within the glass house is similar to the technoscientific gaze of modernity that structures Minke's consciousness. Indeed, like Minke, Pangemanann's perceptive field has also been deepened by scientific knowledge and he views himself as separated from most natives by his education. However, Pangemanann's gaze is also the negation of modern science's truth-capturing gaze. It has a more circumscribed ambit. It is clearly limited to the Dutch Indies. Exiled in Holland, Wardi, Soendari, and Marco "have escaped from my *Glass House*, [and are] beyond the reach of my surveillance" (*RK*, 249; 235). Hence, whereas Minke's nationalist consciousness is regarded as the rightful inheritor of enlightenment, Pangemanann's gaze is a perversion of modernity's truth and light. It is a synecdoche for the colonial state's stance in relation to whatever undermines its domination. It is an archiving, secret-policing rationality that is not limited to actual acts of surveillance.

If we recall Pramoedya's earlier characterization of the colonial state as the incarnation of instrumental reason, we might understand the peculiar relationship of similarity and negation between modern reason and statist rationality not as a mere opposition between two static, self-contained, and irreconcilable terms, but as a dynamic *contradiction* arising from reason's diremption into critical and instrumental reason. We saw how this bifurcation led Pramoedya to distinguish between good and bad forms of spectrality. It should therefore not be surprising that colonial statist rationality

---

1. Compare *RK*, 207; 194; and 233; 220.

is indelibly marked by a neurosis about ghosts that signal the living national body's return. In dialectical logic, this prepares the way for the negation of the negation. Decolonization is the historical form of this process, where the dialectical contradiction between the Indies people and the colonial state is resolved by the Indies people's reincarnation as the popular Indonesian nation-state in which freedom is actualized.

The quartet's structure also reflects this dialectic. *Rumah Kaca* is the dark counterpoint of the first three volumes. It is the moment within the larger dialectical totality where the national spirit portrayed in the earlier books undergoes determinate negation. Thus, the same events (from 1912, the year of Idenburg's appointment, until Minke's exile) portrayed in *Jejak Langkah* are stood on their head. *Rumah Kaca*'s picture of the Indies and Pangemanann's worldview are inverted mirror images of the other novels. I have suggested that whereas the first three volumes make up a bildungsroman that charts Minke's moral development into a pioneering Indies national consciousness, *Rumah Kaca* is an antibildungsroman tracing the degeneration of Pangemanann, who devotes his life to destroying the *pergerakan* despite his conscience. But this also means that the anti-*Bildung* of the Indies nation is part of the larger dialectic of national *Bildung*. This anti-*Bildung* is emblematized by the erosion of Pangemanann's humanity and moral personality and his descent into alcoholism after his wife and family leave him:

> For forty years I made myself the man I wished to be. I formed myself with the utmost discipline. [But] in the past dozen years or so, a power greater than my own has given me a new character, one which conflicts with and has destroyed the self I had earlier created and whose form was set. That's why what I am now is a bundle of scraps, losing bits of my self one after the other. This is I. (*RK*, 173; 163)

This moment of mirroring, in which Pangemanann recognizes himself in the present by referring back to the shadow of his past self that his present self has negated, captures *Rumah Kaca*'s structural dynamic. It suggests that any moment of negation necessarily contains within itself that which it negates because it is defined through the act of negation. This means that negation also contains within itself its own negation. The negation of the negation is thereby promised in the future. This future anterior is intimated at various levels. First, *Rumah Kaca* is a parasitic text that does not make sense without the earlier volumes. It must continually refer to them. This is why Pangemanann obsessively pores over Minke's notebooks. Second, Pangemanann's actions, which are designed to destroy the growing nationalist movement, ironically give Minke and his "progeny" an afterlife. This is because the high esteem he receives from the colonial state is premised on the existence of the nationalist movement. His official position exists only in order to negate the *pergerakan,* which must therefore exist for him to exist.

But more importantly, the official consciousness Pangemanann represents is internally structured by a peculiar inverted doubling. For he is not the simple opposite to Minke and what he represents. He is in many respects very similar to Minke and shares many of his capacities and aspirations. But he betrays these ideals and develops in an antithetical direction. A hole develops in Pangemanann's being, which articulates these unfulfilled ideals in their violation and signifies the unbridged gap between him and Minke, who represents what he could have become. This curious doubling-cum-inversion is enacted through intentional acts of mimicry that continue throughout the book. In the first chapter, we learn that like Minke, Pangemanann is also an ELS graduate who feels different from other, less-educated natives (*RK*, 4; 4). But at the same time this similarity is declared, a crucial difference is also marked: unlike Pangemanann, Minke "is a Native ELS graduate who has no government office" (*RK*, 5; 5). He has chosen to be the eyes and voice of his people over an official position. When he learns that he has to obstruct Minke, Pangemanann experiences an internal struggle. He confesses his respect and admiration for Minke as a teacher figure and regrets his actions against him. He initially identifies with Minke but then learns to identify *with* his office, *against* Minke:

> It seems I'm not so good at acting a part, at wearing two faces. Pretty much like him all along, I think, I was a man with one face and one heart—but a *priyayi* of course! But he is more faithful to himself. He remains with a single human face. . . . Actually, I ought to be helping a man with so good a heart and with such good intentions towards his Native people. And I will help him, so help me God. He as an individuality, I as another individuality, so help me God. Give me the strength. . . . I must take the side of progress, of the progressiveness of history itself. So says my conscience. Quite pure. No personal interest involved. . . . In the last resort, this means I will have to con-

tinue manipulating the activity/movement of the man whom I admire the most, by actions, methods and endeavors that are outside the law. . . . I, a police officer, a servant and executor of the law. (*RK,* 17–19; 16–18)

Because of this ongoing struggle between his career and his moral principles, Pangemanann persistently measures his conduct and life against Minke's, often to the point of obsession. He makes notes like Minke. He wants to copy Minke's actions and be faithful to his teachings: "The truth is that I am writing partly because of the influence of his writings, and I'm not afraid to admit it" (*RK,* 176; 166). At the very end of the novel, he tries to emulate Minke's act of generosity towards his Ambonese maid: "I remembered that when Minke was about to go home to Java, he gave all that he owned to Auntie Marietje. I will do the same" (*RK,* 359; 337). On his promotion to the General Secretariat, he moves into Minke's former house, symbolically stealing his life: "I just stood there lost in reflection: this house is the former residence of Raden Mas Minke. I should be delighted to live here. . . . To be in a position to occupy this house, you got rid of Raden Mas Minke!" (*RK,* 77; 73).

At a psychical level, this inverted doubling that constitutes Pangemanann's official consciousness is a form of haunting: the return of a phantom double. The more his official personality develops and his drive for mastery increases, the more sadistic he becomes. As he grows to enjoy his control over Minke and his progeny and becomes patronizing and condescending in his imaginary addresses to them, Pangemanann is increasingly afflicted by visions of ghosts. These revenants are the traces left behind by any act of destruction, the indelible marks of the absence of what is destroyed but cannot be exorcised. They herald an eventual return and reincarnation.

These metaphorics of haunting are obviously part of Pramoedya's organismic conception of the *pergerakan.* Pangemanann describes his efforts as the work of death: "How ironical. *Edison gave life to dead objects, while the two of us destroy the living*" (*RK,* 253; 239; emphasis added). He sees himself as an evil mercenary who lives off destruction: "My job description is: handling Native organizations. Not to help them develop, but to smash them, to open a path for them which they do not choose themselves, but which I choose for them." (*RK,* 166; 156; cf. 53; 51). He first begins to see ghosts after he is promoted for destroying the Si Pitung bandits and develops a nervous hiss in reaction.

But my responsibility for the annihilation of the forces that fight despotism continued to weigh on my mind and my heart. I felt that I was a guilty man.

To forget this burden, I tried to immerse myself in the files on Pitung. . . . [L]ater, gradually, a shadow of Pitung's face loomed up. . . . Shadows like this made a deep and ineradicable effect on me. . . . They refused to leave me, indeed, insisted on following me everywhere like my own shadow.

. . . During the ceremony of my promotion to Adjunct Commissioner, it was all I could do to prevent myself from shaking my fist to get rid of the shadow of Pitung. . . . Zihhh—my hiss to exorcise Pitung's satanic shadow. And only then did it vanish. . . . Thus my promotion to Adjunct Commissioner was accompanied by the habit of hissing *zihhh* in order to exorcise the specter of Si Pitung. (*RK*, 44–45; 42–43)

This haunting is not just a personal psychological disorder of someone with an uneasy conscience. Pangemanann's psyche is the site of a struggle between opposite sociopolitical forces: the ghosts of the Indies people that haunt him and the office that possesses him and makes him suppress his conscience. He tries to resolve his internal struggle by identifying with the state. He uses the government as a talisman to exorcise the ghosts lodged within his conscience: "Ah, I replied, the State is more powerful than my conscience. To hell with it! . . . The State has beaten you both, Pitung, Minke! So don't put on any airs" (*RK*, 77; 73). After he is entrusted with the task of monitoring educated natives, Pangemanann becomes completely possessed by the state. He sees himself as an integral part of the official "we":

One of those [*mereka*] who determine the fate of the Netherlands Indies—its human beings, its land, and the land's resources. And now I've become one of them. As a group, we [*kami*] are the brains of the might of the Netherlands Indies, as I learned later on; and even the Governor General over there on the other side of that wall is merely a bemedalled and epauletted uniform, which carries out whatever plans we have devised. (*RK*, 84; 79–80)

This shift from "them" (*mereka*) to the exclusive "we" (*kami*) marks the educated native's capture by the colonial state. Pangemanann's co-option exemplifies the betrayal of the emergent nation by reactionary forces.

But the ghosts haunting Pangemanann cannot be exorcised because they are inseparable from modern knowledge. Pitung's ghost is partly summoned up by Pangemanann's reading of his files on the case. Modern knowledge is a conjuration with spirits. It enables Pangemanann to gain a more complete picture of the bandit and to incorporate him as an artifactual body without actually meeting him in person. Indeed, such modern ghosts turn out to be the proxies of life. They are convertible into flesh and the exorcism of the colonial state is coextensive with their incarnation. The haunting of Pangemanann by Minke's image is the inevitable haunting of the colonial state by the emerging nation-people. The government plays a role in the dissemination of modern learning because it needs to produce more native officials and clerks for corporate enterprise. But the spirit of modern historical progress also creates in the educated native a phantom that confronts the state and undermines its authority: "Educated natives! They will become the eternal enemy of the power of the Netherlands Indies! This colonial power is jealous of the educated Natives!" (*RK*, 51; 49). Reason has unfolded itself into a concrete reality that can overcome the colonial state's deadly work. Minke is the modern Pitung, the sublation of Pitung's ghost and the spectral might of modern knowledge. He is the pioneer who gives the national body life.

THE HAUNTING OF THE COLONIAL STATE BY MINKE'S AFTERLIFE

We know that the Indonesian nation had a future beyond the colonial period of the quartet's setting. *Rumah Kaca* tries to show us why the nation had *that* particular future. It further suggests that the spirit that secured that future for the nationalist movement beyond colonial suppression also promises a future beyond the New Order state. The work of memory is crucial to this future. For the nation to survive, the initiator of the awakening must be able to leave footprints in the colonial mud for others to follow, tracks that will not sink into oblivion on marshy ground. The colonial state exiles Minke to remove him from the natives' public gaze. It seeks to avert the possibility of an actual national awakening by destroying his presence. As Hendrik Frischboten, Minke's legal adviser, leaves for the Netherlands, he urges the natives not to forget: "My parting message to you is: do not forget him. It was he who was the Originator, for he was the first to give enlightenment to his people and to give you leadership" (*RK*, 109; 103).

Will Minke have an afterlife, a life beyond his death as an individual? Will his ideals and achievements be preserved in public memory for posterity instead of vanishing without a trace?

From the state's perspective, the preservation of Minke in the native public sphere's collective memory is a haunting. Pramoedya links the return of this ghost to the possibility of a future beyond death and human finitude. The mnemonic trace is not a revenant, although it appears to the colonial state as such. It is a living past event that has been interiorized by memory so that it can be revivified. Pramoedya suggests that while the state can destroy individuals, the *pergerakan* and its initiator's spirit will triumph over this work of death because it will live on eternally through modern native organizations. Such organizations and the nation they engender are a stronger rational response to human finitude than the state. For the state, however, native organizations are not quite modern. The official Orientalist or colonialist position expressed by Meneer L. is that although some natives are semi-Europeans in native bodies because they have absorbed some European knowledge, native organizations are still different in spirit from organizations in Europe. Despite their modern methods, they still exact mass obligation through awe and charisma (*RK*, 28; 27). Hence, native organizations are not institutions. They cannot endure because they are not based in reason, which provides stability, calculability, and predictability. Charisma is transient because it depends on the charismatic leader's presence. Native organizations are therefore based on contingency. They collapse with the leader's disappearance. Pangemanann makes a similar distinction between the awakenings in Asia and Europe. Although the SDI under Minke's leadership is an exceptional example of native awakening, he is misunderstood by his successors who remain mired in the native worldview and historical confusion of the Indies. They are inadequately educated and wield modern European concepts they do not fully understand like talismans. Hence, Pangemanann concludes that he "cannot see a continuation of the values created by our Modern Pitung. New leaders have come forward, but in each case no surplus value is added to the struggle. And what in their eyes is seen as progress, is actually nothing more than the stage-decor behind Minke" (*RK*, 286; 271).

Rumah Kaca reaffirms Pramoedya's views of the *pergerakan* as a vital organism that sublates the European individualist determination of modern freedom and the intimate solidarity of traditional communities by showing us how Pangemanann himself, the awakening's nemesis, gradually changes his views about native organizations. Throughout the novel, when he is haunted by his intellectual and moral conscience, Pangemanann often speaks as Pramoedya's mouthpiece, sometimes even evaluating different native organizations with the same vitalist criteria Minke used in the previous volume. With dismay, grudging admiration, and shame, he is gradually compelled to foresee his own defeat by the *pergerakan,* whom he acknowledges as the spirit of history. The *pergerakan*'s afterlife—the promise of the negation of the negation of life—is nothing but the infinity of modern reason itself that resides in all human beings. Modernity is the age of reason's triumph over brute force and terror. Pangemanann emphasizes more strongly than Minke that a modern native organization can have infinite life. An abstract creature over which the state has no legal coercive power as long as it behaves in accordance with the law, the modern organization is an entity with an existence that outstrips the finitude of its leader and individual members. It outlives them:

> It turns out that the organization of the Syarikat *did not die* when it lost its leadership. In the same way, though various leaders of the Chinese movement were expelled from the Indies, their organization too *did not die* as a consequence. In fact, both became larger and larger. *The State cannot act against organizations,* because in various respects an organization is more than a set of individual human beings. *The State can control individual human beings, but has no power over this kind of abstract creature.* (*RK,* 120; 114; emphasis added)

The organization's abstract nature is moreover not inimical to life but augments it. An organization can teach its members using technomediatic organs. Through a newspaper, the brains of an organization can speak to the members that make up its body, thereby propagating the organization's life infinitely. We see here the same organicization of *techne* found in all political organicisms, indicated by the uncanny interimplication of printing machinery and the human brain:

> Behind the modern newspapers stand not only printing machines but thinking machines. *Sin Po* is directed by a Chinese nationalist thinking machine, *Peroetoesan* by the Syarikat's thinking machine, and *De Expres* by the thinking machine of the Indische Partij. By means of these newspapers the brain

speaks to the limbs of its own body, annihilating distances of hundreds of miles. (*RK*, 134; 126)

Unlike the traditional magical power conferred by mantras, the magic of modern organizations is relational. It does not emanate from a simple substantive source. Its causality is modern reason's self-recursive causality. It involves the reordering or rational rearticulation of power relations between parties to produce a certain result. Using modern methods, the Indies natives can be organized into a force strong enough to make demands on the colonial regime, thereby altering the balance of power. Precisely because power is relational and not a substance, the *pergerakan* can never be killed off by the state. The fever of native organizational activity (*demam berorganisasi*) is a self-sustaining and self-propagating life force. As Pangemanann reluctantly acknowledges, this world in motion cannot be stopped because it expresses nothing less than the life and spirit of progress in/of history: "Native society is not simply changing, it is now in motion [*bergerak*] in search of an adaptation to the modern age. It now contains within itself a new element. It is moving in order to change its own form and content. And there is no human power that can block its path" (*RK*, 140; 133).

Pangemanann's changing views amplify the quartet's authorial message. In his reading of Minke's notebooks (the quartet's first three volumes), Pangemanann shows the reader how Pramoedya wishes the quartet to be read. He rehearses all the questions an alert reader ought to raise about the quartet's themes, genre, and function: the earlier volumes concern the impingement of modernity on the native world in the early twentieth century, and these changes are reflected in the changing consciousness of the narrator himself as an exemplary educated native. Minke is a connecting bridge between European and native worldviews, someone with a hybrid culture (*peranakan kebudayaan*) that shades between the two different worlds (*RK*, 177; 166). Pangemanann begins to grasp what Pramoedya wants the reader to see: that Minke is not simply a concrete individual but an ideal sociological type. The Minke personified in the first three volumes is not an individualistic private autobiographical subject: "He has manifested himself in the midst of various situations as the Modern Pitung, defender of the little people and the defenseless. He acts as a witness to the conditions of his epoch. He places far more importance on these conditions than upon his own existence [*kenyataan*]" (*RK*, 193; 182). The historical accuracy of the events and world portrayed is that of an abstractive or constructive realism that selects and amplifies features in order to distill the epoch's essence. The same goes for Pramoedya's own portrayal of Tirto Ardhi Soerjo as Minke.

The important point here is that this method of typical abstraction corresponds to the moment in historical teleology where reason has become incarnated into organizations.

> In this manuscript too, the role of individuals, no matter whether named Raden Mas Minke, or si Ana or Anu, has not the least importance. The (new) age has ensured the birth, growth and development of organizations, both as containers and as contents—which it sustains. Of course, the individual has left behind traces that are deep and perhaps will become permanent in the future life of the organization, *but what is much more important is how the organization will position itself within the history of the modern Indies, how it will change the Indies and its human beings, in line with the ideals its espouses, fights for, and develops as the contents of the organization's own self.*
>
> The role of the Adjunct Commissioner named Pangemanann is also unimportant. No matter what he does to hold back the development of the organization, he will lose in the end. The progressiveness of history will march on according to its own inner law. Pangemanann merely represents the interests of Dutch Indies power. *But the progressiveness of history is a life-movement of human beings across the planet, a frontline for the life of humanity.* Whatever opposes this force, no matter whether it be a group, an ethnicity, a people, or even an individual, will be defeated. Including the Netherlands Indies and I.
>
> (*RK*, 178; 167; emphasis added)

The inevitable negation of the colonial state is secured by the dialectic of world history. This dialectic is the life that pulses through the veins of organizations. They have replaced individuals as the effective agents of history and are nothing other than reason in its effectivity.

Whether the different native organizations Minke's activity engenders facilitate the propagation of life after his exile ultimately depends on whether their guiding principles are appropriate to the Indies people's needs within a given sociological conjuncture. This part of the novel reiterates the same organismic criteria Minke used to evaluate native organizations in the preceding volume. In his monitoring activity, Pangemanann characterizes both the SDI and IP organisations as weak and deformed specters. They are no longer strong and healthy integrated bodies that pose a threat to the colonial state because they can never unite to complement each other's strengths (*RK*, 131; 124). The IP, which is led by the triumvirate of Wardi, Tjipto, and Douwager, has a higher political consciousness and seeks to unite all modern Indies people. But it cannot do anything because it consists only of Eurasians and educated natives. It lacks any basis in concrete living activity because Eurasian culture is not rooted to the Indies earth. Without a mass following, it is only a shadow party without any strength. It spreads new ideas in the Indies, but its members are unable to act on those ideas (*RK*, 141; 133). Following a more or less Marxist tropology that sees ideas as the mere phantom reflection of living actuality, the IP is figured as a parasitic, vampiric being, without a real body that is rooted to the earth. In contradistinction, the SDI (now renamed Sarekat Islam) has a large membership. But inadequate political leadership makes it an apathetic, bloated body incapable of action. It has been sapped of its strength because, after Minke's exile, its members have surrendered responsibility to their leaders, Tjokro and Samadi, who put their personal interests before the organization's needs and life-pulse (*RK*, 126; 119).

In light of the SI's apathy and the IP's impotence, it is Marco and Siti Soendari who emerge on the scene as Minke's true progeny and the bearers of vital movement. Pangemanann finds structural features in Marco's writings that indicate the rise of a modern national consciousness similar to those in Minke's writings, especially "the ability to depict the spirit aroused by fundamental shifts in values and in social and economic life" (*RK*, 188; 177). Marco is another example of how European ideas can influence natives to produce a new force that can tear apart the hierarchical native world and oppose Europe itself. Like Minke, Marco is also a cultural hybrid. But because his immersion in European ideas is more haphazard, he embodies the most extreme traits of native and European worlds and becomes very dangerous to the colonial state. Through his actions, he sows the seeds of anarchy in Indies life. Similarly, Pangemanann describes Siti Soendari as someone who has "absorbed the dynamic life of Europe" (*RK*, 209; 197). More educated and refined than Marco, Soendari, like Kartini and Minke, is from the *priyayi* caste. However, she is dissatisfied with the apathy of both BO and IP. Soendari's drive and sense of justice makes her the incarnation of Minke's ideals: "She was clearly a spiritual child of the Modern Pitung, a woman of perseverance and manifold activity. It was clear that the words of the Modern Pitung lived on in her" (*RK*, 245; 231).

Viewing these developments as a disinterested social scientist, Pangemanann acknowledges that this fever for organization is a sign that Minke's legacy still lives on and that life is stirring in the Indies: "Yes, yes, a new era, a new way of living, with new conditions of life, and new terminologies and appellations. All of this was a portent of a future way of life of constant movement [*hidup yang bergerak*]" (*RK*, 230; 217). It becomes clear that this life force has grown into a new phase of anticolonial resistance: the phase of nationalism in which Europe is confronted with its own product, a movement consisting of newly born modern natives who spring forth as a new people bereft of capital, but full of energy, not only in the cities but wherever there is European business. Unlike premodern patriotism, modern nationalism involves *organized* resistance driven by pen and paper. Through modern organization and knowledge, the specter that haunts the colonial state has become flesh in the nation-people who now confronts a colonial state weakened by the First World War.

In Pangemanann's eyes, these spontaneous uprisings against European capital are even more powerful than the revolt in France against Louis XVI. Meanwhile, beyond the Indies, the Russian revolution indicates the actualization of a new form of power analogous to the Indies *pergerakan*: "Once again, I was up against a new logic, which felt and sounded crazy, but which had become a reality, emerging and giving itself form in the overthrow and the fall of a tsar with all his absolutist power" (*RK*, 291; 275). This combination of political events within and beyond the Indies compel Pangemanann to admit that these native organizations are the true legatees of modernity's ideal project: "So it was clear that this new development was not for me an adversary. It was a development that was quite natural, even though its spread is more passionate/fiery than anything Europe itself had experienced. With the possible exception of France on the eve of the Revolution" (*RK*, 231–32; 218). Indeed, he suggests in true dialectical fashion that Minke is no longer Javanese but European. Even if he has never studied European philosophy, he has inherited European philosophical ideals and methods through historical absorption and activated them in his endeavors to foster Indies nationalism:

With his modicum of science and knowledge, he dreamed the rise of Indies nationalism without being able to comprehend its course. Here we have a Javanese Native, dressed in Javanese costume, who was absolutely no longer Javanese. *He is a European who founded his life on reason, not on Javanese illusions, and not on Javanism. . . .*

The man beside me is possibly the only Javanese Native who has shed all his illusions as a people and as an individual. With a scientific knowledge still far from adequate he is groping, scrabbling through every twig and blade of grass to awaken Indies nationalism.

. . . A Javanese who is not Javanese is none other than a revolutionary in this age in which I live. I know he never studied Western philosophy. Only the capital of healthy reason has proved capable of liberating him from atavism.

It may be that he is the first Javanese realist. (*RK*, 305–6; 288–89)

This teleological discourse of the passing on of the world-historical spirit from Europe to decolonizing Asia is also a discourse of the transcendence of finitude through knowledge. Minke lives beyond his time. He is able to outstrip and overcome the limitations of his age and the atavistic worldview of his culture of birth. By the sheer strength of his imagination, he is able to project a future for himself and for his people beyond their present and, indeed, beyond any given present. This projection of a future beyond his own individual death at the hands of the colonial state is figured as the leaving behind of footprints in his wake that others can trace and follow, leaving yet more footprints for a posterity that remains infinitely open: "Even if has failed as a doctor, Minke has succeeded in building a kingdom, and in starting to pioneer a transformation. And all modern Native movements will follow in his tracks [*jejak langkahnya*]" (*RK*, 143; 135–36).

Pangemanann tries to erase Minke from public memory by censoring all reports of his death in the native papers. But he is not forgotten: "It turns out people are coming upon his tracks and retracing them, and in their turn leaving tracks more numerous and stretching still farther ahead. I've seen it all with my own eyes" (*RK*, 332; 313). *This* Minke, the Indonesian national spirit, has grown too large for the iron grip of Pangemanann's statist hand: "In another sense, in another reality, it's not merely that my hands and fingers are too small and weak to grasp you, but you yourself are too great for me to grasp" (*RK*, 298; 282). Hence, notwithstanding

Minke's oblivion immediately after his death, he continues to leave an impression on the collective memory of the Indies social body. In the first place, he leaves a deep impression on Pangemanann, the person who tries to obliterate him and all public memory of him. In the end, a delusional Pangemanann would like to see himself as Minke's sole heir. He claims to be Minke's only true admirer, the one who truly understands him, who knows him even better than Marco, his follower. The Syarikat has become a dead child dissociated from its parentage and Pangemanann tries to stage a scene of inheritance from father to son, teacher to student, by promising to resurrect Minke's memory in the future when he is recognized as an expert on colonial affairs (*RK*, 334–35; 315–16).

The quartet's ending is morally fitful but predictable. Pangemanann is denied the inheritance he wishes to receive from Minke. He never receives the official recognition he thinks he deserves. Because Governor-General Van Limburg Stirum no longer takes such a repressive stance towards the *pergerakan*, the colonial state no longer holds Pangemanann in high esteem. He loses his will to work, his interest in his office, and even his will to live. When he visits Minke's grave, he finds that while the state has forgotten him, Minke is still remembered by the Jamaitul Khair, an Arabic organization in the Indies. This suggests that the national *pergerakan* is a better response to finitude than the state. But the narrative does not stop with the poetic justice of Pangemanann's downfall. To intimate the positive dimension of the negation of the negation of life, to point more forcefully to a future beyond the colonial state, Pramoedya makes the dying Pangemanann the *active agent* of the national spirit's preservation.

A figure from Minke's youth enters into the twilight of Pangemanann's life. Nyai Ontosoroh, Minke's spiritual mother and the origin of his political drive, returns once again into the narrative's purview. Her story illustrates that life is possibility and hope. As such, she attests to the truth of Minke's manuscripts. Now married to Jean Marais and a legal resident in France, Madame Sanikem returns to the Indies in search of Minke. Pangemanann, whom the French Consul has ironically assigned to assist her, brings her to Minke's grave, where she surmises that he was responsible for his death. For the Sorbonne-educated Pangemanann, who has maintained an idealized image of France, Sanikem is the representative of France who has come to judge him for betraying his vocation as a person of education. If the confirmation of Minke's enduring legacy in the earlier grave scene suggests that the nation is a better response to finitude than the state, this second grave scene stages life's promise and death's future defeat. Humbled into self-loathing and acknowledgment of the extent of his *Mißbildung*, Pangemanann recognizes himself as the bringer of death. But more importantly, he also realizes that his mission of annihilation has failed:

> You, Pangemanann, you once received a good education in Europe, the best education obtainable in the world in this century. Now you bow your head at the grave of a man much younger than you. Was it really for this death that you received all that education from Europe? Is this all that you could achieve in your life? Whereas that Sanikem who stands beside you, she built [*membangunkan*] whatever it was possible for her to build. And you, was all you could manage destroying it? Even then you could not destroy it entirely?
>
> (*RK*, 357; 336)

Before dying, Minke had also pointed to the promise of the future. He had told his secret-police tormentors that the state cannot ban political activity because it is the essence of human existence:

> Everything is connected to politics! Everything proceeds by organization. . . . And tell me who it is who can free himself from organization. Wherever there is more than two people gathered together, organization arises. . . . From the time of the prophets up till today . . . no human being can escape the power of his fellowmen, except for those who are isolated in madness. Indeed even those who from earliest times exiled themselves in the midst of jungles or open seas, still carried with them the traces of the power of their fellows. And so long as there are those who are ruled and those who rule, those who are dominated and who dominate, men will act politically. So long as a man finds himself in the midst of a society, no matter how small, he will organize and be organized. (*RK*, 313; 296)

This organismic energy of humanity as a political species is precisely what secures a future for the Indies national spirit. Pangemanann's final actions suggest that this promise is not just a utopian hope. He sends Minke's manuscripts together with his own documentation of the colonial state's workings, *Rumah Kaca*, to Nyai Ontosoroh in France. This literary totality, which contains the truth of the national awakening, is destined for the land of liberty's origin, outside the quartet's colonial setting, where it can be kept intact, preserved from the contaminations of an oppressive state, until a yet-unforeseeable time when the national spirit can be reincarnated as the popular Indonesian nation-state.

MORBID INTERROGATIONS: THE CONSTITUTIVE POSSIBILITY OF DEATH WITHIN THE LIVING NATIONAL BODY

I have argued that Pramoedya's affirmation of Indonesian nationalism, which attempts to resolve the contradiction between life and death, the nation and the state, by promising the overcoming of death, is organized by Hegelian dialectics. However, it is crucial to remember that in dialectical speculation, the line separating life from death is not an impermeable border. Sublation (*Aufhebung*) is precisely the overcoming of binary oppositions, where the dividing line between the two terms is removed by having one term subsume or absorb its other within itself. As Jacques Derrida observes, "the Hegelian concept of contradiction (*Widerspruch*), . . . as its name indicates, is constructed in such a way as to permit its resolution within dialectical *discourse,* in the immanence of a concept capable of its own exteriority, capable of maintaining what is outside it right next to it."[2] "Hegelian idealism consists precisely of . . . a resolution of contradiction into a third term that comes in order to *aufheben,* to deny while raising up, while idealizing, while sublimating into an anamnesic interiority (*Erinnerung*), while interning difference in a self-presence."[3]

For Hegel, the concept's ability to be at home with itself in the other is the source of life. Pramoedya makes a similar argument about the national organism. The state is the product of inhuman capital. It is an abstract body that is alienated from humanity, negates life, and needs to be reappropriated. The nation, which maintains a better connection to living human needs, is the agent and product-effect of this reappropriation.

---

2. Jacques Derrida, *Positions,* trans. Alan Bass (Chicago: University of Chicago Press, 1981), p. 101 n. 13.

3. Ibid., p. 43.

Decolonization is the nation's attempt to inspirit the state, to subsume this other within itself so that it can be mobilized to serve the people's interests. This contradiction between nation and state is also a conflict between the good spectrality of modern knowledge and the bad spectrality of Javanist ideology and colonialist instrumental reason. It is resolved when bad spectrality is exorcised and good spectrality is incarnated as a popular nation-state. In all this, death is not so much eradicated but sublated. It is returned back to, subsumed by, and interned within the movement of self-present life as *its* determinate negation. Death is a limit to life that life can know and comprehend because it has posited this limit within itself, and in its knowing of this limit as its *own* limit, as a limit proper to or belonging to life, life thereby transcends this limit that is death.

But the quartet's organismic theme needs to be heavily qualified if we consider it as a literary *example* of national *Bildung* that preserves the national spirit and summons it up in contemporary Indonesian readers in the face of the neocolonial New Order state's active forgetfulness. For with the failure of decolonization, the heralded self-actualization of freedom in the reincarnated national body is at best a remote possibility in the spheres of politics and economics. It can only be promised in the realm of culture. The overcoming of death in and through the living nation can only be performed and actualized in literature, of which the quartet is an example. But here a series of reservations must be raised. Pramoedya's affirmation of the nation is premised on our ability to distinguish between life and death, the nation and the state, so that the former can know and subsume the latter as its limit. Yet, if the quartet is read against the grain of its dialectical discourse, its organismic vitalism becomes problematic for two reasons.

First, the nation-people is infected by death from its birth because the formation of modern native organizations, its embryos, is inherently contaminated. Second, the national spirit can only be preserved under compromised conditions. I am referring firstly to the survival of Minke's manuscripts or the quartet's narratological condition of possibility, its structure of address or how it interpellates readers to participate in national *Bildung,* and only secondly, to the actual publication and dissemination of Pramoedya's writings. The important narratological role of Pangemanann in the transmission of Minke's manuscripts is also a form of original contamination that points to the mutual haunting of the nation and the state instead of the former's dialectical sublation of the latter. This irresolvable haunting implies that the nation and the state are the *différance* of each other in Derrida's sense of an originary difference that cannot be interned within self-presence.[4]

PUBLICNESS AND THE SPECTRAL GAZE OF STATE SURVEILLANCE

The problematization of Pramoedya's organismic vitalism can be located at two levels: the thematic presentation of the *pergerakan*'s rise in Indonesian political history and the quartet's formal narrative structure. Let us first consider the thematic aspect. The promise of life's triumph over death is premised on the political morality or right of the state. The light of publicness can incarnate or give phenomenality to a ghost (the nationalist movement) that haunts the state and holds it accountable because modern political authority is based on reason. We have seen this in Pangemanann's affliction. The colonial state's vulnerability to international public opinion is a more objective form of haunting. When the government exiles the IP triumvirate, Pangemanann is directed to give an official public justification so that the colonial state is not accused by the native and overseas English presses of arbitrary action exceeding its rightful power (*RK*, 158; 148–49).

But these epistemological metaphors of modern light and the enlightened gaze—that of the newly emergent native public sphere and its organizations, Minke's accusatory gaze, Sanikem's gaze that pierces through Pangemanann's heart—are also double edged. The transparency rendered by critical publicness can also be the visibility of the glass house. The light of modern reason reveals the truth of actors and things by bringing them into phenomenality. But it also allows them to be monitored by the state in one and the same movement. To be educated and to be able to write in public is also to be completely legible to the state, to be susceptible to its manipulation. At the same time that technomediation enables the government to be watched, the government is also able to watch its watchers through the same apparatus. Through the phenomenon of publicness, both sides are constitutively attached to each other as phantom doubles.

---

4. Jacques Derrida, "Différance," in *Margins of Philosophy*, trans. Alan Bass (Chicago: University of Chicago Press, 1982), pp. 1–27.

This should not be surprising. The native awakening is, after all, partly a product of the Ethical Policy, a product that strays from its prescribed mold. The state tries to correct this errancy. This is the bind of reason's transparency, the *restance* of a ghostliness that is not necessarily destined for incarnation into a living body. We have seen this spectrality only as the haunting that afflicts the state. But as the condition that allows the state to haunt the emerging nation-people, the spectrality of modern reason is also a remainder that cannot be converted into living flesh. From the start, the colonial state's attempts to dam the tide of native nationalism by channelling it into a more suitable path takes the form of the gaze of surveillance that sees without being seen. Pangemanann says eerily of Minke, "I often see him. But of course he doesn't recognize me, and for the time being there's no need for him to do so" (*RK*, 6; 8). The same invisible gaze is directed at Marco and Siti Soendari.[5]

The paradigm for this seeing-without-being-seen is note taking and reading, even literary criticism, since the material condition of this invisible gaze is the spectrality of written or printed knowledge. People become files on Pangemanann's desk and are ensconced within his glass house. He is able to monitor his targets primarily through press stories about them and, more importantly, by reading their own writing, which gives him a sense of their subjective interiority. For instance, without Minke actually saying it, he is able to infer from Minke's writings that he has modelled the Syarikat after Sun Yat Sen's ideas: "All of this can be gleaned from his editorials in *Medan Priyayi*, the newspaper he himself edits, even though he rarely mentions China or the Chinese" (*RK*, 3; 3). As Pangemanann later observes:

> *From a person's writings I can see the shape of his thoughts and feelings,* his desires, their general direction, his dreams, his stupidities and flaws, his intelligence, his cleverness, and his knowledge—and all of *these are intertwined like clear threads of glass.* Each text forms a world of its own, which drifts about between the world of reality and the world of dreams.
>
> (*RK*, 103; 97; emphasis added)

---

5. See *RK*, 191, 197, 208, 214, 225; 180, 185, 195, 201, 212.

Thus, the newspapers through which native organizations speak to their members "also speak to me [Pangemanann], with the very same words and meanings" (*RK*, 134; 127). Indeed, the more modern an organization's methods, the easier Pangemanann's task because, as someone from the same educated stratum, he has the necessary tools to understand its behavior without needing to refer to Orientalist archives (*RK*, 130; 123).

The native public sphere's constitutive susceptibility to monitoring also means that it can be influenced and bent to serve the state's interests. The dissociation of Hindia (the Indies) from Belanda (Holland), the separation of the territorial people from the administrative state, thus becomes extremely complicated and may even be impossible. On the one hand, insofar as the state can to some degree regulate the technomediatic apparatus that allows the people to be visualized and to visualize themselves, its actions are an important determinant of what the people is. But, on the other hand, the state also cannot control this spectral world completely because it is also the condition of possibility of its hegemony. Hence, it is also haunted and can be transformed by this spectrality as deployed by the people in similarly limited degrees. This is why the people and the state haunt each other from the very beginning of the nation's emergence.

This form of spectrality cannot be contained within the quartet's dialectical economy. As we have seen, in philosophical modernity, the line separating life and death is identical to that distinguishing ideality from finite matter. Reason is *the* prophylactic secularized humanity deploys to protect itself from finitude. Thus, normative collective work (*Kultur* or *Bildung* in both its idealist and materialist variants) is always figured in incarnational and organismic terms. Accordingly, the quartet only recognizes two kinds of specters. Good specters are ideals that cross the dividing line between death and life, are reincarnated, and remain once and for all on the side of the living. On the other hand, bad specters such as the colonial state and its apparatuses cross the border in the other direction. They are capital's mystificatory epiphenomena and should be exorcised and banished forever from the world of the living. One destroys a revenant by ensuring that it stays dead and can never return again. What we see here, however, is a specter that interminably crosses and recrosses the border between life and death and renders the border itself unpoliceable and delirious. Yet delirious spectrality is more originary than the other two forms of spectrality. As the sheer possibility of crossing the line between death and life, it is the condition of possibility of good and bad specters. Without originary spectrality, no crossing between life and death would be possible. To be sure, no ghosts would be possible. But by the same token, no exorcism of ghosts and, more importantly, no incarnation or actualization of spirit, no overcoming of finitude would be possible.

Once we begin to see the public sphere primarily as an effect of spectrality or even as spectrality itself, and only secondarily as the expression of critical reason, the canonical argument about the auto-causality of publicness qua mediating movement between the state and the masses articulated into a civil society becomes fundamentally deformed and needs to be rethought from the ground up. We are speaking here of the deformation of form itself. The phenomenality of public light is supposed to confer rational form to social action because the public sphere as an enlightened nation-people is conceived as a self-reflective collective subject. Its spectrality is thus the stain that inheres in the formation of any self-recursive modern consciousness. It can be likened to the tain of the mirror that allows a free subject, of which the people is a case, to reflect itself and to see and know itself in that reflection, and in that seeing-knowing and return-to-self, incarnate and give life to itself. But the tain itself cannot be seen.

This spectrality was always already present in *Jejak Langkah*'s portrayal of the rise of modern native organizations. As we saw earlier, Pramoedya's organismic affirmation of the nation, which is a response to the destruction of traditional communities by modern technology, involves an interplay between *techne* and *physis* which ultimately subordinates *techne* to life. But this move forecloses the fact that the peculiar kind of life exhibited by organizations and, indeed, all modern artifactual communities, is a form of vitality that can no longer be defined in opposition to *techne* and thus to heteronomy and the demonic. Modern organizations are the best examples of a ghostliness that cannot be completely converted to life or quarantined forever on the side of death. Indeed, because such artifactual bodies are essential to the organic development and growth of colonized natives, *techne* is now woven into the very spacing and timing of life. Life has been opened or has opened itself up to welcome this other within it, this supplement that is necessary to (its) life, even if this other can always be an enemy that threatens life. This sheer exposure without return was already implied by Kant's inaugural characterization of the organism as a technic of nature. The invasion of the life-world by technomediation is merely the historical unfolding of the necessary supplementation of organic life.

Closer examination of Pramoedya's account of the rise of modern organizations reveals that a certain sleight of hand or conjuration occurs when he aligns "the people" with living reality and the state with bad spectrality and death. Consider the curious role of print in the native public sphere's epigenesis. By publicizing information about Dutch law in market Malay, the language of trading life, and by opening its offices to villagers with stories of injustice, Minke's newspaper, *Medan,* "has become a saving angel in the lives of Natives in the Indies" (*JL,* 193; 150). Although its parent organization fails, it maintains an independent life and becomes an organ for articulating and disseminating the people's interests to a larger "reading public of Indies society [which] lifts up its head to be able to observe the important events" (*JL,* 207; 161). This public grows into a sphere of public opinion, whose force is feared by the colonial state. The paper's power of critical publicity derives from its organic unity with the people. This unity presupposes that the interests of natives are initially separate from the state. Through the paper, which is an organ deployed to voice these extrastate interests, the natives come together and become the people, represented by an autonomous public. As a source of justice and truth, the paper is "healthy and energizing food" that nourishes the people (*JL,* 236; 184). As a forum that expresses their interests, it gives them phenomenality and light. Minke observes:

> Natives, my people, now you have your own newspaper, a place where you can register your own complaints and concerns. Don't be hesitant. There is no crime in the world that is not ashamed and embarrassed before the gaze of the world. You now have *Medan,* a place for your opinions and your thoughts, a place where each one of you can weigh sentiment and justice. Minke will bring your cases before the judgment of the world! (Ibid.)

This unity between the people and the organ through which they express their interests and in which they find themselves reflected gives the paper life. It belongs to the people and the people feel they belong to it. Hence, Minke feels that his destiny is "bound to the earth and the people and the *bangsa* of the Indies. My commitment is here in the Indies. Only in the Indies can I build something that matters. In another country, I would probably become merely a withered leaf tossed about in the wind" (ibid.). He is alive because unlike a dead leaf, he is not cut off from the living soil.

Now, for the paper to fulfill its optimal function as a medium in which the people or the public representing it can see and know itself, articulate its interests, and use this self-knowledge to make critical demands against the state, the interests of both paper and people must be clearly delineated from the state. If either is contaminated by the state, the organic unity between them would crumble and publicity would lose its autonomous critical power. But matters are complicated by the fact that the technomedia is not simply an instrument but is actually constitutive of native organizations and the people. Despite the fact that Minke figures the rise of a native public as an awakening from sleep, the people does not exist prior to the constitution of the reading public. Popular interests are as much formed by the technomediatic apparatus as they are voiced through it. The people's vital existence is thus haunted from within by the spectrality of print. It flickers, becoming visible and invisible, appearing and disappearing with the magical phenomenality of print. We see this ghostly birth at work in Minke's description of *Sin Po,* the organ of Chinese nationalists in the Indies:

> In Batavia, *Sin Po* is now being published to lead and to unite the thinking and activity of the Chinese nationalists in the Indies. . . . This new stage is clearly marked by the role of newspapers in guiding the thinking of its readership. The organization in itself can not be made visible to the public. If the newspaper vanishes from the face of the earth under external pressure, then the leadership of the organization will also vanish. (*JL,* 388; 307)

This passage captures the aporetic logic of technomediation: the organization that is supposedly the subject deploying the paper is invisible to the public eye. It only directs and unites nationalists through a visible organ which is a printing body. We infer the invisible organization's reality from its organ. But once the organ, which is only the organization's prosthesis or stand-in, disappears, the organization whose actuality we have inferred from its organ will also vanish (even though we have never seen it), and with it, the nationalist social body it seeks to bring into existence.

This ghostly birth of the people indicates that in addition to forcible repression, the state can have a hand in the shaping of the people from the start by regulating the technomediatic apparatus. Publications have to be registered with the relevant state office and a set number of copies of each issue need to be sent to the appropriate authorities. The state can also shape the world of print and, through it, the people by influencing the content of papers to serve its interests. Nyai Ontosoroh warns Minke of the paper's constitutive susceptibility to the state when she points out that the *priyayi* can abuse the paper's advice to get around the law and the government can use the magazine to implement its regulations properly, to produce natives who know the law (*JL*, 191–92; 149–50). Indeed, Governor-General Van Heutsz describes Minke to European journalists as someone who "is now helping the State with his weekly newspaper, for *Medan* explains and strengthens Law" (*JL*, 211; 164). When Van Heutsz offers to fund *Medan*, Minke recalls Nyai's warning: "You'll be turned into a publicist/propagandist [*juru penerang*] by your own will. He'll use your influence without hiring you, without paying you. Be careful, don't let your ability, your influence, and your experience lose its direction" (*JL*, 220; 171).

In the same way, the educated native can also be an instrument of the Ethical Policy, which is an epiphenomenon of sugar interests and other forms of European capital. As Van Kollewjin, a member of the Dutch parliament, explains to a younger Minke, "[We will] equip [natives] . . . with what they will need to be able to enter the new age. The very best bridge for this purpose is the educated Native" (*JL*, 26; 20). Pramoedya painstakingly describes how *ethici* such as Van Aberon (Abendanon) exploit the publication of Kartini's letters to further their own political ambitions and how these manipulations are a public relations exercise to attract more capital to the Indies (*JL*, 385–87; 304–6). He documents how Governor-General Idenburg uses the funeral of Kartini's husband against the *ethici* who wish to elect Van Aberon as the next Indies Governor General (*JL*, 456–57; 360–61). The *ethici* also support the establishment of more Dutch schools with a government curriculum to the point that they outnumber and displace nongovernment schools.

The point here is not just to denounce such incidents as examples of manipulative official publicity but to account for how and why the people's interests can be channelled by the colonial state, how and why the living people are, in the very moment of their constitution, susceptible to the state's stultifying imperatives. We would be mistaken to think that this bad publicity is in the first and final instance qualitatively different from the pure or good publicness that generates and expresses the nation-people's freedom. The two forms of publicness cannot be separated once and for all, and the good protected from the bad, because the national organism does not exist prior to the spectrality of modern knowledge and technomediation. It is constituted by and, indeed, is nothing but this spectrality. The fact that publicness can bifurcate into a good and a bad modality only attests to the fundamental undecidability of constitutive spectrality. Publicness can easily modulate from being the giver of life to being the agent of death because it is the state's and nation's genetic attachment to each other. This suturing can never be broken as long as the nation-people is the public sphere of civil society and modern state authority needs to find legitimation and secure its hegemony in and through the public sphere.

Organizations and the market are similarly tethered to the state. An organization does not simply reflect society's interests as Pramoedya suggests. Instead, native society exists within a space generated by the organization that claims to represent it before the law. Once again, it is the artifactual body or prosthesis, thought in analogy with the legal personality of the European, which induces the living people that it purportedly represents. Such prostheses allow one to think of society as an integrated body with rightful claims on the Indies earth, thereby opening up a space separate from that of the colonial state, even as the existence of such progressive organizations depends on legal recognition by the state. As they seek to become political parties, native organizations are always haunted by the refusal of legal recognition. Likewise, because market activity occurs under government supervision, the interests of native traders as a *kaum bebas* or *kaum merdeka* (free class) can also be channelled by the state. The most noteworthy examples of this are the scission that occurs within the SDI over resistance to the Sugar Syndicate because some traders do not think that they share the same interests with peasants, and the anti-Chinese feelings and hostility towards Chinese business instilled in some SDI members by the state, which is worried that Chinese progress will upset the balance of colonial society.

The spectral public sphere enables the congenital deformation of native political activity by the colonial state. Pramoedya suggests that this is the root of the historical enmity between the Chinese and the natives in Indonesia. Worried that Chinese and native organizations will oppose European interests and erode loyalty to the state, Pangemanann spreads anti-Chinese feeling and ignites popular anti-Chinese pogroms. This destroys the international public esteem of the SI, which the foreign press had regarded as an example of native awakening, and also diverts Chinese loyalty back to the colonial state, which plays protector to the Chinese community:

> So, Mr. Raden Mas Minke, you will see how your eldest son will be ripped apart and will lose the confidence of the foreign press. And nothing will be left that could be called 'the awakening of the Native bourgeoisie.' . . . I've already formulated the actions that will have to be taken to further this policy: discredit the leadership of the Syarikat as ringleaders of the rioters and the brains behind the pogroms. . . . International esteem for the organization will be made to crumble, and international opinion will have to forget it as an organization with any value for the future. (*RK*, 124; 117)

Since native organizations are the products of the Ethical Policy, the best way to deal with them is not to eliminate them but to turn them into the state's de facto agents. As long as they are not forced underground, their discussions of policy are public and subject to state monitoring: "These organizations will have an open character. At any point we can peer through their windows or their doors" (*RK*, 231; 218). "The right thing is for the State to stretch out its hand to guide, not to destroy. With the right kind of guidance, these organizations need no longer cause the State difficulties—on the contrary they can become its effective assistants" (*RK*, 220; 207). The state encourages the formation of ethnic nationalist (as opposed to Indies nationalist) organizations because they are divisive and will impede the spread of Indies nationalism. The legalization of native political activity after the First World War, which establishes a pseudo-parliament in response to the native demand for self-government, causes resistance fever to be replaced by political fever as social organizations opportunistically scramble to transform themselves into political parties in the hope of getting a parliament seat and the respect it brings (*RK*, 347–48; 327–28).

The *pergerakan*'s inevitable susceptibility to state manipulation via the spectral public sphere instantiates the double-edged nature of *techne* in its originary supplementation of organic life. Minke's tragic fate after his return from exile best illustrates the crushing prevalence of spectrality over the living human agent who would claim technomediation as his tool. The father of the national press and the native awakening's initiator who had earlier claimed modern knowledge and technomediation as the paramount instrument to be deployed to awaken the nation now faces a situation that he cannot even recognize. His creation and instrument has escaped his originating grasp. Thus estranged, it is deployed to deprive its creator of public phenomenality. Pangemanann successfully consigns Minke's return and his subsequent death to oblivion by spreading ignominious rumors about him and controlling the native press. Hence, he is prevented from bringing the Syarikat to life again:

> He still has no idea that paid mouthpieces of the State have been spreading rumors throughout the body of the Syarikat, to the effect that R. M. Minke's return to the Syarikat will bring a catastrophe down on the head of each of its members, for it is he that was responsible for the pogrom against the Chinese four years ago.
>
> And there's still more. The State's mouthpieces also whisper that he was involved in embezzlement at his Bank so that all its assets were seized. . . . No one knows better than I that the further these mouthpieces are from me, the dirtier, the darker and the more threatening their tone. . . . This man must be isolated from his sheep. (*RK*, 310; 293)

The founder of the native press is ironically made invisible to the public eye. He wanders around like an aimless ghost, revisiting the life the state has stolen from him.

> That his return to Java escaped the press's attention was because of my pretty tight control of it. He can't be permitted ever again to attract the public's attention. He must forever be separated from his lamp, the world of journalism. It's really ironical that a pioneer of the Native press can no longer find any place in the newspapers at the most critical juncture of his life. . . . From my desk, I can ensure that the press will do nothing that will permit Minke ever again to be noticed publically. (*RK*, 327; 309–10)

Deprived of any recourse to the life-giving light of public reason and, hence, of any possibility of reincarnating the national spirit by organizing again, Minke is as good as dead.

Life has once again been stultified and obstructed by the bad spectrality of colonialist instrumental reason. However, this fundamental ambivalence of originary *techne* cannot be captured by a Marxist discourse about the oppression of the creator that results from the estrangement and alienation of his or her creations. Paradoxically, we no more originate technomediation than it originates us qua free agents who act according to the imperatives of public reason. The state of publicness, the condition of public man or of being-public, necessarily involves an irreducible and constant paranoia that we are always being watched, always haunted by the spectral other who sees without being seen. It is always possible that we are under manipulative surveillance. As Pangemanann himself comments, if natives manage to achieve self-rule, they could easily take over his apparatus and place him within his glass house: "My *House of Glass will* become empty, and it is possible that even I myself will be put inside it. If up to now I have been the watcher, if they have their own government, who knows? Perhaps everyone will be able to watch me inside it" (*RK,* 337; 318). The interception of life is merely the historical unfolding of an irreducible susceptibility inscribed within the national public sphere's openness to light. It is the constitutive possibility of death in the very promise of life.

COUNTERFEIT LIFE

We have been considering Pramoedya's thematization of the infelicities of Indonesian political history. That the national organism's actualization has been obstructed by death until now does not necessarily mean that Pramoedya's dialectical resolution of the contradiction between life and death is untenable. What we have established is merely that the Indonesian nation has not been successful in incarnating itself as the vehicle of freedom in history. This incarnation remains as a promise projected into a future present that we cannot yet foresee. The concession that the nationalist project has been and remains blocked does not mean that it will always be frustrated. Consequently, the idea of freedom as the self-actualization of reason, and the related philosophemes of culture and life as analogues of the incarnational process remain intact. Indeed, one of the quartet's key ideas is that the national spirit itself has migrated into literary culture because this form of *Bildung* is the best hope of keeping it alive in the current neocolonial conjuncture. The actualization of freedom would not be primarily posed from within the political and economic spheres. It would be relocated in the sphere of culture, thereby affirming culture as the original ontological paradigm of the political.

An onerous burden thus falls on the quartet's interpellative power, its narrative structure's ability to catalyze and intensify the national *Bildung* of its Indonesian readers. Hence, if the narrative structure cannot fulfill this promise of keeping alive the national spirit, of preserving and transmitting it intact, then culture and life, the two key philosophemes of the modern understanding of freedom, would be undermined in their very operation. Such a failure of national *Bildung* would mark not only the contamination of life by death, but the eruption of death in the *promise* of life. The sheer possibility of transcending finitude would be undermined. This is exactly what the quartet performs.

I suggested above that Pangemanann is the active agent who preserves the national spirit. He is the condition of possibility for the survival and transmission of Minke's manuscripts, which make up the quartet's first three volumes. Indeed, from a narratological point of view, we necessarily read them over his shoulder, via the filter of his interpretation, because he is the only person who has access to them. Hence, the national spirit's complete transmission depends entirely on our ability to trust Pangemanann. In other words, Pramoedya can only promise the future return and reincarnation of these ghosts of early Indies nationalism if they are able to impinge on Pangemanann's official consciousness. For us to be able to see and recognize these ghosts as something to be incarnated in the future present, Pangemanann must first be able to see them despite his own degeneration. He must be able to see them so that we can see them through his narrative. Thus, for the quartet's narrative project to work, he must be an educated person with a moral conscience and an innate sense of decency who is able to judge himself throughout his unconscionable campaign against the *pergerakan*. We must be able to trust Pangemanann's own assessment of the *pergerakan* and his condemnation of himself and the colonial government. His self-judgment indicates that the negation of life (official consciousness) contains within itself what it negates and, therefore, promises the negation of itself and the national spirit's reincarnation. Pangemanann's internal struggle, which is rendered in a confessional tone, is compelling reading precisely because we see him fall despite his clear self-knowledge of his own corruption by the colonial state.

But exactly at this point, an insurmountable narratological problem presents itself. For we really have no way of assessing the veracity of what Pangemanann relates to us, and this includes even the manuscripts he passes on. No one else has access to Minke's manuscripts except Pangemanann. He has appropriated them for his personal possessions by reporting to his superiors that they are valueless. As the sole condition of possibility of their phenomenality within public light, he has complete power over them. He can always burn them and smother the life they represent:

> There's only one thing that can be charged against me: my superficial analysis of Raden Mas Minke's manuscripts, which I assessed as "valueless." I kept these manuscripts at home as my personal possessions. . . . I'll continue to maintain [to my superiors] that these manuscripts have more of a private than a public character. And I'll say I've burned them at the office, in the little metal container in my room. (*RK*, 217–18; 204–5)

As the condition of possibility of these manuscripts qua texts to be read by others, Pangemanann is also their first and most conscientious reader. He claims to approach them with a literary critic's careful rigor even though he confesses that his French secondary school literature classes have not prepared him to analyze a text of such historical complexity: "What I don't know is whether a text about these texts will turn out interesting. But not to write would be an error, since perhaps I am the only one in the world who has had the complete freedom to control/have possession of [*menguasai*] these texts which, it seems, were never intended for publication" (*RK*, 177–78; 167). The use of the politically charged verb "*menguasai*" (to control or to possess power over something), is indeed appropriate since we are speaking of control over manuscripts containing the possibility of life's triumph over death, that is, ideas that can challenge colonial domination. Such control over the transmissibility of manuscripts that no one will read or that will only be read through his commentary (since these manuscripts will see the light of day only because of his analysis) means that the originals are usurped by and mediated through Pangemanann's writing. It also implies the possibility of falsification and fabulation. He could always have forged those manuscripts to further his ambitious desire to be a colonial expert on native affairs.

Pramoedya forecloses the possibility of falsification by suggesting that as an educated native and product of the French enlightenment, Pangemanann possesses a will to truth and a moral conscience that finally humbles him and facilitates the manuscripts' secure transmission to Sanikem. Pramoedya also emphasizes that although Pangemanann opposes the *pergerakan* in his official capacity, he is a meticulous archival historian of the awakening. He edits and reproduces in entirety Marco's autobiographical account of his origins, with corrections of his colloquial Malay, because he feels it is an important record of historical change (*RK*, 183; 172). Furthermore, in a unique occasion, the ghost of Minke actually inspirits Pangemanann with national feeling and speaks through him. When Pangemanann is approached by his nephew who wants to form a Menadonese organization, he gives him good advice about the importance of language to nationalist movements, cautioning him against ethnolinguistic exclusivism by pointing out that a language opens or closes up an organization to connections with other organizations, although this advice is patently at odds with his official interests (*RK*, 166–67; 156–57).

Yet the entire quartet ultimately depends on the very slender trust readers ought to have in Pangemanann's authority as a narrator. There is enough evidence from his prealcoholic phase for us to question this because it suggests that he has a disturbed psyche. In the first place, he admits that he has a nervous affliction (*gangguan syarat*). He sees ghosts. Secondly, even if these ghosts are the return of repressed life itself, the national spirit that awaits reincarnation in the person of Minke and his manuscripts, there is an uncanny incident that indicates that these manuscripts and indeed, even Minke himself, may be Pangemanann's distorted inventions. In the first chapter of *Rumah Kaca*, Pangemanann relates an incident, also recounted in *Jejak Langkah*, where he hands over the manuscript of *Si Pitung* to Minke to consider for publication. Only here, Pangemanann admits that he did not in fact write the manuscript but has passed it off for his own. It was written by a distant relative of the same name. But he has read and revised it so often, augmenting it with information from the police archives that he feels it is his own:

The manuscript had been with me quite a while, and I had fixed it up in various places in line with the archives at police headquarters. But still its author did not emerge. And I read and studied the text so often that I started to feel as if it were my own. The writer was also a Pangemanan, but only with one n, and merely a Protestant. (*RK,* 17; 16)

This disquieting plagiarism almost exactly describes the relation he has to "Minke's" manuscripts, the first three books he tells us are written by Minke. He pores over them with an obsessiveness that borders on insanity because they fill the empty hole in his life, and he begins to write *Rumah Kaca* in emulation of Minke's manuscripts (*RK,* 173; 163). Hence, if at a thematic level Minke's manuscripts supplement the lack in Pangemanann's official consciousness, then at the formal and narratological level, it is Pangemanann who provides the necessary supplement to the manuscripts. He makes them into a complete whole by adding his own notes. He brings them into the light of day by sending the completed totality to Sanikem. The dividing line between Minke's narrative voice and Pangemanann's narrative voice and the opposed consciousnesses they express begins to waver. Even if Minke is a fictive version of Tirto Ardhi Soerjo, we have no way of ascertaining from reading the quartet *as narrative* whether the construction of the historical type of the modern Pitung and the portrayal of the national awakening possess the ontological truth countersigned by the authorial signature, "Pramoedya Ananta Toer." This is because the possibility of falsification is built into the very narrative structure of the quartet: as a whole, it is framed by *Pangemanann's* narrative, the authoritativeness of which is questionable.

Because Pramoedya sees the quartet as the incarnation of the living national spirit in a cultural object that will enable the *Bildung* or epigenesis of the nation, the dividing line between the two narrative voices is also the dividing line between life and death. However, the wavering that takes place here is emphatically not the dialectical resolution of the contradiction between life and death that Pramoedya envisions. I noted earlier that a dialectical resolution requires the return of life, which would negate and sublate death as its other. The limit to life would be removed by life itself because life would know this limit as its own limit. In contradistinction, the wavering of the border between life and death that we witness in the quartet's narrative structure is irresolute. It is the fundamental undecidability between life and death that occurs because life (the national spirit captured in Minke's manuscripts) expresses itself through an other, death (the state represented by Pangemanann's official consciousness) and runs the permanent risk of losing itself in this other, which is no longer *its* other, an other *for* it. For death is no longer a determinate limit, the limit *of* and *for* life, the limit that properly belongs to life that life can transcend. Instead of being annulled by life, the limit to life has become a limitless limit, a limit that needs to be interminably experienced and negotiated. In other words, the promise of life beyond death through the nation—whose objective correlative is these manuscripts of the initiator of Indies nationalism—must pass interminably through the constitutive possibility of death.

The Buru Quartet illustrates that without this precarious movement, the transformation of historical reality into a more truthful "literary reality" by engaged literary *Bildung* and the dialectical victory of life over death would not be possible. This interminable passage is what I have been calling the spectrality of the nation. The nation is spectral because it is nothing but this interminable crossing of the border between life and death. This is not merely a metaphysical paradox or aporia of literary figuration. The politicosociological topography that opposes the national public sphere of civil society to the state is a political organicism. Spectrality, which is the mutual haunting or constitutive interpenetration of nation and state—the opening-up of the living nation to the death-dealing state and vice versa—complicates this topography. It is also the irreducible possibility of the becoming-ideological of nationalism, where the nation becomes a mystification the state deploys in the service of global capital. This should not be understood as a rejection of the decolonizing nation, the uncompleted nationalist project as a vehicle of freedom, or the necessity of the ideal of freedom itself. What it does imply is that the idea of freedom needs to be fundamentally reinvented because the transcendence of finitude or the overcoming of death through collective rational work is enabled by something other to reason and life.

Decolonizing nationalism is arguably the most salient historical performance of this revision of the philosopheme of freedom. On the one hand, it indicates the persistence of the nation-form as the most viable political vehicle for freedom in modernity. On the other hand, insofar as the transcendence of neocolonial globalization is not in sight, the nation-people finds itself in a permanent conflictual embrace with the postcolonial state. It wants to remake the state in its own image. But in the current conjuncture, the state always runs the risk of being neocolonial, an instrument of global capital that infects the nation with death. The postcolonial state within capitalist globalization is a limitless limit to life, a kind of death that has to be interminably experienced and negotiated because it cannot be negated and sublated by the nation.

One manifestation of the aporetic embrace between nation and state in neocolonial globalization is the peculiar fact that in some cases, the national spirit, while it awaits incarnation as the popular nation-state, can only survive outside the neocolonial territorial state it hopes to inspirit and transform. This is another modality of the nation's spectrality, another negotiation with death: life (the national spirit) can only preserve itself, gather itself unto itself as a living presence by being outside its proper self, by being in the centers of capital. But it is only from this outside that it can continue to haunt the neocolonial state. Nothing illustrates this breaching of the quartet's dialectical economy as suggestively as the role of Nyai Ontosoroh at the end of the narrative. As we know, Sanikem, a representative of the modern ideal of freedom sublated in the body of a modern native person, returns to the Indies to search for Minke and to judge his destroyer. She personifies the spirit of the emerging modern Indonesia. As the recipient of Minke's manuscripts, she is also the trustee of its future. Yet the narrative logic implies that, paradoxically, the Indonesian nation's future can only be secured by being dispatched beyond the colonial world: to France, the nation where modern freedom was first born. But—another paradox— since the spirit of freedom was also betrayed by French colonialism, it can only live on in the future of the Indonesian nation whose agent is—yet another paradox—the modern native expatriate.

The nation lives on abroad, so to speak, awaiting to be returned to itself, that is to say, to be repatriated. But meanwhile, it lives on uncannily (*unheimlich*), from outside its own home. Until recently, Pramoedya's own writings had the same *unheimlich* existence. They were banned in Indonesia and were only accessible to the intended subjects of Indonesian national *Bildung* through Malaysian imprints, English translations, and reviews and critical studies by commentators outside Indonesia.[6]

---

6. The first extensive book-length study of Pramoedya is A. Teeuw's *Pramoedya Ananta Toer: De verbeelding van Indonesië* (De Geus, Netherlands: Breda, 1993). Most of Pramoedya's works are published in Bahasa Malaysia (which is slightly different from Bahasa Indonesia) by the Kuala Lumpur–based publishing house, Wira Karya, run by Jomo Sundaram, a Harvard-trained professor of political science at the University of Malaya. The quartet's English translation was first published by Penguin Australia. The Cornell-based specialist journal, *Indonesia,* is the most important source for English translations of Pramoedya's shorter fiction and nonfictional prose and is also a continuing forum for critical writing on Pramoedya.

THE NEOCOLONIAL STATE AND OTHER PROSTHESES OF THE POSTCOLONIAL NATIONAL BODY: NGŪGĪ WA THIONG'O'S PROJECT OF REVOLUTIONARY NATIONAL CULTURE

The Kenyan writer Ngūgī wa Thiong'o also has an *unheimlich* relationship to the postcolonial state. In October 1986, he published a novel in Gikuyu, entitled *Matigari ma Njirũũngi,* about a patriot from the period of the independence struggle who has returned from the forests and wanders around the country asking politically unsettling questions because the postcolonial condition does not seem very different from the colonial era. The novel literally conjured up a specter that haunted Daniel Arap Moi's one-party state. "For a short period in 1987," Ngūgī observes,

Matigari, the fictional hero of the novel, was himself resurrected as a subversive political character. . . . By January 1987, intelligence reports had it that peasants in Central Kenya were whispering and talking about a man called Matigari who was roaming the whole country making demands about truth and justice. There were orders for his immediate arrest, but the police discovered that Matigari was only a fictional character in a book of the same name. In February 1987, the police raided all the bookshops and seized every copy of the novel. Matigari, the fictional hero, and the novel, his only habitation, have been effectively banned in Kenya.[1]

---

1. Ngūgī wa Thiong'o, *Matigari,* trans. Wangui wa Goro (Portsmouth, N.H.: Heinemann, 1990), viii. Hereafter cited as *M.* See also Ngūgī wa Thiong'o, "Matigari, and the Dreams of One East

There are some broad similarities between Indonesian and Kenyan political history. In both, radical popular nationalist resistance movements (the *pergerakan* and the Mau Mau) culminated in an initial postindependence period of charismatic socialist leadership (Sukarno and Jomo Kenyatta) that degenerated into corrupt and repressive one-party neocolonial regimes (Suharto and Moi).[2] Pramoedya and Ngũgĩ have both been subject to state persecution. But more importantly, their projects share a claim to a certain spiritual exemplarity. The spirit of Bandung tacitly informs the Buru Quartet. Ngũgĩ explicitly foregrounds *Matigari*'s exemplarity in his prefatory address: "This story is imaginary. // The actions are imaginary. // The characters are imaginary. // The country is imaginary—it has no name even. // Reader/listener: may the story take place in the country of your choice" (*M,* ix). The novel's fable-like quality suggests that the Kenyan postcolonial experience, from which many of *Matigari*'s key events are clearly derived, is exemplary of the general crisis of contemporary Africa.

The key characteristics of the "African tragedy" have been amply documented in social-science literature. It begins with the failure of formal decolonization to constitute a decisive break with colonial administrative institutions and economic infrastructures despite the desire to Africanize each country's economy and political life.[3] Within the framework of the uneven development of global capital, the initial momentum of popular-

Africa," in *Moving the Centre: The Struggle for Cultural Freedoms* (Portsmouth, N.H.: Heinemann, 1993), pp. 159–76. Hereafter cited as *MC.* On the Kenyan state's attitude towards Ngũgĩ and his writings, see Henry Chakava, "Publishing Ngũgĩ: The Challenge, the Risk, and the Reward," in *Critical Essays on Ngũgĩ wa Thiong'o,* ed. Peter Nazareth (New York: Twayne, 2000), pp. 321–33; and Carol Sicherman, "Ngũgĩ wa Thiong'o as Mythologizer and Mythologized," in *From Commonwealth to Postcolonial,* ed. Anna Rutherford (Sydney: Dangaroo Press, 1992), pp. 259–75.

2. On Mau Mau's relationship to Kenyan nationalism, see Carl G. Rosberg Jr. and John Nottingham, *The Myth of "Mau Mau": Nationalism in Kenya* (New York: Praeger, 1966); and Bruce Berman and John Lonsdale, *Unhappy Valley: Conflict in Kenya and Africa* (London: James Currey, 1992). On the differences and continuity between the Kenyatta and Moi regimes, see Jennifer A. Widner, *The Rise of a Party-State in Kenya: From Harambee! to Nyayo!* (Berkeley: University of California Press, 1992); B. A. Ogot and W. R. Ochieng', eds., *Decolonization and Independence in Kenya, 1940–93* (London: James Currey, 1995); and Angelique Haugerud, *The Culture of Politics in Modern Kenya* (Cambridge: Cambridge University Press, 1995).

3. See Colin Leys, *Underdevelopment in Kenya: The Political Economy of Neo-Colonialism* (London: Heinemann, 1975); "Confronting the African Tragedy," *New Left Review* 1, no. 204 (March–April 1994): 33–47; and Giovanni Arrighi, "The African Crisis: World Systemic and Regional Aspects," *New Left Review* 2, n.s., no. 15 (May–June 2002): 7–36.

nationalist social, political, and economic reform has been actively retarded and suppressed by the establishment of neocolonial states run by a comprador indigenous elite in collaboration with multinational capital. The economies of these countries, which are crippled by the heinous cronyism or theft capitalism of the native elite, are also repeatedly subject to internationally imposed structural-adjustment policies. Their political lives are plagued by ethnic and tribal conflict and varieties of undemocratic authoritarian rule. The failure of constitutionalism and the poor human rights records of many African states routinely descried by the Northern media are only the most extreme symptoms of a profounder crisis that cannot be solved by formal legality and the protection of abstract human rights on a case-by-case basis.

The exemplarity of Ngũgĩ's project is not limited to the pessimistic reflection of this degraded reality. In his 1996 Clarendon Lectures, he notes that the Kenyan writer is exemplary in two active senses. His censorship and repression indicate the oppositional relation between radical literary culture and the postcolonial African state. But more importantly, they also emblematize the universal (Platonic) theme of art's relation to the state.

> What has happened to Kenyan writers is symptomatic of the general condition in contemporary Africa. . . . [T]he writer in contemporary Africa had been seen as the enemy of the post-colonial state. His art is often regarded as an act of war against statesmen, a justification of the state's declaration of war against art and artists. . . . The situation in Africa raises in turn the wider issues of the relationship between the art of the state and the state of art, between rulers and writers. . . . There is a war going on between art and the state. Writing is more dangerous than killing, says the state.[4]

In Ngũgĩ's view, art has this oppositional power because it is "creativity and freedom" itself. Art is "the embodiment of dreams for a truly human world . . . where the state is so subject to the social control of the majority as to wither as a coercive power outside and above society. The goal of human society is the reign of art on earth." "It behoves art to join all other

---

4. Ngũgĩ wa Thiong'o, *Penpoints, Gunpoints, and Dreams: Towards a Critical Theory of the Arts and the State in Africa* (Oxford: Clarendon, 1998), pp. 1–3. Hereafter cited as *Penpoints*.

social forces in society to extend the performance space for human creativity and self-organization and so strengthen civil society. . . . [D]reaming to change the conditions that confine human life is the mission of art."[5]

The fundamental premises of Ngũgĩ's argument are as follows: Global capital reproduces neocolonial relations within postcolonial space by attaching various prostheses onto the popular-national organism. A prosthesis is a secondary, artificial object that is added onto a more substantial original body.[6] Although it is prima facie a foreign body that intrudes upon the proper human body's organic wholeness, a prosthesis can supplement a deficiency and provide essential support if it is properly attached and utilized. For instance, as long as they receive life from and are animated by the organic body, artificial teeth and limbs augment and restore the body's original integrity. The organic body remains self-supporting precisely because the prosthesis has been organicized and made an integral part of its proper self. In contradistinction, a bad prosthesis acts as a conduit that makes the body vulnerable to hostile foreign elements. Instead of becoming an organic member of the body, it opens the body to external forces and even makes it dependent on them. Thus, an export-oriented comprador economy and neocolonial cultural images are malignant prostheses that alienate the nation from its proper self so that it can be remade in the image of dead capital. The neocolonial state is the deadly prosthesis par excellence.

Ngũgĩ's project fuses the incarnational power of radical nationalist *Bildung* to the Marxist idea of living labor's dissolution of the coercive bourgeois state through reabsorption and reorganicization. He argues that neocolonial prostheses can be dissolved by a more salutary prosthesis that is integral to the national organism's epigenesis: a revolutionary people's culture. Thus, Ngũgĩ's work is in many ways a more apposite test case than the Buru Quartet for evaluating whether culture possesses the self-recursive organismic causality that makes it the bearer of freedom. First, the continuity between his idea of revolutionary national culture and German idealism's organismic ontology is more direct. Ngũgĩ explicitly acknowledges this by

---

5. Ibid., pp. 131–32. The preceding quote comes from p. 6.
6. As a medical term it refers to "that part of surgery which consists in supplying deficiencies, as by artificial limbs, teeth, etc." (*OED*). *Webster's* stresses that the original body is "human" and the addition is "an artificial part."

marking his filiation to Marx and Fanon. Second, the importance of missionary activity in Kenyan colonialism makes the link between cultural activity and Christian incarnation patently visible. This link can also be found in Pramoedya's Marxism, but it is partially obscured by Islam's dominance in Indonesia. But most importantly, Ngũgĩ directly addresses the impact of a neocolonial global cultural economy on revolutionary national culture's power of self-recursive mediation. Most of his fiction has a contemporary setting where the rise of a global "culture industry" (q.v. the Frankfurt School) through the rapid development of global communications and technomediation threatens to erode and deform national culture.

It is important to emphasize that culture's power of self-recursive mediation is central to social-science debates about contemporary Kenyan politics. According to the Marxist view, the neocolonial state is a mechanism of the ruling class, "an organization for the protection of the possessing class against the non-possessing classes."[7] In liberal accounts of Moi's one-party state, the party is no longer a forum for articulating the interests of different economic groups or for mobilizing support for the regime through interest aggregation. It has degenerated into "an adjunct of the executive or office of the president" that "has assumed the role of transmitter and enforcer of policy decisions, with executive police powers."[8] In both cases, the oppressive party or state is essentially an alienating prosthesis that is inappropriate to the people and fails to respond to their needs. Conversely, accountability to the people, the essence of multiparty democracy, is the reappropriation of a defective prosthesis by the national organism.[9] The problem with many postcolonial African regimes, Ngũgĩ notes, is that "they never see their inspiration as coming from the people, because they know very well that their being in power is not dependent on Somalian people, on Kenyan people, on Zairian people. . . . They don't feel accountable to the people."[10] Culture once again supplies the ontological

---

7. W. R. Ochieng' and E. S. Atieno-Odhiambo, "Prologue: On Decolonization," in *Decolonization and Independence in Kenya,* ed. B. A. Ogot and W. R. Ochieng', p. xiv.

8. Jennifer A. Widner, *The Rise of a Party-State in Kenya,* pp. 5–6.

9. See William Acworth, "Interview with Ngũgĩ wa Thiong'o," *Ufahamu: Journal of the African Activist Association* 18, no. 2 (spring 1990), pp. 42–43.

10. Ngũgĩ, "Moving the Center: An Interview by Charles Cantalupo," *Paintbrush* 20, nos. 39–40 (spring/autumn 1993): 215. Hereafter cited as "Cantalupo Interview."

paradigm of the political. Yet, as a close reading of *Matigari* and *Devil on the Cross* (1982) shows, Ngũgĩ's project of radical national *Bildung*, the first step towards accountability to the people, encounters problems that put the people's self-recursivity and self-propriety or -appropriation into question.

NATIONAL CULTURE AS SELF-RECURSIVE MEDIATION

In Ngũgĩ's view, national culture has a paramount importance in the overcoming of the Kenyan people's economic and political alienation because it is crucial to securing neocolonial political and economic control in the contemporary U.S.-dominated world order. This understanding of neocolonialism is informed by Lenin's argument that imperialism, or the domination of finance capital, has superseded the territorial imperialism characteristic of the colonial era.[11] Echoing Fanon and Cabral, Ngũgĩ likens the nation's evolution to an organic body's development according to its inner biological processes and its interactions with external surroundings.

The air and food the body takes from its contact with the external environment are digested and become an integral part of the body. This is normal and healthy. But it may happen that the impact of the external factor is too strong; it is not taken in organically, in which case the body may even die. Floods, earthquakes, the wind, too much or too little air, poisoned or healthy food . . . are all external factors or activities that can affect the body adversely. The same with society. All societies develop under conditions of external contact with other societies at the economic, political and cultural levels. Under 'normal' circumstances, a given society is able to absorb whatever it borrows from other contacts, digest it and make it its own. But under conditions of external domination, . . . the changes are not as a result of the working out of the conflicts and tensions within, and do not arise out of the organic development of that society but are forced upon it externally. This may result in the society becoming deformed, changing course altogether or even dying out. Conditions of external domination and control, as much as those of internal

---

11. Vladimir Lenin, *Imperialism: The Highest Stage of Capitalism*, in *Essential Works of Lenin*, ed. and trans. Henry M. Christman (New York: Dover, 1987). For Ngũgĩ's reliance on Lenin, see *MC*, p. 6. For his description of the historical genesis of U.S. neocolonialism, see *MC*, pp. 48–49.

domination and oppression, do not create the necessary climate for the cultural health of any society. . . . Hence, [I insist] . . . on the suffocating and ultimately destructive character of both colonial and neo-colonial structures.

(*MC*, xv–vi)

This distinction between "good" organic development typified by the inner-directed ingestion of external elements, and unhealthy externally dictated modes of force-feeding necessarily pertains to all finite beings. All finite beings are constitutively vulnerable to the outside because living is a perpetual struggle with externality. Echoing Marx's metaphor of the human metabolism with nature, Ngũgĩ points out that

our external life is an integral part of ourselves. None of us can live without breathing in air. . . . Yet at the same time, air is out there, external to us. It's give and take or die. By emphasizing the ideal of organic development, I mean that whatever comes from outside . . . must not deform internal development. Taking in air supports our internal organs, yet if there is too much, like a blast of air, it can hurt one as much as a lack of air. This is a kind of healthy struggle and a system which must not be deformed by either external circumstances or by such internal imbalance so as to completely deform the possibilities of development.[12]

The same logic applies to the use of prostheses. The colonial state exposed the national body to the capitalist world system and linked it up to an entire series of prosthetic processes such as commodification, financial circulation, and so on. With the transformation of the nation's useful labor into abstract labor-power, the people's products become alienated and no longer augment its own life. Instead, they reflect and further impoverish the nation's already depleted and fragmented body, which is now reduced to spare parts for the global capitalist machine. Decolonization was supposed to restore the nation's integrity by removing the colonial state. But in fact, a similar foreign prosthesis has been reattached onto the nation and continues to harness and bend it towards multinational capital's inhuman interests. This is the neocolonial state with its oppressive military apparatus

---

12. "Cantalupo Interview," p. 223.

and foreign gadgets. The indigenous elite, "pampered with military gadgets of all kinds with which to rein in a restive population, has often turned an entire country into a vast prison-house. Africa is a continent alienated from itself by years of alien conquests and internal despots. . . . *The Man Died; Things Fall Apart; No Longer at Ease; The Beautyful Ones Are Not Yet Born; From a Crooked Rib;* the titles of many novels in Africa speak clearly of this alienation, or this dismemberment of parts that could have been made whole" (Ngũgĩ, *MC*, 107–8).

For Ngũgĩ, the national organism's liberation from neocolonial domination is a matter of rationally regulating its opening-out onto the external other, which fundamentally affects its self-creative or productive capacity. Hence, the unfinished nationalist project must remove the neocolonial state. Culture, a *psychical* prosthesis, has a paramount but fundamentally ambivalent role in this ongoing project. Following Marx's definition of creative labor as the actualization of ideal forms and the philosopheme of *Bildung* as autonomous, rational purposive work, Ngũgĩ characterizes the national body's productive capacity as its ability to form externality in its own image so that it can develop itself. This autonomized image is a good prosthesis because it can be fully integrated, absorbed until it becomes part of the national body. *Popular national culture* is the paradigmatic example of a good prosthesis for two mutually reinforcing reasons: It originates from the people. But more importantly, through collective psychical incorporation, it also plays a crucial role in the nation's continuing self-formation. In Ngũgĩ's words, "culture gives [a] . . . society its self-image as it sorts itself out in the economic and political fields" (*MC*, xv). As long as these cultural images are self-prescribed and their ingestion inner-directed or self-determined, as long as culture is genuinely national, it will have the self-recursive recognitive structure of Hegelian spirit. Through this movement of reflection from the outside back to itself, the nation gets to know and position itself within the world so that it can better appropriate it for the purposes of its development. A people's culture is thus the formative attachment and ingestion of a self-prescribed rational image, the interiorization of an other that the national organism posits for itself. It is an ideational form that is externalized and given objective shape so that it can be reappropriated by the national body in the process of its epigenesis. Like a pilot in a machine, genuine culture directs the national body's interaction with economic and political forces so that it can finally return home to itself from externality. The nation recognizes itself in the world, which thereby becomes a world *for* it.

This self-recursivity does not make African national culture a static natural entity. Like Cabral and Fanon, Ngũgĩ emphatically rejects a simple return to traditional structures. Instead, national culture is the territorialization of freedom's auto-causality.

> Culture, in its broadest sense, is a way of life fashioned by a people in their col-
> lective endeavour to live and come to terms with their total environment. . . .
> In the course of their creative struggle and progress through history, there
> evolves a body of material and spiritual values which endow that society with
> a unique ethos. . . . No living culture is ever static.
> It is surely not possible to lift traditional structures and cultures intact into
> modern Africa. A meaningful culture is the one born out of the present hopes
> and especially the hopes of an impoverished peasantry, and that of the growing
> body of urban workers.[13]

Hence, culture is the basis of a people's resistance to domination and of their political and economic freedom. Indeed, Ngũgĩ suggests that a people are born anew in the very act of resistance: "It is when people are involved in the active work of destroying an inhibitive social structure and building a new one that they begin to see themselves. They are born again. . . . If we are to achieve true national cultures we must recognize our situation. That means we must thoroughly examine our social and economic structures and see if they are geared to meeting the needs and releasing the energy of the masses. We must in fact wholly Africanize and socialize our political and economic life."[14] Indeed, genuine (popular national) culture is in a relation of symbiotic feedback with revolutionary struggle to the point that they are synonymous. Because it adequately expresses the masses' needs, such culture is a source of sustenance for organized anti-imperialist politics, which necessarily involves "the patriotic defence of the peasant/worker

---

13. Ngũgĩ, "Towards a National Culture," in *Homecoming: Essays on African and Caribbean Literature, Culture, and Politics* (London: Heinemann, 1972), pp. 4, 12. Hereafter cited as *H*.
14. Ibid., pp. 11–12.

roots of national cultures."[15] By the same token, true national culture is itself "a people's fighting culture," "the fighting culture of the African peasantry and working class . . . [that is] a product and reflection of real life struggles going on in Africa today" (*MC*, 45).

Ngũgĩ's account of national culture is thus another example of the reversion of politics to culture. It connects the Marxist topos of appropriation in the political and economic spheres to the recognitive structure of national *Bildung*. The project of appropriation is therefore also a cultural repatriation or "homecoming," the task of building "a true communal home for all Africans" (*H,* xix). Whether other African writers agree with Ngũgĩ's socialist inclinations, his definition of national culture as a mediating prosthesis that enables a people's self-return through self-incarnation and recognition in the external world and his understanding of education as giving "people the confidence that they can in fact create a new heaven on earth" are central to most theories of African literature.[16] Chinua Achebe similarly points to the prosthetic function of culture in his characterization of art as "man's constant effort to create for himself a different order of reality from that which is given to him; an aspiration to provide himself with a second handle on existence through his imagination." The cultural ideals of African socialism, negritude, and so on, he suggests, are "all props we have fashioned at different times to help us get on our feet again."[17]

But like any prosthesis, culture can also be malignant. As a product of capitalism, it is an "anti-human culture," "a culture that is only an expression of sectional warring interests" (*H,* 12). Ngũgĩ argues that the global circulation of neocolonial cultural images generated by intellectual centers in the North and the Northern-controlled international media maintains alienation and undermines nationalist *Bildung* through ideological brainwashing. Whereas economic globalization reshapes the material world in the image of the North, cultural globalization molds the spiritual world to perpetuate Northern hegemony:

15. Ngũgĩ, *Decolonising the Mind: The Politics of Language in African Literature* (Portsmouth, N.H.: Heinemann, 1986), p. 2. Hereafter cited as *DM*. This symbiosis is also seen in the connection Ngũgĩ draws between Africanization and the socialization of political and economic life, African communalism and socialism.

16. Ngũgĩ, *Barrel of a Pen: Resistance to Repression in Neo-Colonial Kenya* (Trenton, N.J.: Africa World Press, 1983), p. 90.

17. *Hopes and Impediments: Selected Essays* (New York: Doubleday, 1989), p. 45. The previous quote is from p. 139.

The *entire economic and political control is effectively facilitated by the cultural factor.* . . . The maintenance, management, manipulation, and mobilisation of the entire system of education, language and language use, literature, religion, the media have always ensured for the oppressor nation power over the transmission of a certain ideology, set of values, outlook, attitudes, feelings, etc. and hence *power over the whole area of consciousness.* This in turn leads to the control of the individual and collective self-image of the dominated nation and classes as well as their image of the dominating nations and classes. By thus controlling the cultural and psychological domain, the oppressor nation and classes try to ensure the situation of a slave who takes it that to be a slave is the normal human condition. (*MC*, 51; emphasis added)

Neocolonial cultural control retards the formation of a collective subject of national resistance by blunting the perceptions of mass consciousness about modern imperialism and planting doubts in the minds of the African people about the moral rightness of their struggle.

In the cultural sphere, therefore, unhealthy ingestion is an unhealthy form of *identification.* It is not only the introduction of a foreign toxin into the blood stream, but the mistaking of an alien body for the nation's real body. Worse than ingesting poison, it is the internalization of forces within one's own body that will produce the means and desire to kill oneself. Cultural alienation is more dangerous than economic or political alienation because it makes the enemy indistinguishable from the self. It makes death the vocation of a neocolonized people. Neocolonial culture

makes [the oppressed] want to identify with that which is furthest removed from themselves. . . . It makes them identify with that which is decadent and reactionary, all those forces which would stop their own springs of life. . . . The intended results are despair, despondency and a collective deathwish.

(*DM*, 3)

Echoing Fanon and Cabral, Ngũgĩ argues that the national organism can only restore its original integrity and dynamism by transcending the finitude of these oppressive conditions. The people need to recognize that neocolonial capital and its prostheses are their alienated products, which they can reappropriate. But because neocolonial cultural control obstructs this recognition, cultural reappropriation or repatriation—the reversal of cultural alienation—is the first step to "a liberated people's consciousness and creativity" (*MC*, 57). At this point, however, Ngũgĩ's argument is riven by a fundamental ambivalence. On the one hand, since the masses are mystified by the neocolonial culture industry, cultural reappropriation will only take place if the masses are educated by the Third World writer or intellectual worker to see the truth of neocolonialism. The latter's task is to create pictures that harmonize with revolutionary forces and to be a conduit that introduces these sanguine, patriotic images into popular consciousness. When they identify with these cultural images, the oppressed masses will be instilled with hope, clarity, and strength. They will be organized and transformed into a collective subject of resistance capable of realizing their vision of a new future. In other words, the postcolonial intellectual should be the catalyst and facilitator of nationalist *Bildung*, which will lead to the sublation of the neocolonial system.

But the intellectual's socioeconomic position makes him or her a fundamentally ambivalent mediation that can either facilitate the national body's self-return or exacerbate cultural alienation and lead to deeper self-loss. First, the postcolonial intellectual can also willingly serve neocolonial interests. He or she can be "trained and cultured into drawing pictures of the world in harmony with the needs of US imperialism" (*MC*, 53). Second, even benevolent intellectuals who act on behalf of the masses—and here, Ngũgĩ includes first generation postcolonial African leaders like Kenyatta and Nkrumah—inevitably fail to achieve a true homecoming if their thought and action remain imprisoned within European languages. The nation sends these individuals abroad to learn, but they "will never bring home their share of knowledge" (*Penpoints*, 89). These intellectuals literally personify nonrecursive *techne*, instruments that refuse to be part of the organic whole:

> For Africa the thinking part of the population, the one with the pool of skills and know-how in economics, agriculture, science, engineering, is divorced from the agency of social change: the working majority. At the level of economics, science, and technology, Africa will keep on talking about transfer of technology from the West. . . . Yet the African intellectual élite, with their *episteme* and *techne*, refuse to transfer even the little they have already acquired into the language of the majority below. . . . There can be no real economic growth and development where a whole people are denied access to

the latest developments in science, technology, health, medicine, business, finance, and other skills of survival because all these are stored in foreign languages. (*Penpoints,* 90)

Ngũgĩ's well-known decision to write criticism and literature in Gikuyu, which was first elaborated in *Decolonising the Mind,* is not a dogmatic nativism but a component of this larger project of national *Bildung.*[18] Its basic premise is that a language organic to a people is the necessary precondition of a nation's spiritual and material integrity, its ability to recognize itself in and return to itself from the world. This argument inventively combines the Fichtean idea that language is the sensuous expression of a people's spiritual values with Marx's idea of "the language of actual life [*wirklichen Lebens*]," where "language *is* practical, actual consciousness."[19] An organic language is fundamental to national culture's organic development because language is the bearer and transmitter of the cultural values through which a people view themselves as a self-identical unity, an organismic whole with a particular place in the external world *and* the ability to persist, develop, and grow through historical time. "Language as culture is the collective memory bank of a people's experience in history" (*DM,* 15). But more importantly, although language is a product of history, it does not merely reflect material life. It can be an effective, actual historical cause because it is crucial to the formation of human agents. "Language as culture," Ngũgĩ writes,

is an image-forming agent in the mind of a child. Our whole conception of ourselves as a people, individually and collectively, is based on those pictures and images which may or may not correctly correspond to the actual reality of the struggles with nature and nurture which produced them in the first place. But our capacity to confront them creatively is dependent on how

18. For a fuller discussion, see Simon Gikandi, "Ngũgĩ's Conversion: Writing and the Politics of Language," *Research in African Literatures* 23, no. 1 (spring 1992): 131–44; and Modhumita Roy, "Writers and Politics/Writers in Politics: Ngũgĩ and the Language Question," in *Ngũgĩ wa Thiong'o: Texts and Contexts,* ed. Charles Cantalupo (Trenton, N.J.: Africa World Press, 1995): 165–85.
19. *Marx, Die Deutsche Ideologie,* 15, 20; *The German Ideology,* 3rd rev. ed. (Moscow: Progress Publishers, 1976), 42, 49.

those images . . . distort or clarify the reality of our struggles. Language as culture is thus mediating between me and my own self; between my own self and
other selves; between me and nature. Language is mediating in my very being.

(*DM*, 15)

Marx's idea of language as practical consciousness only referred to its
practical origins as a communicational instrument integral to the social
process of creative labor. The practicality of language consists in the fact that
the ideas and images it expresses are "immediately [*unmittelbar*] interwoven
with the material activity and intercourse of men."[20] The agency Ngũgĩ
accords to language as culture, however, is a type of mediation that actually forms consciousness. Optimally, it should approximate or recover the
immediacy of the language of actual life by drawing truthful images that
enable a subject to recognize the true nature of external reality. It would
then be a self-recursive mediation that facilitates the subject's self-proximity
or presence to itself, thereby maintaining at the collective level the national
organism's integrity. In Ngũgĩ's words, "language is what most helps in the
movement of a community from the state of being in itself to a state of
being for itself and this self-awareness is what gives the community its
spiritual strength to keep on reproducing its being as it continually renews
itself in culture, in its power relations, and in its negotiations with its entire
environment."[21] But by the same token, language can also be an agent of
constitutive ideological alienation. Historically, the language policies of
colonial regimes imposed a foreign tongue on some African peoples,
which facilitated the inculcation of negative self-images through education
and religious doctrine that justified colonialism as a civilizing mission.
Echoing Fichte, Ngũgĩ suggests that a child educated in the colonizer's
language conceptualizes in a manner utterly alien to his everyday life-
experiences. He can no longer be at home in the immediate world of his
family and community because he sees them through the culture of the
imposed language. Whereas genuine *Bildung* generates living bodies, linguistic alienation produces phantom monstrosities. It involves

---

20. Ibid., 15; 42.
21. "Europhonism, Universities, and the Magic Fountain: The Future of African Literature and
Scholarship," *Research in African Literatures* 31, no. 1 (spring 2000): 3.

an active (or passive) distancing of oneself from the reality around; and an active (or passive) identification with that which is most external to one's environment. It starts with a deliberate dissociation of the language of conceptualisation, of thinking, of formal education, of mental development, from the language of daily interaction in the home and in the community. It is like separating the mind from the body so that they are occupying two unrelated linguistic spheres in the same person. *On a larger social scale it is like producing a society of bodiless heads and headless bodies.* (DM, 28; emphasis added)

The postcolonial intellectual undertaking the task of radical nationalist *Bildung* must therefore contend with the historical legacy of his own formation. The intellectual must first undergo a process of counter-*Bildung*, or unlearning, that will return him to the masses who have not been linguistically alienated. Before the intellectual can teach the masses, he must first communicate to and learn from them because they continue "to breathe life into our languages" and "help to keep alive the histories and cultures they carried" (*MC*, 35). We saw a similar exhortation to return to the origin in the Buru Quartet. But the task is necessarily more problematic for Ngũgĩ, who not only confronts the existence of a neocolonial global culture industry, but also the fact that most African literature is written in a colonial language. Dutch was never a serious contender as a lingua franca amongst the different Indies *bangsa*. In the Kenyan case, however, there is no spoken or written lingua franca that can easily be used to replace English, the same way that Malay could serve an emerging vernacular public. A critical public sphere of vernacular print needs to be created almost from scratch. But in which vernacular? Gikuyu, Swahili, Kalenjin, Somali, or one of the country's other languages?

THE ONUS OF NARRATIVE FICTION

Because Ngũgĩ intends his literature to be a practical exemplar of his theoretical writings, the literary works that follow his fuller understanding of nationalist *Bildung* seek to fulfill two tasks: First, they must depict the cruel reality of neocolonial Kenya in a stylistically cogent manner that will shock their implied reader, the Kenyan people. This exposure of the neocolonial state's nonsubstantial and fictional nature continues Marx's depiction of the distorted, upside-down world haunted by Monsieur le Capital and Madame la Terre. Postcolonial national *Bildung* is more challenging. Paradoxically, the neocolony's hyperbolical excesses are so normalized in daily existence that the depravity is difficult to represent fictionally. "How does a novelist capture and hold the interest of the reader," Ngũgĩ writes, "when the reality confronting the reader is stranger and more captivating than fiction? . . . How do you shock your readers by pointing out that these [African leaders] are mass murderers, looters, robbers, thieves, when they, the perpetrators of these anti-people crimes, are not even attempting to hide the fact?" (*DM*, 78, 80).

The same quandary also gave rise to magical realism, which in Salman Rushdie's estimation, "expresses a genuinely 'Third World' consciousness," and "deals with what Naipaul has called 'half-made' societies, in which the impossibly old struggles against the appallingly new, in which public corruptions and private anguishes are somehow more garish and extreme than they ever get in the so-called 'North' where centuries of wealth and power have formed thick layers over the surface of what's really going on."[22] Ngũgĩ's project is more affirmative. He represents degraded reality in order to sublate it. His fiction not only aims to thematically portray the national organism's teleological time—the national spirit's genesis from colonial resistance and its survival and promise of full actualization beyond the profane neocolonial present—but also to be an active part of its unfolding. It is intended to create a collective subject of resistance through its structure of address. This Marxist conception of activist literature that participates in the incarnation of a new reality with greater *Wirklichkeit* than the degraded present is similar to Pramoedya's idea of literary reality.

The success of Ngũgĩ's project of cultural repatriation and, indeed, the coherence of its representational schema and ontological presuppositions, depend on the ability to make a rigorous distinction between good and bad prostheses, the inside and the outside. The nation can only transcend the finitude of neocolonial reality if it recognizes and reappropriates its original cultural self, which has been alienated from it. If it fails to distinguish between a cultural device that is its own and one that originates from

---

22. *Imaginary Homelands: Essays and Criticism, 1981–1991* (London: Granta, 1992), pp. 301–2.

the other, it will be heteronomously determined and deprived of its bodily integrity. It is important to stress that cultural repatriation does not seal off the national body from the outside world. For instance, from *Petals of Blood* (1978) onwards, Ngũgĩ's fiction welds the revived Christian topos of incarnation to a Marxist discourse of transcendence on the basis that revolutionary nationalism expresses the true content or rational kernel of historical, positive forms of Christian doctrine because it locates the true God in the people, even though both Marxism and the Bible are foreign imports, and Christian education, which preaches quietism, is complicit with British colonialism and contemporary neocolonialism.[23] These appropriations indicate again that Ngũgĩ's revolutionary nationalism is not a nativism, but a process of *Bildung* in which the nation can digest foreign elements and make them part of its organic body. The problem lies rather with foreign prostheses that are mistaken for organic products and expose the nation to the perpetual risk of losing itself without the possibility of return. We have already broached the possibility of irretrievable self-loss in terms of the ambivalent sociological figure of the postcolonial intellectual, who is simultaneously the exemplary agent of cultural repatriation and also the most likely channel for neocolonial cultural influences. But does Ngũgĩ's own fiction convincingly demarcate good from bad prostheses, the living body from death and finitude, in its thematization of the teleological time of national incarnation?

MONSTROUS BODIES AND NONFUNCTIONAL ORGANS

Ngũgĩ's novels evoke the teleological time of the nation's birth and imminent resurrection through recurring images of pregnancy. But because the nation cannot be fully incarnated within a neocolonial order, the portrayal

---

23. The ontotheological analogy between the nation and the incarnation of divinity in man was always present in Ngũgĩ's early fiction. He characterized patriotic sacrifice as religious transfiguration and repeatedly drew parallels between central characters such as Waiyaki in *The River Between* (Portsmouth, N.H.: Heinemann, 1965), and Kihika, in *A Grain of Wheat* (Portsmouth, N.H.: Heinemann, 1967; rev. ed. 1986), and Biblical figures like Christ and Moses. *A Grain of Wheat* is hereafter cited as *GW*.

of decolonization is not marked by the unqualified euphoria that greets an infant's accomplished delivery, but by the anxious expectation of "a woman torn between fear and joy during birth motions" (*GW*, 203). In *A Grain of Wheat*, the scene of nativity that supposedly ends colonial alienation is haunted by the shadow of death. After he encounters a former colonial employer, Lieutenant Koina, a freedom fighter, is filled with doubt:

> Why were all these whites still in Kenya despite the ringing of Uhuru [Inde-pendence/Freedom] bells? Would Uhuru really change things for the likes of him and General R? Doubts stabbed him. Dr. Lynd's unyielding presence became an obsession. It filled him with fear, a kind of premonition. . . . Even now, as he ran, the thought of the unexpected encounter made him shudder. The ghost had come to eat into his life; the cool Uhuru drink had turned insipid in his mouth. (*GW,* 215)

General R. is likewise troubled by misgivings that the exorcism of colonial-ism has failed when he sees collaborators celebrating Uhuru:

> Koina talked of seeing the ghosts of the colonial past still haunting Indepen-dent Kenya. And it was true that those now marching in the streets of Nairobi were not the soldiers of the Kenya Land and Freedom Army but of the King's African Rifles. . . . Kigondu's face was now transformed into that of Karanja and all the other traitors in all the communities in Kenya. The sensation of imminent betrayal was so strong that General R. trembled in his moment of triumph. (*GW,* 220–21)

In Ngũgĩ's earlier novels, this sense of foreboding always gives way to a redemptive hope that the degraded present will be transcended. *A Grain of Wheat* ends with a more promising figure of pregnancy. Gikonyo's plan to carve the image of an expectant mother onto a wedding stool symbolizes teleological time as the sheer possibility of human labor (*GW*, 247). In stark contradistinction, the figure of pregnancy in *Devil on the Cross* is marked by a radical ambivalence. Mūturi, a former freedom fighter and the personification of the urban proletariat, observes, "This country, our country, is pregnant. What it will give birth to, God only knows. . . . [O]ur country should have given birth to its offspring long ago. . . . What it lacks now is a midwife. . . . The question is this: who is responsible for the pregnancy?"[24] This rich allegorical question could be soliciting the identity of the midwife who can facilitate the birth of a new national existence without exploitation and suffering. But it could also be pointing to the fetus's indeterminate parentage. For under a neocolonial regime, it is unclear whether what is awaiting birth is the child of God or the Devil, the living people or dead capital.

For the most part, *Devil on the Cross* seems to support the first interpretation. Its plot charts the *Bildung* of its two main protagonists, Warĩĩnga, a village girl forced to become a secretary in Nairobi after being seduced and abandoned by a rich old man (the archetypal tale of "traditional" patriarchal oppression of women), and Gatuĩria, a research fellow in the Department of Music at the University of Nairobi who plans to compose "a truly national piece of music," an oratorio for an orchestra made up of the instruments of all the Kenyan nationalities (*DC*, 60). They embark on a journey from Nairobi to Ilmorog in a shared cab where they meet Mũturi, Wangarĩ, a representative of the peasantry, and other sociological types. Along the way, they attend a Devil's Feast, the novel's set piece, where various indigenous capitalists compete for the title of the King of Theft and Robbery, and witness a failed uprising against neocolonial forces. Warĩĩnga also meets the Devil on a golf course and resists his temptations. Warĩĩnga and Gatuĩria's romantic relationship is an icon of the alliance between the organic intellectual and the masses that will engender a corporeally self-proximate nation. The organic intellectual who creates a patriotic culture that displaces the ideological myths of neocolonial culture is both father and midwife who guides the nation into healthy life.

Accordingly, the novel repeatedly juxtaposes two different forms of corporeal augmentation. On the one hand, augmentation through human labor and social cooperation is salutary. It forms a collective human heart, a humanity that transcends the circuit of exchange.[25] Communal endeavors are figured as the mutual cooperation and interdependence of corporeal organs. On the other hand, the novel is filled with images of the national body's profanation by neocolonial forces that oppress creative labor and suppress humanity. As Mũturi puts it, "there are two hearts: the heart built

24. Ngũgĩ wa Thiong'o, *Devil on the Cross* (Portsmouth, N.H.: Heinemann, 1982), pp. 45–46. Hereafter cited as *DC*.
25. See Mũturi's speech in *DC*, pp. 51–53.

by the clan of parasites, the evil heart; and the heart built by the clan of producers, the good heart" (*DC*, 53–54). At the Devil's Feast, one competitor dreams of becoming the personification of capital's prosthetic powers. He wishes to set up a factory that can manufacture spare parts for the human body so that the rich man can be the prosthetic body par excellence: "every rich man could have two mouths, two bellies, two cocks, two hearts—and hence two lives! Our money would buy us immortality! We would leave death to the poor!" (*DC*, 181). In a grotesque reinscription of the Marxian topos of man's enslavement by the machine, another competitor wants to set up a farm where electrical machines are attached to the bodies of workers to milk their sweat, blood, and brains for commodification and export to feed foreign industry (*DC*, 188–89).

In an earlier speech, Gatuīria had attempted to locate the origin of exploitation definitively in a foreign source: "Kenya, our country," he asserts, "has no killers or eaters of men, people who drink blood and kidnap the shadows of other men" (*DC*, 67). However, the grotesque images of the Devil's Feast depict the form of alienation Ngũgĩ fears most. The postindependence state, originally intended as an instrument of popular interests, has become a prosthesis serving the indigenous bourgeoisie, the agents of global capital, and has so completely possessed the nation-people that they are not aware of their own exploitation. This is, in other words, an alienation that originates from within the nation itself, where the foreign prosthetic body becomes indistinguishable from the real body and death emerges from within life itself.

Ngũgĩ attempts to maintain the boundary between life and death by counterposing the living nation to these images of living death. As the novel draws to a close two years after the initial journey, Warīīnga has earned the right to assume the authority of the national voice. Politically educated about the structural and systemic causes of her past sufferings, she now earns a living as a mechanic. In a blazonlike sequence, the narrator celebrates Warīīnga as the personification of the self-reliant, organically united, popular national body:

The Warīīnga of today has decided to be self-reliant all the time, to plunge into the middle of the arena of life's struggles in order to discover her real strength and to realize her true humanity. . . . Today, Warīīnga strides along with energy and purpose, her dark eyes radiating the light of an inner courage

... the courage and faith of someone who has achieved something through self-reliance. What's the use of shuffling along timidly in one's own country? . . . Warĩĩnga of the mind and hands and body and heart, walking in the rhythmic harmony of life's journey! Warĩĩnga, the worker! (*DC*, 216–18)

The novel's final chapter is set on the day of her wedding to Gatuĩria. This consummation would be an apposite figure of the nation's teleological promise since it symbolizes the union of the intellectual with the worker necessary to cultural repatriation. But this consummation does not take place. The nation's resurrection is indefinitely deferred. As it turns out, Gatuĩria's father is the rich old capitalist who had seduced and abandoned Warĩĩnga. Transfigured into "a people's judge," Warĩĩnga shoots him and departs, miraculously unrestrained, into a utopian horizon (*DC*, 253). But Gatuĩria cannot follow her because he is unable to renounce his class and family ties: "Gatuĩria did not know what to do: to deal with his father's body, to comfort his mother or to follow Warĩĩnga. So he just stood in the courtyard, hearing in his mind music that led him nowhere" (*DC*, 254). Here is how the novel ends: "Warĩĩnga walked on, without once looking back. But she knew with all her heart that the hardest struggles of her life's journey lay ahead . . . " (*DC*, 254).

The ending is simultaneously a step forward and a moment of paralysis. The utopian moment of poetic justice and Warĩĩnga's flight is the projection of the nation's future coming-to-be, the promise of the negation and transcendence of the neocolonial system in the form of a deferred hope. But this figuration of teleological time is also arrested and interrupted. In Ngũgĩ's theory of national *Bildung,* the postcolonial intellectual is an important agent in the freeing of the national body from possession by death-dealing prostheses it mistakes for its real self. Yet, in the novel's ending, the agent of corporeal self-proximity becomes a nonrecursive, inorganic prosthesis that blocks the teleological time of national incarnation. Frozen into corpselike inaction, Gatuĩria "stood there in the yard, as if he had lost the use of his tongue, his arms, his legs" (*DC*, 254).

Devil on the Cross thus dramatizes how the socioeconomic status of the postcolonial intellectual, on the margins of the same class as the comprador elite, makes him a chameleon with a vacillating social and psychological makeup, both able and likely to collaborate with reactionary forces or to serve the masses. Earlier, the problem is phrased as a repeated question lodged within Warīīnga's and Gatuīria's streams of consciousness: "We the intellectuals among the workers, which side are we on? . . . [A]re we like the hyena which tried to walk along two different roads at the same time? Warīīnga . . . was pursuing similar thoughts: We who work as clerks, copy typists and secretaries, which side are we on?. . . . Who are *we*? Who are *we*? Who are *we*? Warīīnga's heart beat in time to her question, raising problems to which nobody could provide her with solutions because they concerned the decision she would have to make herself about the side she would choose in life's struggle" (*DC*, 205–6). The novel aims to induce the same self-questioning in its Kenyan reader.

Now, this rich Marxist theme of the intellectual's sociopolitical responsibility has always been posed as a *sociological* question, in terms of the individual moral and existential choices of the privileged life-form we call "human." In fact, it raises the more profound question of culture's *formative* role in the actualization of freedom. For the intellectual only has this impact on postcolonial national *Bildung* because Ngũgĩ views nationalist culture as an exemplary prosthetic process that maximizes the nation's capacity for life. This means that the impossibility of definitively distinguishing between good and bad prostheses is logically implied in the idea of *Bildung*. One has to remember that the concept of culture refers to a self-directed, organic process of cultivation according to a rational and ideal image. *Bildung* presupposes an inner susceptibility to the prosthetic use of images. The danger of possession by alien prostheses thus arises from the initial possibility of supplementing or completing the body with an image.

We are speaking here of the vulnerability of life itself. In the organismic conception of the social and political body, life, however difficult, is inherently rational. It is not blind like mere matter. Life is conducive to human purposiveness precisely because it requires effortful struggle. But as we saw in the first part of the book, the teleological time of organismic causality is always vulnerable to disruption by an inhuman *techne* that is not within rational control, although, paradoxically, it is this *techne* that enables the self-recursive causality by which an organism generates itself. The postcolonial intellectual's Janus-like oscillation is a case of the inhuman *techne* that shadows the postcolonial nation's life and complicates its efforts at self-incarnation. This is why Ngũgĩ figures Gatuīria as an inorganic prosthesis.

THE SURVIVING OF SURVIVING

The nation remains haunted even in *Matigari,* which assumes that the popular nation has been incarnated and actively challenges the neocolonial state. The novel's primary concern is not the intellectual's equivocation about the nationalist struggle's rightness. The struggle's universal imperativity is asserted and the reader is drawn into the nation's teleological time by a contract that must be accepted before stepping across the book's threshold: "Reader/listener: may you allocate the duration of any actions according to your choice! // So say yes, and I'll tell you a story! Once upon a time, in a country with no name . . ." (*M,* ix). The nation's incarnation is embodied in the book's title character, Matigari ma Njirūūngi, a messianic Christlike figure, whose name, a footnote in the translation tells us, means "'the patriots who survived the bullets'—the patriots who survived the liberation war, and their political offspring" (*M,* 20).[26] Matigari ma Njirūūngi has buried his weapons, put on the belt of peace and seeks to return home. As a common noun, then, "Matigari" refers to the patriot, an exemplary member of the nation. It is the mark of *survival,* the nation's survival after colonialism, and the promise of its survival beyond neocolonialism, "in a future time when," as Simon Gikandi puts it, "the 'Matigaris' would return from the forest to reverse the betrayal of independence."[27] When Guthera, the main female character, hears Matigari's name, she says, "a patriot? Are you one of those left behind in the forest to keep the fire of freedom alive?" (37).

An allegory for the unfinished nationalist project, Matigari's homecoming is an attempt to find habitation in one's land when it has become so alien that it is no longer a home, a place to which one belongs. His repatriation thus involves at least two tasks. First, there is no returning home until the home belongs to one, that is, until political and economic alienation have been overcome. Ngũgĩ figures the people's reappropriation of the country's economic infrastructure and political superstructure as Matigari's

26. Simon Gikandi notes that "Matigari" was "a reference to leftovers of food or dregs in drinks" but, around 1963, became a signifier for the Mau Mau and referred to recalcitrant independence fighters who remained in the forest, whom the Kenyatta regime regarded as a threat. See "The Epistemology of Translation: Ngũgĩ, *Matigari,* and the Politics of Language," *Research in African Literatures* 22, no. 4 (winter 1991): 161–62.
27. Ibid., p. 162.

attempt to repossess and rebuild his house. But this is not enough, for the home is not an empty edifice but the seat of organic familial generation. As Matigari keeps repeating, he will not go home until he has found his people: "he reminded himself that he had not yet found his people. He could not go home alone" (12). The children are a synecdoche for the people. They can inherit and defend the home in the future by assuming the nationalist vocation: "A child belongs to all," Matigari observes, "a nation's beauty was borne in a child, a future patriot" (48). Colonial education is a sin because it stole the nation's future by corrupting the children of the indigenous elite. But the neocolonial state commits an even more heinous crime. When Matigari attempts to tell the children that "the years of roaming and wandering are over," that they "shall all go home together," he discovers that the children of the masses have been dispossessed (10).[28] They have become street urchins who live in a scrap yard, in the shells of discarded foreign cars, so dehumanized that they fight amongst themselves like scavenging animals.

As he wanders throughout the country seeking truth and justice, Matigari is absolutely confident in the nation's second coming. Thrown into prison, he exhorts his fellow prisoners:

> Truth never dies, therefore, truth will reign in the end, even if it does not reign today. My house is my house. I am only after what I have built with my own hands. Tomorrow belongs to me. I invite you all to my house the day after tomorrow. Come to a feast and celebrate our homecoming! (64)

As word of his deeds begins to spread after his miraculous escape from prison, he becomes a mythical figure who threatens the state by challenging its official views of reality. He is likened to Christ and Marx. Commentators have been critical of Ngũgĩ's mystical portrayal of Matigari, arguing that his supernatural powers undermine the historical-realist aspects of the novel that are more appropriate to the portrayal of Kenyan politics.[29] But

---

28. See Human Rights Watch, *Juvenile Injustice: Police Abuse and Detention Of Street Children In Kenya* (New York: Human Rights Watch, 1997).

29. See Lewis Nkosi, "Reading *Matigari*: The New Novel of Independence," *Paintbrush* 20, nos. 39–40 (spring/autumn 1993): 197–205; and Simon Gikandi, "The Epistemology of Translation." Both view this as evidence of a crisis of representation in the postcolonial African novel. See also

this misses the point: Matigari is not a realistic character, but the personification of the national spirit. Matigari himself points out that he embodies the entire history of nationalist struggle: "I did not begin yesterday. I have seen many things over the years. Just consider, I was there at the time of the Portugese, at the time of the Arabs, and at the time of the British—" (45).

Hence, although the rumors about Matigari are not empirically true (we find out that he escapes from the prison not because he made the prison walls open but because Guthera gave herself to a policeman and stole his keys), and although he displays all the attributes of a finite person, for instance, the political naïveté of someone out of touch with the contemporary world, his intentions and actions still represent a higher truth. This truth is neither the reflection of empirical reality governed by immutable mechanical causal laws, nor the official interpretation of reality disseminated by the Ministry of Truth and Justice through its radio program, the *Voice of Truth,* to justify neocolonial exploitation as an unchangeable reality. Matigari embodies a projected future reality that is reconciled with human ideals and has greater actuality than the neocolonial state. Matigari's truth is ontological and performative. It concerns a transfigured reality that will arise from united human labor: "The children would come out of this graveyard into which their lives had been condemned. They would build their lives anew in the unity of their common sweat. A new house. A paradise on earth. Why not? There is nothing that a people united cannot do" (16).

Indeed, what is of primary importance about Matigari's appearance in the narrative present is his amorphousness and nondeterminability, the impossibility of locating him in a physiological individual. Even as a proper name, "Matigari" refers to a shape that seems to mutate endlessly by feeding off the energy of the people who talk about him, so much so that the soldiers who try to capture him cannot determine who or what he is: "Who is Matigari? . . . How on earth are we going to recognise him? What does he look like? What nationality is he? Is Matigari a man or woman anyway? Is he young or old? Is he fat or thin? Is he real or just a figment of the people's imagination? Who or what really *is* Matigari ma

---

Gikandi, "The Politics and Poetics of National Formation: Recent African Writing," in *From Commonwealth to Postcolonial,* ed. Anna Rutherford, pp. 259–75. James Ogude, in *Ngũgĩ's Novels and African History* (London: Pluto, 1999), argues that Ngũgĩ has an idealistic view of historical change that is not anchored in reality.

Njirũũngi? Is he a person, or is it a spirit?" (170) Paradoxically, Matigari's effectivity does not lie in his actions' being believable to the novel's other characters (and, by implication, to the reader), but in the commotion he generates. His fabulous qualities lead to the diffusion and dissolution of his proper name into a common noun, "patriot," that can apply to all the people. The novel depicts this dramatically in the form of a question the people repeatedly ask themselves: "Who is Matigari ma Njirũũngi?"—that is, "Who is the patriot?" The refrain, which spreads through the entire country each time his parable is transmitted through oral narrative, also serves as an interpellative structure that reincarnates the imagined community of the nation in the same way that the Indonesian nation was conjured up by the magic of vernacular print in the Buru Quartet.

But unlike the formally similar "Who are we?" in *Devil on the Cross*, the refrain in *Matigari* does not lead to an equivocation in the questioning subject's identity. It is more like a rhetorical question that suggests the answer in advance, where the speaker-cum-addressee is supposed to reply "I am Matigari" or at least, "I can be Matigari." As long as the people think that Matigari is a messiah who will miraculously save them, the nation will never be reincarnated. It will only be actualized if the proper name is dissolved into a common noun, appropriated by each person through a commitment to patriotic action. The teleological time of national reincarnation is a practical-humanist messianism. Matigari tells the children that

> the God who is prophesied is in you, in me and in the other humans. He has always been there inside us since the beginning of time. Imperialism tried to kill that God within us. But one day that God will return from the dead. . . . He will return on the day when His followers will be able to . . .say in one voice: Our labour produced all the wealth in this land. . . . Let the earth return to those to whom it belongs. . . . But that God lives more in you children of this land; and therefore if you let the country go to the imperialist enemy and its local watchdogs, it is the same as killing the God who is inside you. It is the same thing as stopping Him from resurrecting. That God will come back only when you want Him to. (156)

Despite the patriarchal nature of Ngũgĩ's vision—Guthera is a Mary Magdalene figure whose role is to aid Matigari—*Matigari* is a more successful attempt at nationalist *Bildung* than *Devil on the Cross* because it draws more hopeful images. In sharp contrast to Gatuĩria's indecision and the failed student uprising in the earlier novel, Matigari decides that justice cannot be achieved by peaceful means. He burns down the house of John Boy Jr., the son of the cook of his former settler employer, who has now become a rich landowner, and vows to build a bigger house with better foundations. Led by chants from the children, the gathering crowd sets fire to the cars and houses of other comprador tycoons. Although Matigari dies at the end of the novel, he is succeeded by Mũriũki (the Resurrected), a street child who has retrieved his guns and inherited his mantle.

But this is only a novelistic depiction of how the nation survives and reincarnates itself through the interpellative power of oral narrative. The more important question is whether *Matigari,* the book, has been as successful in interpellating its readers in the real world as the character in its fictional world. In other words, does the novel also successfully embody and perform what it thematizes such that it is a self-recursive cultural prosthesis that prepares the way for the popular reappropriation of the neocolonial state? And is its performance of the nation's survival a full reincarnation or merely a haunting of the state? As I noted from the outset, the book conjured up a specter that haunted the Moi regime, which tried to arrest "Matigari" and then banned the book. Under such conditions, the theme of survival is necessarily doubled. One must consider how the novel qua embodiment of the nation's survival itself survives. Perpetually shadowed by state censorship, the survival of survival becomes problematic enough to cause the teleological time of the nation's epigenesis to waver.

Like *Devil on the Cross,* Ngũgĩ wrote *Matigari* in Gikuyu, incorporating elements of orature, popular music, and popular culture so that, through oral performance, it would become organic to the Kenyan people and organize them into a collective subject of resistance. Through his commitment to the nationalist struggle, he tries to solve by personal example the problem of the intellectual as nonrecursive *techne* that Gatuĩria personified. But despite his best intentions, the combined effects of political exile and censorship have not been salutary. In the first place, as Christopher Wise points out, however much they may try to simulate orature, "authentic" novels are not oral narratives like the West African griot epic because they lack the face-to-face communal setting of the griot's performance and the dynamism of the story's repeated regeneration and transformation through collaborative work with different audiences.[30] One can of course argue that novels can be converted into oral narratives through public readings, as *Matigari* presumably was. But even here, censorship generates a ghostly supplement that haunts and undermines the living Gikuyu original even as it enables its survival. The novel survives predominantly in its English translation. But this means that many specific historical connotations that threatened the neocolonial state's rhetoric and activity are lost.[31] For instance, the novel's title loses its Mau Mau allusions and simply becomes the central character's name. But more importantly, the need for an English translation also ironically integrates Ngũgĩ into the global circuit of cultural commodification, which assists the usurpation of the original by its English double. As Simon Gikandi notes, "the two texts function in a political situation where English is more powerful than Gikuyu. . . . [T]he eloquent English translation of *Matigari Ma Njirũũngi* defeats Ngũgĩ's intention of restoring the primacy of the African language as the mediator of an African experience. The act of translation is hence a double-edged weapon: it allows Ngũgĩ's text to survive and to be read, but it is read and discussed as if it were a novel in English."[32]

Matigari survives uncannily, out of its proper home, and becomes generally inaccessible to its intended audience, the Kenyan masses. But it can only live on by being misdestined to the North Atlantic, where it becomes part of "African national culture," a commodified cultural identity within the international circuit of cultural exchange and consumption.[33] Indeed,

---

30. "Resurrecting the Devil: Notes on Ngũgĩ's Theory of the Oral-Aural African Novel," *Research in African Literatures* 28, no. 1 (spring 1997): 134–40.

31. This and the following arguments in this paragraph come from Simon Gikandi, "The Epistemology of Translation," pp. 165–67.

32. Ibid., p. 166. For a fascinating analysis of the Anglocentric nature of academic scholarship on African literature, see Bernth Lindfors, "Sites of Production of African Literature Scholarship," *Ariel: A Review of International English Literature* 31, nos. 1–2 (January–April 2000): 153–77. Lindfors notes the lack of conversation between non-African and African scholars; that no book has been written about Ngũgĩ in an African language; that since 1973, Kenyans have only produced six book chapters on Ngũgĩ, four of which were for books published outside Africa, whereas non-Africans have written 68 book chapters most of which are published outside Africa; and that Ngũgĩ is well-known abroad but has not been introduced to other language groups in Kenya.

33. For an amusing metafictional portrayal of the commodification of the African writer, see J. M. Coetzee, *The Novel in Africa*, Doreen B. Townsend Center Occasional Papers, no. 17 (Berkeley: University of California, 1999).

the global *academic* industry may even have infected the aims of Ngũgĩ's critical writings from the early 1990s onwards. Simon Gikandi suggests that as a political exile, Ngũgĩ no longer shares the same communicative sphere as his intended audience, the Kenyan people. Hence, even *Mutiiri*, the Gikuyu journal he started, is "driven not so much by the concerns of Kenyan workers and peasants, but by the rhetoric of American identity politics and postcolonial nostalgia."[34] We should, however, not confuse the uncanniness of the Kenyan national spirit with a celebration of diasporic transnationalism. Ngũgĩ's desire for repatriation is patent. The melancholy irony is that the combined effects of neocolonial oppression, geographical deterritorialization, translation, and the global culture industry are such that national culture necessarily undergoes an accompanying alienation in its attempt to be the people's self-recursive mediation. Intended as linguistic repatriation, the act of writing in Gikuyu subjects the project of home-coming to an expropriating movement.

One can understand the dilemmas of Ngũgĩ's project of nationalist *Bildung* in at least three ways. Following the Third Worldist nationalist position associated with Bandung, one can argue that they indicate the limits of the current conjuncture. Although the nation cannot fully incarnate itself because national reappropriation at the economic, political, and cultural levels has not been accomplished, it will be able to transcend the finitude of the neocolonial world system in due time. Conversely, one can argue that Third Worldist nationalism has entered its terminal phase today. Other signs of its impending demise would include the nation's fragmentation by tribal or ethnic conflict, the lack of historical-material basis of utopian or messianic visions of popular struggle united by socialist ideals such as Ngũgĩ's, and the inherent violence of nationalism, which imposes a false unity that is rapidly undermined by contemporary globalization. The primary rational-choice policy suggestions for solving the African tragedy endorsed by international agencies are either the neoclassical model of a non-interventionist state, market liberalization and structural adjustment, with the aims of attracting foreign investment and creating an export-oriented industrial economy, or the East Asian model of hyperdevelopment (as opposed to African underdevelopment) under a strong state with an effective

---

34. "Traveling Theory: Ngũgĩ's Return to English," *Research in African Literatures* 31, no. 2 (summer 2000): 194.

bureaucracy following the examples of South Korea, Taiwan, and Singa-pore.[35] A recent post–Cold War variation has also stressed the importance of formal democratic reform, which provides a secure environment for foreign investment and is sometimes tied to foreign aid.[36]

Although these rational-choice policies differ in content from Third Worldist nationalism, they are underwritten by the same concept of incarnation. Echoing in degrees Kant's faith in world trade and Hegel's statism, their proponents see them as better institutional models for the incarnation of freedom. Yet it is not clear that they can alleviate the neocolonial dereliction that Ngũgĩ depicts. The Asian economic model has lost its shine after the financial crisis of 1997. The intellectual critique of U.S. neoliberalism's hypocritical and destructive nature has been painfully confirmed in the public imagination by the corporate-management scandals of 2002.[37] But more importantly, they fail to address the uneven, exploitative character of the global capitalist system. As Giovanni Arrighi observes, "for the casualties of so-called globalization, first and foremost the peoples of Sub-Saharan Africa . . . [t]he real problem is that some countries or regions have the power to make the world market work to their advantage, while others do not, and have to bear the costs. This power . . . has . . . deep roots in a particular historical heritage that positions a country or a region favourably or unfavourably in relation to structural and conjunctural processes within the world system."[38]

If we accept that a progressive nationalism making demands on the state with the aim of achieving the people's repatriation and reappropriation of

---

35. Following the Berg Report of 1981, the World Bank endorsed the first model in the 1980s but abandoned it by 1997. See Giovanni Arrighi, "The African Crisis," pp. 5–10. On the East Asian model, see Howard Stein, ed., *Asian Industrialization and Africa: Studies in Policy Alternatives to Structural Adjustment* (New York: St. Martin's, 1995). Some of these ideas have influenced African leaders; see Richard W. Stevenson, "Africa Decides to Flirt with Free-Market Capitalism," *New York Times,* 2 June 2002.

36. See Rachel L. Swarns and Norimitsu Onishi, "Africa Creeps Along Path to Democracy," *New York Times,* 2 June 2002; and Daniel Yergin, "Giving Aid to World Trade," *New York Times,* 27 June 2002.

37. See Joseph E. Stiglitz, *Globalization and Its Discontents* (New York: Norton, 2002); Robert Brenner, *The Boom and the Bubble: The U.S. in the World Economy* (New York: Verso, 2002); and Edmund L. Andrews, "U.S. Businesses Dim as Models for Foreigners," *New York Times,* 27 June 2002.

38. Arrighi, "The African Crisis," p. 34.

their alienated products still remains important in the current conjuncture, we can understand the troubled character of Ngũgĩ's nationalist *Bildung* in yet another way. It can be seen as a *problematization* of the idea of freedom as the power of self-incarnation or -actualization and its association with the self-recursive causality of organic life and culture. It indicates that repatriation through nationalist *Bildung* is always haunted, that the living people's epigenesis is always marked by a certain kind of death. The putative nation-people finds itself constitutively inscribed within a global force field that it cannot transcend or control in its efforts to return to itself. Even socially sustainable development requires foreign capital, which makes the nation vulnerable to financialization and other foreign prosthetic processes. This sheer vulnerability is constitutive of *Bildung* as self-recursive mediation. Despite his intentions, Ngũgĩ illustrates that the nation survives through a certain corruption; it undergoes alienation when it attempts cultural reappropriation. How can the concept of culture, which supplies the ontological paradigm of the political, be reformulated to take into account such radical contamination? What does this imply for the future of postcolonial nationalism?

EPILOGUE. SPECTRAL NATIONALITY: THE LIVING-ON OF THE POSTCOLONIAL NATION IN GLOBALIZATION

I have traced the organismic metaphor of the social and political body from its inception in Kant's philosophy and the prototypical institutional forms it has assumed from idealist cosmopolitanism, idealist nationalism and statism, and materialist cosmopolitanism to socialist decolonizing nationalism and revolutionary national culture in the postcolonial world. Although these territorialized and deterritorialized models conceive of the teleological time of freedom's actualization through analogies with culture and the organism's striving to maximize its life, they are haunted by figures of finitude that are the very opposite of freedom: death, specters and ghosts, lifeless machines, and other forms of nonspiritual *techne* or nonrecursive prostheses. The uncontrollable proliferation of such figures is especially pronounced in Pramoedya's and Ngũgĩ's projects of postcolonial nationalist *Bildung*. Even as the postcolonial nation haunts the state in its promise of reincarnation, it is also shadowed by the state.

Unless the writer is also an activist who can translate theory into practice and transform both theory and reality, the relation between academic writing and political events is one of mere reflection. The responsible thing to do is not to indulge in armchair activism and self-righteous sermonizing about what the world ought to be, but to transform theory passively by asking what it can learn from events. What then does the disruption of the postcolonial nation's teleological time mean for the concepts of freedom and culture? The organismic metaphor marked the gradual shift from absolutist to enlightened conceptions of the political body between the eighteenth and nineteenth centuries. If political organicism is now being deformed in contemporary globalization, what is the most apposite metaphor for freedom today? Michael Hardt and Antonio Negri have recently articulated a vision of liberation based on Gilles Deleuze's nonorganic vitalism.[1] In stark contrast to other aphilosophical approaches to globalization, they argue that liberation should be situated in the proliferation of new subjectivities (the multitude) *immanent* to global processes rather than the ability of revolutionary Third World nationalism to *transcend* global capital. They make three arguments against nationalist politics: the nation-state's efficacy as a juridico-economic structure has been eroded by global institutions; the nation-form was always ideologically repressive anyway; and, most importantly, the flexible organization of labor that follows from the decentralization of production and the consolidation of the world market has broken down the geography of uneven development from which Third World nationalism derived its radicalism, and this has led to the creation of a new deterritorialized proletariat.[2]

My critique of organismic vitalism, however, is not premised on the people's punctual death. Neither the nation-state nor the division of center and periphery have been superseded. First, the persistence of revolutionary postcolonial nationalism indicates that the nation is not a mere ideological formation that can be easily exorcised as Marx envisaged. Second, as we have seen, for Fanon, Cabral, Pramoedya, and Ngũgĩ, the decolonizing nation is not an archaic throwback to traditional forms of community based on the blind ties of blood and kinship, but a new form of political community engendered by the spectrality of modern knowledge, techno-mediation, and modern organization. Finally, globalization does not render

---

1. Deleuze reconceives life as an immanent plane that exceeds the possibility of both death and transcendence. See Deleuze, "Immanence: A Life," in *Pure Immanence: Essays on a Life,* trans. Anne Boyman (New York: Zone Books, 2001), pp. 25–33. On Deleuze's nonorganic vitalism, see Giorgio Agamben, "Absolute Immanence," in *Potentialities: Collected Essays in Philosophy,* trans. Daniel Heller-Roazen (Palo Alto: Stanford University Press, 1999), pp. 220–39; and Keith Ansell Pearson, *Germinal Life: The Difference and Repetition of Gilles Deleuze* (London: Routledge, 1999).
2. See Michael Hardt and Antonio Negri, *Empire* (Cambridge: Harvard University Press, 2000), pp. 332–39.

the nation-form obsolete. Labor flows are not as free as Hardt and Negri suggest.[3] Notwithstanding increased transnational labor migration in the contemporary era, the deterritorialization of peoples remains limited for reasons structural to the global economy. As Samir Amin has argued, in the really existing capitalist world system (as opposed to the generalized world market and mode of production that Marx envisaged), the most deprived masses of humanity are largely confined to national-peripheral space. The globalization of production—liberalization of trade and capital flows—involves the global integration of commodities and capital but stops short of an unlimited integration of labor, where the developed centers would be open without restriction to migrant workers from the less industrialized peripheries where the bulk of capital's reserve army is located.[4] Consequently, "the mobility of commodities and capital leaves national space to embrace the whole world while the labour force remains enclosed within the national framework" (*RPP*, 74). Instead of producing large groups of deterritorialized migrant peoples who prefigure the nation-state's demise and point to a postnational global order, Amin argues that *uneven* globalization makes popular nationalist movements in the periphery the first step on the long road to social redistribution.

The metaphor that has replaced the living organism as the most apposite figure for freedom today is that of the ghost. It is epitomized by the post-colonial nation, whose haunted life or susceptibility to a kind of death that cannot be unequivocally delimited and transcended suggests the need to reconceptualize freedom's relation to finitude. I conclude with an elaboration of the lineaments of this new metaphor.

The haunted character of postcolonial nationalism is the logical outcome of the idea of freedom as the transcendence of finitude through rational human endeavor, whether this is conceived spiritually or in materialist terms. Like all normative political discourses, postcolonial nationalism is a secularized version of a traditional discourse of finitude that contrasts the

---

3. Examples from hyperdeveloping Southeast Asia, such as Singapore and Malaysia, contradict their assertion that "countries that still maintain the rigidities of labor and oppose its full flexibility and mobility are punished, tormented, and finally destroyed by global monetary mechanisms" (*Empire*, 338).

4. Samir Amin, *Re-Reading the Postwar Period: An Intellectual Itinerary,* trans. Michael Wolfers (New York: Monthly Review Press, 1994), p. 74. Hereafter cited as *RPP*.

finitude of humanity with an infinite self-causing divine Creator who gives us being. We justify our given existence and give it and ourselves meaning through our faith in the infinite. In a secularized world, organic life and the sphere of culture are often associated with the auto-causality of the Absolute because of their inherent rationality and purposiveness. The organismic metaphor transfers infinite attributes to the ideal social or political body, which thereby becomes the institutional basis for the transcendence of finitude and the actualization of freedom. But although the popular postcolonial nation appears to be the most viable basis for actualizing freedom for the world's masses, it has not been able to actualize itself as a popular nation-state that can transcend global capital. The living people have reinspirited or reappropriated the state during decolonization and in subsequent moments of postcolonial resistance or revolution. But it has never become an enduring ethical substance because in an uneven world system, the forces of dead global capital have reinfected the state and contaminated the people through it and other prosthetic devices such as official national culture.

Throughout the book, I have connected this irreducible heteronomy that also afflicts other political organicisms to the idea of constitutive finitude, a finitude that inhabits teleological time and constitutes every act of freedom understood as the rational process of transcendence, incarnation of ideals and self-actualization. These cases concern a living body's susceptibility to externality in the epigenetic processes that maintain its form, such as ingestional activity. Thus, the idea that we can transcend our natural existence through *Bildung* or the concept's self-recursive mediation renders us vulnerable to an other, an image, by means of which we transform ourselves. All rational purposive endeavor thus involves a supplementary movement that can disrupt teleological time *if* the image is malevolent and leads to alienation. But this means that the possibility of alienation is always already inscribed within freedom. The question is why this is so. I offer an answer with the help of another discourse on ghosts, this time philosophical and not literary: Jacques Derrida's reflections on spectrality. Derrida's work delineates a radical contamination that necessarily accompanies and interminably circumscribes the incarnational work of freedom. His "hauntology" is especially productive for fleshing out the mutual haunting of nation and state because it refers to a condition of originary prosthesis that is distinct from ideology even though it is the condition of possibility of ideological mystification.

Derrida defines spectralization as the incarnation of autonomized spirit in an aphysical body that is then taken on as the living subject's real body:

> The specter is *of the spirit,* it participates in the latter and stems from it even as it follows it as its ghostly double. . . .
>
> The production of the ghost, the constitution of the *ghost* effect is not simply a spiritualization or even an autonomization of spirit, idea or thought, as happens *par excellence* in Hegelian idealism. No, once this autonomization is effected, with the corresponding expropriation or alienation, and only then, the ghostly moment *comes upon* it, adds to it a supplementary dimension, one more simulacrum, alienation or expropriation. Namely, a body! In the flesh (*Leib!*)! For there is no ghost, there is never any becoming-specter of the spirit without at least an appearance of flesh, in a space of invisible visibility, like the dis-appearing of an apparition. For there to be ghost, there must be a return to the body, but to a body that is more abstract than ever. The spectro-genic process corresponds therefore to a paradoxical *incorporation.* Once ideas or thoughts (*Gedanke*) are detached from their substratum, one engenders some ghost by *giving them a body.* Not by returning to the living body from which ideas and thoughts have been torn loose, but by incarnating the latter *in another artifactual body, a prosthetic body,* a ghost of spirit.[5]

The specter is a waste-product or undesirable residue of *Bildung* as human self-objectification or self-actualization through individual or collective rational work. Worse still, it is the incorporation of an idealization "in a body without nature, in an a-physical body, that could be called, if one could rely on these oppositions, a technical body or an institutional body" (*SM,* 127).

But the specter is not identical to the nonactual phantom forms that political organicism was at pains to exorcise, for instance, Marx's denunciation of ideology or money as the alienation and corruption of living labor. The specter is not an ideologem, a mere mystification that is confused with and lived as concrete reality. An ideologem is an illusion, an alienated ideational prosthesis that begins from the living body and ought to be referred back in the final instance to its material historical conditions

---

5. Jacques Derrida, *Specters of Marx: The State of the Debt, the Work of Mourning, and the New International,* trans. Peggy Kamuf (New York: Routledge, 1994), pp. 125–26. Hereafter cited as *SM.*

by immanent political critique. Spectrality, however, is an interminable process that necessarily follows from our radical finitude as beings in time. Derrida suggests that the persistence or living-on [*sur-vie*] of the *form* of a present being through time—that which makes it actual and allows it to be materialized, the persistence of which represents a momentary arresting of our dying in any given instant—is a minimal idealization before idealization proper that is constitutive of all finite bodies.[6] Without this formal survival, nothing can be present because this is what allows us to identify any present being as the *same* throughout all its possible repetitions. This survival gives life to an organism by enabling it to be self-recursive. It confers an identifiable form that the organism can preserve in its interactions with externality. But paradoxically, this survival of form is also a type of death because it is not a principle *of* the living body. For time is what we do not have. It is not something we can possess and, therefore, something we can give to or receive from another, whether this is someone else, ourselves, or a higher being. As Derrida puts it,

> how can a time belong? What is it *to have time?* If a time belongs, it is because the word *time* designates metonymically less time itself than the things with which one fills it, with which one fills the form of time, time *as form*. . . . Therefore, as time does not belong to anyone as such, one can no more *take* it, itself, than *give* it. Time already begins to appear as that which undoes this distinction between giving and taking, therefore also between receiving and giving, perhaps between receptivity and activity, or even between the being-affected and the affecting of any affection.[7]

The giving of time is thus a peculiar dynamism that exceeds the opposition between heteronomy and freedom, blind mechanism and the self-recursive causality of organic life and culture. It is not the brute existence of a datum or given because it is not deterministic. It generates spontaneous life. But this process of giving is not the teleological time of self-giving since it cannot be attributed to the rational purposiveness of a human subject,

---

6. For an elaboration of "living-on," see Derrida, "Living On/Border Lines," trans. James Hulbert, in *Deconstruction and Criticism*, ed. Geoffrey Hartman (New York: Continuum, 1979) 75–176.
7. *Given Time: I. Counterfeit Money*, trans. Peggy Kamuf (Chicago: University of Chicago Press, 1992), p. 3. Hereafter cited as *GT*.

teleological nature, or an absolute self-causing being. There is a gift, for forms persist and there is living presence, but the gift is not an object and has no donor-subject or origin.[8] Second, this differing-deferral (différance) of a present being in the *iterability* of its form is a paradoxical automaticity that cannot be understood through the nature/culture opposition. It is clearly not the auto-causality of freedom that cobelongs with *human* reason; the rational-purposive formations of society, culture, *techne,* or language; or organic life conceived in analogy with human teleology. But it is also not an effect of the mechanism of nature because it constitutes both spontaneous life and inanimate nature. It is a spectral double that embodies "the contradiction of *automatic autonomy,* mechanical freedom, technical life" (*SM,* 153). The specter is both dead and alive: it seems to animate and spiritualize itself like an organism, but all the while, it remains "an artifactual body, a sort of automaton, a puppet, a stiff and mechanical doll whose dance obeys the technical rigidity of a program" (ibid.). Iterability is thus a radical heteronomy that is not just dependence on another person, thing, or even objectivity in general. It is exposure to an alterity that makes any and all presence possible but is not, itself, of the form of presence. It is the trace of the inhuman and unnatural spectral other within presence.

How does the ghostly gift of time weigh on the political organism's teleological time? Teleological time is the fundamental structure of the rational purposive work through which we transcend finitude and achieve freedom. In contradistinction, spectrality is coextensive with our *radical* finitude. It refers to the sheer persistence of beings in time, the continuing temporalization where our presence is given (to us) by an alterity. What Derrida points to is the *original* exposure of any body to alterity, not only in the maintenance of its already constituted form, but in the constitution of its very form, in the process of its self-identity, its being proper to itself. This other is not a secondary reflection a living body generates to reproduce and transform itself. It precedes and constitutes the body even though it does not *belong* to it as its other. This alterity is so radical that it is not a thing or another present being, not even an infinite, absolute, self-causing presence called God. It is absolutely contingent, but it is, at the same time, the absolutely necessary condition of our existence. Unlike

---

8. See *GT,* p. 24: "the subject and the object are arrested effects of the gift, arrests of the gift."

finitude traditionally conceived, radical finitude is nontranscendable because there is no refuge of eternal presence into which we can cross over.

As the original opening up of any present being by or to alterity, spectrality is the condition of possibility of the incarnation of human ideals in external reality. This pregnancy with the movement of alter-ing allows something to change or transform itself and external reality in time. But the same exposure to alterity is also the condition of possibility of contamination because it allows us to be changed, transformed, or altered by another. According to Derrida,

> all the grave stakes we have just named . . . would come down to the question of what one understands, with Marx and after Marx, by effectivity, effect, operativity, work, labor [*Wirklichkeit, Wirkung,* work, operation], living work in their supposed opposition to the effects of virtuality, of simulacrum, of "mourning work," of ghost, *revenant* and so forth. . . . [D]econstructive thinking of the trace, of iterability, of prosthetic synthesis, of supplementarity, and so forth, goes beyond this opposition and the ontology it presumes. [It inscribes] the possibility of the reference to the other, and thus, of radical alterity and heterogeneity, of differance, of technicity, and of ideality in the very event of presence, in the very presence of the present that it dis-joins *a priori* in order to make it possible. (SM, 75)

We are broaching the condition of possibility of causality as such. Spectrality allows something to act on and affect itself or another (and also to affect itself as an other) or to be acted on or affected by another (and also by itself as an other). It allows any action (transitive and intransitive) or occurrence—which is to say, production and also creation in general—to take place. But it is also the inscription of *techne* within the living body: it opens up every proper organic body to the supplementation of artifice. We commonly understand culture as an alteration we introduce into nature through rational artifice. Spectralization is a form of inhuman culture, before culture *and* nature, that makes both possible. We have already seen this in Kant's idea of a technic of nature, which turned out to be a technic of the other. This inhuman *techne* or culture is the original ground of all historical instances of contamination and can lead to our infection by ideological images and other nonrecursive prostheses that facilitate political, economic, and cultural alienation. Alienation is so difficult to overcome because original contamination cannot be transcended.

The disruption of teleological time is, however, not an impasse that leads to nihilism or apolitical quietism. Since spectrality also sets teleological time in motion, it is not a matter of rejecting the hope that freedom can be actualized through cultural work but of understanding the conditions of the (im)possibility of incarnation. The experience of radical finitude is a practical experience that gives rise to imperativity and responsibility. Without our persistence in time, no incarnational work or action and, therefore, no political event, can take place. However, we can never be guaranteed of our own persistence in time beyond any given instant. In each and every instant, we live only *in and through* the possibility that in another instant, perhaps the next, we might die. Living is always shadowed by death. But the specter also enjoins us to act in the here and now (which is no longer, even as we speak), without waiting and thinking too much, before it is too late. The source of imperativity is not the knowledge that life is short (carpe diem), but the undecidability of not knowing how much more time we will have to actualize our ideals. Each time we have survived into the next moment, each time we unexpectedly receive the gift of time again, we are born anew. We are grateful, but also anxious because this may already be a surfeit of life, and we don't know whether it will occur again. As Derrida notes,

> this anxiety in the face of the ghost is properly revolutionary. If death weighs on the living brain of the living, and still more on the brains of revolutionaries, it must then have some spectral density. To weigh (*lasten*) is also to charge, tax, impose, indebt, accuse, assign, enjoin. And the more life there is, the graver the specter of the other becomes, the heavier its imposition. And the more the living have to answer for it. . . . The specter weighs, it thinks, it intensifies and condenses itself within the very inside of life, within the most living life, the most singular (or, if one prefers, individual) life. The latter therefore no longer has and must no longer have, insofar as it is living, a pure identity to itself or any assured outside. (*SM*, 109)

Thus, even as spectrality disjoins the present, it also renews the present in the same movement. The returning spectral other (revenant) tears time conceived as the linear succession of "now"-s (efficient causality), or a teleological circle. But it is precisely the rending of time that allows the new to emerge and rejuvenate the present by giving it the promise of a future. Totalitarianism, Derrida argues, is continuous with the belief that our ideals are fully present in reality or that reality is *fully present* to itself.[9] But an infinite reality is one that is petrified and immutable, eternally bonded to itself. It no longer has a future because it has removed itself from temporalization. In fact, the substantialization of our ideals is always exposed to heteronomy. It can always go awry because an expropriating movement automatically shadows our appropriation of external reality and even the original self-recursivity of being-proper-to-ourselves. But precisely because substantialization is never complete, the incarnational work through which we become free can have a future. Thus, even as spectrality contaminates and compromises all our rational efforts at incarnating ideals or, better yet, precisely because it compromises these efforts, it also generates the unerasable promise of a future to-come. The future to-come is not the future present of teleological time, for example, the ends promised by Hegelian, Marxist, or revolutionary nationalist teleology. It is something that is always arriving but which never arrives finally. Derrida calls this "the messianic without messianism"—a messianism that has been purged of content and an identifiable messiah, a nonteleological eschatology.[10] Unlike teleology, which always involves a return to self, messianic affirmation is the sheer loss of self through exposure to an alterity that cannot be anticipated. But this exposure to the absolutely other is always presupposed by any teleology for it is the gift of time itself.

Derrida brings us very close to the mutual haunting of the postcolonial nation-people and the state. In a postsocialist age, we can only hold on to the impossible necessity of transcending global capitalism by referring the postcolonial nation's continuing alienation back to a more radical contamination. This is not a matter of rejecting national *Bildung,* but of interminably accounting for its limits. Commenting on Marx's and Stirner's organismic vitalism, Derrida writes that

> Both of them love life . . . : they know that life does not go without death, and that death is not beyond, outside of life, unless one inscribes the beyond in the inside, in the essence of the living. They both share . . . an unconditional preference for the living body. But precisely because of that, they wage an endless war against whatever represents it, whatever is not the body, but

9. See *SM,* 90–91.
10. See *SM,* 28, 59, 65, 89–90.

belongs to it, comes back to it: prosthesis and delegation, repetition, differ-ance. The living ego is auto-immune, which is what they do not want to know. To protect its life, to constitute itself as unique living ego, to relate, as the same, to itself, it is necessarily led to welcome the other within (so many figures of death: differance of the technical apparatus, iterability, non-uniqueness, pros-thesis, synthetic image, simulacrum . . .), it must therefore take the immune defenses apparently meant for the non-ego, the enemy . . . and direct them at once *for itself and against itself* (SM, 141)

In its desire for sustainable development, the national organism's relation to the bourgeois state is an interminable experience of the aporia of life-death, where death is irreducibly inscribed within the living present. The postcolonial nation lives-on, in and through a certain kind of death that also renews life. It can only maximize its well-being and come to freedom by attaching itself to the state. Through the state, it is exposed to techno-logical flows, flows of foreign direct investment, cultural images, and so on, transnational forces that are crucial to development. However, in an uneven global system, national development in the periphery is frustrated because of state adjustment to the dictates of transnational capital. The state can resist capitulation to transnational forces only if it is transformed from an inorganic prosthesis into a popular national state. This is the hope we saw in Fanon, Anderson, Pramoedya, Ngũgĩ, and others, the belief that popular rearticulations of the nation are not ideologies, but ethically imperative spectralizations of the state. However, the exclusionary dimen-sion of popular nationalism can always be manipulated by state elites to hinder postcolonial national *Bildung*. There is a persistent flickering between death and life, ideology and the people's spontaneous will. The state is an uncontrollable specter that the national organism must welcome within itself, and direct, at once *for itself and against itself,* because the state can also possess the nation-people and bend it towards global capitalist interests.

I hasten to add that Derrida does not sanction this line of thought. The contemporary theoretical climate is not supportive of nationalism, and Derrida is no exception. Just as economic transnationalism is widely touted as the solution to problems of underdevelopment and authoritarian-ism in the South, Derrida also dresses spectrality up as the scene of migrancy and transnationalism. Regardless of how contentless he purposely leaves the future to-come, it is definitely antinationalist:

awaiting what one does not expect yet or no longer, hospitality without reserve, welcome salutation accorded in advance to the absolute surprise of the *arrivant* from whom or from which one will not ask anything in return and who will not be asked to commit to the domestic contracts of any welcoming power (family, State, nation, territory, native soil or blood, language, culture in general, even humanity) . . . messianic opening to the event that cannot be awaited as such . . . to the event as the foreigner itself, to her or to him for whom one must leave an empty place, always, in memory of the hope—and this is the very place of spectrality. (*SM*, 65)

Derrida does not say that the specter is a migrant to whom we must play absolute host. He does not put it so vulgarly or bluntly. In *Aporias*, he carefully notes that the *arrivant* is indeterminable, does not cross a threshold separating two identifiable places, and should not, therefore, be reduced to a traveler, an émigré, or a political exile, refugee, or immigrant worker.[11] Nevertheless, he clearly dismisses nationalism as a discourse that does not allow for the promise of the messianic.

Nationalism cannot give place because it is an ontopology, an outmoded doctrine of self-present place:

Inter-ethnic wars are . . . proliferating, driven by an *archaic* phantasm [presumably not a specter because it is tied to a past present] and concept, by a *primitive conceptual phantasm* of community, the nation-State, sovereignty, borders, native soil and blood. Archaism is not a bad thing in itself, it doubtless keeps some irreducible resource. But how can one deny that this conceptual phantasm is, so to speak, much more outdated than ever, in the very *ontopology* it supposes, by tele-technic dislocation? (By *ontopology* we mean an axiomatics linking indissociably the ontological value of present-being [*on*] to its *situation*, to the stable and presentable determination of a locality, the *topos* of territory, native soil, city, body in general).

(*SM*, 82; bracketed interpolation is mine)

---

11. Jacques Derrida, *Aporias: Dying-Awaiting (One Another at) "the Limits of Truth,"* trans. Thomas Dutoit (Palo Alto: Stanford University Press, 1993), p. 33. Derrida's understanding of globalization through the figure of transnational migrancy is even clearer in the list of ten injunctions in *The Other Heading*, trans. Pascale-Anne Brault and Michael B. Naas (Bloomington: Indiana University Press), pp. 77–79. Cf. Gayatri Chakravorty Spivak, "Limits and Openings of Marx in Derrida," in *Outside in the Teaching Machine* (New York: Routledge, 1993), pp. 111–15.

Contemporary population transfers have rendered the nation-form obsolete, and ethnonationalist conflict attests to its violence:

> in the general dis-location to which our time is destined—as are from now the places of lovers, families, nations—the messianic trembles on the edge of this event itself. . . . [I]t would no longer be messianic if it stopped hesitating: how to give rise and to give place [*donner lieu*], still, to render it, this place, to render it habitable, but without killing the future in the name of old frontiers? Like those of the blood, nationalisms of the native soil not only sow hatred, not only commit crimes, they have no future, they promise nothing even if, like stupidity or the unconscious, they hold fast to life. (*SM,* 169)

An ontopology is not an ideology in the Marxist sense. However, the archaic phantasm of the nation is definitely not the life-death of the specter. It is simply on the side of eternal death and cannot cross over the undecidable border between life and death because it can promise no life. Thus, although Derrida is critical of the opposition between rational work and mystical belief in Marx's organismic ontology, he inherits Marx's treatment of nationality as a subcase of religious mysticism that globalization has made effete. Marxism, he notes, is "in principle non-religious, in the sense of a positive religion; it is not mythological; it is therefore not national—for beyond even the alliance with a chosen people, *there is no nationality or nationalism that is not religious or mythological, let us say "mystical" in the broad sense*" (SM, 91; emphasis added).

But why is the nation-form so resolutely ideological and not spectral? In light of postcolonial nationalism's failed promises *and* its continuing imperativity as an agent of ethicopolitical transformation in uneven globalization, Derrida's dismissal of nationalism is too hasty. His understanding of globalization is limited to the broad figure of migration. His predication of the future as transnational migrancy forecloses the implications of uneven globalization for postcolonial nationalism. For instance, what does it mean for a country in the South to practice hospitality without reserve as a host for transnational capital? If, as Derrida suggests, globalization brings about "new forms of a withering or rather a re-inscription, a re-delimitation of the State in a space that it no longer dominates and that moreover it never dominated by itself" (*SM,* 94), then instead of dismissing examples of popular nationalism in the postcolonial South that arise in resistance to economic transnationalism as essentially and irredeemably ontopologo-centric, one can see them as spectral promises.

Contemporary theory is fixated on the crisis of culture. I have argued that culture's vocational task and its organismic vitality have not withered away. Its ghost, however, no longer lingers in the narrowly conceived sphere of culture. Culture as freedom is persistently performed and undone in radical postcolonial nationalist *Bildung*. The postcolonial nation is a creature of life-death because, by virtue of its aporetic inscription within uneven globalization, the state stands between the living nation-people and dead global capital, pulling on both even as it is pulled by both. I end with a concrete example that is also a promise of work to come. As is well known, the financial crisis which is still hampering Asia today became visible in June 1997, triggered by a massive attack on the Thai baht by currency speculators from 14–15 May 1997. This crisis became a free fall into deep economic recession across industrialized and industrializing Southeast Asia and East Asia, indicated by increased inflation, declining production, and rising unemployment. What is so surprising about the collapse of the "Asian economic miracle" is its suddenness. Almost overnight, the strong economic fundamentals of many of these countries—the economic well-being of the nation conceived as an organic body—which were widely regarded by international financial and economic authorities, such as the World Bank, not only as sound but also as models for African and Latin American countries to follow, were driven down by global financialization.

The ghost of money has clearly contaminated the realm of real production. But more importantly, these rapidly developing postcolonial national bodies have been spectralized by the ghost of foreign money which they cannot *not* welcome within themselves in order to develop, even though this exposure is also a certain kind of death, a form of auto-immunization. Indeed, prior to the collapse, those countries had ironically colluded with the Northern liberal picture of the fiscalization of the globe, world trade liberalization, and foreign direct investment—"growth for all, leading to transnational solidarity"–by touting themselves as the success stories of flexible or disorganized global capitalism in their official cultural self-representations in the international public sphere.

Here are instances of both sides of the aporia, where the postcolonial national body must accept the other within but cannot clearly discriminate between what it welcomes into itself. On the one hand, as Prime Minister

Dr. Mahathir Mohamad of Malaysia notes, even after the crash Malaysia regards "genuine foreign direct investors" as *vital* contributors to the country's industrial development: "We have always treated them as *special guests* of the country."[12] On the other hand, the very conditions that can secure future foreign direct investment, such as acquiesence to IMF directives, are themselves harmful. Using Indonesia as an example, one commentator notes that "some of the IMF policies are wrong and deadly. Asking the IMF for assistance may well cause a moderately sick patient to develop a serious and life-threatening disease that will take much suffering and many years to get out of, if at all."[13]

Far from being rendered obsolete by globalization, the living-on of the postcolonial nation in the wake of the currency crash can be seen in the rise of both popular and official nationalisms in Southeast Asia in response to both economic neocolonialism and IMF manipulation: protest by the Malaysian state against unregulated currency speculation, peasant protest in Thailand and student radicalism in Indonesia that led to the fall of Suharto's New Order regime. The postcolonial nation must be seen as a specter of global capital (double genitive): it is originarily infected by the prosthesis of the bourgeois state as the terminal of capital. But it is also a specter that haunts global capital and awaits reincarnation, the undecidable neuralgic point that refuses to be exorcised. This is why it is the most apposite figure for freedom today.

---

12. "Dr. M: We don't need 'hot money,'" *The Star* (Kuala Lumpur), 14 June 1998;, emphasis added.
13. Martin Khor, "IMF 'cure' pushes Indonesia to crisis," *The Star,* 11 May 1998.

INDEX

Compiled by Chad Wellmon

accountability, to the people, 272, 353, 354

Achebe, Chinua, 358

actuality (*Wirklichkeit*)/actualization of freedom, 1, 3, 59, 142, 145, 160, 169, 170, 177, 206, 209, 229, 237, 252, 370, 379, 381, 384; Hegel's concept of, and the idea of the state, 1, 144–49, 170, 176–78; as incarnational activity and the realization of ideals, 147, 160, 246, 356, 384; and Kant's moral freedom, 103, 105, 111; Marx's understanding of, 179, 192, 196, 198, 199, 200–208; in the nation, 212, 221, 227, 364; in Pramoedya, 251, 252, 263, 264, 271, 289, 299, 301, 324, 336; and reason, 116, 137, 141–45, 221, 289; relation to culture, 99, 166, 199, 216, 235, 264, 379; role of literature in, 143, 243; in the state, 373

Adorno, Theodor: account of commodity culture, 236; *Dialectic of Enlightenment* (with Horkheimer), 20, 94, 236; and myth, 58; and Pramoedya 282. *See also* Frankfurt School

aesthetics, 24, 257n, 258, 263

aesthetic ideology, 130, 130n, 137

Africa: the African tragedy, 377, 378nn35–38; failure of constitutionalism in, 351; human rights in, 351; theft capitalism in, 351

alienation: cultural, 271, 358, 359, 360, 379, 388; and externalization, 166, 202n41; and freedom, 384; linguistic, 129, 362; Marx's theory of, 195, 196, 205, 207, 219, 341, 385; political, 169, 170, 177, 243, 312, 354, 356, 359, 366, 368, 371

alterity: Hegel's understanding of, 143, 150, 153, 177; and iterability, 387; of nature, 102, 109; and spectrality, 13, 112, 303, 390

Amin, Samir: on popular nationalism, 237, 249, 383; theory of uneven development, 230–32, 383

Anderson, Benedict: *Imagined Communities*, 3–4, 187, 225–28, 238; and literary *Bildung*, 238, 242, 255; on nation vs. administrative state, 226–29; and philosophical nationalism, 3–4; on print

Anderson, Benedict (*continued*)
  capitalism and *techne,* 238, 266; on
  Third World nationalism, 225–26,
  391
anthropomorphism: in Kant's
  teleology of nature, 102–5, 109, 112;
  modern worldview as anthropologistic, 36, 42, 241, 281
Anwar, Chairil, 257, 257n16, 258n20,
  259
appropriation: cultural, 11, 87, 358, 359,
  360, 375, 379; and expropriation, 112;
  and Fanon, 219, 221; and Hegel, 165,
  204; relation to national integrity
  and national culture, 216, 219–21,
  232, 245, 329, 353, 354, 371, 377; and
  proletarian world revolution, 10,
  191–200, 205–6
Arendt, Hannah, 64n11, 200n
Aristotle, 48–53, 88, 149n, 155; account
  of *physis,* 48, 50, 52; on causality, 50,
  53; on organic life, 48–50; and
  organic state, 48; and *techne,* 52
Armah, Ayi Kwei: *The Beautyful Ones
  Are Not Yet Born,* 240, 245–46
Asian economic miracle, 394
Asian financial crisis, 378, 394–95
automaton, 27, 35, 37, 51, 68, 69, 311,
  387

Balibar, Etienne, 125–26n19
Bandung Conference, 283; non-
  alignment and national
  development, 230; spirit of
  Bandung, 1, 230, 350, 377
Bauer, Otto, 209, 210
Benjamin, Walter, 236, 241
Bildung: as autocausality, 42, 56; in
  Cabral, 216–17, 219–21; connection
  to culture and organicism, 8, 11, 38,
  47; as cultivation, 39–42, 58; and
  decolonizing nationalism, 220, 237,
  239, 240, 246, 330, 375, 390; in

Fanon, 219; and ideology, 8, 137; as
  incarnation of freedom, 45, 112;
  literary, 137, 210, 238, 240, 242, 330;
  literature as, 239, 240–42, 261; as
  moral action 40, 71, 77; *Mißbildung,*
  311, 328; Ngũgĩ's theory of, 358,
  360–65, 369, 377, 379; and *physis,* 47,
  56; postcolonial, 7, 11, 237, 370, 391,
  394; in Pramoedya's writings, 249,
  255, 261, 263–65, 273–80, 303, 311,
  312, 315, 330, 345–48. *See also* Fichte;
  Hegel; Kant; Marx
bildungsroman: and *Bildung,* 11;
  definition, 244; and demagicking
  (*Entzauberung*) 241; and homelessness, 243; and postcolonial nation,
  239, 240, 265; and teleology, 241,
  245, 273
Bildungstrieb: and *Bildung,* 88, 217; and
  Cabral, 217; and culture, 90
Blumenbach, 54; Hegel's critique of
  152, 152n47; and Kant, 86, 88; rejection of preformationism, 54–56
border: in Fichte, 118–19, 124, 136,
  138–42; freedom as transcendence
  of borders and limits, 119, 127–28,
  141, 191, 218, 330, 342, 346; between
  German and non-German, 125–28;
  between labor and capital, 197;
  between life and death, 117, 125–28,
  175, 246, 329, 333, 345, 393; as self-
  limitation, 127; between sensible
  and supersensible worlds, 118, 124;
  territorial, 127, 128

Cabral, Amilcar: on culture, 129, 181,
  219, 223, 224, 237; on nationalism,
  214, 222, 266, 354, 359, 382;
  similarities to Fichte, 129, 216, 219
Canguilhem, Georges, 51n68, 52, 53, 56
capitalism: and colonialism, 232, 302;
  global capitalist system, 209, 222,
  251, 351, 358, 390, 394; and

romanticism 22–23; and rationalization, 284, 290

causality: auto-causality, 34, 39, 42, 44, 49, 57, 59, 63, 67, 90, 103, 112, 125, 132, 192, 357, 384; culture as form of, 2, 8, 41, 42, 43, 75, 76; of freedom, 10, 34, 35, 67–69; mechanistic, 26, 29, 35, 41, 47, 69, 290, 294; organismic, 11, 55, 56, 63, 80–89, 91, 96, 100, 107, 132, 136, 238, 241, 245, 246, 295, 352, 370, 379, 386; purposive, 54; and spectrality, 387, 388, 389; and *techne*, 48, 51, 71, 102, 110; and the will, 67, 69

center-periphery distinction, 181, 231–32, 382–83, 391

Chatterjee, Partha, 3, 5n8, 267–68, 268n, 283n41, 303; theory of Indian nationalism, 225–26; and *techne*, 227

Chinese, the: anti-Chinese feeling, 254–55n12, 338, 340; contribution to Indies nationalism, 255, 265, 277; in Indonesia, 285, 302, 336;

Christianity: complicity with British colonialism and contemporary neocolonialism, 365; doctrine of incarnation, 353, 365

civil society: Hegel's theory of, 10, 116, 143–45, 153–61; Indies, 256, 299, 300–302, 338, 346

colonialism: antimodern ethos of, 282, 309; complicity with traditional authority, 223; and instrumental reason, 268, 286; Marx on, 188–89; native subservience to, 254

colonial state: as agent of death, 265, 290, 298, 302, 305, 308, 310, 311; haunting of, 282, 287, 307, 319–29, 331; and surveillance, 331–41

community: vs. capital, 225; linguistic, 116, 121–25, 160, 227, 301, 362; organic, 4, 17, 18, 20, 21, 25, 33, 38, 62, 84, 92, 132, 235, 242; relation of

national, to modernity, 171, 225, 242, 280, 284, 286, 290, 294, 298, 302; vs. society, 14, 157; world, 181–90

comprador, 5n8, 222, 231, 351, 352, 369, 375

compradorization, 232

contamination, 9, 10, 112, 113, 137, 140, 144, 177, 178, 226, 229, 294, 329, 342, 379, 384, 388, 390, 396

cosmopolitanism: and bourgeois society, 184; and culture, 8; Kant's, 62, 78, 79, 89–99, 100; proletarian, 181, 185, 191, 205, 208, 209, 229; socialist, 11, 231. *See also* Fichte; Hegel; Marx

culture: as auto-causality, 44, 76; and bildungsroman, 240, 242; Cabral's views on, 11, 215–17, 219, 245; cosmopolitan, 89–99; and epigenesis, 97; Fanon on, 217–19; Fichte's theory of, 117, 119–21, 122, 129, 137, 139; as freedom and autonomy, 8, 13, 77, 97, 165, 166, 394; global culture industry, 12; Hegel's theory of, 10, 152, 163–69, 171, 174; as incarnational activity, 7, 8, 25, 44, 95, 97, 199, 249, 341; indigenous, 223; Kant's theory of, 10, 73, 75–80, 87, 89–99; as language, 361–63; Marx's critique of, 182, 199, 216; and organicism, 10, 37, 38, 47, 56, 57, 87, 163, 230, 232, 241, 290, 352, 384, 386; as paradigm of the political, 7, 45, 46, 129, 166, 201, 216, 235, 237, 259, 342, 353, 358; patriotic, 11, 367; as political activity, 45, 152, 166, 235; and politics, 58, 129; prosthetic function of, 356, 358, 370; as response to modernity, 37; revolutionary national, 209, 213, 219, 223, 229, 353, 381; revolutionary people's, 245, 259, 352; as second nature, 43, 241; and the state, 171,

culture (*continued*)
174, 219; as transcendence of finitude, 42, 56, 76–77, 124
death: and capital, 198; as contamination, 112, 117, 128, 297, 342, 389; moral, 310; and nation, 1, 116, 121–25, 139, 140, 175, 178, 188, 224, 229, 263, 294, 329–31, 341, 346, 369, 382; negation of, 56, 59, 81, 99, 119, 134, 137, 162, 229, 235, 312–19, 320, 328, 343, 346, 365; and neocolonial state, 246, 256, 298, 299, 302, 307–12, 326, 335, 359, 391, 393, 394. *See also* border
decolonization: Algerian, 213; in Asia and Africa, 1, 174; failure of, 6, 181, 330, 350, 355; and German idealist nationalism, 213; as incarnation of freedom, 181, 315; Indian, 255, 315, 330; Indonesian, 251; Kenyan, 366; relation to socialism, 10, 11, 25, 178, 179, 181, 208–32
Deleuze, Gilles, 382, 382n
DeMan, Paul, 130n
Derrida, Jacques: account of spectrality, 12, 384–91; and actualization of freedom, 4, 126; critique of nationalism as ontopology, 392; *différance*, 112n, 331; on globalization, 393; and Hegel, 329; iterability, 387; radical finitude, 387, 389; *Specters of Marx*, 385; and teleological time, 109, 387
Descartes, René, 21, 27, 51, 88
development: "good" vs. "bad," 355; sustainable, 379, 391; uneven, 213, 350, 382
dialectic: contradiction in dialectical logic, 58, 315; Hegelian, 201, 202, 250, 329; of nationalism, 251, 252, 258, 261, 309, 341
discipline, 77, 97, 98, 103, 110, 114, 120, 138, 164, 315

education: and *Bildung*, 39, 40, 45, 237n6, 130, 159, 163; and colonialism, 5, 255, 281, 308, 319, 328, 358, 362, 365, 372; cultural, 44, 77, 78, 94, 136, 178; Fichte on, 130, 138, 139; Kant on, 79, 94–98; of the "masses" 218; moral, 94; and political state, 94
Enlightenment, the: ideals of, 23, 36, 40; and Pramoedya, 262–63, 267, 268, 280, 283, 288, 302, 306, 308–10, 314; and universalism, 3, 6, 8
epigenesis: classical, 48, 50, 56; and culture, 97; of labor, 191–200, 206; and Mau Mau uprising, 356; modern, 54, 55; of nation, 261, 295, 345, 352, 356

Fanon, Frantz: on culture, 2, 129, 181, 217, 219, 223, 224, 237; and Hegel, 218, 219; on the Mau Mau uprising, 218; and nationalism, 222, 266, 309, 354, 359, 382; and Voice of Algeria, 221; and teleological time, 222
Farah, Nuruddin, 240
Fichte, J. G.: *Addresses to the German Nation*, 117, 120, 121–32, 134–41; and *Bildung*, 124, 128–36, 139; and cosmopolitanism, 116, 117; on culture, 116–20, 122, 124, 129, 132, 139; on the foreigner, 128; idea of divine life, 124; and idea of the original people, 121, 126; on language and nation, 121–25; and the living nation, 117, 121, 127, 130, 137, 139, 140, 141; on nationalism, 121, 129, 130, 135, 136; and patriotism, 116, 161, 130; philosophy of freedom, 10, 116, 118, 119, 125; *Science of Knowledge* (*Wissenschaftslehre*), 118; and self-activity, 118, 119, 126, 128, 129, 135, 136; and self-positing, 118, 119, 127; similarities to Cabral, 129, 216, 219; on the transcendence of finitude, 120

finitude: and culture, 56, 75, 76, 96; as exposure to alterity, 111; radical or original, 305, 386, 387; traditional conception of, 70, 72, 77, 235, 383; transcendence of, 2, 12, 20, 24, 34, 42, 56, 59, 76, 105, 119, 124, 127, 128, 147, 153, 160, 162, 191, 198, 207, 223, 230, 237, 326, 342, 346, 359, 377

Frankfurt School: culture industry, 288, 353: on instrumental vs. critical reason, 142, 207, 268

freedom: actualization of, 3, 6, 9, 10, 37, 99, 103, 104, 108, 110, 125, 141, 144, 160, 165, 177, 199, 201, 207, 229, 252, 370; as antithesis of mechanism, 35, 118; as autonomy, 67–69, 71, 103; through culture, 7, 8, 56, 74–80, 96, 97, 121, 165, 166, 217, 235, 259, 389, 394; deterritorialization of, 181–91, 232; economic, 2, 144, 215, 357; and the Enlightenment, 36, 262–63; as ghost, 209, 381, 383; from the given, 36; and heteronomy, 386; individualist determination of, and life, 5, 32, 34, 64, 230, 298, 301; through the nation, 135, 136, 281–89; and organicism, 2, 80–89, 63, 64, 195, 262, 263; political, 2, 24, 34, 45, 92, 93, 128, 144, 219, 357; as power of causality, 64; practical, 35, 66; as self-actualization, 137, 116, 227, 330, 341, 379; as self-causality, 34, 35; as transcendence of finitude, 2, 12, 59, 230, 383; transcendental idea of, 34, 38, 152, 262. *See also* Fichte; Hegel; Kant; Marx

French Revolution, 26, 29, 90n, 93, 93n, 108, 131, 276, 286, 310, 311; Kant's views on, 90n, 93, 93n, 108; Hegel's critique of, 166—67n76; in Pramoedya's novels, 278, 286, 310, 311

Gadamer, Hans-Georg, 47

gift: and the given, 36, 75; and nation, 396; nature's, 96, 101, 108; of organic life, 100, 102, 109, 112; of time, 89, 113, 247, 387, 389, 390

globalization: cultural, 358; economic, 2, 6, 20, 200, 209, 215, 228, 232, 249, 246, 377, 378, 382, 383, 393; neo-colonial, 245, 289, 346, 347

Goethe, Wilhelm von; on *Bildung,* 38, 56; organicism, 56; *Wilhelm Meisters Lehrjahre,* 241

Guha, Ranajit, 3

Habermas, Jürgen: and literary *Bildung,* 238, 255; on publicness and public communication, 93, 208, 238; and Pramoedya, 255, 266, 288; *Structural Transformation of the Public Sphere,* 93n, 158n60

Haller, Albrecht von, 52

Hardt, Michael, and Antonio Negri, 382

Hegel: on actuality, 144, 160, 170, 177; *Aesthetics: Lectures on Fine Art,* 149n43; on the animal organism, 149–53; on *Bildung,* 152, 154, 156, 159, 160, 161–78; and consciousness, 152, 159, 160, 162, 163, 171, 173, 175; critique of civil society, 155–61; critique of cosmopolitanism, 116; critique of public opinion, 157–59; critique of social contract theory, 157; on culture, 116, 142, 163, 165, 166, 171, 174; definition of the concept (*Begriff*) 147; *Encyclopedia Logic,* 146, 147, 149; and finitude, 145, 147, 153, 160, 162, 170; *Philosophy of Nature,* 150–53; *Philosophy of Right,* 141, 144, 145, 148, 149, 153–58, 160–61, 162, 164, 166, 169, 170, 175; and Pramoedya, 250, 259, 261, 306, 329; on relation of ideal state to

Hegel (*continued*)
individuals, 2, 145, 148, 154, 169; on spirit, 162; theory of freedom, 116, 141, 145, 176; theory of the organic state, *see Sittlichkeit;* theory of organism, 144, 149–53; idea of *Volksgeist,* 170

Heidegger, Martin: and culture, 7, 41–42, 46

heteronomy: definition of, 67; as inhuman, 207; and iterability, 387; and mechanism, 106; of nature, 69, 70, 100; and organic life, 106, 150, 304, 384; relation to moral freedom and opposition to freedom, 67, 111; and *techne,* 69, 76, 110, 165, 306, 334

historical materialism, 9

historicism: and Hegel, 177n; and Marx, 9; as self-actualization, 9

Hobbes, Thomas, 3, 26, 27, 28, 30

humanism, 279

human rights, 55, 231, 351

hylozoism, 84, 85, 86

idealism: and the decolonizing nation, 303, 352; German, 2, 5, 9, 19, 20, 21, 29, 31, 34, 46, 58, 60, 117n4, 130n, 191, 192, 200, 352

ideology: national community as, 18–25; Marx's critique of culture, 7, 8, 183, 204, 361, 385, 393

indigenous culture, 223, 232

Indonesian nationalism: and decolonization, 266, 283, 346; and the New Order regime, 253, 258; role of modern organization in, 302, 325, 339; role of native printing press in, 264, 266, 268, 270, 288–89, 296, 302, 335; similarities to Kenyan nationalism, 350

international division of labor, 231

international media, and Northern hegemony, 358

Javanism, 254, 281, 282, 298, 299, 302, 326

Kant, Immanuel: *Anthropology from a Pragmatic Point of View,* 62, 63, 93, 94, 97–98nn44–45, 98; anthropomorphism, 102, 109; anti-mechanism in, 67, 69; on archetypal understanding, 100, 103–5, 109, 110; on *Bildung,* 71, 77, 78–79, 95, 112; and *Bildungstrieb,* 85, 86, 88, 90; on cosmopolitan federation, 61–62, 78, 79, 93, 98; *Critique of Practical Reason,* 68, 69; *Critique of Pure Reason,* 65–66, 67n, 70, 104n; *Critique of Judgment,* 80–89, 90, 96–114; critique of hylozoism, 84; freedom as spontaneity, 65, 68, 69; historical writings, 74–80; Idea for a Universal History, 76–79; juxtaposition of mechanism and freedom, 69, 72, 81; on nature, 62–63, 69, 73, 75–76; on organicism, 82–89; and Pramoedya, 262, 294, 298–99, 304, 334; relation of ideas of organic life to political thought, 89–99; theory of culture, 76, 97; and vitalism, 84–85, 97

Kenyan nationalism, similarities to Indonesian, 350

Kenyatta, Jomo, 350, 360, 371n

Kohn, Hans, critique of German nationalism, 2, 18, 20, 21nn6–7

Kulturnation, as spiritual organism, 125–29

labor: division of, 7, 37, 38, 167; as epigenesis, 191–200, 206; global community of, 59, 185; international division of, 231; living, 5, 10, 197, 198–200, 212, 289, 352, 385; as self-conscious activity, 9, 164, 165, 193,

203, 215; and trade, 383; truncation of labor flows, 383; as transcendence of finitude, 194. *See also* Marx

language: colonial language policies, 129, 359, 362; and Fichte, 121–25, 138; as life, 129, 301, 302; and nation, 116, 121–25, 211, 232, 361; practicality of, 361; relation to *Bildung*, 160, 161n, 362; and spiritual life, 122, 362

Leibniz, 51

Lekra, 250, 257, 258

Lenin, V. I.: definition of imperialism, 215; theory of national self-determination, 210–12

life-world, 99, 207, 296, 306, 335

literature: and actuality, 261, 330; agency of, 255, 260; historio-graphical function of, 259, 260–61; and life, 262, 263; literary *Bildung* and vernacular languages, 241, 359, 361, 363; and nationalism, 129, 202, 239, 244; and public memory, 266; and public sphere, 258, 263

Lukács, Georg, theory of the bildungsroman, 242

Lyotard, Jean-François, 108n, 111n

machine-state: as absolutist state, 26; and Aristotelian model 27–28; Fichte's critique of, 131, 138; and French Revolution, 29; Hegel's critique of, 29, 142, 156, 157

magic: and capital, 197, 198, 287; magical realism, 364; of modern knowledge, 269, 276, 286, 288, 293, 302, 312, 322; and the novel, 242; and print, 336, 380

Mannheim, Karl, critique of political organicism and conservatism, 22–25

markets: globalization of, 181; liberalization, 383

Marx, Karl: analysis of alienated labor, 197, 207; anticulturalism and

dismissal of culture, 7, 10; on appropriation, 193, 199, 200, 205, 216; and *Bildung*, 186, 197, 199, 200; *Capital*, 192, 196, 200, 232; and colonialism, 188, 189; *Communist Manifesto*, 182, 190, 200; critique of capital, 184, 196–200, 215; critique of cosmopolitan bourgeois society, 181, 182, 184, 186; critique of nation as ideology, 180, 183, 189; on disappearance of national state, 184, 191; *Economic and Philosophical Manuscripts*, 184, 193, 194–95n29, 195, 197–99, 202–4, 206; on externality, 202, 203, 204, 205; on finitude, 194, 195, 204, 207; on freedom, 181, 185, 191, 195, 199, 209; *German Ideology*, 184–85, 187, 193, 204–5, 361–62; *Grundrisse: Foun-dations of the Critique of Political Economy*, 194n28, 195, 198, 206; and Hegel, 179, 182, 186, 193, 194, 197, 202, 203, 205, 206, 208; on money, 197, 198–99; on Polish and Irish nationalism, 180, 188, 189, 190; theory of the labor process, 191, 194, 195–96; theory of proletarian revolution, 179, 186, 195, 196, 199; on self-activity, 199; and vitalism, 181, 200, 208

Márkus, György, xi, 37, 39n43, 40n45, 43, 51n78, 163n65, 174n87, 200n36

Mau Mau uprising, 218, 350, 356, 371, 376

mechanism: antimechanism, 67, 69; as antithesis of freedom, 33, 35, 37; Cartesian, 50, 52; and industrialism, 37; of nature, 35, 36, 43, 47, 54, 58, 71, 78, 86, 96, 106, 387; vs. teleology, 51, 51n, 73

Meinecke, Friedrich: *The Age of German Liberation*, 26; *Cosmopoli-tanism and the National State*, 121

memory: public, 254–55n12, 266, 320, 326, 327; relation to dialectics, 330

messianism, 371, 374, 377, 390

Mettrie, Julien Offray de La, 51

mimeticism: as basis of political freedom, 106; and *Bildung,* 48; in Kant, 88; of *physis* and *techne,* 50, 52, 88, 102, 106, 112; of political and divine design, 28

modernity: European experience of, 6, 37–38, 144; European models of, 223, 325; ideals of, 36, 308; of knowledge, 270–73, 282, 284, 286, 288, 291, 295, 299, 301, 308, 313, 318, 319, 338, 340; modern vs. traditional rationality, 37; non-Western models of, 286; progress in scientific knowledge in, 284; relation to capitalism, 196; relation to colonialism, 243, 283, 268, 269, 280, 281, 302

Moi, Daniel Arap, 349, 350, 350n2, 353, 375

Nancy, Jean-Luc, 59n; and Philippe Lacoue-Labarthe, 57

Napoleon: and German nationalism, 6, 26, 120; and Third World decolonization, 5

narrative: function of, 11, 241, 253, 331, 342, 345, 347, 363–65; and modern personality, 271, 273; and national consciousness, 254; oral, 374–76

nation: as appendage of bourgeois state, 187; bases of national unity, 210; as *differánce* of state, 331; distinguished from a community of race and blood, 125; as haunted, 269, 303, 371, 381, 383, 384; as ideological phantasm, 227; as incarnation of freedom, 225, 341, 378, 384; and internal border, 127, 129, 137–39, 141; as linguistic community, 121–25, 361; national development, 230; obsolescence and disappearance of, 182; as organic community, 39, 291; as organism, 19, 120, 303, 305, 289, 354; pro-letarian, 190, 209, 212; phantomatic, 117; and spirit, 171–78, 315, 319, 326, 329, 330, 340, 342, 344, 347; as supplement to the state, 138, 169–76

national consciousness and national awakening, 212, 218, 224; and comparison, 279; in the Indies and in Indonesia, 250, 253, 264, 266, 267, 268, 269–73, 279, 281, 294, 302, 311, 315, 324; native awakening, 296

nationalism: basis in organismic vitalism, 6, 18, 19, 100, 224; and Cabral, 129, 214, 216, 222, 224; cultural vs. political, 8, 117; decolonizing, 19, 116, 137, 141, 178, 212, 215, 226, 235, 239, 266, 346; dis-tinguished from cultural chauvinism, 125, 299; and the Enlightenment, 8, 18, 23, 267; and the expatriate, 347; Fanon's concept of, 216, 222, 224, 226; and fundamentalism, 1, 2; German, 2, 5, 20, 25, 26, 59, 213; "good" vs. "evil," 2; as humanist messianism, 390; Indian, 3, 225; Indonesian, 253, 258, 283, 302, 308, 309, 325, 329, 339, 342, 346, 350; Kenyan, 350, 350n, 365; and language and vernacular culture, 116, 289, 363; Marx's views on nineteenth-century European, 180, 186–88, 190; and patriotism, 134, 161, 136; and philosophy, 3, 4, 21; popular vs. official, 225, 228; postcolonial, 3, 6, 8, 12, 20, 212; vs. premodern patriotism, 325; radical, 239, 283; romantic, 18, 23; as statist ideology, 130, 228, 268; unfinished project of, 221, 229, 251, 252n5, 304,

356, 371; and universalism vs. particularism, 2, 8

National Socialism, 18, 20

nation-people, 121, 131, 136, 208, 224, 226, 227, 228, 231, 246, 256, 261, 265, 272, 284, 288, 298, 293, 296, 304, 319, 325, 330, 332, 337, 338, 346, 368, 379

nativism: Cabral's critique of, 2, 222; Fanon's critique of, 2, 222; relation to indigenous bourgeoisie, 222–23

neocolonialism: definition of, 353; neocolonial global culture, 245, 353, 358, 363

Ngũgĩ wa Thiong'o: and the academic industry, 377; on *Bildung*, 352, 354, 356, 360, 362, 363, 365, 369, 370, 377; *Devil on the Cross*, 354, 366–70; figures of ghosts in the writings of, 366, 376; *A Grain of Wheat*, 366; on language, 362–63; *Matigari*, 349, 371, 373–76; on national culture, 352–63; on neocolonialism, 354, 360, 365; *Penpoints, Gunpoints, and Dreams*, 351; *Petals of Blood*, 365; and prostheses, 352, 355, 364, 365, 369, 370; on the relation of art to the state, 351; on the responsibility of postcolonial intellectuals, 360, 370; and the task of literature, 363; and *techne*, 360, 370, 375

novel, the: as analogue of nation, 238; and nation, 239, 240, 241, 242; social, vs. bildungsroman, 244

office, and death, 310, 311

official consciousness, 316, 317, 342, 345

organism: as actualization of freedom, 37; as analogue of freedom, 57, 58, 59, 81; animal, 145, 149–53; and auto-causality, 39, 42, 55, 63, 87; and culture, 10, 12, 38, 47, 56, 57, 58; as distinct from artifice, 26, 33, 54, 56, 64; formative drive of (*Bildungstrieb*)

86, 88, 90, 132, 152; organicism and ideology, 19; as political body, 10, 18, 19, 25, 27, 33, 62, 89–99; and political conservatism, 22; purposiveness of, 47, 53, 81, 84, 89; and rationality, 23, 59; as systematic whole, vs. aggregate, 83. *See also* Kant; Hegel; organization

organization: as conjuration, 294; and imagination, 295; of nation-people, 297, 330; in nature, 84, 86, 90, 103, 107; and organic life, 63, 64, 67, 85, 88, 90, 96, 99–103, 106–7, 109–12; and organized matter, 84, 86; rational, 80, 136, 157, 214, 219, 268, 290, 323; political, 107, 90, 93, 256, 265, 294, 321, 328; self-, 26, 82n, 87, 176, 238, 242, 352; social, 5, 32, 265, 294, 300

organizations, modern, and the law, 338

patriotism, 174, 175, 176, 187; civic, 161, 142, 172; premodern, 325. *See also* Fichte

pergerakan, 265–66, 307–9, 315–17, 320–22, 325, 327, 331, 339, 342

Philippines nationalism, 286; role of José Rizal in, 240, 280

physis: and *Bildung*, 47; relationship to *techne*, 64, 206, 229, 291, 293–94, 302, 334

political body: artificial, 28; as mechanism, 27, 28; as organism, 2, 7, 18, 22, 27, 33, 58, 62, 89–99, 176; and Rousseau, 31

political organicism, 9, 111, 136, 142, 144, 189, 209, 227, 229, 232, 245, 246, 289, 294, 346, 382, 385

postcolonial: *Bildung*, 7, 11, 370; bildungsroman, 242; nation, 11, 209, 226, 242, 280, 289, 304, 306, 370; nation-state, 229; state, 4, 225, 237,

253, 346, 349, 351; the role of, intellectuals, 360, 363, 365, 369, 370

Pramoedya Ananta Toer: and Adorno, 282; *Anak Semua Bangsa* (Child of all nations), 273–76, 277–79, 286–92; and auto-causality, 262, 290, 334; and bildungsroman, 315, 265, 241; *Bumi Manusia* (This earth of mankind), 269–73, 276, 280; critique of colonial instrumental reason, 268, 281–89, 290, 302, 314, 330, 340; critique of Javanism, 254, 281–82, 298–99; and the Enlightenment, 262, 267, 268, 280, 282, 283, 288, 302, 308, 314, 344; figures of ghosts in, 298, 303, 310, 312, 315, 317, 318, 319, 342, 344; ideas of freedom, 251, 252, 257, 258, 259, 261–63, 281–89; on Indies national consciousness, 250, 264, 266, 269, 271, 273, 277, 279, 281, 294, 296, 312, 315, 324; *Jejak Langkah* (Footsteps), 265, 280, 285–86, 292–306, 335–37; and Kant, 262, 268, 294, 299, 604, 334; and Lentera, 350; literature as actuality, 330, 341; on modern rationality, 281, 282; and national consciousness, 250, 253, 264, 267, 268, 269–73, 281, 294, 302, 311, 315, 324; and the national public sphere, 256, 259, 261, 263, 266, 289, 341, 346; and organization, 280, 289–96, 304, 321, 338; portrayal of the *pergerakan*, 265, 266, 301, 307, 308, 309, 315, 317, 320, 321, 322, 325, 327, 331, 339, 342; and prostheses, 338; and public sphere, 253–64, 288, 289, 292, 320, 331, 333, 334, 335, 338; relationship to Lekra, 250; relationship to Suharto, 250, 254, 254n11; relationship to Sukarno, 255, 256; reliance on Hegelian-Marxist discourse, 250, 259, 308; *Rumah Kaca* (Glass house), 282, 308–48; similarity to Hegel,

260–61, 329; and vitalism, 249, 256, 257, 259, 264, 297, 330, 331

preformationism: Blumenbach's critique of, 54, 56; and Cartesian mechanism, 52

print media, 266, 268, 273, 276, 277, 289, 297, 303, 304, 321, 332, 335, 336, 363, 374

priyayi, the, 281–82; Pramoedya's critique of, 254, 297, 298, 311, 316, 324; Sarekat Priyayi 296–97. *See also* Pramoedya Ananta Toer, critique of Javanism

prosthesis, 198, 205–7, 208–9, 223–24, 239, 246, 293, 336, 381, 384–85, 388, 391, 395; and culture, 364, 370, 388; definition of, 352; and financialization, 355; modern organizations as, 338; and neocolonialism, 352, 359

publicness (*Öffentlichkeit*), 92, 93, 93n, 169, 169n80, 238, 255, 256

public sphere, 92–93, 100, 159–60, 238–39; critical, 95, 239, 253; as effect of spectrality, 334, 338; and the nation, 237, 240, 266; in Pramoedya, 253–64, 266, 288, 289, 331, 333; spectrality of, 288, 289, 320, 366

purposiveness; and *Bildung*, 48; human, 102, 106, 107, 110; and Kant, 80–81, 84, 85, 89, 102, 149; and Marx, 193, 194; moral, 100, 106; natural, 53, 54, 62, 74, 96, 101, 105, 109. *See also* organism

reason: actualization of, 10, 137, 141–44, 145, 146, 147, 170, 221, 341; critical, and the nation-people, 288; critical vs. instrumental, 207, 314; and freedom, 34, 35, 65, 66, 75, 143, 145, 148, 269; instrumental, 99, 268, 281–89, 302, 314, 330, 340; moral, 65, 92, 111, 112, 116; and organic vitality, 34, 156, 289; transparency of, 266, 331, 332

Renan, Ernst, 17–19, 29
resistance, 250, 283, 299, 303, 306, 325, 339, 348, 357, 359, 360, 364
revolution, Russian, 325. *See also* French Revolution; Marx
Rizal, José, *Noli Me Tangere,* 239, 240
romanticism: German, 18, 19, 21–23, 33; as critique of capitalism, 22–23
Rosca, Ninotchka, 240
Rousseau, Jean-Jacques: conception of the political body, 31; *Discourse on Political Economy,* 30; Hegel's critique of, 157n; *The Social Contract,* 30; and vitalism, 29

satanic, the, 263, 286, 287, 288, 290, 312
Schmitt, Carl, 59
self-activity. *See* Fichte; Marx
Sittlichkeit (ethical life, ethical sub- stance), 156, 159–60, 166–68, 172–73, 173n, 384
society, as organism, 157, 159
spectrality: and *Bildung,* 303; and causality, 388; definition of, 346, 386, 388; and fetishism, 299; "good" vs. "bad," 289, 293, 303, 314, 340; of Javanist ideology, 330; of modern knowledge, 270, 289, 291, 299, 302, 330, 338, 382; of modern print, 277, 332, 335, 336; of the nation, 12, 269, 302, 303, 346, 347; in Pramoedya, 269, 289, 291, 302, 303, 314, 330, 336, 338, 340, 346, 347; and the public sphere, 334; and spirit, 277
spirit: Hegel's theory of transition from animal life to, 162–64; national, 170–73, 255, 259, 263, 264, 279, 315, 326, 327, 328, 329, 330, 340, 341, 342, 344, 345; products of, 171
spontaneity: of *Bildung*/culture 42, 56–57, 120, 136–37, 263; and moral freedom, 35, 44, 45, 57–59, 65, 67–69, 89, 92, 112, 123; of *physis* 25,

42, 49, 50, 53–55, 64, 81, 85–87, 150; of popular political movements 4, 201, 218–19, 226, 289, 325, 391; and publicness, 93; and reason, 34
state: art and, 351; censorship of literature by, 254n, 351, 375, 376; colonial, 209, 228, 239, 243; as *differánce* of nation, 331; as human machine, 27; and the individual, 46, 58, 78, 132; as instrument of nation, 130, 135, 136; as machine, 10, 21, 26, 27, 28, 31, 32, 45, 89–99, 117; neocolonial bourgeois, 229; organic, 10, 18, 26, 32, 117, 142, 144–49, 153, 155, 157, 160; poetic, 31; postcolonial, 225, 237, 253, 346; and radical literature, 249, 255, 258; republican, 78, 90; as supplement to nation, 11
structural adjustment, 377
subaltern studies, critique of national- ism by, 3–4, 187, 225, 283, 303
Suharto, 250, 253, 254, 395
Sukarno, 252, 255, 256, 258, 258n19, 283
surveillance, by the colonial state, 255, 287, 313, 314, 331–41

techne: Aristotle on, 49, 52; heter- onomy of, 82, 132; in Kant, 68, 70, 71, 76, 78, 79, 96, 99–113; in Marx, 205–6; and nation's incarnation, 221–22, 224, 273, 290; nature as, 69; in Ngũgĩ's writings, 360, 370, 375; organicization of, 177, 224, 227, 228–29, 303, 321; and organic life, 102, 107, 117, 236, 294, 304, 388; and political organicism, 107, 321
technology: development in modernity, 270, 282; print, 268, 270; relation to nationalism, 334
technomediation, 270, 279, 291; heteronomy of, 334; of print, 336; as supplement to life, 265, 334, 335, 339

teleological time: definition of, 73, 73n; disruption of, 106, 109, 110; and Fanon, 222, 223; and finitude, 89, 365; and Ngũgĩ, 364, 365, 366, 369, 370, 371, 374, 375

teleology: as actualization of freedom, 110; and bildungsroman, 241, 245; distinction between classical and modern, 51; and epigenesis, 53; and judgment, 107; and Marx's theory of labor, 195; and mechanism, 51, 52n80, 85n29; relation to morality, 73, 105, 109

Third World and postcolonial intellectual, 252, 257n17, 267, 367, 369; as member of the comprador elite, 222; sociopolitical responsibility of, 263, 360, 363, 370

uneven development and uneven globalization, 6, 209, 213, 228, 350, 378, 382–84, 391, 393–94

Weber, Max, 281, 290; ideal type in, 290

will: causality of, 81, 96, 107; and freedom, 34, 65, 67, 70, 155; moral, 35, 65, 69, 75, 77, 98; to organize, 279, 295, 296; in Rousseau, 30